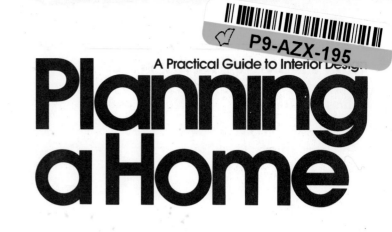

A Practical Guide to Interior Design

Planning a Home

reproduced on the cover
A home designed by Michael and Cindi Sands.
(Photograph: Philip L. Molten)

cover design
Karen Salsgiver

Holt, Rinehart and Winston
New York   Chicago   San Francisco   Atlanta
Dallas   Montreal   Toronto   London   Sydney

Sarah Faulkner

A Practical Guide to Interior Design

Planning a Home

Editor Rita Gilbert
Picture Editor Joan Curtis
Production Assistants Laura Foti, Barbara Curialle
Production Supervisor Nancy Myers
Illustrator Sandra E. Popovitch
Associate Illustrator Richard N. Pollack, A.I.A.
Designer Marlene Rothkin Vine
Associate Designer Karen Salsgiver

Publisher Judith L. Rothman

The line illustrations and special halftone combinations in this book
were conceived by Joan Curtis and executed by Sandra E. Popovitch.

Figs. 258, 266, 269–270 adapted from *Nomadic Furniture* by James Hennessey
and Victor Papanek. Copyright © 1973 by Victor J. Papanek and James Hennessey.
Adapted by permission of Pantheon Books, a Division of Random House, Inc.

Library of Congress Cataloging in Publication Data

Faulkner, Sarah.
    Planning a home.
    Bibliography: p. 371
    Includes index.
    1. Interior decoration. I. Title.
NK2110.F93   747 ′.8 ′83   78-22021
ISBN 0-03-045471-9

Composition and camera work by York Graphic Services, Inc., Pennsylvania
Color separations and printing by Lehigh Press Lithographers, New Jersey
Printing and binding by Capital City Press, Vermont
9 0 1 2 3 138 9 8 7 6 5 4 3 2 1

Preface

Planning a Home is a comprehensive introduction to interior design for college students and for the generally interested reader. As the subtitle implies, it is written from a practical, problem-solving point of view. Some of the information in *Planning a Home* has been adapted from an earlier book, *Inside Today's Home*, which I coauthored with my husband, Ray Faulkner. But, except for standard tables and lists, the text in this volume—and nearly all the illustrations—are new.

When we wrote *Inside Today's Home*, in the early 1950s, we envisioned a world—and a home—quite different from those of today. We assumed then that a large segment of the population would enjoy the opportunity of having their homes custom-designed and built, tailored specifically to the needs of their families. We assumed, too, that most people would live in *houses*, and moreover would live in those same houses for most of their lives.

Over the last quarter century, much has changed. The costs for land and construction have placed the individually designed house virtually beyond the means of all but the rich. Ever larger numbers of people prefer to, or must, live in apartments, condominiums, mobile homes, and other nontraditional dwellings. Above all, we have become a mobile society. It is the rare family today that puts down roots in one place, where all members live out their life cycles.

In the course of four editions, *Inside Today's Home* has changed to take account of these shifts in life style, and will continue to change in the future as new patterns of living emerge. However, Rita Gilbert, my editor and friend for many years, saw the need for another book on a somewhat different level and with a very practical approach to the interior design of homes as they are today. She proposed such a text, and a spark was struck. I decided this book should recognize the fact that most people live in spaces that are circumscribed and not ideal, and that many must work within a limited budget. I wanted to show how such limitations can be overcome in a variety of ways—ways that may be equally useful to people who have more leeway. Finally, I wanted the book to meet the needs of those who hope to make careers in interior design. Thus was born *Planning a Home*.

Chapter 1 of *Planning a Home* introduces the underlying concept of the book: that design is successful only in the context of the people for whom it is created. This chapter includes a detailed profile questionnaire, formulated to determine the needs, desires, tastes, and life styles of those who will live in the home, whether the reader's family or the reader's clients. Subsequent chapters deal with the floor plan, design elements and principles, lighting and color, and major features such as floors, walls, windows, and furnishings. Three chapters treat the three principal types of spaces within the home—social spaces, private places, and work spaces. Another chapter deals with the personalizing qualities of accessories, and a final one broaches the necessary subject of budgets and planned buying. *Planning a Home* concludes with a Glossary of Period Styles, a Glossary of Terms, a Bibliography, and an Index.

The illustrations for *Planning a Home* presented a special challenge. Certainly many authors of interior design books, and their editors, have grappled with the problem of how to show variations and contrasts: Why is one design more effective than another for a given space—more balanced, more unified, more interesting? Line drawings can be dull and often do not give a sense of how actual furnishings will look. Photographs limit the choices, for it is almost impossible to find pictures of the same space designed in different ways.

Joan Curtis, picture editor at Holt, devised a unique solution for some of the illustrations in *Planning a Home*. Scattered throughout the book are photo-line drawing composites—sprightly line drawings onto which have been superimposed photographs of real furnishings. This technique made it possible, for example, to show side by side the same room (in line) with two different design solutions (in photo and line).

Altogether there are more than 50 photo-line composites in *Planning a Home*, plus numerous line drawings and some 320 photographs, 50 of them in full color. I have endeavored to choose examples of effective design in all price ranges, but concentrating on a wide spectrum of middle-income budgets. The book is based on a deep conviction that exciting design need not cost a great deal of money. Imagination, skill, and flair cost nothing. All of these can be enhanced by training, and this is the major premise and purpose of *Planning a Home*.

Acknowledgments

As in any book of this magnitude, there are more people deserving of thanks than space could ever allow. Particularly helpful were comments supplied by scores of interior design teachers who filled out a questionnaire circulated by my publisher. For detailed reviews of the manuscript in progress I am indebted to Shirley M. Camp, of Iowa State University; Elaine Meisch, of Dakota County Area Vocational Technical Institute; and Victoria Brinn Feinberg, of California State University, Northridge.

The task of gathering illustrations was made easier because of the generosity of several photographers who opened their files to us. My special thanks go to Morley Baer, Joshua Freiwald, Norman McGrath, Philip L. Molten, Robert Perron, Gordon H. Schenck, Jr., and Ezra Stoller, who supplied so many of the pictures in *Planning a Home*.

As mentioned earlier, Rita Gilbert, my editor at Holt, Rinehart and Winston, provided the inspiration for *Planning a Home* and continued to inspire her staff through the seemingly endless months when the book was in production. That the book has appeared at all is due to her, first and last; she has my heartfelt thanks.

The mechanics of illustrating a book like *Planning a Home* involve an enormous amount of detail—coordinating text, illustrations, and captions; hunting down likely sources of photographs; gathering possibilities and permissions; and keeping all of these elements floating freely in the mind until just the right placement becomes obvious. Only someone as devoted and brilliant as Joan Curtis could deal with such complexity.

I am indebted to Marlene Rothkin Vine for the book's elegant design, which so beautifully exploits the quality of the illustrations. She and Karen Salsgiver collaborated to create a stunning, contemporary layout. Finally, Laura Foti and Barbara Curialle bore the responsibility for holding together the millions of details that have coalesced into this printed book. Without their efforts, there would be no *Planning a Home*.

Stanford, California   S. F.
March 1979

For Ray

Contents

Planning
for People

1

nterior design is above all a human endeavor. It is done by and for people. The basis for planning a home must always be the comfort, well-being, and pleasure of those who will live in it. But people vary in their needs and wants. What to one person would be the perfect home might be unworkable for another. Moreover, needs differ not only among households, but also within the *same* household, as members are added or subtracted, and as people proceed through the life cycle or change their mode of living.

Most people design their own homes without professional help. Others may call upon an interior designer to advise them. The advice given by a professional designer could be anything from a brief consultation about a few purchases to the plan and execution of an entire home.

Whether the design is to be undertaken by household members or by a professional, the same factors must be taken into consideration. These factors include:

- Who will live in the home, in what manner, and for how long?
- What are their psychological responses to people, space, and color?
- What are their aesthetic likes and dislikes?
- What resources are available?

Each of these elements must be examined and then balanced in relation to the others. Whether you are designing for yourself or for a client, certain questions must be asked about the person or persons who will live in the home. In some cases the answers to these questions will provide detailed information about design decisions; in others they will offer a general background for the plan.

Before undertaking a project, interior designers may ask their clients to fill out a questionnaire. Once completed, the questionnaire becomes the basis for all kinds of design choices. It is important that all those involved in the final approval of the design have an opportunity to respond to the questionnaire. This will eliminate the guesswork in selecting colors, furniture, and other items, and especially in making decisions that may affect individuals in specific areas of the home.

After reading the background information in this chapter, you might begin this study of home planning by filling out a profile questionnaire on *your own* life style and tastes. (See pp. 24–30.)

1. Successful home design takes into consideration the needs of those who will live in the home. Living space must be planned with *people* in mind. Architect Bob Kindorf planned this home for the life styles of its family members. The fireplace, wood beams, and hanging lantern create a rustic atmosphere, and help to connect the home with the outdoors. One family member can prepare a meal without being excluded from the conversation. (*Photograph: Philip L. Molten*)

right: 2. People influence the design of a home. A living room with a built-in seating platform along one side wall can accommodate many people and a casual life style. A shaggy rug seems comfortable to young people and a dog; the rattan chairs and stool can be moved around wherever they are needed. Edward L. Barnes, architect. (*Photograph: John T. Hill*)

below: 3. A living room more formal than the one in Figure 2 would seem better suited to a family without young children. The numerous small pieces, many evoking the seaside setting, personalize the space. (*Photograph: Philip L. Molten*)

People

The number and relationships of the people who make up a household will be a primary factor in designing the home. This seems obvious, but it has broad implications. It will influence everything that follows. A household with children will have very different needs from one composed entirely of adults. Even if all are adult, relative age can still make a difference. Elderly people or those with physical handicaps have very special requirements.

Anthropologist Paul Bohannan defines the household as "... a group of people who live together and form a functioning domestic unit. They may or may not constitute a family, and if they do, it may or may not be a simple nuclear family."*

---

* Paul Bohannan, *Social Anthropology* (New York: Holt, Rinehart, and Winston, 1963), p. 86.

4. A well-designed home has space for the specific demands of hobbies. While most families probably would not include a gymnasium, this active family considers it essential to their life style. (*Photograph: Dan Wynn*)

This definition could be extended to include the following:

- a single person
- two or more unrelated people
- two or more blood relations
- a married couple
- a nuclear family (husband, wife, children)
- an extended family (a nuclear family plus grandparents, uncles, aunts, cousins)
- two or more nuclear families living together
- a commune

Furthermore, this basic household structure may be broadened by:

- live-in household help
- short-term guests
- long-term guests
- boarders
- family pets

In planning the home, some attempt must be made to answer at least partially the requirements of each of these individuals and to reflect the relationships among them. Some families are gregarious, entertaining a steady stream of guests. Others are very private. All of this adds up to what might be called a *life style*.

Life Style

Many aspects of life style influence the design of a home. Perhaps most essential is the personal concept of what a home should be. Some people consider a home as just a place to sleep and sometimes to eat; they spend most of their waking hours in other places. At the opposite extreme is

the totally home-centered family devoted to communal meals and group amusements. The interior of any home must reflect these preferences if it is to work well.

Some people watch television a lot, others like to listen to music, and many spend hours doing both. Work, hobbies, and games make specific demands. How can all these activities be accommodated?

One aspect of life style that is sometimes overlooked is the amount of time spent in maintenance. At one extreme is the compulsive housekeeper whose home would always pass a white-glove inspection. At the other is the person who cleans only in the frantic few hours before guests arrive—if then. Most of us probably fall between these two categories. We would like provision for tasks to be done with as little fuss and bother as possible.

above: 5. The bedroom of this home also serves as a study and den. Sections were added to create double dressing rooms and extra storage space. The entire family uses the room. Albert Herbert, designer. (*Photograph: Dan Wynn*)

below: 6. Architect Sevilla Weber designed her loft with a balcony that functions as a work area. The plan makes the most of the room's wood floors and high ceilings. This is a serviceable, streamlined design that uses few partitions for dividing living space. (*Photograph: Dan Wynn*)

7–8. Two very different life styles call for different dining arrangements.

left: 7. It is important to the owner of this home to have a formal dining room for entertaining, complete with a crystal chandelier, although the rest of the home is not particularly formal. The chandelier and sculpted chairs contrast with the straight lines of the floor tiles and glass panels. The table combines the sleekness of glass with the ornamentation of carved wood. Don Loomis, architect. (*Photograph: Philip L. Molten*)

below: 8. In a loft renovated by Polly Myhrum and Myron Adams, the kitchen/dining area is more informal for casual entertaining and drop-in guests. Cookware and dishes are displayed rather than hidden from view. No attempt is made to conceal pipes, and furniture is eclectic. The room is both functional and cozy. (*Photograph: George Gardner*)

Equally as important as the functions that take place in the home is the character of the space and its furnishings. It can be formal or informal—even chaotic to some eyes. The space may be geared to entertaining or to basic family activities. Contemporary or traditional style, or eclectic—a mixture of styles from many sources—simple or complex, the character will influence the inhabitants and the way they choose to live. (See Plate 1, opposite.)

Plate 1. The owners of this apartment furnished it with 19th-century antiques and farm furniture, reflecting their desire to create a tranquil home amid the frantic pace of a large city. A modern sofa divides the living room into separate sections, but its simple design coordinates well with the rustic American pine cupboard, blanket chest, and other country furniture. Mary Emmerling, designer. (*Photograph: Robert Perron*)

above: Plate 2. The home of designer Luís Baragan, with its broad areas of open space and simple furniture, creates a cool atmosphere in contrast to the warm Mexican climate. The almost bare, light pink walls and blonde furniture complete the effect. (*Photograph: Hans Namuth, Photo Researchers, Inc.*)

right: Plate 3. Furniture painted in bright colors enlivens the atmosphere of this child's room. The curtains and quilt are striped with the same cheerful colors as the room divider. Mandy Haas, designer. (*Photograph: Philip L. Molten*)

right: Plate 4. The walls of this bedroom have been stained a deep earth red, giving a feeling of cozy warmth. The feeling is amplified by the low ceiling and the soft light from small lamps. The carpet, pillows, and patchwork quilt pick up the dark color of the walls for a unified effect. John Saladino, designer. (*Photograph: Norman McGrath*)

below: Plate 5. Chinese red against white highlights the effect of boxes within and upon boxes in this apartment. The ceiling-height cutouts at left contain guest bunks, reached by means of the ladder with its plants removed. A full wall of storage cubes holds magazines and books. George and Ann Hartman, designers. (*Photograph: John T. Hill*)

Plate 6. This kitchen, part of a remodeled 200-year-old forge, is fully equipped with modern facilities, yet retains a charming rural atmosphere. The large window faces south, letting in plenty of sunlight. Work and storage spaces are organized for efficiency. John Saladino, designer. (*Photograph: Norman McGrath*)

Mobility

In our society, mobility is a fact of life. One out of every five households moves to a new location each year—around the corner or across the country. Many people must move; some just like to.

The planning of a home might well reflect this, if it is obviously temporary or only semipermanent. Furniture could be lightweight; or modular, so that it can be arranged in different ways in different places; or even demountable, capable of being taken apart and easily transported, in keeping with today's mobile society.

above: 9. Modular furniture is ideal for the mobile family. It is easily moved, and can be arranged different ways to accommodate changes in life style. This arrangement makes the most of a small space.

below: 10. The same number of modular units is used here as in Figure 9. In a more spacious room, however, the pieces can be spread out for more casual seating.

right: 11. This desk, designed by Jerry Johnson, can be completely taken apart and easily assembled. The concept of demountable furnishings is old, but still practical, and today's designers give these furnishings a fresh, contemporary look. (*Photograph courtesy Landes*)

below: 12. Built-in shelves and furnishings are ideal for children's rooms, because they minimize clutter. Gamal El Zoghby, designer. (*Photograph: Robert Perron*)

Demountable furnishings have received well-earned attention from designers lately, but the concept is quite old. Some of the earliest furniture consisted of folding stools and chests with handles for easy carrying to new locations.

There are other possibilities. Some people "scavenge" old furniture in junk shops, garage sales, and the town dump, then restore it for at least temporary use. It may be sold to the next tenant, left behind—or taken along in a friend's pickup truck or van if it has become a treasured and necessary possession.

At the opposite end of the scale are families who expect to stay put for a number of years. They can indulge a liking for large, solid pieces, or perhaps for fragile but lovely furniture that would require careful packing and handling if moved. The ultimate in permanence would be built-in furniture that is part of the house shell.

Location, Climate, and Orientation

Where we live—location and climate—enters into our conscious thinking primarily in regard to an urban/suburban home or a vacation home. It may seem logical that an urban dwelling be more formal and precise, the mountain cottage casually and sturdily outfitted. These differences reflect the activities of the people occupying the places, continuously or intermittently, as well as the locale. (See Plate 1, p. 7.)

The climate and location will, or should, have primary influence on the shelter itself. A house in the tropics should be as open to breezes as possible, while capable of being tightly shut against storms. A home in the snow belt needs a roof properly constructed to shed snow, well-insulated windows and walls, and windows angled to catch the sun in winter but protected from what may be a very hot summer sun.

13. A poured concrete dune house by architect William Morgan is an excellent example of a structure in tune with its surroundings. The exterior is covered with sand and sod. The focal point of the living room is the ocean view, but the house is protected from wind and surf. Furnishings soften the stonelike walls and ceilings. The house becomes one with the environment, and, at the same time, a haven from it. (*Photograph: Alexandre Georges*)

The orientation of a home, chiefly window exposure, opens it to sun and breezes as well as views. These are certainly important considerations, greatly influencing window treatment. Curtains, shades, and draperies control light and privacy, as well as revealing or concealing the outdoor scene.

The interior design of a home, however, can go even further by creating an appropriate atmosphere—of warmth or coolness, snugness or airiness, according to climatic conditions. A home finished in light colors and containing broad areas of uncluttered space will make people feel cooler (Pl. 2, p. 8).

Those who live in chill, wet climates may choose to counteract the depressing effects of the weather by using warm colors—reds, oranges, yellows—to bring the quality of sunlight indoors and compensate for its absence outside. Fabrics will help too. Contrast the feel of a sleek plastic, or even a fine silky satin, against a textured, heavy woven wool.

Of course, the demands of location and climate are not absolutes. People who love rustic country furniture can re-create a rural farmhouse in a city apartment (Plate 1, p. 7). Conversely, a home in the country can be dignified. An 18th-century Colonial home furnished in the gracious style of its period would be an example. Such a home would be comfortable in its location, an old New England village, perhaps, but hardly rural in its atmosphere.

14. In a cold climate, many patterns, textures, and accessories can give a room a feeling of snugness. Draperies covering the windows serve a dual purpose. They are functional, insulating the room from cold, and aesthetically harmonious, since they complete the impression of a cozy, closed-in nook.

above: 15. Warm climates often call for an uncluttered design. The smooth surfaces, tiled floor, and shuttered windows create a feeling of openness appropriate to the climate.

right: 16. The skylight and windows are exploited by this city apartment's design. Potted trees, doubled in the mirrored walls, thrive in the abundance of natural light. Since the trees need misting daily, the sofas are sensibly covered in waterproof raincoat fabric. Arthur Scott and Mark Sephton, designers. (*Photograph: Charles Wiesehahn*)

Proxemics

Environmental psychologists, social anthropologists, and designers have studied people's responses to other people and to the kinds of spaces they occupy—a field known as *proxemics*. These experts can predict where we probably will sit, at what angle, how close to a stranger or friend, and how much interaction there will be. They will also tell us that most people tend to forsake formal living rooms, gravitating to informal social spaces such as kitchens or family rooms. This seems to confirm what we already know but do not always put into practice—because we do not *really* consider a given group's likely responses.

Response to space as space has not been studied so intensively. The subject does not lend itself to objective analysis, although subjective appraisals abound. We all have our own instinctive reactions and ideas on the subject. They will differ according to each person's own psychological makeup.

Claustrophobia—the fear of enclosed spaces—afflicts many people. In its mildest form it causes discomfort when one is seated in a hemmed-in location. The opposite, agoraphobia, creates a feeling of insecurity in the absence of walls or other protective features.

Many of us, of course, have no specific fears. We may just know that we like cozy, snug, secure places; or that plenty of open, uncluttered space and vistas beyond the immediate room make us feel free and unfettered. Sometimes these feelings will change, according to our moods, the weather, the work we have to do. Ideally, a home will include both types of spaces to take care of everyone and their changing needs for privacy or conviviality.

People in Relation to their living space.

17. A child's special nook for privacy is a design feature many busy adults would treasure. Architect Murray Whisnant designed his home with many windows, soaring ceilings, and individualized spaces for all family members. (*Photograph: Gordon H. Schenk*)

Light and Color

As we will explore in detail in Chapters 5 and 6, light and color are one, color being simply the evaluation by our visual sense of light reflected by an object. The words *visual sense* give us a clue—our responses to light and color are first of all physical. We cannot escape them. Light enables us to see, and it usually awakens us. We cannot see in the dark, and dark may put us to sleep.

As with all the factors, people vary in the amount of light they prefer, and even need. Someone with poor eyesight will require more light than the person with 20-20 vision. The people in a household may like a sunflooded room in the morning, a candlelit room at night. These needs and desires should be considered when designing a room.

There has been quite a lot of research done on color preferences and effects, but much of it is contradictory. All of us know that we have certain color preferences and beliefs. We may not know why a sunny yellow room will seem pleasant on a dull winter morning, or why a room decorated primarily in shades of red will seem oppressive on a hot muggy afternoon. Bodily responses are not absolutes; they are affected by psychological impressions, so that what we *think* we feel is what we actually feel. (See Plate 3, p. 8; Plate 4, p. 9.)

It cannot be denied that people do have varying reactions to colors. There are those who, given a choice, will pick cool colors; others gravitate to the warm end of the spectrum; still others like the neutrals. Perhaps we choose colors not only because we relate to them psychologically, but also because they compliment our physical appearance. If you were to walk into a room painted in a cold green and lit by harsh fluorescent lighting, you would not want to look in a mirror. Color response simply is not predictable, except for individuals, and then within certain limits. Therefore, in designing for a group of people, compromises may be needed to please everyone.

Style: Taste, Character, and Personality

The word "style" has many meanings. In the context of interior design it is often used to mean the type of furnishings that were popular in a particular country, at a certain level of society, at a given period in history. Louis XIV or French Provincial would be examples.

But style can also mean the distinctive flair with which someone furnishes the house. We say that a person or home has style—a characteristic look, a personality served up with verve and originality.

Among the most revealing indications of personality is taste, which at a very simple level can be defined as the particular likes and dislikes of an individual or a household.

Taste is an outgrowth of daily observation of the immediate environment, supplemented by all that we do to broaden our experiences. The various media—books, magazines, and newspapers; plays and

opposite and right: 19–20. Individual taste influences design decisions. One person may prefer a rustic country look (**19**), with exposed brick walls, wood floors, and furnishings to match. Another may prefer a more elegant setting (**20**).

motion pictures; museums and friends' houses; travel—all influence our aesthetic sensibilities. Our tastes develop and change over the years as new experiences are added.

To a large extent taste is governed by an individual's *values* and the ways in which a home reflects or encourages them. Values are a measure of the things people consider important or worthwhile. Often they are instilled in early childhood and are absorbed from the family group; but sometimes they develop as a *reaction* to the values held by one's family. For example, a child growing up in a family that placed high value on money and material possessions might rebel against this and as an adult choose to live more simply.

A household that is entirely centered on family life might consider comfort, safety, security, and companionability to be the most important values expressed in the home. Another household, in which one or more members are achievement-oriented and upwardly mobile, might place more stress on prestige or nonconformity. It is not necessary to discuss which of these values may be "good" or "bad," but only to know what they are for an individual or household and how they affect design decisions. The question of values is related to one aspect of life style: what you expect a home to be—or what you want people to think about you from seeing your home.

Because our tastes inevitably influence our choices, it is helpful to explore just what they are and to develop our own design criteria. Then the character of the home will unfold and become a positive extension of our individuality, rather than a random outcome. We will create our own distinct style. (See Plate 5, p. 10.)

Design Aesthetics: Criteria for Judging

In talking about taste, many people become concerned with acquiring "good taste." They believe that simply by following established rules or hallmarks, "good taste" will evolve. But there is no single version or definition of this term. Taste is an elusive concept, changing with time and circumstances.

However, we can suggest some criteria against which any design can be evaluated, to determine if it is well-designed and suited for its particular purpose.

21. Emy Leeser designed this studio apartment to be as functional as possible. Every square inch of space is utilized. Note how the dining area is clearly separate from the living area. Seating is comfortable and encourages conversation; lighting is subtle but sufficient. Casements on panel tracks offer a novel window treatment, allowing a view without compromising privacy. (*Photograph courtesy Belgian Linen Association*)

22. The opposite view of the apartment in Figure 21 shows the dining area, which also acts as a work area and library. Oriental prints create points of interest, and natural material abound. (*Photograph courtesy Belgian Linen Association*)

As an example, let us consider a choice to be made among chairs. A chair is right for its intended use if it:

- gives comfortable support; if it fulfills its *function*
- is worth the price, plus the time, energy and money necessary for its maintenance; if it is *cost efficient*
- gives pleasure when seen or touched; if it has *beauty*
- suits the household so well that it belongs, yet has special qualities of its own; if it has *character*

Some or all of these four criteria can be applied to any design decision you have to make in planning a home.

Function

We want a home that works. Its spaces and furniture should serve the purposes for which they are intended. For example, social spaces should encourage group interaction: seating should be comfortable; storage convenient and ample; lighting and heating appropriate and functional; and work spaces organized for efficiency. (See Plate 6, p. 10.)

Cost Efficiency

Money inevitably enters into our design decisions. However, there are other factors to consider in addition to the price. Can you afford the installation or maintenance expenditures of both time and money at this particular time?

Beauty

As we all have been told, beauty is in the eye of the beholder. It is the quality that pleases the senses and lifts the spirits—but whose? Beauty is not an absolute. What is trash to one person can be treasure to another.

Certain design elements and principles (Chaps. 3, 4) give us a language with which to discuss beauty. We can refine and define our appreciation of what we think is beautiful by study and observation, but it will still be a subjective judgment. This is liberating. We can express our own ideas of beauty, and in doing so, reveal particular tastes and preferences that characterize us as individuals.

Character

All the qualities that differentiate one piece of furniture or one home from another combine to give a good definition of character. But we should make certain it is the character we want. Character is most successful when it comes naturally from interests and preferences, tastes and personalities. It is most convincing when it develops from fundamental life styles, rather than from an attempt to follow design movements and fashion. And character should have its own inherent qualities of excellence and authority.

Resources

Answers to the questions in the profile will provide a starting point on the financial aspects of planning a home. However, more than purely financial resources are involved. The management of human, material, and environmental resources also enters in. Of equal importance is the fact that we may start out with assets—both in possessions already acquired, that may or may not need repair and/or updating—and in abilities that can be turned to good use.

Financial Resources

The first practical consideration is the amount of money available for furnishing a home. It is important to realize that prices will have some relationship to the quality of furnishings (within limits), but cost does not necessarily affect the results possible.

Human Resources

Human resources consist of our abilities, plus our use of time and energy. People's productivity is influenced by the environment in which they work, so it is cost-efficient to make this environment as easy to work in and as pleasant as possible. The whole household benefits when a kitchen is planned to make the best use of a cook's capabilities. The amount of time required for maintenance must be balanced against that desired for other activities.

23. In a home designed by Francis Palms, an interesting and unique bed has been made by converting an old Victorian sofa. A carved fragment from the bottom of the sofa is now positioned above the bed, adding special emphasis. (*Photograph © Morley Baer*)

Material Resources

A survey of what is already owned is constructive. An old chair may be fundamentally of better quality than a similar piece in our price range today. Reupholstering may be the answer. Other pieces can be put to new use—a trunk into a coffee table, for example. Imagination, a human resource, is most useful when applied to material assets.

Given this background information, you should now be ready to answer the questions on the following pages. The profile questionnaire is designed to alert you to the wide range of needs and desires that must be taken into account in planning a home. In answering the questions, assume that you are about to have your home designed by a professional consultant. The results will depend on the accuracy and completeness of your responses. The word "you" is used in both the singular and the plural, for you as an individual and for a group of people living in one home, as the case may be. By working through the questionnaire you will learn much about the design process. And you may even learn something about yourself.

Profile Questionnaire

I. People

1. Who will live in the home?
a. *Adults:* number _____ approximate ages _____
    special needs _____
b. *Teens/young adults:* number _____ approximate ages _____
    special needs _____
c. *Children:* number _____ ages by sex _____
    special needs _____
d. *Elderly/handicapped people:* special needs _____
e. *Pets:* number _____ kind(s) _____ size(s) _____
    special needs _____ outside only _____ inside _____
f. *Guests:* occasional _____ frequent _____
    long visits _____ short visits _____
    mainly relatives _____ mainly friends _____
Do they become members of the family? _____
Or are they more formally treated? _____
g. *Other:* boarders _____ live-in help _____
Do you expect the composition of the household to change in the
    next five years? _____ ten years? _____
    children will be added _____
    grown children will leave _____
    adult relatives will move in _____
    explain: _____

II. Life Style

1. What type of home do you live in?
one room _____ apartment _____ house _____
    mobile home _____ other _____
own the home _____ rent _____ board _____

2. How do you like to live?
casually _____ informally _____ formally _____
    inexpensively _____ moderately _____ luxuriously _____

3. How do you like to entertain?
a. *Casually:* never _____ infrequently _____
    occasionally _____ often _____
b. *Informally:* never _____ infrequently _____
    occasionally _____ often _____
c. *Formally:* never _____ infrequently _____
    occasionally _____ often _____

4. What do you do for entertainment in the home?
a. *Talk:* in living room _____ family room _____
    kitchen _____ outdoor terrace, porch _____ other _____
b. *Read:* in solitude _____ in a social group _____
    aloud _____ in living room _____ family room _____
    bedroom(s) _____ study _____ other _____
c. *Watch television:* in living room _____ family room _____
    bedroom(s) _____ kitchen _____
How many television sets do you need? _____
Should television be segregated from other activities? _____

d. *Listen to music:* radio _____ where? _____
stereo _____ where? _____
How much stereo equipment must be accommodated? _____
Is placement of components for good listening important? _____
Do you need storage space for records and tapes? _____
e. *Play music:* piano _____ portable instruments _____
drums _____ amplification equipment _____
Where will music be played? _____
Will the instrument(s) be used for practice? _____
Or will they be used for entertainment only? _____
f. *Games and active play:* bridge _____ backgammon _____
other board games _____
played regularly _____ occasionally _____ never _____
Do you like a permanent card table _____
folding card table _____
Or do you use the dining table _____ coffee table _____
floor _____
Do you need space for active indoor play (dancing, billiards,
ping-pong, etc)? Type and location
_____
Do you need space for outdoor sports? Type and location _____
Do you need to provide for children's play? _____
indoors: bedrooms _____ family room _____
outdoors: play yard _____ lawn _____

5. What are your eating habits?
a. *Place for meals* (percent of time): living room _____
living-dining room _____ dining room _____
kitchen _____ living-kitchen _____ family room _____
outdoor terrace _____ restaurants _____
in various places, according to people and occasion _____
b. *Types of meals* (percent of time): pot-luck _____
casual _____ on the run _____ informal _____
buffet _____ sit-down _____ formal _____
Does everyone eat together? _____
How often and where are snacks eaten?
_____

6. What kind of cooking facilities do you like?
very simple _____ average _____ elaborate _____
separate kitchen _____ living-kitchen _____ living
area _____ outdoor barbecue _____
Do two or more people often cook at the same time? _____
Do you have a large library of cookbooks? _____
Do you have any specialties (such as baking) that would benefit from
having separate facilities? _____

7. What is your approach to housekeeping?
wary _____ resigned _____ average _____
compulsive _____
Who is responsible for cleaning the home? everyone _____
one adult _____ all adults _____ teenagers _____
children _____ hired help _____
Where is most of your laundry done? wash basin _____
in-home washer/dryer _____ laundromat _____
apartment washer/dryer _____ commercial service _____

8. What kinds of hobbies do you have?

large-scale _____ small-scale _____ quiet _____
   noisy _____
special needs _____

9. Do you have any collections that should be accommodated or displayed?

special needs _____

10. Do you work at home?

desk work _____
   other _____
special needs (desk, files, drawing table, typewriter,
   etc.) _____

11. What are your personal habits?

a. *Smoking:* Do you smoke? _____
Do other members of the household smoke? _____
Do you permit guests to smoke in your home? _____
Should smoking be segregated in one room or section of the
   home? _____
Should furnishings and colors be selected so as not to show the
   effects of smoke? _____
Or would you tolerate the extra maintenance involved so as to enjoy
   light colors and fabrics? _____
b. *Drinking:*
Do you enjoy soft drinks or alcoholic beverages?
   seldom _____ occasionally _____ often _____
Do you serve beverages to guests?
   seldom _____ occasionally _____ often _____
Would you like provision for a separate bar or drink caddy:
   in living room _____ in family room _____
   in kitchen _____ outdoors _____ portable _____
c. *Communication:*
How important to you is the telephone?
   very _____ somewhat _____ not at all _____
In which rooms would you like to have a telephone?
   kitchen _____ living room _____ bedroom(s) _____
   family room _____ bathroom _____ outdoors _____
   other _____

III. Mobility

1. How long will you live in your present home?

less than five years _____ five to ten years _____
   indefinitely _____

2. How will you move?

alone _____ with help from family and friends _____
   professional mover for large items _____
   for everything _____

3. Where will you move?

to a different dwelling _____ to a different community _____
   to a different climate _____ to a different country _____

4. Do you or will you have a second home? _____
Will each be completely furnished? _____
Will you move some furnishings between the two places (television
    set, sleeping bags, knock-down furniture)? _____

IV. Location, Climate, and Orientation

1. Where do you live?
city _____   suburb _____   country _____
cold climate _____   warm climate _____
    temperate climate _____   dry climate _____
    damp climate _____

2. Do you have pleasant views?
from all windows _____   from some windows _____
    not at all _____

3. Do you need to provide for privacy?
during the day _____   at night _____   always _____

4. Do you need to provide for insulation against heat and cold?
too much sun _____   too little sun _____   cold winds _____

V. Proxemics—Response to Space and People

1. How do you respond to space?
Do you feel the need for space in which to spread out?
    physically _____   visually _____
Do you like to feel enclosed and protected?
    physically _____   visually _____

2. How do you respond to people?
Do you like to be in physical contact, even if only casually? _____
Or do you prefer visual contact without physical contact? _____
Do you have varying needs according to moods or work? _____
Do you like to be alone: most of the time _____   often _____
    occasionally _____   never _____   hate it _____
Do you like to be part of a group: most of the time _____
    often _____   occasionally _____   never _____
    hate it _____

3. Is most of your day spent: outside the home _____
    in noisy group situations _____   in quiet groups _____
    at home, mostly alone _____   with young children _____

VI. Light and Color

1. Natural light:
Do you seek sun _____   or shade _____
Does daylight make you feel energetic? _____
Do you have any eye problems related to amount of light? _____

2. Artificial lighting:
Do you prefer: indirect, even lighting _____
    dramatic, focused lighting _____
Do you need special lighting for certain tasks? _____

3. Color:

How do you respond to color? slightly _____ moderately _____
  strongly _____
Do colors affect and/or express your moods? _____
Do you like a lot of color? _____ or restraint? _____
Do you like colors that are:

  bright _____ clear _____ dominant _____
  clashing _____ deep _____ rich _____ intense _____
  positive _____ exuberant _____ dark _____
  glowing _____ mellow _____ delicate _____
  light _____ soft _____ subdued _____ cool _____
  variegated _____ contrasting _____ raw _____
  monochromatic _____ neutral _____

VII. Taste and Personality

1. Are your clothes: tailored _____ trim _____
  neat _____ casual _____ thrown together _____
  comfortable above all _____ flowing _____
  relaxed _____ conservative _____ wild _____
Do you like to keep up with the latest styles? _____
Or do you stay with styles that suit you? _____

2. Do you consider your personality to be: forceful _____
  shy _____ boisterous _____ quiet _____
  romantic _____ sensible _____ worldly _____

3. What does a home mean to you?
Check each of the following values that you would like your home
  to express or foster:

  prestige _____ aesthetics _____ conformity _____
  nonconformity _____ security _____
  independence _____ comfort _____ nature _____
  privacy _____ sociability _____ leisure _____
  achievement _____ family ties _____ economy _____
  serenity _____ convenience _____ eccentricity _____

4. What do you want for your home?
already know _____ have seen exactly what you want _____
  want to explore the possibilities _____
  would like a professional to suggest solutions _____
  like tried-and-true solutions _____ like to experiment _____

5. Who will make the design decisions?
Will you, as an individual, make all the decisions for the
  household? _____
Will other members of the household participate in the actual
  design process?
  husband or wife _____ children _____ roommate _____
Will a professional designer assume full control? _____
other _____

6. Style
Does the architecture of your home follow a certain style? _____
Do you want the interior to follow the same style? _____
Must everything conform to the same style? _____

Or would you like to mix styles and periods, choosing individual
pieces that you like? _____

Can you envision a mixture that would be compatible (lively but not
chaotic)? _____

Do you want to evolve your own style to express you and your
life style? _____

VIII. Resources

1. Inventory your present possessions:

	have sufficient	need or want to replace
beds	_____	_____
chests	_____	_____
chairs	_____	_____
sofas	_____	_____
coffee tables	_____	_____
side tables	_____	_____
lounge chairs	_____	_____
pull-up chairs	_____	_____
dining table	_____	_____
dining chairs	_____	_____
cabinets for china, glass, silverware	_____	_____
bookcases	_____	_____
carpets	_____	_____
area rugs	_____	_____
curtains	_____	_____
draperies	_____	_____
window shades	_____	_____
lamps	_____	_____
works of art	_____	_____
range	_____	_____
oven(s)	_____	_____
refrigerator	_____	_____
dishwasher	_____	_____
trash compactor	_____	_____
kitchen tools	_____	_____
clothes washer	_____	_____
clothes dryer	_____	_____
ironing board	_____	_____

2. What will you need to buy right away?_____

What can wait until a year from now? _____
five years from now? _____

3. How much money do you have?

The budget is: skimpy _____ enough for basics _____
ample _____ the sky's the limit _____

The money: is at hand _____ will be available for the first
year _____ will be available over a five-year period _____
will be available later _____

4. What abilities or skills do you have?

a. *Sewing* (curtains, upholstery, etc.) _____

b. *Weaving* or other fabrication techniques _____
c. *Carpentry:* small repairs _____ putting up bookshelves _____
   making furniture _____ skilled cabinetwork _____
d. *Painting:* furniture _____ walls _____ anything _____
e. *Other:* _____

5. How much money do you want to spend on upkeep?
   minimum _____ average _____ no limit _____
How much time do you want to spend on upkeep?
   minimum _____ average _____ no limit _____

6. Are you concerned about conservation of energy and natural resources?
Which of the following would you like to explore:
   solar energy _____
   noncentral heating (wood-burning stove, etc.) _____
   insulation against heat and/or cold _____
   recycling _____
   biodegradability _____

Planning for Space

2

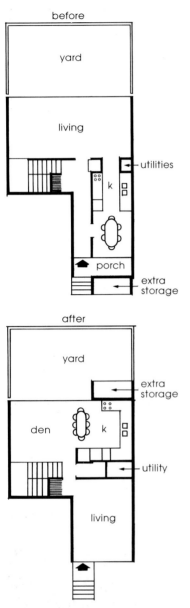

before

yard

living

utilities

k

porch

extra
storage

after

yard

extra
storage

den   k

utility

living

above: 24. Often the information supplied by household members can be used to make a dwelling more suited to their needs. A plan for a low-income housing project (*top*) reworked in response to a user survey (*above*), not only resulted in an apartment more in keeping with the probable life style of the occupants but also opened up the spaces to make the most of available square footage.

right: 25. A floor plan can be an imaginative and personal expression of the needs and desires of those who will live in the home. A beginning exercise in planning a home might be to imagine a fanciful ideal dream house such as a child would design. An example is *Underwater Hideout* by Allison Williams, 11, and Michelle Hill, 12, students of Nancy Renfro. From the exhibit "Kids As Architects," Renwick Gallery, Washington, D.C., 1977–78.

F inding out about people—their tastes and personalities, their life styles, the things they do and have—has given us a start in planning a home for a particular individual or group. When all these factors have been considered, what do we do with them? We start at the bottom—with the floor plan. A floor plan is essentially a two-dimensional diagram of the *spaces* in a home.

People live in space, space that is protected, defined, and limited by floors, walls, and ceilings. Some can plan that space and build it, or have an architect design it and supervise the building. But most of us must search for the apartment or house that most nearly seems to meet our needs and desires.

The initial attraction to a certain home may be its location, the community facilities available, its surroundings, its style, even some distinctive feature, such as an odd-shape room or a splendid fireplace. However, only by seriously considering the organization of its space—the plan—can we determine how well that space will "live." The importance of the plan in shaping the kind of life possible in that space can scarcely be overestimated. The plan not only establishes the basic character of a particular structure but also influences the life style that can flourish there.

For example, suppose the family for whom you are planning—your own or a client's—is composed of very private people who like to pursue their own interests apart from everyone else. A home with large open spaces and very few walls clearly would not work. If possible, this family should choose a different home. Otherwise, you as the designer will have to plan for dividing the space in some way, to accommodate the needs of the individuals.

Assembling and analyzing information about the household members, as we did in Chapter 1, is the basis of functional planning for space. Architects and interior designers often gather this information in informal discussions with their clients, or they may use the more formal written survey as a starting point. Then, they can proceed to visualize the space needs that become apparent.

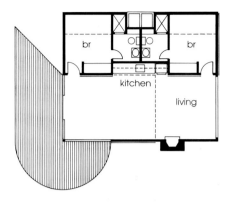

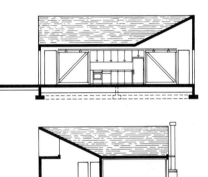

left: **26.** A schematic diagram is the first step in deciding on a house plan. It allows for almost infinite adjustment as plans develop.

right: **27.** The schematic diagram in Figure 26 could be developed into the plan for this year-round vacation house in Puget Sound, Washington, designed by Richard Cardwell. The plan is appealing in its simplicity. Half the house is set off for living and dining, with views facing both north and south. The other half of the house has two bedrooms and two baths.

We will begin this study of space in the home by considering the nature of plans and the various types of plans that exist. Our main purpose will be to investigate ways in which the plan—and therefore the space—can be molded to fit individual needs.

below: **28.** Elevation of the home in Figure 27. *Top:* two sliding barn doors can be closed to conceal the kitchen facilities. *Bottom:* the roof pitch turns 90 degrees over the owner's bedroom, creating an interesting geometry.

The Plan: An Outline of Space

We cannot draw space. We can, however, draw the outlines that shape a space—the walls, floors, ceilings, and other dividers that limit and enclose space. Architects and designers use three basic types of drawings to indicate space: the *schematic diagram*, the *floor plan*, and the *elevation*. The first two of these are bird's-eye views of a home, drawn as though we were looking straight down on it. They differ in that the schematic diagram is loose and informal, the floor plan precise.

An elevation is a side view of a structure, showing how space is organized vertically. It is drawn as though one had sliced off one wall from roof to foundation and sketched the pattern of floors, ceilings, and walls from the side. For our purposes here, the elevation is not so important, and we will not discuss it in detail at this time.

29. Interior view of the home in Figures 27 and 28. With barn doors open, the kitchen is part of the living area.

The Schematic Diagram

A schematic diagram is a freehand drawing of circular or free-form shapes. It *roughly* outlines different space uses. In their proportion to each other, the shapes show the relative size and importance of each area and of the activities that will take place there.

The diagram also establishes relationships between various spaces, such as kitchen and dining area, by means of connecting lines. Arrows on the diagram signify openings as well as circulation patterns. Such a diagram is equally useful in planning a single room.

Sketchy as it is, the schematic diagram can indicate some of the most basic factors in space planning. For instance, it can show the separation of noisy, social areas from quiet areas meant for sleeping or study. Some families may wish to segregate children's spaces, particularly play spaces, from those inhabited by adults. Even an existing space, or a very small one, can benefit from analysis with a schematic diagram. Often, the space can be realigned to meet specific needs.

The advantage of the diagram is that it can be reworked many times, with much adjustment of spaces, zones, and relationships. After these initial decisions have been made, the process of organizing space can begin in earnest.

The Floor Plan

The floor plan is nothing more than a precise, accurate interpretation of the schematic diagram. It shows the exact proportions and placement of spaces, walls, doors, other structural elements, and sometimes furniture.

Once you learn to read and to draw plans, you will find them a marvelous tool for visualizing your ideas and explaining them to clients. Initially, the plan will show you the relative size of different areas, their organization with respect to one another, and circulation paths through the space.

Floor plans always are drawn to *scale.* This means that, while the plan on paper will of course be much smaller than the home itself, all elements will be in correct *size relationship* to one another. The scale $\frac{1}{4}$ inch equals 1 foot is a common and convenient one. Using this, you can fit the floor plan of most homes on a single piece of paper. Thus, if you were drawing a wall that is actually 20 feet long, you would make it 5 inches long on paper. A closet 4 feet wide would be 1 inch wide on paper, and so forth. When planning a single room, you may want to choose a somewhat larger scale, perhaps $\frac{1}{2}$ inch equals 1 foot, to give you more space to maneuver. It makes no difference, provided *everything* is drawn to the same scale.

30–32. You can arrive at a detailed floor plan using the following steps, based on your own room or apartment:

30. Plans can be formulated in a general way by means of a <u>schematic diagram</u> or sketch. *Right:* schematic diagram of an **L**-shape studio apartment; *far right:* an alternative, with the sleeping area converted to work area. The living room now doubles as a bedroom. Schematic diagrams can help when you are adapting existing space to meet changing needs.

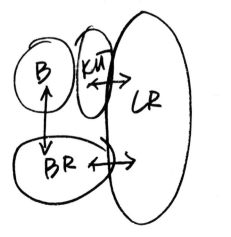

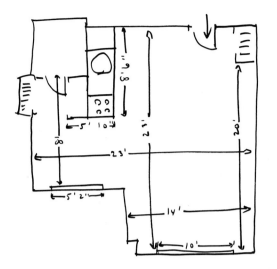

left: 31. The next step after a schematic diagram is the rough floor plan, which shows the important measurements.

below: 32. A detailed floor plan is drawn using the first steps as guides. The main furniture elements are now in position.

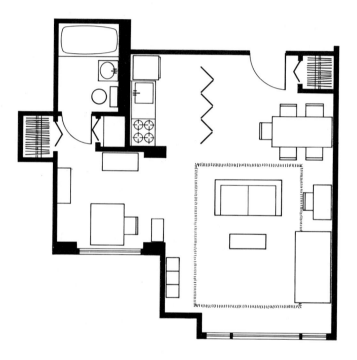

You then can make or purchase templates (outline shapes drawn to scale) of various furniture items, and move them about on the floor plan until you arrive at the best possible arrangements. With a little imagination, you may even be able to project the color sequences that will be seen from different viewpoints. Planning on paper gives you unlimited freedom to experiment and is far less tiring than moving the furniture itself. Anyone working with interior design, from the individual buying a sofa to the professional designer, needs to develop the ability to think and plan in scale.

It is often possible to obtain a floor plan of a home under consideration. However, you must be careful. The plan given to you may not be absolutely accurate, or the scale may have been changed in reproducing the plan. If the plan is off by a few inches in one place or another, has a changed door position, or does not show the correct location of electrical outlets, your design may not work. *Always check the plans and the scale with actual measurements.*

If no plan is available, you can draw your own. This may be as simple or as elaborate as you like, but the more accurate, the more useful. Armed with a precise plan, you will never end up with a sofa that is too large for its intended spot or a dishwasher that cannot be plugged in.

Drawing a Plan   You might begin your plan with a rough outline drawing of the space to be plotted. Do not worry about accuracy at this point, but simply sketch in the approximate positions of all elements, including the following:

- walls, partial walls, indentations, and changes in floor level
- doors, and which way they open
- windows
- closets and cupboards
- staircases
- immovable fixed objects, such as fireplaces and bathroom fixtures
- electrical outlets and switches

Next, measure each distance carefully, with a yardstick or steel tape. Mark the actual dimensions on your rough sketch. If the height of something is important (for placement of a table under a window, for example), mark this on the sketch as well. When all the measurements have been taken, redraw your rough sketch to correct scale.

Let us now consider the various types of plans and how they can be used. The plan may show spaces that are open or closed, laid out horizontally or vertically. By understanding the advantages and disadvantages of each, you will be better equipped to design the space for those who will live in it.

Spaces: Open and Closed

Throughout the world there exist two basic arrangements for space within a home: a single large area in which everyone in the household lives as a group; and a series of tightly segregated rooms that shelter different activities.

In Western industrialized society, this century has brought great changes in life styles and therefore changes in the way living space is organized. Instead of the separated boxes labeled "living room," "dining room," and "kitchen," we may have living-dining rooms or family-kitchens, or bedroom-workrooms—or simply spaces opening into one another with little or no separation.

Our lives today are less formal, with fewer social rituals. So our homes have changed to meet the needs of active, informal, mobile life styles. We still see both types of space organization—open and closed—as people choose the plan that is right for their way of living. Sometimes the best solution is a compromise, with one part of the home open, another closed.

Open Plans

Open plans have few fixed, floor-to-ceiling partitions. They allow for as much flexible social space as possible. Space is organized so that it flows from one section to another, and often to the outdoors. This greatly expands the potential for use and design of any one particular area.

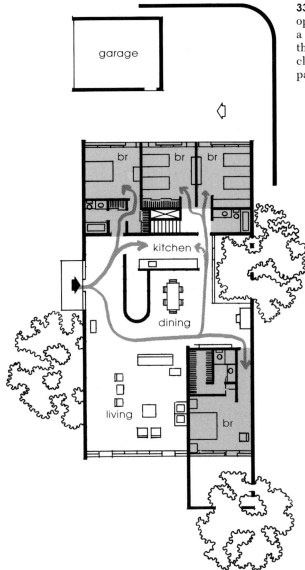

garage

33. With today's less formal life styles, open plans, like the one shown here, offer a maximum of flexible social space. In this example, noisy and quiet areas are clearly defined, and the main circulation paths, as indicated, are very direct.

The advantages of open plans include:

- a sense of spaciousness, particularly for a small home
- diversified use of space
- recognition of the flow of life and the interaction of many activities
- freedom from isolation, perhaps of the cook from the party

But open plans also have certain disadvantages:

- Noisy activities may interfere with those requiring quiet.
- There may be no place to get away from it all.
- The space may seem barnlike if not well planned.

These drawbacks can be overcome in several ways. The space can be:

- shaped with partial walls, floor levels, or furniture placement
- planned for noise control with surfaces that absorb sound
- provided with isolation areas for noisy play or quiet solitude

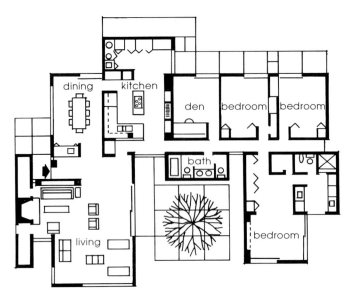

34. A closed plan offers privacy, dividing space into different rooms for different activities. The **U**-shape of this particular plan accentuates the privacy of each individual room. Donald Gibbs and Hugh Gibbs, architects.

Closed Plans

The closed plan divides space into separate rooms. It appeals to many people and has a number of good points, including:

- **privacy** for different age groups and conflicting activities
- **varying upkeep,** with some areas, such as a family room, maintained more casually and others kept relatively neat
- **energy conservation,** through the ability to close off areas not in use

Against the closed plan are:

- a feeling of constriction, which many people cannot tolerate
- lack of flexibility in the use of space
- rigidly controlled circulation paths
- restricted sight lines, cutting off long views

The only way actually to overcome these disadvantages is to remove one or more walls, but this is not always possible. In some cases, the space can be made to *seem* more open through the use of light colors and minimum furniture.

Spaces: Horizontal and Vertical

In addition to open and closed plans, we can divide the treatment of space into horizontal and vertical—one-story plans and multistory plans. Both have been popular at different times. The choice between them may depend upon availability and cost of land, family size, and architectural interest, among other things.

Horizontal Plans

One-story plans always have been suited to small houses and apartments (apartments being essentially one-story homes stacked on top of each other). In this century one-story plans have spread over the land in so-called "ranch style" houses. Their popularity is so widespread that they have become the "typical" suburban home in many areas.

Such plans have many advantages, including:

- elimination of stairs to climb
- ready access to the outdoors
- easy supervision of children
- a horizontal silhouette that fits well on level land

Apartments, of course, do not have all of these advantages. But they are cheaper to build this way, because identical units can be stacked, resulting in shorter plumbing and heating lines, for example.

There are also disadvantages to the horizontal plan, most of them related to conservation of resources. These include:

- increased use of space, on a person-per-acre basis
- greater cost for land
- higher cost for structural elements
- inefficient use of energy for heating and cooling

It costs far more to heat or cool two rooms side by side than two stacked rooms. Heat generated from below will rise to an upper room; a second story protects a lower floor from summer sun.

Vertical Plans

The multilevel floor plan has become increasingly popular again for good reasons—the main one being the pressure of limited space. As suggested above, the cost factor—in land and structural elements—is much less. Other advantages include:

- Heating and cooling are less expensive.
- Vertically separated rooms simplify zoning.
- An upper story may catch cooling breezes or a nice view.

below: 35. This house, with only 1,000 square feet of space, is a good example of a horizontal plan. It was designed in the early 1950s by Bruce Walker and has stood the test of time, perhaps because it features four distinct but integrated areas for group living: an all-purpose space and conversation alcove indoors, a terrace and screened porch outdoors. The arrangement allows for an easy flow of movement, but also for stabilized furniture groupings. Bedrooms and bath are well segregated in a unit away from the group spaces, with a sound barrier of coat closet, heater room, linen storage, and bedroom closets. The children's bedrooms occupy a small separate wing.

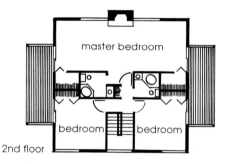

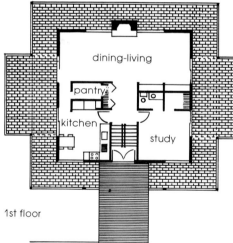

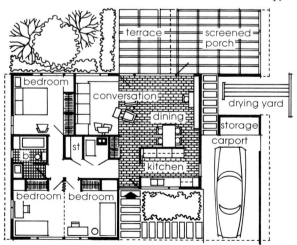

above: 36. A vertical plan has many advantages. This one, being square, encompasses the most space with the least foundation, exterior walls, and roof. Because it has two stories, exterior maintenance and heating costs are reduced. A potential problem is solved by a first-floor study that can double as a bedroom or sickroom. The balconies off the bedrooms give the second story access to the outdoors, while the split-level entry is convenient to both floors. This house has excellent zoning and circulation.

But these benefits must be weighed against the faults:

- **Stairs** can be a nuisance, especially when there are small children, and those children have toys. To an elderly or handicapped person, they are a major obstacle.
- **Separation of zones** causes much running up and down those stairs when someone is ill or there is a baby in the house.
- **Maintenance** is more difficult, unless a complete set of cleaning supplies is kept on each floor.

Good planning can help to solve these problems. A bedroom and bath on the main floor can double as a nursery, sickroom, or in-law room as needed, then revert to a guest room or study. Properly designed storage at the top and bottom of the stairs can serve as a catch-all until a trip up or down comes naturally.

The multilevel plan seems especially suited to cluster and row houses or townhouses because of its ground-saving feature. It is also showing up in duplex apartments, where the two-story layout somehow seems more "homelike."

Open Vertical Plans

A major innovation in house planning today involves the manipulation of vertical space, of volume. Soaring interior spaces generate a sense of excitement that many architects have explored. Even "development" or "tract" houses now often have high ceilings with balconies or openings into second-floor areas. This trend is a radical departure from the 8-foot ceilings that were standard for so long.

In part this is a response to shrinking land area. Tall interiors counteract our awareness of smaller floor areas and give a sense of spaciousness. In hot and humid climates, a plan that opens vertically will draw air up and through the house, to be vented at the top.

37. Amherst Hills, Mass., is a project of more than 1,500 condominium townhouses, duplexes, four-plexes, and detached units, plus a 34-acre commercial center. The floor plan below is for a two-story townhouse with two bedrooms. Figure 43 shows the first floor interior. Callister, Payne and Bischoff, architects.

2nd floor

1st floor

38–39. So-called "tract" houses historically have lacked originality of design, but innovative architects face the challenge in new ways. Whalers' Cove Apartments in Foster City, California, is an unusually well-designed single-family housing development with soaring interior spaces.

right: 38. In the plan illustrated, note that the living room height is two stories. Flexibility in the floor plans provides for formal living and dining areas or more casual treatment of space. Circulation paths are excellent. Fisher-Friedman Associates, architects.

below: 39. A view from the balcony overlooking the two-story living room reveals an arched window looking out over the water. Individuality throughout the Whalers' Cove Apartments is emphasized by treatment of windows, varying combinations of bay, arched, porthole, or dormer designs. Fisher-Friedman Associates, architects. (*Photograph: Joshua Freiwald*)

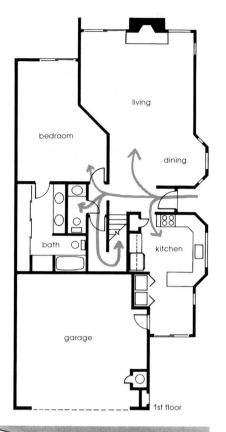
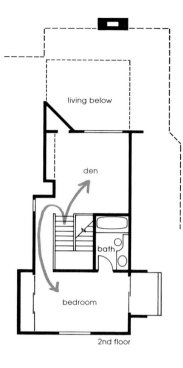

40. In an open home designed by architect Bob Cabrera in collaboration with Marlene Rothkin Vine, a fan (top right) directs heat down so that energy is not wasted. (*Photograph: David Vine*)

Such a plan also has drawbacks:

- Heat rises, which may be good in the summer but wastes energy in winter. Much of the heat generated ends up in those soaring but unused spaces.
- High windows pose a cleaning problem and a hazard.
- Noise also rises, making zoning for quiet more difficult.

As with other arrangements, each household must balance the aesthetic advantages against the practical difficulties.

Circulation

Space is not something we look at. We use it, and to use it we must walk to it and through it. The paths of circulation established will influence the success of any home plan. Generally speaking, these paths should radiate from the home's *principal* entrance, be it back door or front.

Short and direct are probably the key words; least interference with other activities the key concept. Ideally, it should be possible to get from the entrance to any room in the home, and from room to room, without going through the middle of a living area. There are some exceptions:

The dining space, used only at certain times during the day, can double as a circulation space without too much interference.

A family room often becomes the nucleus of the household. People will be trooping through in all directions, and the room should be planned accordingly.

A kitchen can also be the hub of the house. If it is large enough, it can be designed so that people moving through do not interfere with the activities of the cook.

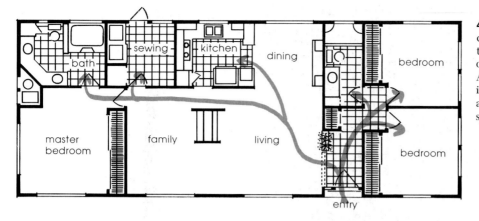

41. A home has good circulation if you can get from the entrance to any room in the home, and from room to room, without going through a furniture grouping. A mobile home, although restricted by its basic 24-by-64-foot size, achieves separation of parents' and children's private spaces. (*Courtesy Balboa Mobile Homes*)

Most of the time, the architectural structure of the home determines circulation *between* rooms or areas. The designer can do little or nothing to control these paths. But the circulation *within* a room often remains quite flexible. To a large extent this depends upon furniture placement. It is a good idea to draw traffic paths between and within rooms on your floor plan *before* considering the arrangement of the furnishings. Then, after everything is in the place you have decided upon, sketch in the traffic patterns again, to make sure there is an easy unobstructed flow.

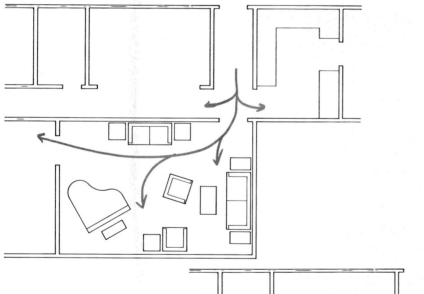

42. The circulation paths within a room are important. Furniture must be placed so that there is an easy flow. The living room (*left*) is an example of poor circulation. The furniture has been placed without attention to traffic pattern. The room *below* is better arranged.

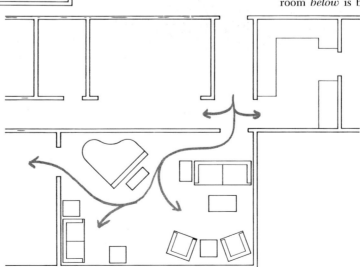

Evaluating a Plan

A large part of this discussion about space has been abstract. The focus has been on types of plans, their good and bad points. How does all this relate to you or your client? Most of the time you will be confronted with an existing space—a home in which the family already live. A more fortunate situation is being able to decide about a future home or to choose between two or more possibilities. Either way, the ability to evaluate the plan will help you to make many design choices. Following is a series of questions that will influence these choices:

Is the total amount of space adequate? As a rule of thumb, a home should provide at least 200 square feet of space for each occupant, although 500 square feet gives more comfortable living. To find the square footage, measure the interior floor space, adding all stories together. Do not count in unfinished cellar, attic, or garage. Then, divide this figure by the number of occupants to calculate the per-person quota. If the amount of space per person is less than 200 square feet, you may have to design very carefully to allow any privacy.

As the number of household members increases, the space required by each individual diminishes somewhat, because they overlap in certain

43. The Amherst Hills kitchen (plan in Figure 37) is conveniently arranged so that the cook will not be excluded from any gathering, whether in the dining area on one side or the living area on the other. At the same time, the size of the kitchen floor space will allow another person to pass through at any time. Architecture and planning by Callister, Payne and Bischoff; interior design by Virginia Anawalt and Marianne Myers. (*Photograph: Ezra Stoller* © *ESTO*)

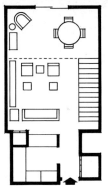

above: 44. Space is appropriately allocated if it is designed to suit the activities of those who live in it. The same floor plan, with different furniture arrangements, can serve varying needs and life styles. The tenant who is rarely home during the day has little need of a view; the seating area has been brought inside and assumes the quality of a library. (*Courtesy Apartment Ideas, Summer 1972.* © *Meredith Corporation, 1972. All rights reserved.*)

right: 45. As the plan for Figure 44 shows, dining space has been de-emphasized and removed from the kitchen, since the owner seldom has occasion to eat at home.

social areas. But households with a spread of ages and interests may need more space per person than a relatively quiet, homogeneous group. Flexible and multiuse space lessens the overall size of the space needed.

Is the space appropriately allocated? Within the same amount of space, one plan may have smaller bedrooms to allow for larger social spaces. Another plan will cut down on the group areas to provide larger bedrooms and baths for those who like privacy.

The space devoted to cooking can vary from a one-person cubicle to a large living-kitchen where all gather to supervise or help or simply talk, in a companionable atmosphere. The plan may allow for only one general space—a living room—or two or three. There may be a bedroom for each person, or else the necessity of some doubling up. Answers to the questionnaire in Chapter 1 will help you to decide which of these arrangements will work.

Is the space well zoned? Are social areas well removed from private areas, such as bedrooms? Are potentially noisy spaces segregated from quiet ones? If desirable, are children separated from adults, at least part of the time?

The indoor-outdoor relationship should be considered. A living room opening onto a protected terrace or lawn unites the home and the outside into a social zone. Too often a living room will face the street, making this difficult.

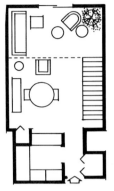

above: **46.** The apartment in Figure 45 lends itself to another plan. Cooking and entertaining are more important to this occupant, so the dining table is adjacent to the kitchen.

top right: 47. In this arrangement the window—bringing light, air, and view—has been left unobstructed for the tenant who spends more time at home. (*Courtesy Apartment Ideas, Summer 1972. © Meredith Corporation, 1972. All rights reserved.*)

Is the circulation well plotted? Some questions to consider are:

- Can you get to the bedrooms without passing through the major group area?
- Can guests get to a bathroom without passing through a bedroom?
- Can you move through the kitchen without interfering with cooking operations?
- Are hallways wide enough for two people to pass each other comfortably?
- Are entrance areas large enough to give a welcome to the home, without dumping guests straight into the middle of a party?
- Are staircases wide enough to permit passage of furniture? (Spiral stairways are very popular now, but they lose some of their charm when you imagine carrying a queen-size bed up them.)
- Are doors well situated to allow for a flow of traffic and comfortable furniture arrangement?
- Does the home have a "heart"—where people automatically congregate? Are paths to that area unobstructed?

Are the rooms of suitable size? You must consider *usable* size as well as *actual* size. A room with one wall of glass eliminates that wall space

Table 2.1
Typical Square Footages for Certain Portions of the Home

Room	Small	Medium	Large
entrance	25–30	35–40	45+
living space	150–200	220–280	300+
dining area	100–130	150–180	200+
dining space in kitchen	25–40	50–70	80+
kitchen	75–90	100–140	160+
bedroom	80–130	140–190	200+
bathroom	33–35	40–45	50+
utility room	12–15	18–25	30+

for placement of furniture, reducing usable area but expanding the room visually. The size of the furniture will have considerable bearing on room size needed. Contrast a Victorian dining room set against a glass-and-chrome table with sleek plastic chairs.

Some typical square footages are listed in Table 2.1. Some households will be happier with fewer but larger rooms; others would rather have more separate, though smaller, spaces.

Will the rooms take furniture required for the planned activities? There are several variables here: the shape of the room, the location and size of openings, the activities, and the type of furnishings. These questions will be examined in more detail throughout the book.

Is there adequate storage space? No one ever seems to have enough storage space. We might concentrate on the word "adequate." This means well-planned storage for specific use, such as a linen closet, as well as some raw space for the many things we cannot bear to throw away just yet. Depending on the household involved, "adequate" storage might be room for: a thousand books, five pairs of skis, 50 pounds of dog food, an extensive wardrobe, a collection of antique rifles, or almost anything else. Again, the answers to the questionnaire will help to determine what is adequate.

Is the plan well oriented? The relationship of individual rooms to the outlook and the street, to the sun, wind, and trees, will affect interior design in many ways. Must window coverings be planned to screen unpleasant views, or to block early morning or hot afternoon sun? Will draperies need insulation to cut icy northern winds? Can passersby look directly into the home during the day or at night?

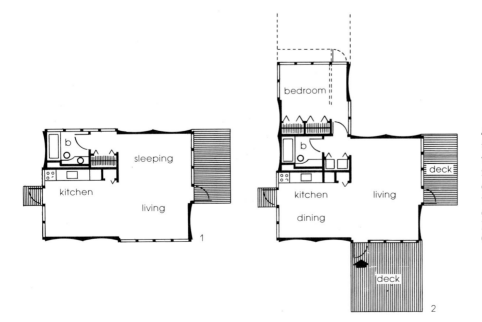

48. An interesting aspect of some industrialized houses is their ability to expand, with minimum disruption, as family needs change. This version begins as a compact unit and grows with the addition of a bedroom wing and deck. Several other arrangements are possible. Mark Hildebrand, designer, for Rudkin-Wiley Corporation.

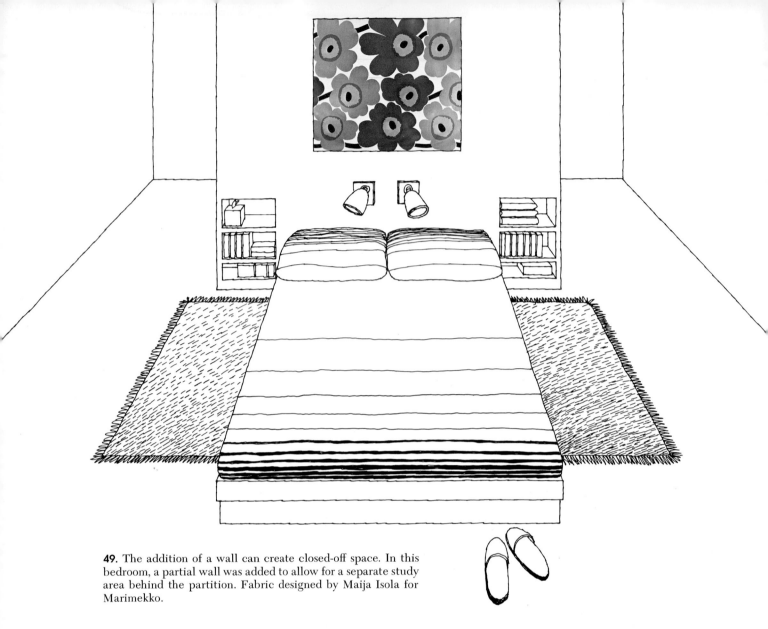

49. The addition of a wall can create closed-off space. In this bedroom, a partial wall was added to allow for a separate study area behind the partition. Fabric designed by Maija Isola for Marimekko.

Does the plan lend itself to change? This question should be considered on two levels. Can the plan be changed immediately to suit present needs? Can it be changed as life patterns evolve? The needs of a household alter as children come and go, a small budget may give way to a more ample one, and tastes change, inevitably, over the years. A flexible plan will allow the home to change and develop as the tastes and life styles of the occupants do.

Modifying a Plan

Given an existing architectural structure, there are two basic ways in which a designer can shape a plan: *physically* and *visually.*

A physical change means a real structural change. The potential for this will be determined by two factors—whether the occupants own or rent, and the money available. As a rule, you cannot make permanent structural changes in a rented house or apartment. The owners might object, and the investment would not be worthwhile. There are, however, *semi*permanent structural changes possible in a rented dwelling, such as erecting a partial wall not attached to the floor.

The physical changes you can make in a plan include the following:

- Removal of a wall to open up the space. This entails major reconstruction with *load-bearing* walls, the walls that actually hold up the structure. But often interior walls can be eliminated quite easily, with little effort.
- Addition of a wall or partial wall to close off space, for example, creating a separate dining room from a large kitchen.
- Installation of sliding or folding doors to open space for large gatherings or subdivide it for greater privacy.
- Construction of a platform floor to separate one part of a group space from another. If not permanently attached, this can be added to a rented dwelling. Two gentle risers, at least, are necessary to alert people to such a change, or the platform may become a hazard. A low railing, plants, or furniture will call attention to the shift in horizontal plane.

50. A platform floor, depending on its shape, can virtually change the floor plan. Shown here, a platform created for the sleeping area provides extra seating at the end of the bed. If desired, storage space can be built into the platform.

- Lowering of a ceiling to separate parts of a group space or to create a more intimate spot. A false ceiling over a fireplace seating area or a dining area will dramatize a change in function.
- Construction of a balcony for sleeping or work. This is a time-honored solution to the problem of limited space in a one-room apartment. It could well be adapted to larger homes (especially ones with high ceilings) to make more flexible use of space.
- Opening of an attic for more living space. The refinished attic could become another bedroom or a playroom; in an upside-down arrangement it might even be the new living room, with bedrooms and cooking/dining areas underneath.

The *visual* changes possible in a plan are more limited in their effect but virtually *un*limited in the varieties. They include:

- wallpapering a certain wall section or leaving bare brick exposed to divide that space from an area with plain walls
- placement of furnishings and screens to create "islands" within a larger space

above: 52. The arrangement shown here makes double use of the existing space. A balcony bed provides additional room for a work area.

below: 53. Movable walls, sliding doors, or folding doors can extend the possibilities for opening up or closing off space. Edward L. Barnes, architect.

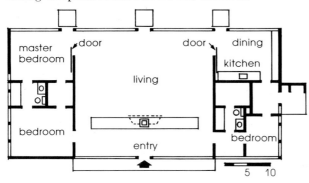

- limited furnishings and/or careful grouping of furnishings to make the space seem more open
- room dividers of furniture, fabric, or plants
- varied floor treatment, such as positioning of area rugs, to give the impression of separate spaces, or carpeting to create a sweep of broad space
- use of light wall colors, furnishings, and fabrics to open up a space; darker, heavier colors and furnishings to bring a sense of closure
- a single color scheme throughout the home to make it seem like one continuous space

The floor plan is the beginning, not the end. Drawing a plan will tell you what you have to work with, but it should also suggest what you *might* have. Imagination and creativeness can overcome many obstacles and sometimes result in truly personal solutions. Your task is to understand and then to manipulate the space in question, as expressed in the plan, to meet the needs of a particular household. And then you are off to a good start, for you have begun the process of design.

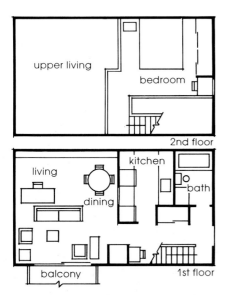

left: 54. Furniture placement alone can establish zones for different activities without cutting up space into little boxes. Dining space, a library-study, and a conversation grouping all borrow from the surrounding areas without intruding on them. George C. Oistad, Jr., architect.

below: 55. Placement and orientation of furniture in a one-room apartment is crucial if the plan is to be workable. Here three separate areas are clearly delineated. A divider of storage cubicles in the center creates two spaces out of one. The dining area is the third. (*Courtesy American Home Magazine*)

Elements of Design

3

When we plan the furnishing of a home, we are dealing with design—design that will affect the people who live in the home. This is what interior design is all about. We plan, and the result is design—good, bad, or indifferent. The most elementary furnishing of a space has some thought behind it, even if it is only considering whether the sofa will fit against the wall where it is supposed to be.

When you place a sofa in a room, you must decide where it will go—against this wall or that or out in the middle of the room. An impulse to leave it where the mover dropped it is a *decision*. You may not know why you decided as you did, but there the sofa remains.

Sooner or later the result of your decision will become apparent. If you placed the sofa in the middle of a traffic path so that it becomes an obstacle to circulation, your decision was a poor one; the design does not work. If the sofa fits neatly against a certain wall but has no relation to other furnishings—no lamp for reading, no tables for holding things—the design could be called indifferent, neither good nor bad. But if you arranged the sofa in a comfortable furniture grouping, with perhaps a chair or two for easy conversation and convenient tables and accessories, you probably have created an effective design, at least in terms of physical comfort.

Effective interior design must be considered from two viewpoints: the *visual* and the *functional*. An attractive home that does not work for its inhabitants will cause them to be frustrated and uncomfortable. A functional design that has no visual appeal will be boring. As a designer, you have one great advantage operating in your favor: Thoughtful planning for function very often contributes to visual attractiveness.

Design is an active process that usually begins with some mental image or idea. This is true whether the thing to be designed is a

56. These are the units of design for a particular room: the room itself, and what will fill it. They are the raw materials to be organized into a total composition. Chair at right by Selig.

57. The units in Figure 56 are arranged here in a way that works visually and functionally.

painting, a chair, a toaster, a room, a house, or a whole city. Regardless of the product, all design has certain *elements* in common, which can be thought of as the raw ingredients of the design. They are: space, form, line, texture, ornament, light, and color. The character of the design will depend upon how these elements are used and combined.

Space is something we cannot touch, but it inevitably touches us. We are within and surrounded by space, and therefore a part of it. Although we cannot make space, we can *mold* and change it fairly easily, to take full advantage of its dynamic qualities.

Form is the basic tangible element, as in the form of a room or a chair. It has substance and shape.

Line gives us the outline of form and separates it from the surrounding space. Line also has the characteristic of being highly expressive, of being able to make subtle or strong design statements.

Texture and *ornament* are surface characteristics of form. Texture is always present, because everything has a surface and thus has texture, be it smooth or rough. Ornament can be considered an extension of texture—an enrichment to give greater visual delight.

Light, like space, is untouchable but touches all. Without it, we cannot see. Varying intensities of light affect our emotions as well as our ability to work, and its composition produces color.

Color, probably the most powerful of the elements, is always present to some degree.

58. A fireplace recessed in an inglenook promises warmth and companionship or a cozy place to read. The hearth raises the level of the fire so it can be seen more easily from the length of the room. Judith Chafee, architect. (*Photograph: Ezra Stoller © ESTO*)

The interior designer manipulates these elements in creating an environment. We live in space, sit on forms, follow lines with our hands or eyes, see and feel texture, and respond to ornament and color, which are made evident by light. For example, in practical terms:

- A living room has so much *space* in which to arrange furniture.
- We need *light* to see and read and work.
- The *form* of a bed may dictate its placement.
- The *line* of a traffic path should skirt the cooking area.
- A *texture* may or may not reveal soil.
- A certain *color* will alter skin tones.

Let us now discuss some of these elements as they relate specifically to interior design. It will become obvious right away that it is almost impossible to talk about one without mentioning the others. The various elements interact continually. We separate them here only for the purposes of analysis.

Light and color are particularly complex topics. They are also areas in which the designer can, perhaps, exert the greatest influence. Each is the subject of a full chapter later in the book.

Space

By erecting walls, an architect or builder carves finite, measurable space out of infinite space. It is three-dimensional, having length, breadth, and depth. It then becomes the interior designer's role to define and mold or modulate that space.

Merely by walking into a room we change its space. What had previously been one unbroken space becomes fragmented, bounded on one side by the shape of the body. Placing furniture in the room further alters the spatial relationships. (See Plate 8, p. 60.)

As we move through space, we gradually accumulate impressions, until a sense of the whole space has been assembled. The dynamics of that space will invariably affect us. A large room with a high ceiling, drawing our gaze upward, will have a very different impact from that of a fireside nook with a lowered ceiling.

We respond to the spaces that envelop us, and we adapt to them—sometimes willingly, sometimes not. The fireside nook would probably make most people feel protected and sheltered, although some might find it confining. In an open plan, where spaces flow into one another, the inhabitants could feel either exhilaration or dangerous exposure, depending upon their personalities.

Space Modulation

The spaces we must deal with can be adapted to our needs, to our likes and dislikes. We use other elements—line, form, light, color, and texture—to mold the space. This is an important design consideration, for it is only when we vary the sizes and shapes of the spaces within a building that space acquires its dynamism.

Fortunately, most homes have some built-in space modulation. We enter through a relatively small hallway, which then opens into a larger living room, and then may contract again into smaller specialized areas. This gives a sequence of impressions to which we respond differently. We can emphasize this pattern of change by furniture arrangement that encloses portions of a room while leaving circulation paths clearly defined. A lowered or raised ceiling height over some sections enhances the sense of spatial variation.

The ideal of space modulation is simply to define an already pleasing space. But few homes or rooms have ideal space. More often, the designer is confronted with a spatial problem to be solved, and there are endless ways to do this.

59. The addition of a floor-to-ceiling wall near the entrance to an apartment divides the space into a foyer plus dining area. (*Photograph courtesy Dunbar*)

60. A bold geometric painting provides a point of strong emphasis in the dining room of a house designed by Charles Moore of MLTW/Moore Associates. (*Photograph © Morley Baer*)

- A too-large, open space can be subdivided by the placement of forms—a screen, a furniture grouping, a room divider, a bank of plants, for example.
- A confining space can be enlarged visually by small-scale furnishings that do not crowd the space.
- An amorphous space, lacking definition, will take on character from a lively pattern in a textile or wall covering.

Plate 7. Apartment dwellers faced with a limited amount of horizontal space may decide to expand their homes vertically by building a sleeping loft, like the one designed by playwright Paul Cherry for his own apartment. There is ample room for books on the walls, and a small office fits cozily beneath the loft. (*Photograph: Dan Wynn*)

Plate 8. Designer John Saladino used light colors and low furniture to make this ceiling seem higher than it actually is. Vertical Venetian blinds and lighting fixtures also contribute to the effect. Brightly colored pillows and flowers add accents. (*Photograph: Norman McGrath*)

Plate 9. Rectilinear shapes are exploited in the design of this dining area, framed by tall shelves on either side. The back wall is dominated by a large set of panels grouped together in a square, while the ceiling beams emphasize the geometric symmetry of the setting. Elizabeth Williams, designer. (*Photograph: Robert Perron*)

above: Plate 10. Antique leaded and stained-glass windows, combined with newly crafted windows of colored and clear glass, comprise the walls of a romantic house in Mill Valley, California. The broad expanses of glass seem to bring the outdoors into the home. William W. Kirsch, architect. (*Photograph: John Dominis, Time-LIFE Picture Agency*)

below: Plate 11. This nylon Jacquard weave fabric from the "La Paz" collection has a stripe pattern enlivened by small triangular shapes that punctuate the design. (*Photograph courtesy Westgate Fabrics*)

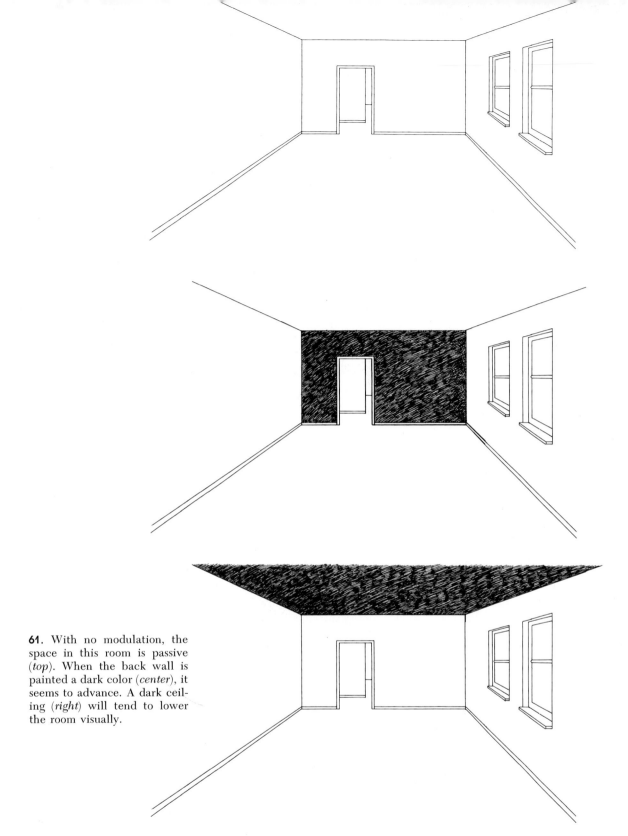

61. With no modulation, the space in this room is passive (*top*). When the back wall is painted a dark color (*center*), it seems to advance. A dark ceiling (*right*) will tend to lower the room visually.

- Colors dramatically affect our perception of space. Light, cool colors make a space seem to expand; warm, dark colors seem to contract space. A room that is too long and narrow, for example, can be made to appear more square by a dark color or active pattern on the end walls.
- Light is also a potent tool in modulating space. A large, open room can be carved into spatial areas by control of natural light or sensitive placement of artificial lighting. (See Plate 10, opposite.)

right: **62.** An easy chair designed by Mario Bellini illustrates the use of *mass* to achieve a desired effect, in this case comfort. (*Photograph courtesy Atelier International, Ltd.*)

below: **63.** This chair's *shape* is its most obvious element. A continuous metal frame covered with rattan makes it very light to move about. The cantilever construction gives a comfortable springiness to the design. (*Photograph courtesy Founders Furniture, Inc.*)

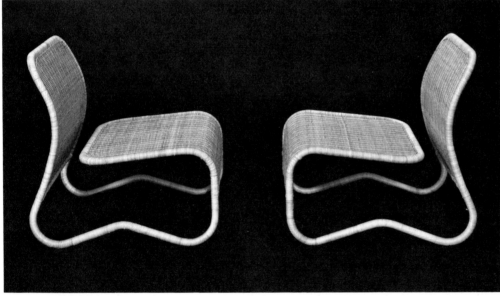

Form

In interior design, form can be defined as three-dimensional shape, mass, or structure. Three chairs illustrate the varied aspects of this definition and the effects produced (Figs. 62–64). In the first we perceive form as *mass*, which fills space solidly. In the second it is the *shape* that catches the eye, reduced in this case almost to lines that define the space both within the outline and outside it. The third chair calls attention to its form by concentrating on *structure*. We examine the fitting together of the various components and realize that the rectangular form has been softened by a slight rounding of the edges.

Form affects us both physically and emotionally. A particular chair is not well designed unless it accommodates itself to the *human* form. So fundamental is this concept that one of the great catch phrases of this

64. Beautiful *structure* is emphasized by the use of superbly crafted wood joints in this chair. The rectangular form is softened by the slightly rounded edges. (*Photograph courtesy C.I. Designs*)

century, in design and architecture, has been "form follows function." This means simply that the form of an object should grow out of its intended use and moreover should *look* as though it does. This would seem self-evident, were it not for some of the tortured shapes concealing their functions that were popular in such periods as the Victorian era.

Today, design is freer, and there are no rigid patterns to follow. Form no longer is dictated by any extreme—either the layers of ornamentation of the previous century or the obsessive streamlining that prevailed in the middle of our own century. If a form pleases the eye and fulfills its purpose, it can be considered effective design.

Shape

The words *form* and *shape* often are used interchangeably, but there are shades of meaning that separate them. As suggested earlier, shape is one aspect of form. Whereas form can encompass many things, shape is specific. It describes the measurable contours of a thing, its outline. When we speak of a rectangular shape or a round shape, a definite picture comes to mind.

There are, of course, an infinite variety of shapes in our universe. But all can be categorized as *basically* rectilinear, angular, or curved. In their purest forms these are geometric figures—rectangle, triangle, circle; cube, pyramid, sphere. While these seldom appear in the natural environment as pure forms, they are well suited to the built environment, because they can be specified precisely for machines.

Rectilinear Shapes   A mathematician might well argue that rectangular shapes are one kind of angular shape, which is certainly true. But the rectangle as such has become so much a part of our lives, so much the basis of the built environment, that we tend to focus on the qualities that make it unique. (See Plate 9, p. 61.)

For the most part our homes are composed of rectangles—the overall shape of a room, the shapes of doors, windows, and furniture, the

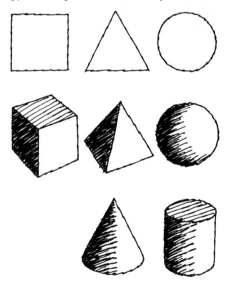

65. The basic geometric shapes and forms: rectangle, triangle, circle, cube, pyramid, sphere, cone, and cylinder.

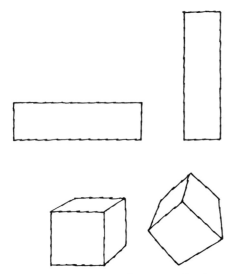

fitting together of the building blocks of room beside or on top of room. Straight line fits snugly against straight line.

It is the predictability of the angles that allows this, always a precise 90 degrees, but it is the shape within that impresses itself upon us. Rectangles can range in shape from linear thinness to cubical fullness. The repertoire is almost endless, and so is the manner in which the rectangles can be used.

Cubes, for example, can vary in size. They can rest stably on one side, insecurely on one edge, or precariously on one corner. The adjectives describe our emotional responses to these placements.

In general, however, it is the stability of the rectangle that commends it to us.

- A long horizontal rectangle has the restful quality we associate with lying down on a bed.
- A vertical rectangle, standing upright on the floor, is still secure, but more lively because we know it is well adjusted to the force of gravity, as we are when we are standing.

Angular Shapes   *Triangles,* and the *diagonals* that comprise them, in general have a dynamic character. Unlike the stable 90 degrees of the rectangle, their angles can vary from sharp to relatively blunt, with a corresponding variety of emotional response. Diagonals imply motion, from the quiet of a long oblique line to the quick flicks of small, interrupted lines.

A fabric with a pattern of triangles will enliven a room, as will a sloping ceiling that leads our eyes up to the highest point. The degree of energy will depend to some extent on the degree and number of the angles, and the size and slant of the diagonals:

above: 66. A rectangle on its side gives us a feeling of security and stability, while a rectangle on its end seems more lively. A cube resting on one side appears immovable, but one standing on its corner has potential motion.

below: 67. In this room, the angular shapes on the rug serve to enliven the surroundings. Choppy, curved lines in the graphic on the wall emphasize the effect. The two fabrics work together to make the room cheerful. (*Photograph courtesy Belgian Linen Association*)

68. Diagonal lines incorporated into a house plan will create an effect of increased space. Thomas N. Larson, architect. (*Photograph: Phokion Karas*)

- Repeated sharp angles and diagonals have a briskness about them, perhaps mentally pricking us.
- Large diagonals generally increase apparent size and generate a sense of expansiveness. The angles are far apart and moderate; we are more aware of the line between and its quiet movement.

Actual triangular shapes in the home usually are concentrated in relatively small-scale patterns or large-scale flat planes, such as the ceiling mentioned. We rarely want to feel sharp angles. They are uncomfortable, and even seeing too many is tiring.

Implied diagonals, however, are very useful. Chairs set at angles that will produce easy conversation between people is a standard and congenial arrangement. A long diagonal sight-line between two rooms can give the impression of more space than is actually there. In this way, we use the dynamics of the shapes rather than the actual shapes.

Curved Shapes   Circles and spheres, cones and cylinders—*curvilinear* forms bring welcome relief into the basically square interior environment. No doubt they remind us of our more or less curved bodies and other natural forms in which the straight, rectilinear line is almost totally absent.

69. Circular rooms like this one, from a Victorian house, are rare but give a feeling of drama. The kitchen makes the most of the available space, imaginatively combining the functional and aesthetic to create a unique design. Gus Dudley, architect. (*Photograph: Robert Perron*)

Circular rooms are not often seen in homes, for they leave too many unusable spaces in between; but circular objects abound. Rounded shapes are most noticeable in dishes and glassware, where the form is sympathetic to our hands. Round tables are popular for bringing people into a friendly circle with easy eye contact. A round pillow is a definite accent against a squared sofa. A round lamp shade spreads light in an even, natural way.

Circles are used as motifs for many patterns in textiles, wallpapers, and floor coverings, when the repetition of such a decided form is in sharp contrast to the flat rectangular surface on which it is placed.

Cones and *cylinders* also appear in the home, but in less noticeable ways. They offer a definite directional movement toward a focal point, especially the cones. As furniture legs, lamp bases, vases, and candleholders, they are usually unobtrusive but pleasing, gently drawing our attention to what they support.

Nongeometric curves are probably the most adaptable, bringing together continuity and constant change. Most seating has some rounded edges to soften its basic rectangularity and make it conform to the shape of the human figure. The softness and pliability of textiles gives them a relationship to curvilinear patterns.

70. The nongeometric curves on this chair give a feeling of both continuity and constant change. "Sausalito," designed by Heinz Meier for Landes.

In some parts of the world, the rounded shape of a hut or tree house is a structural necessity; the material with which the people build dictates this form. We see traces of this structural demand in such areas as ceramics. Cups and plates come naturally off the potter's wheel or from the potter's hands in rounded form. Although machines have long taken over the task of making dinnerware in almost any shape imaginable, the rightness of the circular shape has proven itself structurally and *seems* right to us. So, too, the shaping of a tree limb into a cylindrical or cone-shape support for a table persists, although often the form may become very modified.

These are aesthetic decisions now, not necessities. We use curved lines and forms for their humanizing qualities, their visual appeal, their dynamic attributes.

71. The base of the table in a home designed by Charles Moore and Dimitri Vedensky is in the shape of a tree trunk. Many tables use cylindrical or cone-shape supports as bases—a refinement of the tree-trunk shape. (*Photograph © Morley Baer*)

Line

For so simple a device, line has a tremendous range of expressiveness. Theoretically, it has only one dimension, length, but it shapes the world in which we live. Even its two basic contours—straight or curved—have emotional implications. We "walk a straight line," or alternately, "follow a curved path."

Our eyes trace lines until we perceive the form of a chair, the shape of a room, the pattern of a textile. Among the most expressive qualities of line is its direction. In studying the ways in which direction affects our feelings and our movements, consider the following generalizations:

- Vertical lines imply a stabilized resistance to gravity. If high enough, they evoke feelings of aspiration and ascendancy.
- Horizontals tend to be restful and relaxing, especially when long. Short and interrupted horizontals become a series of energetic dashes to the eye.
- Diagonals are comparatively more active, suggesting movement and dynamism.
- Big upward curves are uplifting and inspiring.
- Horizontal curves connote gentleness and relaxed movement.
- Large downward curves bring a welcome sense of solidity and attachment to the earth.
- Small curves suggest playfulness and humor.

As applied to interior design, these generalizations recommend that verticals be emphasized—high ceilings, tall doors and windows, upright furniture—for a feeling of loftiness and cool assurance. Horizontals—low ceilings, broad openings, stretched-out furniture—would give an impression of informal comfort. Diagonals—sloping ceilings, oblique walls or furniture arrangements—suggest activity.

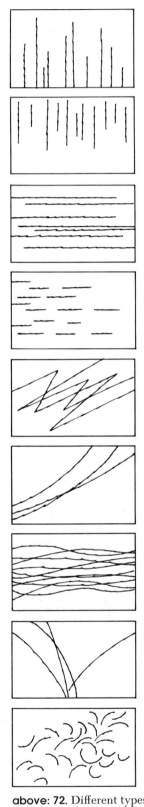

above: 72. Different types of lines evoke different responses.

right: 73. A door designed to seem like part of the wall when closed makes an impressive accent when open, emphasizing the dramatic vertical character of the space. Edward L. Barnes, architect. (*Photograph: John T. Hill*)

74. A great soaring arc that reaches up to encircle the bedroom-balcony of this house exploits the tensile strength of wood. Mark Mills, architect. (*Photograph © Morley Baer*)

Texture

Texture refers to surface quality: how something feels when we touch it, how it looks when light strikes it. There are two basic categories of textures—*tactile* and *visual*.

Tactile or actual textures can be felt by the hand as smooth or rough, as in unglazed brick, rough wood, or plush velvet.

Visual textures, also called illusionary or simulated, may be absolutely smooth to the touch but give the impression of texture. Patterns in fabrics and flooring would be an example.

There is also another method of classifying textures, according to the way in which they are created.

below left: 75. *Tactile* textures are those that actually can be felt. The grain of the wood paneling, the smoothness of the lamp base, the weave of fabric and rattan—all are tactile textures. (*Photograph courtesy California Redwood Association*)

below right: 76. A *visual* texture can give a smooth surface the illusion of texture. The smooth patterns in these printed fabrics resemble the weave of a basket. (*Photograph courtesy Bloomcraft*)

left: 77. The textures surrounding the hearth area all emerge from the structures of the materials, and their fabrication—the grain and knots of wood, a shag rug, smooth ceramic tiles, and a rougher concrete flooring. Callister, Payne & Bischoff, architects. (*Photograph: Charles Callister, Jr.*)

above: 78. A detail of Figure 77 shows the incised marks in the ceramic capitals atop the columns, an example of applied ornament.

Structural textures develop from the way in which an object is made or from its material. Examples include the light-reflecting smoothness of polished chrome or the light-absorbing quality of a nubby tweed fabric.

Applied or external textures are just that—something added onto the underlying structure. Decorative scrollwork or inlay on furniture would fit this definition. Applied textures really bring us into the realm of *ornament*, discussed later.

It is important to realize that every surface has texture, and that it affects us in a number of ways. Texture influences:

- **Physical impressions** of everything we touch. An upholstered fabric, if coarse and harsh, can be actually irritating to the skin. If too sleek, it may look and feel slippery and cold. The most popular fabrics tend to be neither too rough nor too smooth.
- **Light reflection,** and thus the appearance of any form. Very smooth materials—polished metal, glass, or satin—reflect brilliantly. They attract attention and make their colors look clear and strong. Moderately rough surfaces, such as a brick floor, absorb light unevenly, so their colors look duller.
- **Household maintenance**—literally, the amount of work needed to keep surfaces looking clean. The shiny surfaces of brightly polished

metal or glass are easy to clean but show every spot. Rougher surfaces, such as bricks or rugs with high piles, call less attention to dirt but are harder to clean. Smooth surfaces with visual textures combine most of the good qualities of both.

- **Beauty and character.** For instance, an old wooden beam, roughened by time, will cause responses of delight in its age and interest in the way in which its surface sets up patterns of light and dark.

Ornament

Ornament can be seen as an elaboration of texture. It is related to tactile texture, but also to *pattern*, a term generally used in reference to decoration of two-dimensional surfaces, such as fabrics.

Ornament usually is thought of as an enrichment of a surface, something added to enhance the visual attractiveness. However, *added* does not mean "tacked on." In the best designs, ornament emerges from the very quality of the object itself. It could be a pattern printed on cloth, a carved motif on furniture, or a design etched on glass. Any ornament should complement the form, shape, and material of the surface to which it is applied. (See Plate 11, p. 62.)

We might think of ornament as "form applied to form," the two elements being harmonious. The forms of ornament and pattern can be divided into three broad design categories.

Naturalistic designs represent things in the natural world. They arouse associations with the subject matter—flowers, fish, landscapes, and so on.

Stylized designs are simplified. They usually emphasize basic qualities or lines of a form in an attempt to discover its true nature.

below left: 79. The *naturalistic* design of this fabic, "Wisteria," uses motifs of plants and flowers. The pattern complements the material. (*Photograph courtesy Boris Kroll*)

below right: 80. This cotton fabric by Brunschwig and Fils, called "Fossils," has a *stylized* design. The leaves and shells are not strictly representational but rather emphasize basic qualities. Tricia Guild, designer.

Abstract designs have little or no relation to known objects. They are also called *nonrepresentational*, because they represent nothing but themselves. Abstraction seeks to please the eye through a combination of lines, shapes, and colors that are satisfying by themselves, with no reference to familiar things.

Our discussion of space, form, line, texture, and ornament—the elements of design—has been fairly abstract. As mentioned at the outset, these elements, in practice, are closely related. To understand how the elements are combined, we must turn to the principles or concepts underlying effective design.

81. An *abstract* design, such as the one on this fabric designed by Maija Isola, does not represent anything but itself. (© *Marimekko Oy 1961*)

Principles
of Design

4

f the elements described in the previous chapter can be thought of as the raw ingredients of design, the principles outlined here might be considered as the ways in which those ingredients can be combined, and the results of such compositions. They are concepts that have evolved to explain how and why certain combinations and relationships of elements please us, or perhaps seem unpleasant.

The number of principles is not set. We will consider seven that are useful in creating or analyzing any design: *scale* and *proportion; balance, rhythm,* and *emphasis; variety* and *unity.* It is important to remember

82. The room shown here illustrates many of the elements and principles of design. Its *scale* is small and *harmonious,* making it look comfortable. The furnishings are in *proportion* to one another. *Variety* is provided by the combination of an American Indian theme and modern furniture, unity by the *repetition* of patterns. *Rhythm* is also set up by repetition. The *focal point* of the room is the fireplace, *emphasized* by the way accessories are grouped around it. The plates near the ceiling are symmetrically *balanced;* the hanging over the fireplace is an example of radial balance; the items on the mantelpiece set up asymmetrical balance. Chair at right by Selig.

83. This home has been scaled down so children can be as comfortable in it as adults. Furnishings are low and shallow; spaces between things are relatively narrow. At the same time, there is ample seating and walking space for adults. Caswell Cooke, architect. (*Photograph: John T. Hill*)

that these are not rules to be followed strictly. In fact, they are often used intuitively: the designer may have an almost subconscious feeling about where to place furniture for a balanced or unified arrangement, or, conversely, feel that a room lacks variety.

Often, the design principles come most strongly to our attention when something is wrong. Perhaps we have sketched or even executed a design, and somehow it does not work. Then, when we analyze the results, we see that the design is lacking in balance, or in points of emphasis, or whatever. Correction of these problems may successfully pull the whole design together.

We can evaluate a design by studying how the various principles have been employed. They do not, however, tell us whether a given design is good or bad. They are only general truths, serving as a means of communication. As with all concepts, they are subject to changing interpretations and discoveries.

Scale

The idea of scale was introduced in Chapter 2 as it relates to the floor plan. There we were concerned with maintaining *constant* scale—the same size relationship of things to each other—in transferring from life size to paper size. In treating scale as a principle, we refer to *appropriate* scale. A grand piano placed in a tiny room would seem *out of scale*—equally in the actual room and on the paper floor plan.

The standard of measurement relating objects to each other, to us, and to the spaces they occupy may well be one of the most important principles in interior design. Scale must be adjusted to two often conflicting demands—human scale and architectural scale. Only after these have been considered can other concepts come into play.

Undoubtedly, the primary concern is human scale. Most furniture is built for people who are between 5 and 6 feet tall and between 100 and 200 pounds. A basketball player, often more than 7 feet tall, would be happier with more generously scaled furnishings; a child is much more comfortable with child-size pieces. This takes us back to the very first question posed in Chapter 1: Who will live in the home?

human Scale
Architectural Scale

Architectural scale is another matter. Although the basketball player may well find or build a house with 10-foot ceilings and 8-foot doorways, most of us must live in rooms with ceilings about 8 feet high and doorways 7 feet or less. Indeed, we feel most secure in these dimensions, with perhaps a soaring or dropped ceiling in certain areas for contrast. The overall measurements of a room or home establish a basic scale to which furnishings and other elements must be related. Scale relationships in the home cover the entire range of design: of furnishings to space and to each other; of texture, pattern, and ornament to surfaces and furnishings; and of accessories to larger pieces.

We adapt quickly to a variety of scales, from small to large. However, the success with which scale is used depends on some consistency. It is not simply a matter of size—of placing small furniture in a small room—but of harmonious relationships. A delicate chair upholstered in satin will give an impression of fragility, a rugged leather easy chair a sense of heavy mass, even if both are the same size. They probably would not be used together in a design scheme, because their scales are incompatible.

In working with scale, then, the designer should consider other factors beyond sheer size. For instance, a bookcase filling one wall of a room may be large in size, but if the many shelves are filled with books and other objects—plants, sculpture, perhaps a stereo system—the physical size is counteracted by the smaller pieces and brought into a congenial kinship with the rest of the furnishings. The scale has been humanized. (See Plate 12, p. 95.)

84. The scale of this room is slightly off. The lamp is too large for the table, and a larger piece of art would look better on the wall behind the sofa.

85. The scale of these furnishings is more harmonious.

Proportion

Many people use the terms *scale* and *proportion* interchangeably, and it is not really necessary to make a clear-cut distinction between them. In general, scale is the broader, more inclusive term, proportion the more particular measurement.

The comparative relation between a part and the whole, *proportion* has no set formulas, although many people have tried to find the ideal. The so-called Golden Mean or Golden Section, an invention of the ancient Greeks, is achieved by dividing a line or form so that the smaller portion has the same ratio to the larger as the larger to the whole. This is a safe rule, but its applications are limited. Following the Golden Mean would yield a room of pleasing proportions, but it would be too rigid if applied to bed sizes.

Nevertheless, proportion does have value as a principle. It is an ingredient in balance, rhythm, and emphasis; in relationships between

determines Size & Weight (Visual)

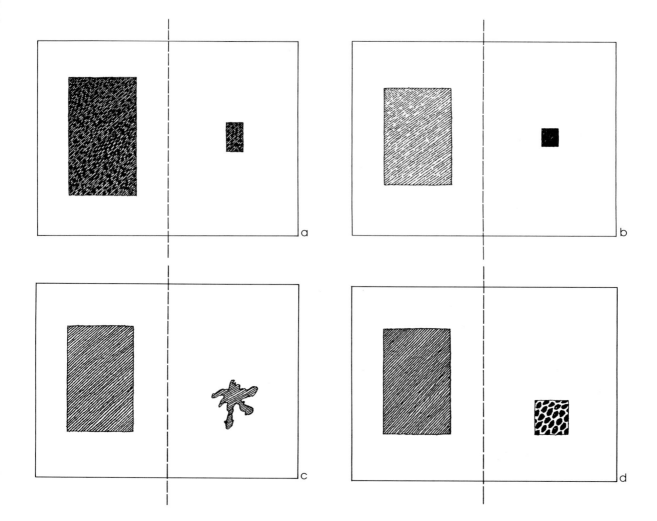

86. a. A large shape has more visual weight than a smaller one, other things being equal.
  b. The small dark shape is equal in visual weight to the larger gray one.
  c. The small irregular shape is equal in visual weight to the larger geometric shape.
  d. The small textured shape is equal in visual weight to the larger, even-tone shape.

the visual weights of parts and the whole; in the rhythmic flow of forms and colors.

The ability to judge and discriminate comes with practice. The designer needs to try out different proportional relationships until the best combination emerges. The "rightness" of proportions will relate to the feeling of balance that is achieved.

Balance

Balance is a fundamental law of physics that expands into most areas of living. It is very evident in nature. A rock sitting solidly on the earth has a static balance; undercut the rock, and it will fall until it achieves a new balance. The human body is a masterpiece of balance. We constantly shift weights and postures to equalize forces that allow us to sit, stand, walk, run, dance, or lie down with minimum effort—in other words, to achieve balance.

In design, we are concerned less with actual weights than with *visual weights*. The visual weight of something means the psychological impact it has upon us, the way it attracts our attention. As with the other design principles, there are no hard rules about this. However, in general terms, with all other factors being equal:

- Large size has greater visual weight than small size.
- Warm, bright, advancing colors have greater visual weight than cool, dull, receding colors. (See Plate 13, p. 95.)

- Rough or busy textures and patterns have greater visual weight than smooth or plain ones.
- Irregular shapes have greater visual weight than geometric shapes.
- Diagonal or jagged lines have greater visual weight than vertical or horizontal lines.
- Brightly lighted areas have greater visual weight than dim ones.

Following these guidelines, the designer might balance a small, brightly colored area with a larger neutral one, or a small, rough-textured object with a larger smooth one. There are endless combinations, some of them illustrated in these pages. The success of the design depends on trying various possibilities until equilibrium is attained.

It is important to note that the balance in a room or home shifts and changes constantly over the course of a day. Two factors in this shift are illumination and people. Think of the way a room looks at night and by day. Windows that in the daytime are bright with sunlight, at night will be dark holes in the wall. Areas that are in shadow by day may be illuminated for reading or work at night. Control of natural light and placement of artificial lighting can have great impact on the balance in a space. (See Plates 16, 17, p. 113.)

People also contribute to nuances of balance. No room is alive unless it is being used. As we walk into a room, the balances constantly change when we view it from various angles, and we ourselves become

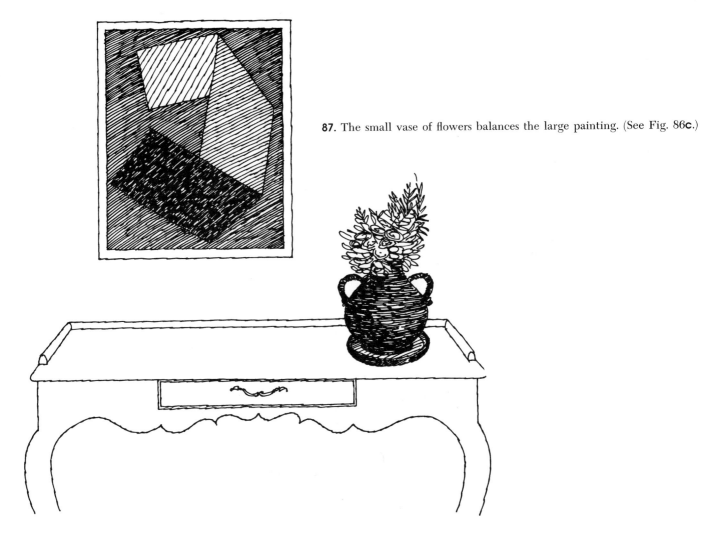

87. The small vase of flowers balances the large painting. (See Fig. 86c.)

88. This room is symmetrically balanced. Identical tables and lamps stand at either side of the sofa. The picture above the sofa and the table and rug in front are centered. This type of design tends to make a room appear more formal, but it can easily become boring.

part of the composition. Not only do we take our own "visual weight" in and out, we also bring in a magazine or some flowers, take out a newspaper, subtly shifting the equilibrium.

What does all this mean? Simply that change is inevitable and should be considered as inherent in the design. A well-considered and decisive balancing of the design elements will be secure enough to withstand minor modifications.

Balance can be classified in three categories: *symmetrical, asymmetrical,* and *radial.*

Symmetrical Balance

Balance that is achieved by having one side of an object or an arrangement the mirror image of the other is called *symmetrical.* Alternate terms are *formal* and *passive.* We all are familiar with the placement of a sofa with identical tables and lamps at each end. The first term, symmetrical, describes its composition: an arrangement of corresponding parts. The other two words describe its effect. It is formal—a conventional, regular array of objects rather than a spontaneous, irregular placement. We know what to expect from it. Also, such balance is usually passive, quiet, and reposed, demanding little from us. We can see easily *how* the balance is achieved.

Most furniture is symmetrical. It fits our symmetrical bodies and balances well so that it sits firmly on the floor. Some furniture arrangements are symmetrical because they work best that way. A rectangular dining table usually has an equal number of chairs on each side so that people can talk together easily and the dining equipment can be comfortably placed.

A symmetrical arrangement also provides a good focal point for some area or object that is to be emphasized. The axis around which like components are placed leads to a natural center of interest that draws our attention. The whole composition becomes steady and stable, easily grasped and appreciated.

Having said all this, however, it must be pointed out that symmetrical balance is usually employed, and is most suitable to, the smaller units in an interior design. Furniture itself is the chief example.

Much classical architecture shows symmetrical balance, as indeed do some houses today. But once beyond the façade of today's symmetrical house, the illusion vanishes. The rooms are disposed for use rather than strict and arbitrary symmetry.

Only rarely does a whole room lend itself to such design. To begin with, the space itself is almost never symmetrical. On occasion windows are evenly placed, but more often they vary in response to outlook and to workable furniture arrangements. Doorways seldom are balanced; the functional house plan would not allow such formality, and the resulting division of space within the room would be difficult to cope with.

We most often see symmetrical balance used around a fireplace or some such dominant element. Perhaps identical chairs or sofas face each

89. A symmetrical arrangement of chairs makes the fireplace a focal point. Attention is directed to the fire, because the chairs are of equal visual weight. The embroidered pattern on the chairs serves to enliven the composition. (*Photograph: New York Times/Aller*)

other across a coffee table. But even here symmetry is rarely carried out in every detail. Different lamps or pillows, end tables, and various enriching objects will break the monotony created by too much likeness.

One of the main objections to strict symmetry in interior design is that it reduces the apparent size of the whole area. By constantly drawing attention to the unit, we ignore what is happening elsewhere. This tendency can be countered by lines, shapes, or colors that lead the eye away from the symmetrical center and enliven the composition.

Asymmetrical Balance

The type of balance in which the visual weights or attractions are equal but not identical is called *asymmetrical, informal,* or *active.* It can be achieved in two basic ways:

- The forms, though dissimilar, may be of the same visual weight and placed equidistant from the center of a composition.
- Quite dissimilar forms may be counterbalanced by their placement at unequal distances from the fulcrum or center—the principle of the seesaw. The heavier object is placed closer to the center.

90. Two dissimilar forms—the vase of flowers and the lamp—are placed on either side of the sofa, and the framed print is off-center, illustrating the concept of asymmetrical balance.

91. above: Two dissimilar objects are placed with their centers equidistant from the composition axis, creating asymmetrical balance.
below: Two dissimilar objects at unequal distances from the axis also achieve a type of balance. This is called the seesaw principle.

92. Four different natural materials—metal, wood, ceramic, and concrete—arranged in simple forms, combine to make an elegant, asymmetrical still life. (*Photograph: Philip L. Molten*)

Asymmetrical balance seems more natural to us, more active, and perhaps more responsive to our informal lives, as its other names indicate. Its energy comes because we instinctively, though unconsciously, seek to find equilibrium in the composition, so that we ourselves are not disoriented.

Our bodies are more or less symmetrical when viewed from the back or front, but they are almost always in a state of asymmetrical balance. We walk and eat, sit with our legs crossed or lie in bed with an arm or leg bent, and yet maintain balance. In fact, it is hard for us to hold a completely symmetrical stance, and we assume it only when we want to appear dignified and formal. Then we discard it as quickly as possible! The static is rarely useful in daily life.

Our homes echo this compromise. As a rule, we have asymmetric arrangements of essentially symmetric furniture. Starting with solidly balanced chairs and tables, we place them for use rather than for design principles, and then achieve poise by an active balancing of visual weights. A lounge chair and ottoman may have the same apparent importance as a sofa and may fit our needs better than two identical sofas; a small red pillow will counterbalance a larger beige one, giving us a choice of color and sizes for comfort and variety. This system allows for flexibility and individuality; we can make changes easily without destroying the whole.

Radial Balance

A circular balancing of parts around a center, *radial* balance is customarily found in smaller items about the home, items that are themselves often circular, such as plates or a bowl, or a round pillow. Radial motifs in patterns are also common, and in occasional larger items, such as a lighting fixture.

93. A round dining table, set for a meal and with chairs ranged around it, automatically establishes a radial balance. The Trova print, partially visible at left, echoes this theme. Kirsten Childs, architect. (*Photograph: Robert Perron*)

Radial balance is not only the exact repetition of forms around a pivotal center, but also circular movement to, from, or around a central focus. The focus may or may not be emphasized. Thus, radial balance can be either essentially symmetrical and static, or asymmetrical and swirling. A table set for dining with a centerpiece would be a good example of the first, a spiral staircase the second. This type of balance is fairly restrictive, but the curvilinear element, as always, makes a refreshing counterpoint to so much rectangularity.

Rhythm

A consideration of rhythm in any design follows naturally after balance, because rhythm depends on balance, as it does in the dance. Balance is observable rhythm. The unity and harmony, character and individuality

94. A circular staircase, although asymmetrical, creates a radial balance that acts as a counterpoint to the straight lines typical of a home's structure. Thomas N. Larson, architect. (*Photograph: Phokion Karas*)

above: 95. The living room of this city apartment is filled with subtle rhythms. Each element has its own rhythm, progressing from the delicate geometry of the pillow fabrics to the stronger pattern of wood parquet covering the radiator, and finally the bold striped carpet. Tom O'Toole, designer. (*Photograph: New York Times/Hausner*)

below: 96. The dining area of the apartment shown in Figure 95 is also full of subtle patterns. The floor tiles, mosaic mirror, Indian motif rug, and cane chairs blend harmoniously; their rhythms interact. (*Photograph: New York Times/Hausner*)

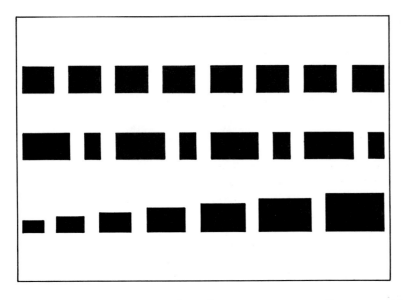

97. Repetition, alternation, and progression: each has a rhythm.

of our homes are in part determined by the continuity of fundamental rhythms. These can be achieved through *repetition, alternation, progression,* or *counterpoint.*

Repetition

Rhythm is perhaps easiest to see in a fabric pattern where the exact repetition of a motif sets up a steady beat.

Almost every home is full of repetition, from window shapes to dinnerware. Sometimes this effect is carried to the point of monotony, as when a furniture "style" is too dominant. But boredom usually results from unthinking repetition; a more discerning eye would repeat the *spirit* of a form or pattern, not the exact lines. (See Plate 14, p. 96.)

Alternation

Interruptions

If we consider the spaces between repeated motifs as *shaped* spaces, alternation inevitably enters. A more dynamic alternation occurs when a second distinct motif or color introduces a gentle pause or a heavier, longer accent in the underlying beat. More broadly, in a home we see it in the alternation of windows and walls, which may set up a steady rhythm or an irregular tempo, according to how they are placed.

Progression

An ordered, systematic progression of space, forms, or colors may have an obvious but subtle beat, slowly swelling or diminishing, or a more dynamic sequence of changes whose underlying rhythm becomes apparent only upon examination. Size may range from large to small, lines alter in quality or direction, shapes change by degrees from square to rounded, colors blend or repeat in sequence.

Progression seems less insistent, more inventive than simple repetition, and for these reasons it has far greater scope. We see it in the movement of lines or forms over an upholstery or drapery fabric, in the building up of a furniture group, in the sequence of spaces within a room or a home.

Progression, too, is almost inevitable, simply because the wall surfaces of a room, and the furnishings, vary in size.

Contrast and Counterpoint

At its simplest, *contrast* is the deliberate placing of forms or colors to create opposition by abrupt transition instead of gradual—round next to square, red by green. It is a favorite device to awaken response. The rhythm produced is exciting. If the manner in which the forms or colors adjust to one another is bolstered by similar transitions elsewhere, it provides the continuity upon which a rhythm is established.

Contrasting rhythm has become an increasingly popular theme in home design, although it has always been used to some extent. We find that old furniture, perhaps with a boisterous, joyful pulsation of curves is set off well against the quiet measure of a chaste background. Or the most severe of modern furniture gains richness against the foil of an ornate Victorian setting.

This can be an exciting and challenging design concept, but one that must be used knowledgeably and with some restraint. We may end up with a result that looks more like a store than a home. The individual rhythms may fall apart into chaos.

All homes make some use of counterpoint. One relentless rhythm would become tiresome and overwhelming. So we use contrasting rhythms—the intricate pattern of an Oriental carpet against the quiet lines of a natural wood floor; brightly patterned upholstery on a sofa contrasted with a subdued stripe on a chair or two.

The key to rhythm, in a dance, a fabric, or a room, is *continuity*—the organized movement of recurring or developing patterns into a connected whole. We do not want to be left with one foot in the air.

Consistency of rhythm—through repetition, alternation, progression, or contrast—establishes a solid foundation upon which grace notes of color or form can flourish. The result, however, is usually better if one rhythm predominates, to avoid the equivalent of a traffic snarl. For this we need our next design principle, emphasis.

98. The Victorian chair in this room emphasizes the simplicity of the space by setting up a contrast. Betsy McCue, designer. (*Photograph: Stephen Hill*)

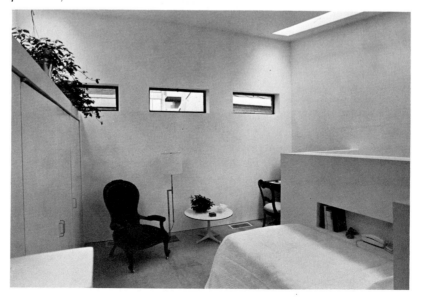

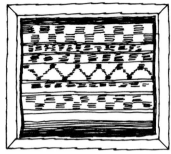

Emphasis

The presence of *emphasis* in both balance and rhythm soon becomes apparent. Emphasis means varying degrees of stress, of intensity, given to the parts of a design. We cannot emphasize one thing without deemphasizing another, automatically setting up a scale of dominance and subordination. We assess the visual weights that are dominant in a design to see what kind of balance is achieved. The beat and scale of intensities establishes rhythm.

The importance of emphasis, in a small design, or in a whole room, is that it gives us stressed points (or *focal points*) and rest areas for the eye. Thus, it is the basis of balance and rhythm. In a fabric design the emphasis might be on a series of bright, repeated motifs.

In a room, the dominance and subordination of the various parts will be broadened to include a scale of significance. Often a focal point, or center of interest, will be the standard against which the other parts are measured. For ease in dealing with the idea, we might set up a four-point scale:

opposite: 99. Placement of the sampler above the chair does not work so well as placement over the chest. In the top example, the designer has not taken advantage of the natural emphasis created by the bulk and weight of the chest, which directs attention toward the sampler in the lower one.

right: 100. A handmade tapa cloth hanging serves as a headboard and gives a focal point to the room. The rug evokes but does not duplicate the design. (*Courtesy House Beautiful. Copyright 1972, The Hearst Corporation.*)

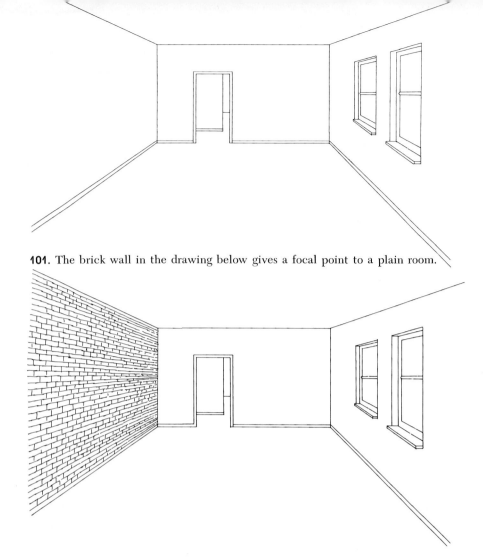

101. The brick wall in the drawing below gives a focal point to a plain room.

- **emphatic**—fireplace or a substantial bookcase, built up with paintings, wall fabrics, or accessories into a strong focal point
- **dominant**—large furniture grouping around this emphatic focus, drawing people into its orbit
- **subdominant**—smaller furniture groups undemanding but supportive; windows lightly curtained for privacy rather than impact
- **subordinate**—floor, walls, ceiling that enlarge the background by being unobtrusive, and accessories that have meaning and visual attractiveness but are not clamorous

102. The grain of the wood paneling on this staircase subtly emphasizes its direction. It would have been easier to have panels all going in one direction, but, instead, a strong decorative detail has been added. Chris Woerner, architect. (*Photograph: Robert Perron*)

left: Plate 12. Although a tall set of shelves dominates one wall of this kitchen area, the collection of cookbooks and dishes makes the scale less overwhelming. Gus Dudley, designer. (*Photograph: Robert Perron*)

below: Plate 13. The kitchen-dining space of a Connecticut home has been designed in warm earth tones, which seem to advance from the off-white walls. More vivid color accents come from the food, cooking utensils, and accessories. Judith Chafee, architect; Christina A. Bloom, designer. (*Photograph: Ezra Stoller © ESTO*)

left: Plate 14. The natural pattern of this staircase has been emphasized by the alternation of black and white paint. The design is echoed not only by the low wall but, unexpectedly, by the banister as well. Carl Pucci and Ben Benedict, Bumpzoid, architects. (*Photograph: Robert Perron*)

below: Plate 15. A design is composed of individual parts brought together, with a unifying theme. Ric Wineshank, Sunshine Design, designer. (*Photograph: Robert Perron*)

Within each of these groupings, however, a similar hierarchy must be established. In using the fireplace as a focal point, for example, it might be the mantel that would most of the time be most emphatic, with a collection of carefully chosen and placed accessories subordinate but influential in strengthening its importance. A painting over the mantel would come next in the scale, dominant because of its size and colors, while a brick hearth and dark fireplace opening would be subdominant. At night, however, a different effect might be apparent, with the flames of a fire drawing all eyes, an irresistible center of interest.

Such levels of emphasis, of course, are natural and inevitable. They bring a quality of life and interest to our homes. Simply the changes of light, during the day and at night, will sometimes alter the focus, as will the presence of people. A successful design will accommodate these changes without losing its balance and rhythm. This can be handled chiefly by restraint. In general, no one feature in a room should be so dominant that it demands constant attention.

Harmony: Variety and Unity

Unifying a variety of diverse forms and colors results in harmony.

Unity is easily achieved by a strong and clear motivating idea. The specific means might be through:

- Sameness or repetition, with walls and ceiling the same color.
- Similarity, one step removed, introduces some variety: walls might be one hue, with the ceiling slightly darker or lighter.
- Congruence of parts: a round table on a round rug; the forms are different in size but they fit together.

103. Unity can be achieved by built-in furniture and a single color scheme, as in this living room. Because the room is less than 12 feet wide, the space is expanded visually with white walls, a white nylon carpet, and the simple furniture. The use of white and beige as the dominant colors, with the accessories providing variety, creates a feeling of harmony. (*Photograph courtesy E.I. duPont de Nemours & Co.*)

- Components that express the basic character desired, such as stress on a positive color.
- Enclosure—a frame around a painting; a conversation pit or encircling modular seating arrangement.

Variety brings vitality. It hardly needs explanation, being only too easily introduced into the home by random purchases, gifts, casual acquisition. Diversity, however, produces welcome surprises and heightens the total effect if it is kept within bounds and has an underlying justification. It can be as subtle as slightly different textures of pillows on a sofa, or as challenging as a polished copper hood above a stone fireplace.

When unity and variety achieve a happy merger, *harmony* results. Small variations of texture and color, form and space are easily assimilated. Sharper contrast will take its place in a harmonious scheme if it seems part of an overall design, perhaps one that stresses the pairing of the rugged with the sleek. Many other themes would be possible. For example, stone and metal have an affinity, both being natural materials, as well as a long history of togetherness.

104. There is a congruence of parts in this kitchen: a round table, globe lights, and wooden chopping boards. The shapes and textures are harmonious. Wood paneling provides a texture different from the smoothness of the countertops and table. The whole room is a pale color, with dark accents to provide variety. John Saladino, designer. (*Photograph: Norman McGrath*)

left: 105. Small variations of form and texture are easily assimilated in this sitting room. Most shapes are geometric, and the ones that are not work as points of contrast, lending variety yet maintaining harmony. John Field, designer. (*Photograph © Morley Baer*)

below: 106. A combination of textures, furniture styles, and objects blend together within an overall plan. Mary Emmerling, owner-designer. (*Photograph: Robert Perron*)

107. Harmony is lively, not bland and monochromatic. The design elements of this home create a feeling of harmony by utilizing variety and contrast as well as unity. Although there is a dominant neutral color scheme, natural woods and boldly colored wall hangings and rugs enliven the surroundings. (See also cover photo.) Michael Sands, architect. Cindi Sands, interior designer. (*Photograph: Philip L. Molten*)

Harmony is perhaps easiest to achieve when most of the design elements—space, form, line, texture, light, and color—are held fairly constant and only one or two ring in a challenge. But harmony does *not* mean a dead level of sameness. As in music, it is the simultaneous combination of different tones, or qualities, that results in a pleasing arrangement.

The animating principle of any design, however, is its spirit—the essence that calls it to life. It is the character chosen by the designer, but more than that, it is the execution of the design with originality and verve. (See Plate 15, p. 96.)

No one can tell a designer just how to achieve spirit. There are no rules or patterns. By allowing imagination free play, however, by trying out an unusual or novel approach, even by deliberately flouting so-called principles, you may discover a refreshing expression, a spirit that can put its imprint on your design.

Our discussion of the elements and principles inherent in all design has concentrated on the aspects important for interior design. In working with the materials, the architectural elements, the furnishings that are examined in later chapters, you will discover just how basic and inescapable these ideas are.

Light

5

Unless one is sealed in a closed box, light is enveloping and ever present. It is such a common thing that we usually forget it is a form of energy, a force to which our eyes react immediately, although subconsciously, and to which our bodies respond. So attuned are we to light that in the absence of daylight, we make light.

Without light there would be no color. White light, although apparently colorless, is composed of all the hues of the spectrum. When light strikes an object, some of its hues are absorbed and others reflected. It is the reflected hues that give the object its color quality. For example, a surface that we call "yellow" actually absorbs almost all hues in light except yellow ones.

Light and color, therefore, are almost inseparable. Because each is so complex and so vital to the dynamics of interior design, we have divided them into two chapters for detailed analysis. However, in this chapter and the following one devoted to color, we will have frequent occasion to mention the ways in which the two elements interact.

The interior designer must be concerned with two kinds of light—natural and artificial. They have many attributes in common, but the methods of dealing with them may be very different. Natural light exists always by day, and the designer's role lies in controlling its effects. Artificial light must actually be created and positioned.

Beyond these two broad categories, the designer must also plan for two different *aspects* of lighting in the home—the functional and the aesthetic. Often, the two are complementary.

Functional lighting is obvious. We need a certain amount of light to see, to read, to cook, to dress, and to perform other tasks.

Aesthetic lighting is a less concrete idea, because it involves psychological responses to light and color. Light represents warmth, wakefulness, and security. Not surprisingly, high levels of light are often associated with high physical and mental energy, whereas subdued light usually accompanies more tranquil activities. It is no accident that

108. The abundance of natural light in this home creates a mood, an energetic feeling intensified by the soaring ceilings and streamlined design. Moore/Turnbull, architects. (*Photograph* © *Morley Baer*)

offices and classrooms tend to be brightly lighted, or that candlelight is favored for intimate dinner parties. In each case the person who planned the lighting wanted to create a certain mood and atmosphere—whether of high productivity and alertness or of relaxed coziness.

Working with light, the interior designer can therefore exercise great influence in determining the atmosphere in a home. Ideally, the lighting should be flexible enough to adapt to all varieties of activities that may take place there.

Light is of the utmost importance in dealing with the other elements of design.

- **Space** can be molded and shaped by light. It may be extended by general lighting or constricted by having light focused on specific areas, such as a dining area.
- **Form** or **shape** can be dramatized by the angle at which light hits it; or it can be made to fade into the background by the use of low, uniform lighting.

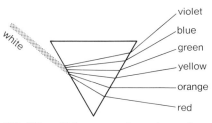

109. When light passes through a prism, the component colors are separated into clearly distinguishable bands.

110. The lighting in this multi-purpose apartment is cleverly designed to be as flexible as possible. Although there are large windows at either end, daylight does not reach the center of the room. Many sources of artificial light have been added, from spotlights to standing lamps. The spotlights, both functional and attractive, can be adjusted to meet varying needs. Georgie Wolton, architect/designer. (*Photograph: Richard Einzig*)

111. Different types of lighting serve different purposes. Some degree of light contrast is both functional and aesthetically pleasing. The interesting architecture of this room has been enhanced by the placement of lighting within the structure. Lamps concealed at the top of the cement-block wall illuminate the timber roof, connecting it with other shapes in the room. The rug is lit by an internally silvered reflector floodlight mounted high and out of the picture to the right, and the floor lamp serves as a useful reading light. Peter Aldington, architect. (*Photograph: Richard Einzig*)

- **Lines** can be produced by a light tube. The outline of an object may be highlighted by back lighting. The lines in any pattern will fade or strengthen according to the amount of light striking it.
- **Texture** and **ornament** also respond to light in varying ways, being thrown into relief or flattened according to the angle and intensity of the light source.
- **Color,** as mentioned, is totally dependent on light. The individual colors and general color quality of a room may be sharply different by day and under artificial lighting at night.

Physical Aspects of Light

The three physical aspects of light that concern us most in interior design are brightness, reflectance, and color quality.

Brightness

Light varies amazingly in brightness. Sunlight is about four hundred thousand times brighter than the light of the full moon. Light bulbs generally in use in the home vary from a low 3½ watt night light to the 350 watt bulb that may occasionally appear in a general lighting fixture. Brightness has great impact on both function and aesthetics.

Glare is an unfortunate side effect of brightness. It can result from:

- bright sunlight streaming through an uncurtained window
- exposed, bright sources of artificial light
- incorrectly designed lighting fixtures
- too much light from one direction
- excessive contrast between lighted areas and shadowed ones

Glare can be tiring or even painful to the eyes. It is especially unpleasant if one is reading or doing close work. The causes of glare listed above almost automatically suggest ways to counteract it.

- Windows that admit strong southern or western light can be curtained with sheer fabric or blinds that admit light but cut glare.
- Bright sources of artificial light can be shaded to diffuse or direct the brilliance.
- Light coming from two or more directions usually eliminates glare.
- A room with strong local lighting for specific activities, such as reading, may also need a low level of general illumination to diminish contrasts. For close work, the working area should be no more than five times as bright as the darkest part of the room. A ratio of 1:10 is undesirable anyplace.

The opposite of glare is *blandness,* which occurs when every part of a room or home is equally bright. This situation is not only boring; it can be fatiguing to the eyes as well. Some degree of light contrast is nearly always desirable in the home, for both functional and aesthetic reasons.

Reflectance

When light strikes an object, the light may be reflected, as from a bright surface such as a mirror or highly polished silver; absorbed by a dull texture, perhaps velvet or brick; or allowed to pass through a transparent substance. Most of the time we expect the larger surfaces in a home—walls, floors, major furnishings—to absorb some light. Other elements provide an accent in reflecting or transmitting light. There are exceptions to this, of course. Kitchen and bathroom floors are often light-reflecting, and an entire mirrored wall is not uncommon. As with brightness, the best plan is usually a mixture of reflective and absorbent textures, to provide contrast.

112. Mirrored tabletops and other light-reflecting accents combine with light-absorbent elements, such as shag carpeting and an upholstered sofa, to provide contrast. Design by Childs-Dreyfus Inc. (*Photograph: Hedrich-Blessing*)

113. A large neon cow adds a whimsical note in a renovated barn. Neon: Joe Bucelli of Jo-Ran Neon. Moore Grover Harper, architects. (*Photograph: Robert Perron*)

Color Quality

True color quality is revealed by white light, but light itself is seldom completely colorless. (See Plates 16, 17, p. 113.)

Noon sunlight comes nearest to white light, but it can be subtly or even drastically altered by haze or smog.

Late afternoon sunlight has a warm reddish cast.

Moonlight is bluish.

Incandescent light bulbs usually cast a faintly yellowish light, but some are manufactured in pale colors. Pink light bulbs, for instance, are favored when it is desirable to cast a very warm glow, flattering to facial tones. By projecting the light through a filter, almost any hue can be produced.

Fluorescent light tubes come in a range from "daylight," which casts a blue light, to the pink of "natural white."

Neon light is somewhat of a misnomer, because "neon" refers specifically to a gaseous element that emits a red-orange glow. Other gases used in the same manner will produce other hues. Many strong, exciting colors are available, their light called neon for convenience. The unique quality of these elements is that they do not so much cast light as *condense* it. In other words, the light glows with brilliant intensity within its own form.

Psychological Aspects of Light

Some of our emotional and aesthetic responses to light are undoubtedly rooted in the physical—the actual reaction of our eyes to light and the stimulation of the organism by varying light levels. But we also have subconscious reactions to the direct radiant energy of the sun, and to the age-old light source of flame, from candles or fireplace. Light is a mood setter, and the interior designer can plan it as such.

114–116. Varied levels of indoor lighting can change the mood of a room dramatically. Marlene Rothkin Vine and David Vine, owners-designers. (*Photographs: David Vine*)

right: 114. Natural daylight streams in through windows and a skylight for an overall cheerful effect.

below left: 115. General artificial illumination brightens every corner of the room to produce a mood suitable for group entertainment.

below right: 116. Subdued night lighting from lamps and the fireplace creates intimate "pockets" of light while leaving the corners in shadow.

- **Bright light** energizes us and has a tendency to foster either hard work or energetic play.
- **Subdued light** makes us feel relaxed, but if too subdued, it may put us to sleep.
- **Too-brilliant light** often causes us to look away, in physical and emotional distress. A bright, focused light can make us feel "in the spotlight," like an actor on the stage; or it can put us "on the spot," as in the legendary police interrogation.
- **Flickering light,** as from a fireplace, nearly always draws attention and physically draws people toward it.
- **Strong contrasts** of bright and dark seem dramatic, but if they are too extreme they can be tiring.
- **Warm-colored light** seems cheerful and welcoming.
- **Cool light** is often more restful.

Lighting designers for the theater use psychological response as their stock in trade. Often the mood of a play is established by the lighting, before the actors speak a word. The interior designer would do well to borrow a page from the theatrical book in planning light for the "cast" who will live in the home and for the different kinds of scenes they will play there.

Economic Aspects of Light

In an energy-conscious era, designers must be aware of the economic aspects of light, both natural and artificial. Natural light streaming into a room through a south window can provide warmth in winter. But in summer the same generous light may bring so much warmth that the room must be cooled artificially.

Until perhaps fifty years ago windows routinely were equipped with shutters or opaque draperies, which would be closed to keep out hot sun and prevent fabrics from fading. Today we have colorfast dyes and air conditioning. Few of us would want to live in such self-imposed darkness. But a careful use of curtains or blinds to temper the light, without blocking it altogether, can cut down substantially on heat entering a room, thus lessening the energy needed to cool it.

117. Artificial lighting should be distributed around a room rather than concentrated in a single fixture. This room has many imaginative light sources that can be used at varying times to adapt to changing needs. Susan Forbes, Forbes-Ergas Design Associates, Inc. Design Consultant: Der Scutt. (*Photograph: Norman McGrath*)

118. The enormous window in this living room provides enough natural light for reading so that artificial light is not needed during the day. The brightness also sets the mood for the room. Plants thrive in the sunlight, and pale colors emphasize the feeling of airiness. Don Solomon, designer. (*Photograph: Joshua Friewald*)

Artificial lighting requires energy for its production. From a purely economic standpoint, it would be desirable to provide for the *minimum* lighting necessary to give the desired effect. In practical terms, this means that the designer should never create a situation in which maximum lighting *must* be utilized. An example would be a room equipped only with general, overhead lighting or a single switch controlling all illumination. Even a kitchen, which needs fairly bright light for food preparation, should have one or two low-level light sources for casual use at other than mealtimes.

Selective switches allow us to turn on or off different fixtures at will. With rheostatic dimmers, brightness of light can be adjusted smoothly, from lowest to highest level. These dimmers are inexpensive and frequently offset the need to install many different fixtures to create varying light levels.

On a positive note, light itself can be an economical design tool. Certainly lighting fixtures *can* be expensive, but they need not be. For the designer working on a tight budget, carefully planned lighting may transform a room or home almost as much as new furnishings—and at a much lower cost. And, if the budget is truly slim, a sparsely furnished room can be given character by imaginative lighting until more money is available for purchases.

Daylight

The light of day enters a home through openings of many types— ordinary windows, window walls, skylights, and glass doors. Ideally, natural light will illuminate rooms sufficiently during the day so that supplementary artificial light is not needed.

119. The light from kitchen windows is balanced by that from the skylight above. The track lighting provides artificial light at night. Ron Friedman, designer. (*Photograph: © Morley Baer*)

Probably the most important factor in producing a pleasant atmosphere is that the light be *balanced.* As mentioned earlier, light entering from one direction only, especially if it is bright, creates an unpleasant glare. The same amount of light balanced by some coming in elsewhere will seem more mellow.

The direction from which light comes also affects its quality:

North light, traditionally demanded by artists, is cool and steady, with few shifting shadows. In a north-facing room, the use of warm color will counteract the possible harshness of that revealing light.

East light appears first in the morning, changing from bright to neutral as the day wears on. An eastern exposure brings morning brightness and wakefulness to a bedroom or kitchen. When bedrooms face east, the designer should know the personalities of those who will occupy them. Some people love to be awakened by light; others cannot face it until they have been up for a while. In the latter case, an opaque or semiopaque window treatment is indicated.

South light seems warm and constantly shifts direction during the day. It may need to be tempered, especially in the summer months. Cool colors will help to counteract its flat brightness, if desired.

West light is sometimes too warm and rich, particularly in the late afternoon. If a room where people gather at the end of the day faces west, the designer will probably need to control the light with blinds or curtains. Again, cool colors will help. Wherever possible, outside elements—trees, trellises, shrubs, or awnings—will give the best defense against excessive light.

The many ways of tempering sunlight coming in through windows and doors will be taken up in Chapter 8. Curtains, draperies, blinds of all kinds can do everything from changing the tint and intensity of the light to shutting it out entirely.

Finally, there are a number of factors relating to natural light that the interior designer usually cannot control but should be aware of in making other design decisions. Light entering near the top of a room illuminates the ceiling and spreads through the room better than light at floor level. Floor-level windows may have more of a tendency to admit glare. Nonglare glass—clear, smoke, or reflecting—will reduce the problems of too much sunlight.

Artificial Light

Light produced as a substitute for daylight gives the designer maximum control in creating a "scene." Referring again to our analogy of the theater, lighting is a vital part of drama, constantly changing and underscoring the mood of the play.

We can use this device, for example, to enliven a party. Flexible lighting allows the hosts to plan a sequence of experiences, perhaps starting with a moderately lighted living room where guests gather, then moving to a highlighted or candle-lit dining table, and then to either bright lights for dancing and games, or subdued lighting for quiet after-dinner music. All this can be accomplished with the different types of lighting and fixtures available.

Artificial light can be discussed in categories, depending upon the way it is produced and the way it is used.

Light Production

There are two basic types of lighting elements—incandescent and fluorescent.

Incandescent bulbs typically have a tungsten filament that is heated by electricity to the temperature at which it glows. They are available in many different shapes, sizes, and amounts of light produced.

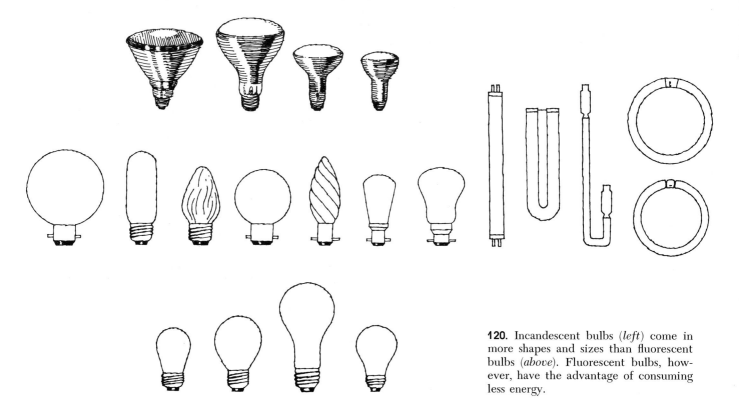

120. Incandescent bulbs (*left*) come in more shapes and sizes than fluorescent bulbs (*above*). Fluorescent bulbs, however, have the advantage of consuming less energy.

121. Ceiling fixtures generate direct light and spread it uniformly throughout the room. The windows provide enough illumination during the day. Smith and Larson, designers. (*Photograph:* © *Morley Baer*)

Fluorescent tubes offer a luminescent or "cold" (not produced by heat) source of light. A glass tube with an inside coating of fluorescent powder is filled with vaporized mercury and argon; then the ends are sealed with two cathodes. When electric current activates the gases, invisible ultraviolet rays cause the fluorescent coating to produce visible light. Although fluorescent tubes come only in straight or circular shapes, they have considerable diversity in color. They are also much less energy-consuming than incandescent bulbs.

Use of Artificial Light

We can divide artificial lighting into three general types:

General Lighting   General lighting illuminates a room more or less uniformly. It breaks down further into two kinds.

Direct lighting comes from such sources as ceiling fixtures or luminous ceilings that shed light downward, or from lamps with translucent shades spreading light in all directions.

above: Plate 16. The high windows of this house let in plenty of sun, flooding the living area with bright, almost white, light. Wendell H. Lovett, architect.

below: Plate 17. In this night view of the scene in Plate 16, small lamps and hidden ceiling lights provide a soft, golden light.

Plate 18. Instead of being discreetly hidden by lamp shades, oversize bulbs are brought out into the open, complementing the casual, informal effect of the primary colors and uncluttered furniture. Ric Wineshank, Sunshine Design, designer. (*Photograph: Robert Perron*)

Indirect lighting is usually concealed, in coves, cornices, or valances. It may also come from a lamp with an opaque shade open only at the top. Light is thrown against the ceiling or washes a wall, and then is reflected throughout the room. It is softer than direct lighting, but often more costly in both installation and operation. When used imaginatively, indirect light can dramatize a space. Otherwise, it may be monotonous and needs to be combined with local lighting.

above: 122. Indirect lighting is concealed here in wood beams over countertops. Direct light is supplied for close work and also is reflected throughout the room. Roth O'Brien, architect. (*Photograph: Philip L. Molten*)

123. A baffle can conceal the source of light. Its placement can direct light two different ways. In the illustration *right* the light washes over the ceiling; at *far right* it washes over the wall, in a downward direction.

124. One disadvantage to the living room of this beach house was its lack of light. Owner-architect Hobart Betts installed larger windows, covering them with white roll-up shades. A solid door to the sunporch was replaced with a glass-paneled one. Various lamps were added to provide focused reading light. (*Photograph: Maris-Semel*)

Local Lighting   Specific activities, at specific locations, need specific lighting. This type of lighting, which may be either task lighting or accent lighting, might be used:

- for reading or other close work
- for sewing and needlework, craft work of many kinds
- for cooking, especially in areas where appliances or knives are employed
- to highlight a painting or other art object
- to illuminate a bank of plants not placed near a window
- to focus on an architectural element
- to break up a large room into "islands"
- to make a small room appear to have several distinct areas, thus visually enlarging its space

Numerous other possibilities will occur to you, some of them suggested by the questionnaire in Chapter 1.

Local lighting can be provided by lamps at strategic points. Fixtures attached to wall or ceiling, under cabinets, alone or in multiples, are growing in popularity. Although fixed and out of the way, they can be very flexible in direction and design.

Many fixtures, although designed specifically for local lighting, have both direct and indirect features, thus providing the room with some general lighting as well.

125. Lighting can separate areas of a room and provide for special needs. The track lighting over the dining area focuses on the painting and defines the space. Concealed lights illuminate objects on the shelves; Gro-lights are suspended over the plants. A lamp by the couch can be used for reading or other close work. (*Photograph courtesy Simmons Company*)

**Table 5.1
Minimum Recommended Light
for Certain Activities**

	Footcandles
General Lighting	
most rooms	5–10
kitchen, laundry	10–20
Local Lighting for Activities	
card playing	10–20
casual reading, easy sewing, makeup, easy musical scores	20–30
kitchen, laundry	30–50
prolonged reading, study, average and machine sewing, difficult musical scores, shaving, benchwork	40–70
fine sewing, any small detail work	100–200

Light for Light's Sake   A play of brilliants or streaks of light, pulsating color—many are the experiments now being done with light. In bygone eras this type of light-as-decoration was provided by crystal chandeliers and candelabra, stained glass lamps, and Christmas trees. All of these are still in evidence, but the repertoire has widened. Now, fixtures with tiny light bulbs or punctured shades may bring sparkle. Thin threads of light hang as a curtain of mystery. Moving, colored lights are exciting—though only for limited periods. Light becomes sculpture. It is a fertile field, to be used with imagination. (See Plate 18, p. 114.)

Lighting for Activities

In planning the lighting for a room or an entire home, you should return to the floor plan (Chap. 2). First determine what activities will take place in which locations, the practical furniture placements, and the availability of natural light. Then you can decide upon the kind and location of artificial lighting. Following are some points to consider for various activities.

Conversation can take place almost anywhere, in almost any light or none at all. The type of lighting may even affect the conversation. Bland general lighting may result in bland, general observations; mood lighting in more intimate talk. Very high-key lighting can spark the mood at a party.

Reading of a casual nature can be done in moderate light, but more sustained reading or study needs direct light balanced by some general lighting to avoid glare.

Close work, such as sewing or certain hobbies, requires even more intense light directed at the work, again balanced by general lighting. Care should be taken to avoid casting shadows on the work.

Active play, dancing, or physical games usually benefit from high levels of general light.

Walking is safer by light. Special needs may include a night light or a focused light to show changes in floor levels.

The international unit of measure for light intensity is the *footcandle,* equivalent to the amount of light produced by one standard candle at a distance of 1 foot. Lighting engineers have determined minimum recommended footcandles for various activities. Light meters that measure illumination are available for those who need precise measurement. For most of us, Table 5.1 is helpful because it indicates the *relative* suggested brightness of light.

Lighting Specific Areas

The discussion on the preceding pages offers general guidelines for lighting throughout the home. But certain areas of the home have specific needs.

Entrance Areas   Diffused light from ceiling or wall fixtures is friendly and welcoming in an entrance. It allows the resident to identify the caller. If the entrance area is arranged so that visitors will remove coats and boots, and perhaps check hair and makeup, the lighting should take this into account.

Living and Family Rooms   Social spaces, such as living and family rooms, need general illumination, preferably both direct and indirect, to bring the rooms into soft perspective. Flexible, direct light is best for

126. In a dining area, the primary emphasis is on the table. Spotlights here focus on the table, and, along with candles, make everything glitter. The candlelight offsets unbecoming shadows cast on faces by overhead light. Joan Regenbogen, designer. (*Photograph: Norman McGrath*)

close work, games, or homework. For parties and other special occasions, a heightened light intensity may be desirable, and some sparkling light would add interest.

Dining Areas   In a dining area, the primary emphasis is on the table and the people around it. Down light makes tableware sparkle, enhances the color of food and beverages. The down light should be countered by some indirect, diffused light or light from the table itself to avoid casting unbecoming shadows on faces.

above: **127.** Lighting in a kitchen can come from various sources. The skylight gives general light; track lights can be directed downward or on specific areas of the room. The lights under the cabinets illuminate counter space for close work. Hank Bruce, architect. (*Photograph: Philip L. Molten*)

below: **128.** In another view of the same kitchen, small wall fixtures supplement the other lighting sources for specific tasks.

Kitchens   In a kitchen, ceiling fixtures or lighted ceiling panels give generous light and should be supplemented by undercounter bands of light at work centers. Sections where dangerous tools, such as knives and electrical appliances, will be used require especially good light.

Bathrooms   A bathroom needs general illumination from a ceiling fixture or two, which is often combined with a heat lamp and/or exhaust fan. Bands of light around the mirror give the most shadowless illumination on the face. Lights on two sides or above and below work almost as well as a full circle.

129. During the day this bathroom is lit by a skylight, a practical alternative to windows. Lights flanking the mirror give brighter light where it is needed most. Donald Loomis, architect. (*Photograph: Philip L. Molten*)

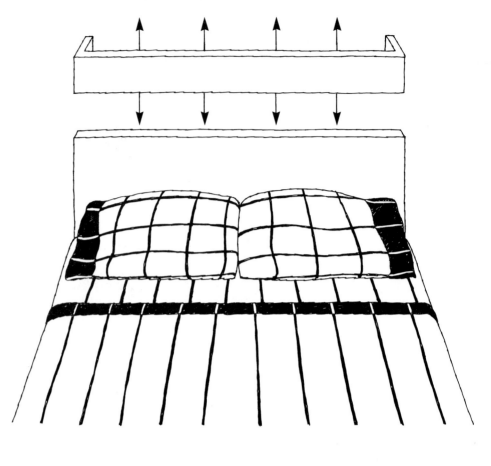

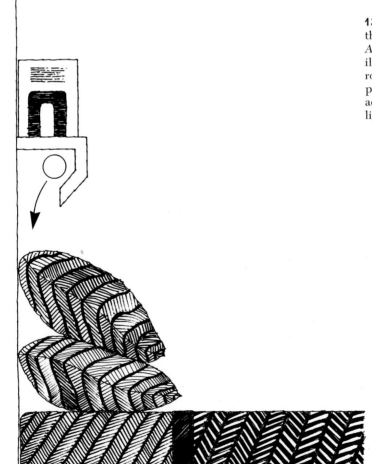

130. The drawings on these pages show three alternatives for lighting around a bed. *Above*, bulbs are concealed, but light still illuminates both the bed and the rest of the room. A bulb hidden beneath a shelf (*below*) provides light specifically for reading. An adjustable lamp (*opposite*) can double as lighting for two areas.

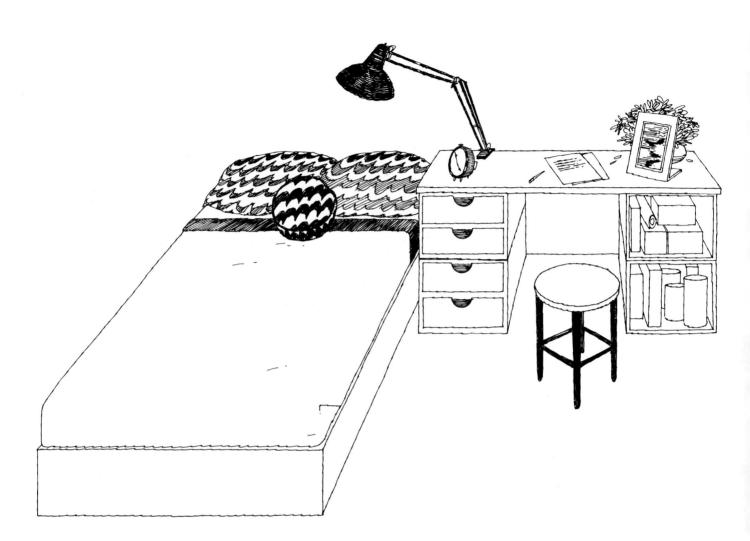

Bedrooms　Some general light is needed in bedrooms for dressing, plus direct light for reading in bed, desk work, or sewing. Many times direct/indirect fixtures will do all that is necessary, but if a makeup/shaving mirror is involved, bathroom-type lighting should be included.

Halls　Some overall lighting from ceiling or wall fixtures is desirable in a hall. Lighting near the floor focuses on the area we need most to see and offers some variety in lighting effects. Colorful, ornamental fixtures can brighten space that is often featureless.

Stairways　Ceiling or wall fixtures that send even, glare-free light downward lessen hazards and help prevent accidents. Switches at top and bottom ensure that light can be turned on when needed.

Exterior Lights　The outside entrance to a home should be well illuminated so that friends can identify it and the house number, and the resident can identify friends. The quality of the interior space also can be enhanced by exterior lighting. Lighted terraces, patios, and gardens eliminate the black windows that result from a lack of balanced illumination. Such light will expand the apparent size of the interior.

131. Many kinds of lighting fixtures are designed to serve particular purposes. They are as simple or ornate as could be desired. (*Photograph courtesy Koch & Lowy, Inc.*)

Switches and Outlets

Every door into a room needs a light switch beside it, preferably a multiple switch controlling different fixtures to be used as needed. Dimmer controls adapt lighting to different needs and moods.

Each separated wall space requires a wall outlet for lamps and appliances. On long walls, two or more outlets will lessen the hazards of extension cords.

Bed lamp switches should be within easy reach of the sleeper. Bathrooms require outlets for numerous appliances; they are safest when removed as far as possible from water facilities.

In a kitchen, many outlets at counter heights are convenient. This is true not only at the backs of kitchen counters for appliances, but also behind the refrigerator, washer, and dryer.

Lighting Fixtures

Ideal fixtures give the kind and amount of light suitable to a particular purpose. Almost inevitably, lighting fixtures contrast with other furnishings in the home, because they meet a very different need. Lighting devices can set up their own pattern of design running through the entire home.

Fixtures come in a bewildering diversity, but the light sources fall into three basic shapes.

- **Lines** include fluorescent tubes, long lighting tracks or plugmold strips, lighted valances and cornices. These lead the eyes in a strongly directional movement. They wash the ceiling, wall, or draperies with light.
- **Orbs** or **Spots,** if large, resemble little suns, radiating light in many directions. If small, as in candles, they are like sparks or stars.
- **Planes** of light illuminate large areas evenly.

right: 132. Lighting can be a unifying thread running through a home. In this house spotlights illuminate certain areas, highlighting artwork and stairs and providing light for reading. Michael Trible, owner-architect. (*Photograph: Gordon H. Schenck, Jr.*)

below: 133. Luminous panels over the table define this dining space and set it off from the rest of the room. Overhead panels also have the advantage of illuminating large areas evenly. Austin & Falk, architects. (*Photograph: Gordon H. Schenck, Jr.*)

134. Ordinarily, track lighting is fixed to the ceiling, but in this home spotlights are attached to pipes. The structure of the home is enhanced by exposed pipes and flooring. Natural materials add to the effect. Gus Dudley, architect. (*Photograph: Robert Perron*)

Architectural and Built-in Lighting

Built-in light assures us that illumination was not an afterthought. It contributes to the overall unity of a space.

Lighted Valances or Cornices   Lighted window fixtures wash the ceiling, wall, or draperies with light and may have a strong direction.

Track Lighting   Plugmold strips or track lighting which is fixed to the ceiling or wall, offers great variety. One strip often holds spotlights, floodlights, and even hanging fixtures that can follow furniture placement around. The tracks can be movable for flexible arrangement.

Ceiling Fixtures   Ceiling fixtures have become common once again, owing to vastly improved design. Some are inconspicuously recessed in the ceiling, or flush with it. They may soften light with louvers or diffuse it with lenses.

Some may be the ceiling itself, soft luminous panels that illuminate large areas evenly.

Shallow glass or plastic bowls, dropped a few inches, reflect light from the ceiling and diffuse it through the bowl. They can also direct a pool of light downward, making an inexpensive three-in-one way to light space for eating, hobbies, or homework.

Many ceiling fixtures are dropped well below the ceiling. Those adjustable in height and position give welcome flexibility. Adjustable spotlights and floodlights, now available with shades in many sizes, shapes, and colors, can be turned on work areas or visual centers of interest for direct light, on the ceiling for reflected light.

Wall Fixtures   Wall fixtures have been brought up to date and retain their popularity for one overriding reason: they remain out of the way and free table and desk surfaces for other things. At the same time, they give direct light where it is needed. Some wall fixtures, however, are used simply to provide gentle overall and balanced illumination.

Portable Lamps

Floor and table lamps can be moved when and where they are needed. They also act as decorative accessories. Chapter 15 discusses the design and selection of portable lamps as enrichment for the home.

Placement of Fixtures

The placement of fixtures affects the atmosphere of the room as a whole and the ease with which tasks can be done. Table 5.2 (p. 128) was developed by lighting engineers, and it should be of considerable value to the interior designer. The wattages given are in terms we are all familiar with. The range of wattage allows for personal variation. Some people see better than others, and some just like more or less light.

Light and Color

As mentioned earlier, light itself varies in color, with type of light and time of day or night. In addition, it can be varied by the color of the light bulb, the fixture, or any shading device.

135. The globe lights on these walls replace table and standing lamps and echo the furniture forms. Henrik Bull, architect. (*Photograph © Morley Baer*)

Table 5.2
Recommended Placement and Wattage of Light Fixtures

Type	Placement	Range of Wattage
wall fixtures (incandescent)	at least 66″ above floor	60–100w every 8′ for general lighting
wall fixtures (fluorescent)	faceboards at least 6″ out from wall, and as high in inches as they are in feet from floor, to shield fluorescent tubes	general lighting—approximately 1′ of channel (10w) for each 15 sq. ft. of floor area special lighting—approximate width of area to be lighted
cornice	at edge of ceiling, sheds light down	
valance	at least 10″ down from ceiling, sheds light up, down, or both	
wall bracket	50–65″ above floor, sheds light up, down, or both	
ceiling fixtures shallow	centered, symmetrically placed, or placed to illumine special areas	120–200w in multiple bulbs; 60–80w in multiple tubes
recessed	as above	30–150w bulbs
pendant	as above; see below when used for reading	120–180w in multiple bulbs
floor lamps (for reading)	stem of lamp 10″ behind shoulder, near rear corner of chair; bottom of shade 45–48″ above floor	50/150w–100/300w bulb; 60–180w in multiple bulbs
table lamps (for reading)	base in line with shoulder, 20″ to left or right of book center; bottom of shade at eye level when seated, about 40″ above floor	as above
wall lamps (for reading)	42–48″ above floor, 15″ to left or right of book center	as above

Table 5.3
Percentage of Light Reflected by Colors

Color	Percentage of Light Reflected
white	89
ivory	87
canary yellow	77
cream	77
orchid	67
creamy gray	66
sky blue	65
buff	63
pale green	59
shell pink	55
olive tan	43
forest green	22
coconut brown	16
black	2

Colors look different under different lights. The colors in a textile can vary quite remarkably under incandescent, fluorescent, or natural light. This is the reason why it is so often recommended that the colors to be used in a home be examined together under the conditions in which they will be used.

Conversely, the colors in a room affect the color of the light. Light reflected from a green wall will have a slightly green tint; that from a pink or apricot colored wall will have a warmer tinge. You might consider this factor in relation to the color used in a bathroom, perhaps, as opposed to that in a room with a window wall facing south or west.

Finally, the amount of light reflected from any surface—walls, and ceiling, floor and furnishings—depends on the color of that surface. Table 5.3 gives the percentage of light bounced back by various colors. As we might expect, white reflects the most light, black the least. Light colors give the most light for the money, dark colors the least.

We turn now to a discussion of color itself, always referring back, necessarily, to its interaction with light.

What a magical word is color! Nearly everyone reacts strongly to colors, and moreover has done so since earliest infancy. When children are learning to talk, the names of colors are frequently among the first words they master.

It would probably be safe to say that color symbolism has been important to every culture and nation, at every period of history. In different contexts, colors symbolize:

- political and national affiliation (the colors of a flag)
- status or rank (colors worn by royalty)
- events (weddings or funerals)
- holidays (the red and green of Christmas)
- professions and vocations (the colors worn by clergy)
- emotions (red for anger, green for envy)
- attributes (yellow for cowardice, red for bravery, blue for fidelity)

The list could go on and on. We mention these ideas here to show how vitally important color is to people's emotional and psychological responses. As a designer, you must consider far more than the visual effect of a color or combination of colors.

Working with color is a science as well as an art. You must know what you want, how to get it, and why the results may or may not turn out to be what you had in mind.

To complicate matters, perception of color varies from person to person. If you give a house painter a sample of the blue-green you want on the walls of a room, you may be surprised at how blue the finished walls appear to you, although another person may see them as green. In addition, perception of color can be influenced by many factors, including light, surrounding colors, texture, reflectance, and size of the color area. In this chapter we will discuss these factors, with a view toward achieving satisfactory and *predictable* results.

Color Theory

Many people have formulated color theories that attempt to explain what color is and how it works. Some have developed elaborate color systems that enable us to communicate with precision about color.

The Munsell system, for example, enables you to pick a color, and find its notation on a series of color charts. In principle, if you told someone you wanted number 5R 5/10 on the Munsell charts, you would get exactly the pure red you chose. This type of precision is, of course, invaluable for those who work intensively with color.

For most of us, an understanding of the simplest, most familiar color theory is adequate. This theory is based on the fact that to describe a color with reasonable exactness at least three terms are needed: *hue, value,* and *intensity.* These properties give us a working vocabulary for dealing with color.

Hue: The Name of a Color

As we saw in Figure 109, when natural light is passed through a prism, it separates into bands of violet, blue, green, yellow, orange, and red. The traditional color wheel is formed by bending these six hues into a circle and placing intermediate hues between them (Plate 19, p. 139). The twelve colors of the color wheel can be divided into three categories:

136. Color influences emotional and psychological responses. Because of the colors used here, and their values, this room divides into two areas. The darker area seems warm and cozy, the lighter open and cheery. Angelo Donghia, designer. (*Photograph: © 1978 Peter Aaron/ESTO*)

- **Primary hues**—red, yellow, and blue. Theoretically, these cannot be produced by mixing any combination of other hues together.
- **Secondary hues**—green, violet, and orange. Each stands midway between two primary hues and is the product of them. Green is a mixture of blue and yellow, for example.
- **Tertiary hues** are midway between a primary and a secondary hue, of which they are the product. For instance, yellow-green is produced by mixing the primary yellow and the secondary green.

The twelve hues on this color wheel are only a beginning. There are an almost infinite number of hues. In nature, this can be seen in rainbows, where raindrops act as tiny prisms, breaking up sunlight and producing a sequence of colors, with one shading imperceptibly into the next.

137. Many contrasting values of light and dark give a lively atmosphere to this room. Wong and Brocchini, architects. (*Photograph: Joshua Friewald*)

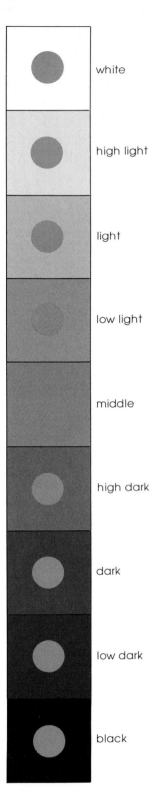

white

high light

light

low light

middle

high dark

dark

low dark

black

138. A gray value scale shows seven gradations between black and white. The central dots are all of identical (middle) value, but, like objects in a room, they appear lighter against a dark background and darker against a light one.

Hue is what we visualize when we think of a color. The world of fashion retailing has invented endless poetical, fanciful names for colors: celery, taupe, avocado, puce, persimmon, fuschia, chartreuse, Grecian sand, carmine, camel, Moroccan red, delphinium. But these are imprecise and could easily mean different things to different people. To identify colors accurately, it is better to name their standard hues, as affected by value and intensity—such as pure, light yellow.

Interaction of Hues When placed next to each other, hues produce effects ranging from harmony to strong contrast. In a general sense, this has to do with their relative positions on the color wheel.

- **Analogous hues** are adjacent to each other on the color wheel, as are yellow, yellow-green, and green. When used together in a room, analogous hues create a sense of harmony. (See Plate 20, p. 140.)
- **Complementary hues** lie directly opposite each other on the color wheel, as do yellow and violet, red and green, blue and orange. When two complementary hues are placed next to each other, they contrast strongly. Each hue is intensified by the other, an effect known as *simultaneous contrast.* (See Plate 21, p. 140.)

Another phenomenon associated with complementary hues is *afterimage.* If you stare directly at an area of vivid red, and then quickly turn your eyes to a white wall or sheet of paper, you will see a faint image in the complement, green, in the same shape as the red area. This is important for the interior designer. In certain circumstances a large area of strong hue might cast an afterimage of the complementary color.

Imagine a dining room with the walls painted bright red, having a white tablecloth on the table. Color fatigue in the diners' eyes could easily result in a faint greenish tint over the table, which would certainly make the food look unappetizing.

Blending of Hues Very small areas of color, when placed next to each other, may lose their separate identities. If you mix some red paint with some yellow, you will get orange. The same thing happens when small areas of color are close together. A textile woven from red and yellow yarns will probably appear orange from a distance.

Temperature of Hues Each hue has its own "temperature" that affects us and our homes in several ways. Red, orange, and yellow are considered warm hues, reminding us of the sun and fire. Blue, green, and violet are thought of as cool hues, as in grass or water.

The warm hues are called *advancing* hues, because they seem to be nearer than they actually are. Conversely, the cool hues are said to be *receding,* for they appear farther away than they actually are.

Value: Relative Lightness or Darkness

The amount of light a color reflects—in other words, its lightness or darkness—determines its value. This is easiest to understand in the neutral gray (Fig. 138). Obviously, white reflects the most light. By gradually increasing the amount of black, less and less light is bounced off, until at the other end black absorbs almost all the light.

Value gradations apply equally to hues. Each color has its *normal value,* corresponding to its relative brightness in the color wheel. These seem natural to us: yellow is bright, violet dark. (See Plate 22, p. 141.)

- A *tint* is a value lighter than a color's normal value. Pink is a tint of the hue red.
- A *shade* is a value darker than a color's normal value. Maroon is a shade of the hue red.

Value is important for two reasons:

- The degree of light reflectance from different values can result in a room that is light and bright or dark and dull, with many variations in between.
- Contrasts in value accentuate differences; similar values blend.

above: 139. This room, decorated in a neutral camel color, has an excellent lighting system that alters values and colors. Light can be heightened or dimmed, blinds raised or lowered. A mirrored wall further expands the possibilities of coloration. Tom O'Toole, designer. (*Photograph: Maris-Semel*)

below: 140. Dark accents in a pale room provide a special emphasis. Built for American Plywood by R.B. Fitch. (*Photograph: Gordon H. Schenck, Jr.*)

141. Pronounced contrasts, such as black and white, are active. The strong pattern in the bedspread echoes the colors that predominate in this room and at the same time provides a refreshing change of shape. Robert Fitzpatrick, owner-architect. *(Photograph: Ezra Stoller © 1969 ESTO)*

A room all in beiges, light values of yellow, will seem at best serene, at worst monotonous. A room in dark browns will absorb much of the light, and may seem dead. But a white rug or white curtains, stark contrasts to the browns, will be exciting and brighten the room.

Intensity: Relative Purity or Strength

Any hue can vary in its purity or strength—the degree to which it differs from gray. This quality is called *intensity, chroma,* or *saturation.* Pink is always red in hue and light in value, but it can be vivid, almost pure pink (*high intensity*); or it can be a neutralized, grayed pink (*low intensity*). (See Plate 23, p. 141.)

A hue in its purest state, unmixed and unmodified, is at the highest possible intensity. To lower the intensity, one can add either some gray (black plus white) or some of the complementary color.

Intensity is apparently changed by the color of light striking it, as well as by adjacent colors. A red will seem to have lower intensity if a red-orange (an analogous color) is placed next to it. The same red will seem to have higher intensity if a green (the complement) is next to it.

Effects of Colors

The effects of colors—of hue, value, and intensity—are interactive and highly variable. We need to actually work with color to develop understanding and a feel for color. Fortunately, of all the areas of home design, color is one of the easiest to perceive directly through poster paints or watercolors, colored paper or color chips, or simply colors cut from magazines. The following are generalizations that hold true at certain times, under certain conditions.

Effects on Feelings   Psychological response to color is a personal thing, but there are certain tendencies we can identify:

- Warm hues, lighter values, and strong intensities are stimulating and energetic. (See Plate 24, p. 142.)
- Cool hues, darker values, and weak intensities seem quiet and subdued.
- Intermediate hues, values, and intensities are relaxing and visually undemanding.
- Pronounced contrasts, such as black and white, are active and stimulating.

Table 6.1
Summary of Effects of Hue, Value, and Intensity

	Hue	Value	Intensity
feelings	warm hues are stimulating, cool hues quieting	light values are cheering; dark values range from restful to depressing; contrasts are alerting	high intensities are heartening; strong, low intensities are peaceful
attention	warm hues attract more attention than cool hues	extreme values tend to attract the eye; but contrasts or surprises are even more effective	high intensities attract attention
size	warm hues increase apparent size of objects; used on walls, they decrease the apparent size of room	light values increase apparent size of objects; but strong contrast with background is equally effective	high intensities increase apparent size of objects; used on walls, they decrease apparent size of room
distance	warm hues bring objects forward; cool hues make them recede	light values recede, dark values advance; sharp contrasts in values also bring objects forward	high intensities decrease apparent distances
outline, or contour	warm hues soften outlines slightly more than cool hues; contrasting hues making outlines clearer than related hues	value contrasts are a potent way of emphasizing contours	intensity contrasts emphasize outlines

Effect on Size and Distance   The apparent size and distance of any object or surface can also be influenced by the interaction of the three color properties:

Warm hues, dark values, and strong intensities usually make an object look larger and nearer. They also make walls look nearer, thus apparently decreasing the size of a room. Therefore:

- A too-large space can be made to seem more intimate with darker, warmer colors.
- A long, narrow space can be visually widened by having one or both end walls warmer, darker, and more intense than the side walls.
- A too-high ceiling can be visually lowered with darker, warmer colors.
- Furniture upholstered in warmer, darker, purer colors will seem more prominent and will stand out.

142. A dark wall strongly emphasizes the upward slope of the ceiling as well as the wall's length. Light furniture becomes more prominent when placed against a dark background. Robert Getz, architect. (*Photograph: Joshua Friewald*)

143. A small room can be made to look larger by a light ceiling with dark beams. The eye is drawn upward; the room gains interest and contrast. James Caldwell, architect. (*Photograph: Philip L. Molten*)

Cool hues, light values, and weak intensities usually make an object look smaller and farther away. Therefore:

- Small rooms can be made to seem larger by the use of cool hues and light values.
- The boxiness of a square room can be relieved by using a cooler, lighter color on one or two walls, or by having that color spread across the ceiling.
- A too-low ceiling can be visually raised by painting the ceiling a lighter, cooler color.
- Furniture upholstered in lighter colors will tend to recede.

144. Strong contrasts are dramatic but tend to make a space appear smaller. Contrast also makes furnishings more prominent. A light sofa stands out against a setting of dark values—a scheme that increases the apparent size of the sofa and emphasizes its contours (*above*). A light sofa against a light wall (*below*) is less prominent; however, the overall space is unified and expanded. A dark sofa is somewhat diminished in size against a light background (*bottom*), though the striking contrast creates much the same spatial effect as in the first version.

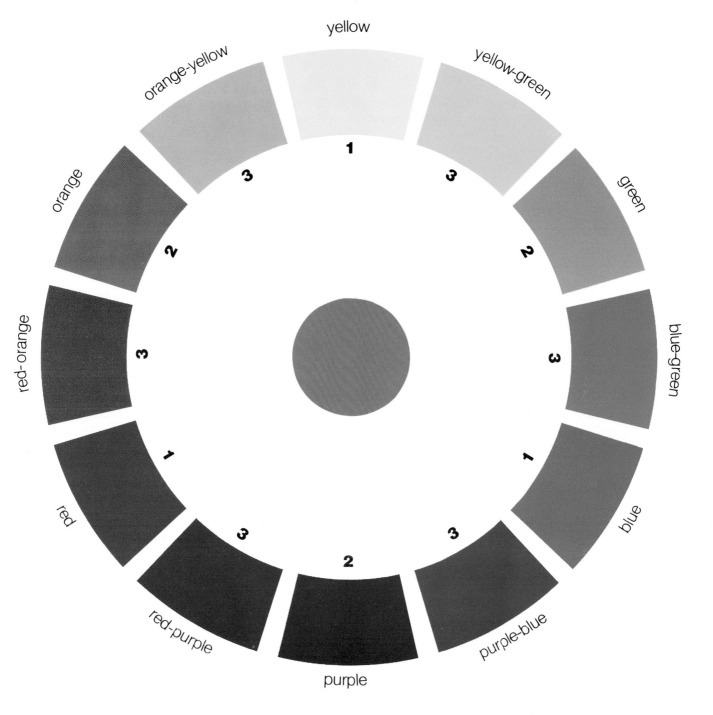

Plate 19. Color wheel showing primary, secondary, and tertiary hues.

left: Plate 20. The unity of design evident here is due in large part to the use of analogous hues against the neutral background colors of the walls and floor tiles. Charles Moore, architect. (*Photograph © Morley Baer*)

below: Plate 21. Sensitively balanced complementary colors seem suited to the simple furnishings of this bedroom. James Caldwell, architect; Phyllis Martin-Vegue, designer. (*Photograph: Philip L. Molten*)

Plate 22. Value scales for green, orange, and violet, showing tints, shades, and normal values.

Plate 23. The two examples of pink shown in **a** have the same value but different intensities. If a hue is placed next to an analogous color (**b**), it will appear to have a lower intensity than when it is placed next to its complement as in example **c**.

above: **Plate 24.** Strong intensities of colors provide a stimulating environment. The area rug, plants, and wallpaper help tone down the potential harshness of this color scheme. Malcolm Holzman, designer. (*Photograph: Norman Mc-Grath*)

right: **Plate 25.** A variety of textures prevents monotony in a monochromatic design. Careful placement of color areas keeps them from becoming overwhelming. Michael Sands, architect; Cindi Sands, designer. (*Photograph: Philip L. Molten*)

145. Dark beams in the ceiling of a predominately pale room provide a focal point, drawing attention to the unusual architectural design. Design by Janet Schirn Interiors. (*Photograph: Hedrich-Blessing*)

Strong contrasts are dramatic, but they also tend to break up unity and contract space. Therefore:

- Similar hues, values, and intensities can unify a collection of furnishings and make a space seem visually larger.
- Contrasts between furnishings and walls make the furnishings seem more prominent.
- Similar colors carried from one room to another increase visual spaciousness.
- Contrasts of hue, value, and intensity emphasize contours.

Color Dynamics

Psychologists, industrial designers, and interior designers have probed endlessly into color preferences and responses. It is fascinating to investigate what colors different people like at various ages, in different countries, under varying circumstances.

In spite of extensive study, however, there is no real consensus. Too many variables are involved. One experiment might suggest that red is a favored color, another experiment just the reverse. Exact conditions of testing are hard to duplicate. One test might have been given on a cool day, the other in blazing heat.

Perhaps the most useful finding to come from all the research is that reactions to color are primarily emotional, subjective, and infinitely varied. For the interior designer, this brings us directly back to the profile in Chapter 1: Who are the people who will live in the home? How do they live? Where do they live? What do they like?

One fact has emerged quite clearly: We are in a colorful age. We no longer concentrate solely on conventional color "schemes," but rather on the dynamics of color, the range of forces that colors set in motion.

Color Harmonies

Traditionally, colors were chosen in terms of definite color schemes or harmonies. Today these formulas seem rather rigid. Few people would want to establish such a scheme and follow it religiously. But color harmonies can be useful in understanding why certain colors work together and others do not. They provide general guidelines and in some cases can offer inspiration.

Color harmonies break down into two broad categories—*related* and *contrasting*. Related harmonies can be further subdivided into monochromatic and analogous.

Monochromatic Harmonies   Based on one hue, varied in value and intensity, monochromatic harmonies bring unity to a room. They can border on monotony if not orchestrated carefully, as with differences in form, texture, and spatial relationships. (See Plate 25, p. 142.)

Analogous Harmonies   An analogous color harmony is composed of hues next to each other on the color wheel. This arrangement also seems automatically unified because of a shared color. An example would be blue-green, blue, and blue-violet. The effect is usually harmonious, with a smooth transition from color to color. Analogous harmonies tend to have more variety and interest than monochromatic ones.

Contrasting color schemes unite hues that are separated on the color wheel. The most common is the complementary harmony, which depends on the symmetrical balancing of color to achieve equilibrium. But there are many variations on this.

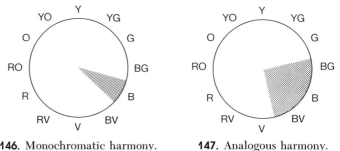

146. Monochromatic harmony.   **147.** Analogous harmony.

Complementary Harmonies   A simple complementary color scheme is based on hues directly opposite one another on the color wheel. Examples would be blue and orange or red and green. Complementary harmonies offer a balance of warmth and coolness, as well as more contrast. They tend to be livelier than either of the related schemes.

The success of such a combination depends on careful handling of value and intensity. Red and green are used at full intensity in Christmas decorations, but they might seem too glaring in the form of a bright red

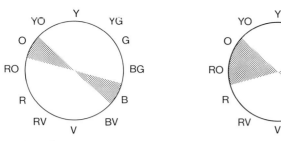

148. Complementary harmony.　　**149.** Double-complementary harmony.

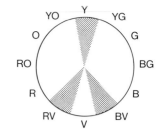

150. Split-complementary harmony.

sofa on a bright green rug. However, if you think of a deep mahogany-red chair placed on a moss green carpet, the combination seems more harmonious. (See Plate 26, p. 151.)

Double-Complementary Harmonies　A development of the complementary scheme, double complementaries are simply two sets of complements. Orange, red-orange, blue, and blue-green in combination would be one example.

Split-Complementary Harmonies　Another variation, the split complementary is composed of any hue and the two hues at each side of its complement. This provides a contrast less violent than in the simple complementary, but still adds interest and variety.

Triad Harmonies　A triad scheme consists of any three hues equidistant from each other on the color wheel. Examples include red, blue, and yellow; or green, orange, and violet. Again, these combinations might sound shocking, but they would seldom be used at full intensity in the home. Green, orange, and violet could translate into sage green, cocoa brown, and dove gray. Triad schemes can be vigorous or subdued, depending upon the designer's intent.

Tetrad Harmonies　Any four hues equidistant from each other on the color wheel produce a tetrad scheme. Such combinations lead to rich, varied yet unified, fully balanced compositions.

One more possibility exists in the contrasting category—color schemes achieved by an active balancing of hues that are not complements.

Asymmetric Harmonies　Asymmetric harmonies are based on two or more colors from one side of the color wheel, but without any shared hue. They provide more contrast than related schemes, and create tension, as any asymmetric design does. They gain equilibrium through an active, dynamic balancing of colors. The typical Mexican hot pink and orange, or sky blue, leaf green, and cream would be examples.

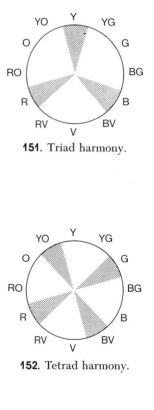

151. Triad harmony.

152. Tetrad harmony.

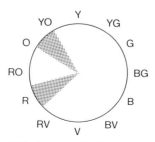

153. Asymmetric harmony.

Planning for Color

The color harmonies described above work very well for analysis, and they may stimulate you to try new ideas and solutions. But in planning the colors for a room, or a whole home, you need not follow any set formula. Above all, you should consider the basics: the people who will use the room, the furnishings, and the space itself.

If you find yourself completely at a loss about how to begin choosing colors, you might work through the following steps.

Consider the people who will live here. Some people have strong color preferences and some do not. Find out if they like:

- a lot of color or just a little
- bright colors or subdued, neutral tones
- strong contrasts or a mellow blending of hues
- traditional colors, such as Williamsburg green, or new, off-beat hues, such as "raisin."

Evaluate what you have to work with. Often, one or more of the colors in a room will be established by some elements that cannot or should not be changed. (See Plate 27, p. 151.) Examples could be:

- a treasured Oriental rug
- a painting or print
- an architectural element that has color, such as a brick fireplace

Decide upon the effect you want. Do you want the room to be:

- energetic or subdued
- formal or casual

154. Subdued colors and soft textures make this room ideal for sleeping, relaxing, or quiet work. Joan Regenbogen, designer. (*Photograph: Norman McGrath*)

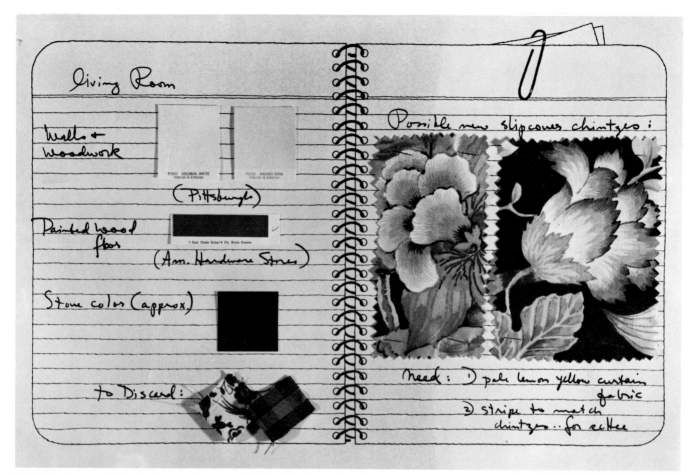

155. Keeping a notebook is a good means of planning for color, since it organizes swatches and paint chips. Rejected colors and fabrics should be saved as well.

- warm or cool
- modern or traditional
- bright and cheery or dim and intimate
- "masculine" or "feminine"
- soft or hard
- sophisticated or down-to-earth

<u>Consider the use of the room.</u> Different types of spaces lend themselves to different color effects. Again, there are certainly no rules about this, but the following guidelines generally apply:

- Rooms intended for noisy group activities suggest the use of vigorous color schemes.
- Rooms meant for sleeping and quiet work are usually in more subdued colors. However, when there is a large family group, a personal bedroom offers the opportunity for each individual to express his or her color preferences, whatever they may be.
- Communal spaces, such as living and family rooms, should have colors that—if they are not the favorites of all household members—at least do not actively offend anyone in the family.
- Bathrooms should have colors that flatter the complexion. Very few people want to face the mirror, first thing in the morning, in a green room. Of course, careful lighting can counteract the effects of unflattering colors.

156. A ceiling is usually neutral, but in this room a bold graphic sunburst draws the eye upward and personalizes the space. Barbara Burke Associates, designer. (*Photograph: Hedrich-Blessing*)

Economies with Color

Color is the most economical of all the elements that make up a home. The color you like is no more expensive than the one you do not like. Especially with paint, color is a powerful but inexpensive tool.

- Paint on walls, floor, and ceiling can revitalize a room almost instantly. (See Plate 28, p. 152.)
- New color can refresh old furniture.
- Painted graphics on walls, painted bands or designs around windows can bring tremendous design impact. They may even substitute for wallpaper or draperies.
- Floors can be painted instead of carpeted.

Perhaps best of all, color can personalize and vitalize the most humdrum or undistinguished space, any style and condition of furniture. It can be truly an extension of the self.

The Shell: Floors and Ceilings

7

The surfaces that enclose space—floors, ceilings, walls, and windows—have a number of roles in the home. They keep us warm and dry, define the space we have to live in, and establish its character. Floors are the most used surfaces, ceilings, the least; walls come in between, literally and figuratively. We will consider these elements separately for their potential in function and their contribution to the design of a home. Although the forms of these elements are usually fixed, we often can modify them to emphasize their positive characteristics, to add to livability, and to conserve energy in the home.

This chapter deals with floors and ceilings; the subsequent one with walls and windows.

Floors

We must consider floors in planning the design of any interior simply because the floor is there and in constant use. Floors take the most wear of any element in the home, so maintenance, replacement ease, and costs of both become important factors. Because floors are the foundation of any room, both physically and visually, their design affects the total design of the space.

The designer can make only minor modifications in the form of a floor. It is possible, for instance, to raise one section of the floor a step or two above the main level, thereby interrupting the flow of space and dividing it into areas. This technique of raising the floor level has led to seating or sleeping platforms that are as much part of the floor as they are furniture.

Basically, however, floors are flat, horizontal surfaces with two main functions—to insulate us from the cold, often damp earth, and to provide a firm, level plane on which to walk and to place furniture. The only exception to this horizontality is in an occasional ramp, introduced when someone in the household cannot cope with steps or when a wheelchair is necessary.

To carpet or not to carpet is often the first question that comes to mind when considering floors. Many floors today are left by the builder in an unfinished state, requiring a surfacing material to complete them.

157. By lowering one section of the floor, architect William Remick created two distinct social areas. A Franklin stove, the focal point in a brick-lined conversation pit, would draw people around it. An Oriental rug designates a second, more open area in another part of the room. (*Photograph: Joshua Freiwald*)

Plate 26. While high-intensity red and green may be too strong for each other in the home, combinations of dark brick red with pale yellow-green (*above*), or pink with dark green (*left*) are more palatable.

below: Plate 27. Sometimes the colors in a room will be chosen to coordinate with part of the architecture itself. This red brick fireplace wall serves as a background for the warm, subdued earth colors of the furniture and carpets that complement it. Roger Larson, architect. (*Photograph: © Morley Baer*)

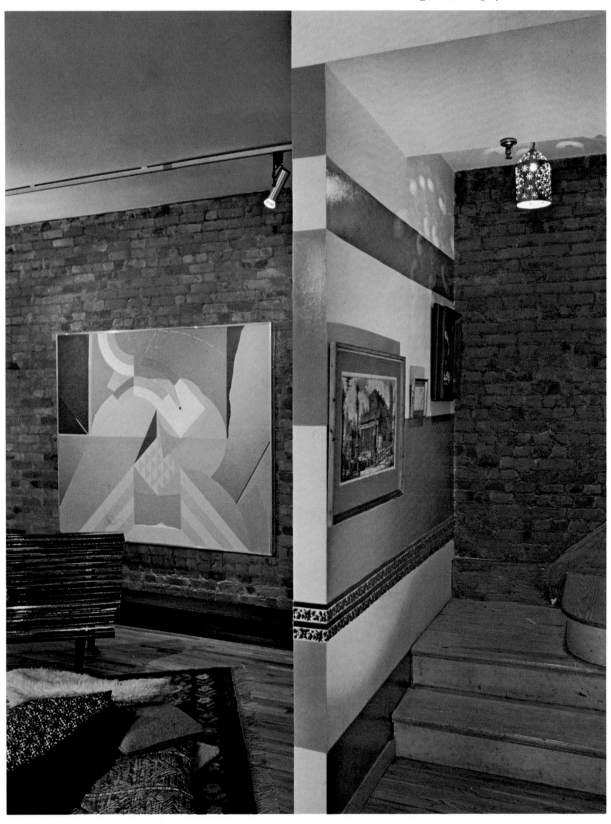

Plate 28. One of the most economical ways to decorate walls is with paint. Here, cheerfully striped room dividers contrast with the red brick walls and display an art collection. Hugh Hardy, designer. (*Photograph: Norman McGrath*)

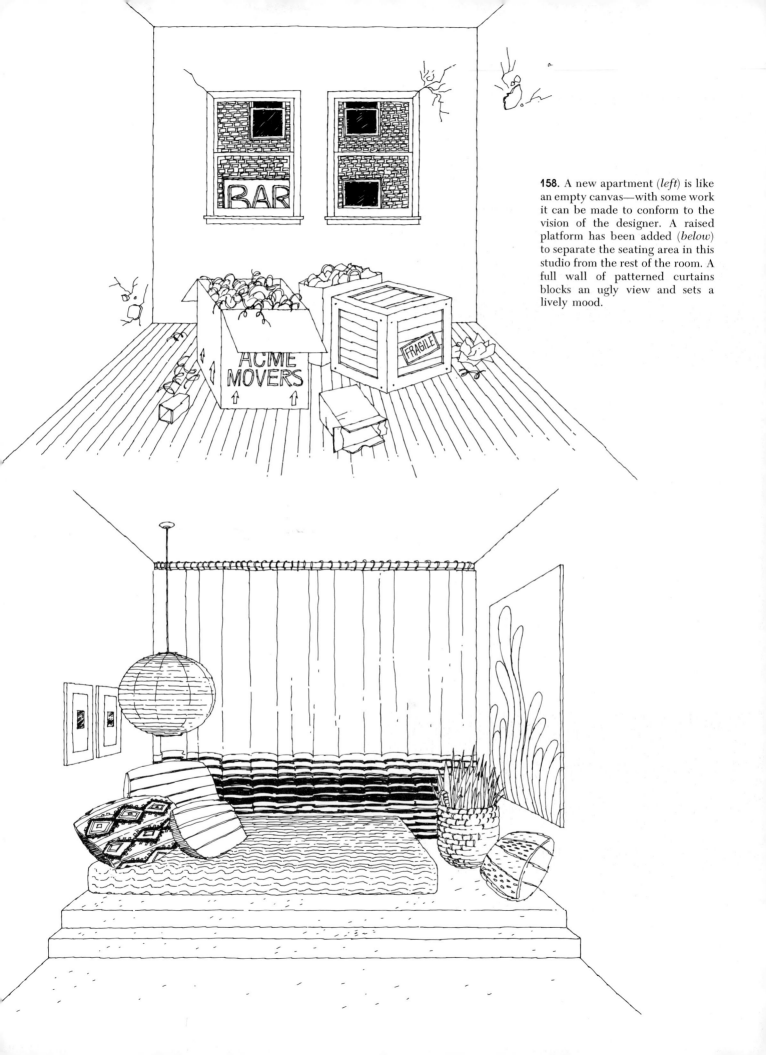

158. A new apartment (*left*) is like an empty canvas—with some work it can be made to conform to the vision of the designer. A raised platform has been added (*below*) to separate the seating area in this studio from the rest of the room. A full wall of patterned curtains blocks an ugly view and sets a lively mood.

Table 7.1
Flooring Materials

Material	Source or Composition	Use	Size and Shape	Patterns
Hard				
concrete cost: least expensive flooring; can be both base and finish flooring	cement, sand, aggregates, and water; can be integrally colored	can be left bare; a base for clay, tile, brick, and stone; coverable with wood, resilient flooring, carpets	usually poured in slabs but tiles available; at times marked off in rectangles by screeds	exposing aggregates gives surface interest; terrazzo has mosaiclike patterns from marble chips
stone cost: very expensive	slate, flagstone, marble, and so on	chiefly entrances and near fireplaces, but can be used in any room	usually not more than 2' square; rectangular or irregular	natural veining, shapes of stones, and patterns in which they are laid
tile and brick (clay) cost: expensive	heat-hardened clay; tile is usually glazed	areas getting hard wear, moisture, and dirt: entrances, hallways, bathrooms, or any place where effect is wanted	tiles are $\frac{1}{2}''$ to $12''$ square or rectangular, hexagonal, and so on; standard bricks are $2'' \times 4'' \times 8''$	tile has varied designs; typical brick patterns come from the way in which the bricks are laid
wood (hard) cost: moderately expensive	oak, birch, beech, maple, pecan, teak, walnut; sealable with liquid plastics, finished with synthetics	any room; often covered by carpets	strips $1\frac{1}{2}''$ to $3\frac{1}{2}''$ wide; planks $2''$ to $8''$ wide; parquet blocks $9'' \times 9''$ and so on	color and grain of wood; usually laid in parallel strips; also blocks of varied parquetry patterns
Resilient				
asphalt tiles cost: least expensive composition flooring	asbestos or cotton fibers, plasticizers, pigments, and resin binders	recommended for laying over concrete directly on ground, especially in much-used areas	standard is $12'' \times 12''$ but others available	tiles are plain or marbleized; laying creates typical tile patterns
cork tiles cost: moderately expensive	cork shavings, granules compressed and baked to liquefy natural resins	floors not subject to hard wear, water, grease, stains, or dirt	squares $9'' \times 9''$ or $12'' \times 12''$; also rectangles	chunks of cork of different colors give fine to coarse textural patterns
rubber tiles cost: moderately expensive	pure or synthetic rubber and pigments vulcanized under pressure	can be laid directly over on-grade concrete floors	$9'' \times 9''$ to $18'' \times 36''$	usually plain or marbleized
vinyl-asbestos tiles cost: inexpensive	similar to asphalt but with vinyl plastic resins	any indoor floor including on-grade and below-grade concrete floors	$12'' \times 12''$ tiles are typical	wide range of patterns, printed or embossed
vinyl-cork tiles cost: moderately expensive	same as cork but with vinyl added as a protective sealer	any floor where heavy-duty durability is not important	same as cork	same as cork
vinyl sheets and tiles cost: moderately expensive	vinyl resins, plasticizers, pigments, perhaps cheaper-grade fillers, heat-formed under pressure; sheet vinyl laid on alkali-resistant backing	any indoor floor; special types available for basement floors; also counter tops, wall covering; foam backed for greater resiliency	usually $12'' \times 12''$ tiles; also by the roll, 6' to 15' wide; new types poured on floor for completely seamless installation	great variety, new designs frequent; marbled, flecked, mosaic, sculptured, embossed, veined, and striated
Soft				
carpeting and rugs cost: wide range	almost all natural and manufactured fibers	recommended over any flooring that is moisture-proof	almost unlimited	plain to ornate, structural to applied

In some older homes, the floors have deteriorated sufficiently to have reached a state where refinishing or replacement is necessary. Carpeting then is considered, because the choice is wide in color, texture, and cost, and carpeting is fairly easy to install and to change.

But many other materials are possible, from hard masonry such as stone or tile, through the wood that was standard for many centuries, to resilient vinyl—a fairly new but useful manufactured material. Each has definite characteristics and optimum uses.

Table 7.1
Flooring Materials (continued)

	Colors	Durability	Maintenance	Comments
Hard				
concrete	limited range of low-intensity colors, but can be painted, color-waxed, and so on	very high except that it often cracks and can be chipped; serious damage difficult to repair	markedly easy if sealed against stains and grease; waxing deepens color and gives lustrous surface but is not necessary	hard and noisy; cold (welcome in summer) unless radiantly heated
stone	usually black, grays, and tans; variation in each piece and from one piece to another; marble in wide range of colors	very high but chipping and cracking difficult to repair	easy—minimum sweeping and mopping	solid, permanent, earthy in appearance; usually bold in scale; hard and noisy; cold if floor is not heated
tile and brick (clay)	glazed tiles in all colors; bricks usually red	generally high but depends on hardness of body, glaze; may chip or crack, fairly easy to replace	easy—dusting and washing; unglazed types can be waxed; porous types absorb grease and stains	satisfyingly permanent and architectural in appearance; can relate indoor to outdoor areas; noisy and cold
wood (hard)	light red, yellow, tan, or brown; can be painted any color	high but shows wear; irradiated types very durable	medium high—must be sealed, then usually waxed and polished; irradiated need minimum care	natural beauty, warmth; moderately permanent; easy to refinish; but fairly hard, noisy
Resilient				
asphalt tiles	full range of hues, but colors are neutralized; becoming available in lighter, clearer colors	excellent but can be cracked by impact and dented by furniture; some types not grease-proof	moderately easy—mopping and waxing with water-emulsion wax	eight times as hard as rubber tile; noisy; slippery when waxed
cork tiles	light to dark brown	moderately high; dented by furniture	not easy; porous surface absorbs dirt, which is hard to dislodge; sweep, wash, and wax	luxurious in appearance; resilient and quiet
rubber tiles	unlimited range; often brighter and clearer than in asphalt	moderately high, resistant to denting; some types damaged by grease	average—washing, wax or rubber polish	similar to asphalt, but more resilient
vinyl-asbestos tiles	almost unlimited	high general durability, resistant to grease, alkali, and moisture; can be dented by furniture	among the easiest; resilient underlay retards imbedding of dirt	somewhat hard and noisy but more easily kept than asphalt
vinyl-cork tiles	same as cork	same as cork, but more resistant to denting, dirt, grease	very easy—sweep, wash, and wax as needed	vinyl makes colors richer; less resilient and not so quiet as cork
vinyl sheets and tiles	wide range including light, bright colors; in some, translucency gives depth in color similar to marble	excellent; cuts tend to be self-sealing; resists almost everything including household acids, alkalies, or grease, denting, chipping, and so on	very easy; built-in luster lasts long; foreign matter stays on surface; can be waxed but not always necessary, especially for some types; dirt collects in depressions of embossed types	pleasant satiny surface; quiet and resilient, some types have cushioned inner core; patterns developed from material itself seem better than those imitating other materials
Soft				
carpeting and rugs	infinite range of hues, tints, shades alone or in rich designs	depends on fiber (see Table 9.1)	daily spot cleaning, weekly vacuuming, sweeping for Orientals; occasional deep cleaning	appreciated for possible beauty, as well as softness, warmth

Flooring Materials

Table 7.1 summarizes the characteristics of flooring materials popular today. With the exception of carpeting and rugs, almost all are durable, cool, either hard or only moderately resilient, more or less stain-resistant, and easy to clean. But, paradoxically, according to their color and texture, some will take more care than carpeting, since they show dust and spots more readily.

159. A slate floor is expensive, but long-lasting. In this room it works well with the brick wall and fireplace and the wood ceiling. (*Photograph: courtesy Buckingham-Virginia Slate Corporation*)

Masonry Stone, such as slate or marble, brick, and ceramic tile floors have high original cost but are long lasting, indoors or out. They can look rugged or formal, according to the way they are set. Masonry floors can *look* cool or warm, depending on their color and texture; but they *are* hard and cold unless radiantly heated. In warm climates this quality can be an advantage, keeping the house cool long after the outdoor temperature has reached an uncomfortable level.

Concrete is being used increasingly as a flooring material, even in highrise apartment buildings. In most cases it is unseen, a sub-flooring upon which a surfacing material is laid to provide resilience, sound absorption, warmth, and a more attractive appearance. Concrete, however, can be integrally colored or inlaid with aggregates, or divided by wood or metal screeds into rectilinear patterns.

160. Ceramic tiles come in many shapes and can be laid in different patterns. (*Photograph courtesy Country Floors, Inc.*)

right: 161. The use of natural materials creates an affinity between a home and its environment. A concrete aggregate floor simulates the outdoors; a sunken bathtub, wood paneling, skylight, and plants add to the feeling of being in natural surroundings. Alex Riley, architect. (*Photograph: Philip L. Molten*)

below: 162. Viewing this living room from above makes it easy to see how the area rug creates a focal point in front of the fireplace. The entire floor is masonry, and the rug provides warmth as well as defining a separate area. Julian Neski and Barbara Neski, architects. (*Photograph courtesy Hastings Tile Co., Inc.*)

Actual surface texture is a factor in maintenance, and especially so in a surface meant to be walked on. Glazed ceramic tile has an impervious finish that resists staining; unglazed brick, unless sealed, will absorb greasy stains that are then difficult to eradicate. On the other hand, the rough texture of brick hides minor spots and dust that will show up on a highly glazed, plain colored tile.

A common design solution today is the combination of masonry floors with area rugs. This choice makes it possible to enjoy all the good qualities of masonry, and at the same time offset the potential drawbacks of hardness and coldness. It offers several advantages, including:

- contrast of color between the more neutral background of the masonry and the color or pattern of the area rugs
- contrasts of warmth and texture
- creation of "islands" for furniture groupings or use areas within the expanse of floor; the flooring provides unity, the area rugs, variety

163. For this floor hemlock decking was sanded, sealed, and stained to create what the architect, Michael Sands, calls "a poor man's hardwood floor." Cindi Sands, designer. (*Photograph: Philip L. Molten*)

164. Painted floors offer a variety of possibilities. Here, the floor was painted to give the illusion of a rug. To preserve the paint, polyurethane could be applied on top, followed by a heavy coat of wax.

Wood   The most popular hard flooring material undoubtedly is wood, with its long history of use and its generally warm appeal. Wood varies in cost, from inexpensive pine to costly walnut parquet, but it is fairly easy to repair and refinish.

Like concrete, inexpensive wood is often used as a subflooring, ready for surfacing with either a better grade of wood or some other appealing finish.

When used as a finish flooring, wood needs to be kept waxed to make it stain-resistant, unless the wood has been irradiated, or impregnated with polyurethane or a similar plastic that makes it cleanable with a damp mop. This type of flooring is high in original cost, but low in maintenance.

Clear urethanes are available for home application, providing a less expensive alternative to irradiated wood and requiring less care than waxed floors.

Painting is also a possibility. Painted floors have come back into favor, because the paint is fairly easy to apply and often useful as a stop-gap measure until more expensive flooring can be installed. Special tough floor paints are available, and the effects can range from a plain foundation color to bright patterns or stenciled designs.

Wood floors usually take one of three forms: narrow, regularly spaced strips; random-width boards; or blocks of solid wood or parquet, laid in simple alternating or quite elaborate patterns.

The actual laying of wood floors has for the most part been left to the professional. Now, however, it is possible to get wood blocks or squares, with or without a self-adhesive backing, that are fairly easy for the amateur to install if instructions are followed carefully.

Long a traditional flooring material, wood has retained its popularity because it has been updated by new finishes and methods of application that make it suitable for use in any room in the house. It provides a subdued but rich foundation that seems right with almost any type of furnishing, any color scheme. Its inherent structural ornament, enhanced by the way it is laid, enlivens a room without being visually demanding.

As with masonry, wood floors often are combined with area rugs, for the same design advantages listed above.

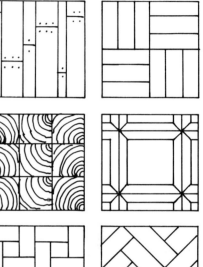

165. Wood floor patterns can range from random plank flooring (*top left*) to a block pattern showing the grain of the wood (*middle left*) to various parquet patterns.

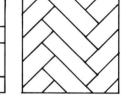

below: 166. The oak floors in this beach house have a polyurethane finish for easy care. A high-pile area rug defines the living area as separate from the dining area. Note that the circular skylight is directly over an oak pedestal table of the same size. (*Photograph: Norman McGrath*)

167. Flooring such as the pre-trimmed, pre-pasted vinyl shown here offers many advantages in a kitchen. It is resilient, attractive, and easy to clean and install. (*Photograph courtesy Collins & Aikman*)

Resilient Flooring   So useful have resilient floorings proven themselves, that it is hard to imagine a home without at least some. Their resiliency is only comparative: not quite so hard as stone, but not nearly so soft as carpeting. They are probably the closest approach yet to the ideal of an attractive, easily maintained, smooth-surface flooring material, making them the flooring choice for areas subject to much wear and tear.

Many types of resilient floorings are now available. Their degree of resiliency varies from the almost-hard of asbestos tile to some of the newer cushioned vinyls that are foam-backed to increase their springiness and warmth.

Choices also are spread between materials that need constant waxing and those that need none at all. Although the foam-backed types usually require no waxing, certainly a time saver, they are often heavily embossed. This results in a slightly uneven surface. Dirt can collect in the depressed areas, requiring a certain amount of scrubbing to dislodge it.

A major decision is the choice between sheet materials and tiles:

- **Sheet vinyl** comes in rolls 6 to 15 feet wide and has fewer dirt-catching seams than do tiles, but it usually must be installed professionally.
- **Tiles** can be installed with less waste if the floor is irregular in outline, and they allow piecemeal replacement of worn areas. The self-sticking versions can be laid by any handy person.

168. Vinyl floor coverings can be designed to complement almost any kind of furnishings. Here a traditional Spanish tile pattern, which is sold in sheets, sets off the straight lines of modern steel and plastic furniture. (*Photograph courtesy Armstrong Cork Company*)

In making a decision about resilient flooring, the first factor to be considered is the type of subfloor. Informed advice is needed here. The condition of the subfloor is important. It should be as level and smooth as possible to avoid bumps in the finished surface, and it should have an insulating membrane to stop the passage of moisture.

Beyond the practical, the choice is wide open in pattern and color. Possibilities range from plain colors to intricate designs that resemble traditional tile patterns, from the kind of structural ornament that comes from the manipulation of the basic material—flows or flecks of color, embedded self-chips—to the applied ornament of embossed designs that vary from abstract to imitations of brick or stone.

Soft Floor Coverings

Carpets and rugs of all kinds—soft floor coverings—add warmth, texture, resilience, quietness, and attractiveness to what must be an essentially firm foundation. We often choose them first for their visual qualities. Carpets and rugs contribute a softness and friendly intimacy to floors that relate them to upholstered furniture, draperies, and even our clothing. Their colors, textures, and patterns establish the foundation on which the interior design scheme can be based.

A few definitions will establish the categories.

- **Rugs** are made in finished sizes and are seldom fastened to the floor.
- **Carpeting** comes by the yard in widths from 27 inches to 18 feet or more. It is cut, and pieced if necessary, to cover the whole floor and is fastened down. It can also be cut to a specific size and bound at the edges, making it in essence a rug.
- **Broadloom** simply refers to the fact that the carpeting was woven, as the name implies, on a wide loom, without reference to any other quality.

Rugs, carpeting, a combination of both, or none can be appropriate for different situations. We will use "carpeting" as an all-inclusive term covering all types of carpets and rugs.

Wall-to-Wall Carpeting   One of the best means of unifying a room or of relating adjacent spaces is wall-to-wall carpeting. If muted in color and pattern, it makes a room seem larger. Because it does not define special areas within a room, it simplifies arranging and rearranging furniture.

169. Wall-to-wall carpeting unifies this room, and the pale color makes the space appear larger. Imagine the same space with area rugs. The result might be too much for the already lively effect. Built for American Plywood by R. B. Fitch. (*Photograph: Gordon H. Schenck, Jr.*)

170. The polished wood floors in this living room are not completely hidden, but an Indian rug defines the conversation area in the center of the room. The pattern of the rug is echoed by the sofa pillows. Paranjpe, designer. (*Photograph: Norman McGrath*)

Wall-to-wall carpeting is more expensive than a rug of the same quality (except handwoven rugs), and it serves as a finished floor covering, eliminating more costly hard-surface flooring underneath.

Maintenance time and effort may be less than for resilient floorings that need constant washing and waxing, but carpeting does need weekly vacuuming and an occasional thorough cleaning by professionals or the homeowner. This is necessary to keep it looking its best and to prolong its life. Embedded dirt is abrasive, and stains can harm fibers.

Rugs Rugs can range from almost-room size, to *area* rugs that define space without enclosing walls, to the small versions that are sometimes called *scatter* or *throw* rugs. If they cover the entire floor or most of it, the effect is similar to that of carpeting, except that most rugs have a fairly definite pattern that makes them more emphatic. This pattern may be simply the binding or perhaps a fringe that creates a frame around the rug.

171. A braided rug contributes to the homey, rustic feeling of this sitting room. Raymond Zambrano, designer. (*Photograph: Philip L. Molten*)

Rugs can be used on hard-surface floorings or on top of carpeting to hold together a furniture group or to accent an area. They protect sections of the floor subject to hard use, and are easily cleaned.

It is the mobility of rugs that makes them particularly useful. Since they are not attached to the floor, they can be moved around in a room, or between rooms and homes, sent off to the cleaners, or even changed with the seasons. Most rooms have traffic lanes and some areas that get more use than others; rugs can be reversed to spread the wear and soil.

Rugs are usually, although not necessarily, striking in color, pattern, or texture. Oriental and Scandinavian rya, hooked or braided rugs, and an infinite variety of handwoven rugs add a special touch of character to a room. They thus play a more dominant role in the total room design than a plain carpet. Exceptionally fine ones often migrate off the floor, to be displayed on walls or over railings.

Carpet Tiles   A fairly recent innovation, carpet tiles come with or without a self-adhesive backing, making them easy for the amateur to lay. They work best in a wall-to-wall application, because the edges are not bound, and they can be cut quite easily to conform to the contours of a room. The longer the pile, the less the seams will show. At times, the squares are deliberately laid to form a pattern with an alternation of color or texture. They can even be cut, perhaps on a diagonal, and reassembled in a more complex configuration.

An interesting variation results in an inexpensive floor covering. Mill-end pieces of carpeting can be bought for very little money and then assembled at home and held together by carpet tape. Texture, color, and pattern will be important to the success of such a project.

Whatever type of soft floor covering is chosen, its quality will be the next consideration. Quality depends on the material and the method of construction, as is stressed in Chapter 10. But more and more, special processing and combinations of fibers are being used to overcome specific disadvantages.

172. Carpet tiles offer the designer infinite variations of pattern. This maize floor covering has a dark-and-light checkerboard pattern. (*Photograph courtesy Stark Carpet Corporation*)

Materials for Floor Coverings

Table 10.1 in the chapter on Fabrics lists the substances used in carpeting, but the following are the most commonly encountered:

- **Wool** retains its age-old popularity, probably because it has so many good qualities and because it appeals to our ingrained love of natural materials. It is resilient and long lasting, takes dye beautifully, and is resistant to burns. Wool needs mothproofing, and some people are allergic to it, but it has few other disadvantages. Costs vary tremendously from the cheap and short-lived reused wool rugs to the antique Orientals that are both art objects and financial investments.
- **Acrylic** yarns are the most wool-like of the synthetics, are nonallergenic and easily spot cleaned. It is important to be sure that the yarns meet flammability standards. Trade names include Orlon, Zefran, and Acrilan.
- **Nylon** is popular for its endurance, easy maintenance, and resistance to insects. It is resilient and nonallergenic. New treatments counteract its tendency to pilling and static electricity. Common brand names are Antron, Cumuloft, 501, or often just Nylon.
- **Olefins** (polyethylene and polypropylene) are growing in popularity because of their low cost and many resistances. They are often

found in the indoor-outdoor types of needlepunched carpets and tiles, as well as in indoor pile carpeting. Herculon is a common brand name, but the fibers may be offered as generic names.

- **Polyesters** share many of the good qualities of manufactured fibers, are relatively inexpensive, and easily washed and dried. They come in a wide range from living room to bath carpeting and colorful throw rugs. Labels may specify Dacron, Fortrel, Kodel, and various generic names.
- **Sisal** and other grasses, in both pile and woven designs, make cool and inexpensive floor coverings well suited to today's natural look. They usually have an unobtrusive pattern resulting from the weave and the way the sections are assembled, although they can be quite fanciful in design.

Construction of Floor Coverings

Next to the type of yarn used, the way it is put together influences quality. In this connection, it is the density of the surface (the weight per square foot) and the firmness of the process that is important.

Carpet backings (as distinguished from separate pads or cushions), are also an important factor in quality. Traditionally of jute but with many newer materials coming into use, they are the ground fabric, the foundation on which carpets are constructed. The backing should be tight and firm.

Often the backing is coated with latex or a similar product to hold the surface yarns securely, or an extra layer of backing may be added for greater strength. Still newer are the carpets with *unitary* backing, in which two layers of backing are bonded together.

A good carpet backing helps to keep the carpet flat, prevents it from skidding, aids in noise control, and adds to its life.

Design Qualities of Floor Coverings

Texture Of all the materials used in the home, carpeting undoubtedly has the greatest diversity of texture within its range of softness. These

173. Sisal carpeting has a natural look and requires little maintenance. It is ideal for a sun porch, as shown in this house designed by Quick Associates. (*Photograph: Gordon H. Schenck, Jr.*)

174. A strongly patterned thick pile rug lends a pronounced accent amid other strong design elements in this room. William Remick, architect. (*Photograph: Joshua Friewald*)

are actual, tactile textures that are also visually very effective. They feel good underfoot, they look pliable and responsive, and they break up light in various ways.

In addition, textures are extremely important in sound control, muting the noise of footsteps, the scrape of furniture, the sound waves from voices, television sets, and music systems.

Many carpets have some kind of pile, cut and uncut loops of varying heights. These result in textural effects that range from coarse to smooth, but the overall result is almost always soft.

Pattern   Texture and pattern are closely allied, because in rugs and carpets pattern is often structural ornament. In other words, beauty arises from the materials themselves, the way they are fabricated, and the resulting texture.

Pattern can result from a combination of textures, as in high and low loop or cut and uncut, or from the colors of the fibers and the way they are put together. Often it is a subtle management of texture—shearing a pile in a seemingly random fashion or in a distinct pattern. Colored fibers can be combined to form almost imperceptible shifts of hues over the surface, or the rich designs of Oriental rugs.

Pattern serves two purposes, and this is especially true in floor coverings. It enriches the surface and it hides soil. Beyond these considerations is the contribution that carpets and rugs of all kinds make to the character of a room. (See Plate 29, p. 169.)

Selection of Floor Materials

Decisions on flooring are big ones because of the actual size of the areas involved, the probable cost, and the long-term consequences. In general,

175. The direction of a carpet's pattern has an effect on the room. When the pattern goes crosswise (*right*), the room seems wider. When the pattern goes lengthwise (*below*), the room seems longer.

176. Types of flooring materials influence the design of the rest of the room. Wall-to-wall carpeting (*right*) enlarges the room visually and links spaces. Area rugs (*below*) break up the space in a room for furniture groupings.

floorings are not easily changed or replaced; their maintenance is time-consuming and incessant. Above all, floors play a definitive role in establishing the total quality of a space.

In deciding on a flooring material, the last comes first: what do you want it to do for a given room? Since a floor lays the actual and the aesthetic foundation of a space, the kind of flooring is usually the first consideration. A flow of muted carpeting will visually enlarge and link spaces, promise a soft warmth. Waxed and polished wood floors have a warm glow and an enduring quality. Area rugs act as frames for furniture groupings, lead the eyes down a hall, bring in bright or subtle pattern and color. Vinyl flooring seems right for relaxed, informal living.

When this decision is made, it is time for research into the many varieties and prices within each subgroup, coupled with a candid review of your own or your client's life style to determine what will be most appropriate and pleasing.

Ceilings

Typically, ceilings are the same size and shape, and parallel to, the floors they shelter, but from there on they bear little resemblance. The choices are far different and many, many fewer. Durability is seldom a factor, except for the weatherproofing of the roof above, and the design has been decided upon by the architect and builder, leaving little to the imagination of the interior designer.

We barely notice ceilings in a great many homes. They are bland, flat, unadorned surfaces, and very little has been done to change them. Perhaps this is just as well. It is usually a good idea to retain one large, undecorated surface in every room for visual respite. Nevertheless, ceilings need not be so plain, if thought has been given to their shape and direction, possible structural and applied surfacings, as well as color and ornament.

Dropped and Elevated Ceilings

A ceiling lowered below the general ceiling level differentiates areas without seemingly limiting the space, as walls, screens, or even furniture arrangement or rugs might do. A dropped ceiling suggests intimacy and

177. An Oriental carpet emphasizes the direction of traffic. Note that it is used on top of wall-to-wall carpeting. Fisher-Friedman Associates, architects. (*Photograph: Joshua Friewald*)

coziness, drawing people around a dining table, perhaps, or conserving the warmth of a fire. Conversely, a sudden elevation of ceiling height gives a feeling of expansion and uplift, freedom from constraints.

Sloped Ceilings

Gabled, or double-pitched, shed, or single-sloped ceilings move from the common horizontal to the diagonal, encouraging us to look up. They activate and increase the apparent volume of a space.

Beamed Ceilings

Beams establish a rhythm, across or down a room, accentuating length or breadth, or up a pitched ceiling emphasizing dramatic height. They can be very demanding or only an accent, according to their color and size, and whether they are embedded in the ceiling, seem to support the ceiling, or are a free structure across space. Of all the ceiling treatments, they are probably the most significant in terms of possible character.

180. The beamed ceiling in a loft renovated by Polly Myhrum and Myron Adams sets a rhythm for the space and emphasizes the height of the ceiling. The natural materials (wood, brick, wicker, cotton fabric, and ceramics) contribute to the character of the room as defined by the ceiling. (*Photograph: George Gardner*)

left: Plate 29. Because it has both visual and tactile texture, carpeting can greatly influence the character of a room. Here, a high-pile area rug adds warmth and texture to what would otherwise be an austere interior. Dan Solomon, designer. (*Photograph: Joshua Freiwald*)

below: Plate 30. While most ceilings are white or off-white, a carefully chosen decided color can become part of a design. Many of the furnishings shown here were chosen to coordinate with the soft blue of the ceiling; the carpet, in contrast, is a neutral color we would ordinarily expect to find above our heads, not beneath our feet. Elizabeth Williams, designer. (*Photograph: Robert Perron*)

above: Plate 31. One of the most common and versatile wall finishes, paint can be used to achieve many different effects. The striking blue wall on one side of this kitchen picks up the unusual blue color of the sink. Claude Stoller, architect. (*Photograph: Ezra Stoller © ESTO*)

right: Plate 32. While most Venetian blinds are made to be as inconspicuous as possible, they can be used to enhance the design of a room. These thin-slat custom-designed blinds are green on one side, yellow on the other. When open, they give a muted view of the patio outside; when partially closed, more color shows. Chinacoff/Peterson, designer. (*Photograph: Norman McGrath*)

Coved Ceilings

When walls and ceilings are joined with a curved surface rather than at right angles, space seems more plastic and flexible. A variation of this creates a recess, a space for cove lighting around the perimeter of a room, washing the ceiling or the wall with light from an unseen source.

Surfacing Materials

The typical ceiling today is surfaced with plaster or with some kind of composition board, and it is painted white or some very pale hue. This is a stereotype that literally designs itself, and for good reasons. It is inexpensive to build and maintain, gives unobtrusive spaciousness, and reflects light well, a very important quality.

Sculptured ceilings were very popular in the days when plaster work was still a living craft, and many remodelers are saving and repairing such examples as survive. The modern sculptured ceiling is a pale comparison, virtually limited to a surfacing of roughened plaster.

Various types of panels or tiles with textured surfaces are easy to install and may give some acoustical control. They set up a repetitive pattern across the ceiling, because the panels must be set into a framework, while the tiles, though interlocked and stapled on, still show lines where they are joined.

Translucent panels concealing fluorescent light fixtures fit easily into the framework system, adding another element—a very useful one.

Wood is another possibility as a ceiling surface, offering a variety of textures. It can be variable in color, and left natural, stained, or painted. A wood ceiling will bounce back noise, and unless very light in color, soak up light, but it will seldom need refinishing unless stained by leaks.

Glass or transparent or translucent plastic occasionally appears in a skylight, bringing illumination from an unexpected source and allowing glimpses of the outdoors.

left: 181. Translucent panels are especially practical for a dressing room or bathroom, since they can provide even light for all areas of the room. Fluorescent lights are concealed by the panels, resulting in an uncluttered look. Jerry Kler, architect. (*Photograph: Philip L. Molten*)

right: 182. The entire ceiling in this kitchen is a glass skylight, bringing the outdoors inside. Plants add to this effect. Note that the cabinets are of the same wood as the beams in the skylight. David Shaw, architect. (*Photograph: Gordon H. Schenck, Jr.*)

Applied Surfacings   Although the possibility is not often considered, ceilings can be surfaced with wallpaper or with stretched fabric, as a wall would be, or fabric can be draped across the ceiling. Because they are unexpected, any of these treatments will have a decided impact unless the material is muted or neutral.

Light and Color

We mentioned that most ceilings are white or pale in color. The practical reason for this is that they then reflect the greatest amount of light. This is a primary consideration in spreading any daylight that comes in across the room, and in making the best use of artificial lighting. But if color is to be used, deciding on the hue for a ceiling brings other considerations.

Ceilings, especially at night, bathe everything below in reflected color. A yellow ceiling would enliven yellows, oranges, or yellow-greens, but would dull any blues or violets.

A strong color on a ceiling is very noticeable, perhaps because of the unbroken area of the color that we see as a whole, or its novelty. For these reasons it will suggest or even limit the colors that can be used elsewhere in the room. (See Plate 30, p. 169.)

Although floors and ceilings are separated by 8 feet or more of space, with usually quite a lot going on in between, they should be considered in combination. The design concepts come into play here. Only as the scales are balanced, the rhythms compatible, emphasis logical but not domineering, will these two major elements take their place in the general scheme of the space as a whole.

below: **183.** An Indian marriage tent draped over a suspended bed gives a canopy-like effect and provides color and bold design in an otherwise simple room. (*Photograph: Dudley Gray*)

below: **184.** The masonry tile on this floor separates the kitchen from the rest of the area and reduces kitchen maintenance. The diagonal lines in the floor tile pattern are repeated in the angles of the sloped ceiling. In general, although much space separates the floor and ceiling, the two surfaces should be considered in combination. Turner Brooks, designer. (*Photograph: Robert Perron*)

The Shell: Walls, Windows, and Doors

8

The untrained designer or homeowner nearly always approaches interior design by asking two questions: What color paint or wallpaper shall I put on the walls? What kind of curtains or draperies shall I buy? These are basic decisions, and from them all other choices flow. The treatment of walls and windows *is* among the most crucial of factors in interior design, because these elements are often the ones we notice first. They may establish the character of an entire room or home.

For the trained designer, however, such questions come much later. Design of a room or space is seen as a totality, with walls and windows playing only secondary roles to the overall design. As we have stressed repeatedly throughout this book, the basic questions should be: What do I want this room to be? Who will live here? How will they use this room? Only after *these* questions have been answered should specific decisions be made.

Walls and windows are large elements. Their treatment can be planned either to *carry* the design or to *blend* with it. For example, the choice of a strongly patterned wallpaper, a vivid wall color, or a striking drapery fabric will *establish* the design of a room. Other elements—furnishings, upholstery, accessories—will be determined by the set pattern in walls or windows. Conversely, a decision to paint the walls white or a pale color, to use neutral fabrics or an unassertive treatment at windows, will *follow* from another strong design element, perhaps a brilliant rug or a large piece of furniture.

Despite their size, walls and windows should not necessarily be considered first. They are part of a whole.

Walls

The shape and size of rooms are determined by walls. We may be able to make small changes, taking down a wall here, or building in a wall divider there. But for the most part our efforts must be directed toward the role of walls in affecting mood, character, and spirit—setting the stage for daily living.

The role and treatment of walls have changed over the centuries. From their first purely functional status of protection from the elements they grew into decorative backgrounds for a relatively small amount of furniture. Today, walls are more "used" in interior design.

- Storage walls unite the enclosing functions of walls with many kinds of storage space, either within the walls as closets, or attached to them as cabinets.
- Walls become furniture, with built-in bookcases, seating, or counter space.
- Walls act merely as space dividers rather than as enclosures, cutting off direct views or segregating activities within a room, without really stopping the flow of space.

Walls always have been pierced by doors for access, and later by windows for ventilation, light, and glimpses of what was going on outside. We cannot talk about walls without mentioning the decisive part that openings in walls play. More and more the distinction between walls, windows, and doors has been evaporating. What was once a solid opaque wall with a heavy wooden door and two small cutout windows becomes a window wall with perhaps half of it a sliding glass door. Not only is the effect vastly different, but there are different problems.

185. A wall can be more than just a room divider. This storage wall serves as a bookcase and also connects the kitchen to the living/dining area. Shutters can be closed to hide the kitchen from view completely. Hank Bruce, architect. (*Photograph: Philip L. Molten*)

Design of Walls

The architect and/or builder has designed and put up the walls. The shapes are there, but what to do with them becomes the designer's problem. Going back to the profile questionnaire in Chapter 1 will give strong hints about possible wall treatments—what might be done to affect the design of walls.

Some questions come to mind that should be considered first.

Formal or Informal Symmetrical balance in window and door placement, pronounced regularity in wall treatment, smooth surfaces, emphasis on verticality—all these contribute to a formal effect. Asymmetric rhythms, rougher textures, lively patterns, and emphasis on an easy flow into and out of the room will seem more informal.

186. The unusual walls in this room give the effect of solid glass. There are, however, many sections of wood as well, against which furniture can be placed and paintings hung. Koberg, architect. (*Photograph: Philip L. Molten*)

187. Walls are either active or passive elements of design. The graphic painted on this bathroom wall makes a strong design statement. (*Photograph: Norman McGrath*)

Active or Passive   Walls can act as background only, passive receptors of whatever is hung on them or placed against them. Or they can be active design statements in their own right if they arouse visual interest. Active elements include wood with its grain, texture, and color; patterned wallpaper; built-in bookcases; accented windows and doors—anything that calls attention to a wall. An alternative would be smooth, noncommital walls activated by the use of bright paint.

Large or Small Scale   Walls can be of tremendous importance in establishing successful scale in a room as a whole. A too-long wall can be shortened by building in a short spur wall that will create an intimate sitting area. A too-high wall can be controlled by cutting it down with a chair rail molding or perhaps a lighted cornice just above head height. Just too much wall can be broken up by variations in treatment that focus attention on one sector at a time.

Permanent or Mobile   Unfortunately, many walls cut space into undesirable cubbyholes. One of the joys of house remodeling is often the removal of walls to open up space. On the other hand, a loft or barn will need additional walls to give privacy where needed. Mobile walls are a

188. A hanging plywood wall panel divides a large kitchen into two spaces—a sitting area and a smaller eat-in kitchen. Original cabinets, counters, and an old gas stove were retained. All furniture was recycled from cast-offs. The ceiling light fixture was converted into a drop light, and other lights were added over the counters. Automobile hubcaps decorate the walls. The lighting fixture behind the hanging panel was constructed from an old wire postcard rack, plastic meat trays, and Christmas tree lights. Designer and photographer: Philip L. Molten.

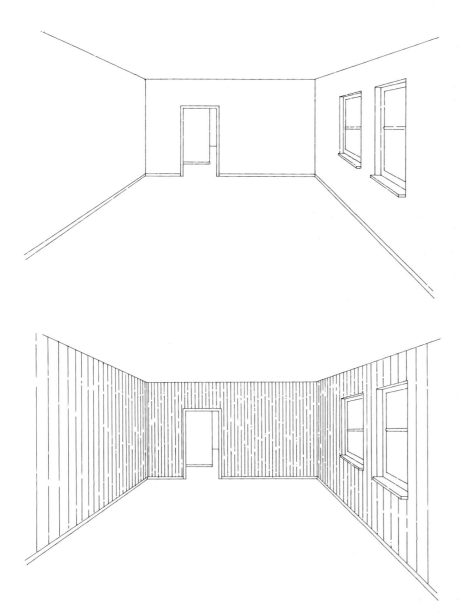

189–191. Different wall treatments make different design effects possible with the same space.

189. An empty room is the starting point for design (*above*). Walls with vertically striped or oriented wallpaper (*left*) appear to be taller.

sensible solution here, perhaps screen dividers not quite ceiling-high that can be moved around as circumstances suggest. Modular storage units can function in this way, too, providing sound as well as sight control.

Open or Enclosing   Opaque, substantial walls, warm dark colors and textures, small windows with heavy draperies create a feeling of protected enclosure. Light-colored walls and transparent, wide doorways leading to other rooms or to the outdoors seem and are less restricting. Continuity of materials, forms, and colors on walls throughout the house emphasizes the flow of space.

Light or Dark   The color of walls greatly influences the livability of a room. A critical factor is how much light is absorbed or reflected by different colors. As discussed in Chapter 6, white reflects a high percentage of the light striking it, black very little. Surface texture is also a consideration. The smoother the surface, the more light will be reflected. This is especially important in a room with small windows, where as much light as possible is needed to brighten the space. The

190. Dark walls make a room seem cozy. The mirrored wall at left expands the space, giving the room an interesting contrast and a certain formal air. Rug designed by Edward Fields. (*Photograph: J.B. Esakoff*)

glass-walled room brings a superabundance of light in the daytime, blackness at night, both of which may need control.

Sound Absorbing or Reflecting   Whether a wall is sound absorbing or reflecting is largely a question of wall construction, but we are not entirely at the mercy of the builder. Much can be done to control sound, whether it is the noise that leaks through walls or the music we want to hear in a room. A room in which music is a favorite recreation should have a well-thought-out mixture of sound-absorbing and sound-reflecting walls to balance the sound.

Hard surfaces bounce and reflect sound. If they predominate in a room, the result is noise. Soft, porous materials absorb sounds and can appreciably lower the decibel level in a room. Some wall panels are engineered to lessen noise reflected back into a room and also noise transmitted through walls to another room.

Heat and Cold Insulation   The way a wall was constructed is the decisive factor in temperature insulation. But there are also things the designer can do, such as applying a second layer of interior wall materials—wood paneling or thick panels of vinyl-faced fiberglass, even carpeting. Beyond these are a number of other possibilities that will be taken up in the discussion on windows and doors, where they are more directly applicable.

Durability and Maintenance   All walls need to be maintained, but the amount of time and money spent on them will vary greatly. Wood, tile, and vinyl plastics are durable and easy to keep. Glass is very easy to clean but shows dust and fingermarks. Some wallpapers are fragile but will be satisfactory on walls that do not get hard use. The basic questions in selection are the usual ones: What kind of use will the wall get? How easily can it be cleaned or repaired?

191. The trellis-type wallpaper, plants, and wicker furnishings in this room combine to suggest the atmosphere of a garden. The shutters also contribute to the outdoor feeling. The overall effect is lively and less formal than the room in Figure 190.

192. Designer Tom O'Toole needed a quiet place in his apartment, where he would not hear his office staff. Felt-covered walls, reflected here by mirrors in the bedroom, absorb sound from the adjoining office. (*Photograph: Maris-Semel*)

193. White painted wallboards and blond woodwork call attention to the many and varied window openings in this room. Turner Brooks, architect. (*Photograph: Robert Perron*)

Wall Surfacings

Table 8.1 lists wall-surfacing materials and may help you to evaluate and compare them. The ones most used in homes, however, have special qualities beyond the purely practical, and these design characteristics will influence your choices.

Wallboards Many new walls today are of drywall construction, with interior walls consisting of one of the various types of wallboards: sheetrock, gypsum, pressed wood, or plastic laminate. They are relatively inexpensive and easy to install. Many take readily to different types of finish and can be refinished. For our purposes, the important differences occur between the totally prefabricated panels and those that need further finishing.

The first, such as plastic laminate panels, are complete in themselves. They already have a fairly impervious skin. Panels are available in a wide range of colors, and many of them have a woodgrain, fabric, or some other pattern.

The unfinished panels are usually an unsightly gray or beige and therefore need paint, wallpaper, or fabric to provide a protective and more attractive surface.

Both types, however, have one characteristic that must be considered when attaching anything to the wall. Being light and not very dense all the way through, they will not support a heavy weight. This means that to suspend anything on the wall, from a large painting to bookcases, you must first locate the wood studs that are the inner structure of the wall. Studs are usually spaced at 16-inch intervals, not always just where you might want them.

The alternative to finding studs is to use the special types of screws (molly bolts or the like) that go all the way through the panel and clamp on the inner side. These will leave unsightly holes when later exposed, but the holes can be filled in with spackling paste and then repainted. Smaller objects can be put up with the usual picture hangers.

Wood As boards, blocks, shingles, or panels, wood is available in an immense variety of grains and colors. Wood paneling in the form of large

Table 8.1
Wall Materials

Material	Character	Use	Finishes	Advantages	Disadvantages
brick (adobe) cost: varies greatly from one locality to another	earthy solidity combined with handcraft informality; large in scale; noticeable pattern of blocks and joints unless smoothly plastered	interior-exterior walls, chiefly in mild climates	stucco, special paints, or transparent waterproofing	unique character: resists fire and insects; newer types made with special binders and stabilizers are stronger and more weather-resistant	older types damaged by water; walls must be thick or reinforced; sturdy foundations required; comparatively poor insulating qualities
brick (fired clay) cost: high but less than stone	substantial and solid, small-scale regularity; many sizes, shapes, and colors; can be laid in varied patterns	interior-exterior walls; around fireplaces	none unless waterproofing necessary; interior walls can be waxed	satisfying texture and pattern; durable, easily maintained; fireproof	none other than heat-cold conduction and noise reflection
concrete blocks (lightweight aggregate) cost: moderate	typically regular in shape, moderately textured, and bold in scale; many variations	interior-exterior walls in mild climates	exterior waterproofing necessary; no interior finish needed but can be painted	durable, easily maintained; fireproof; fair insulator	none of any consequence, except perhaps lack of domestic character
cork cost: moderately high	sympathetic natural color and texture	any room; only plastic-impregnated types suitable for baths and kitchens	none needed but can be waxed	durable, easily kept; sound-absorbent; good insulator	harmed by moisture, stains, and so on, unless specially treated
glass (clear, tinted, patterned, and mirrored) cost: moderately high	open and airy; patterned glass transmits diffused light; mirrored spreads light through a room	interior-exterior window walls; patterned glass for translucency; tinted glass for privacy, glare; mirrored for reflection	none (except for curtaining for privacy and control of light, heat, and cold)	clear glass creates indoor-outdoor relationships; patterned and tinted glass combines light and varying degrees of privacy; mirrors enlarge	breakable; very poor heat-cold insulation unless Thermopane; needs frequent cleaning
paint (water-base, oil-base) cost: moderately low	flat to gloss, smooth to textured; endless color range	any wall; select for specific use	none needed	inexpensive, versatile, colorful	must be chosen and applied properly
plaster and stucco cost: moderately low	typically smooth and precise but can be varied in texture; only surfacing material that shows no joints, breaks; quiet background	plaster in any room, stucco usually for exterior house walls	special weather-resistant paints; paint, paper, or fabric for interiors	moderately durable if properly finished; suited to many easy-to-change treatments; fireproof; special types absorb sound	often cracks or chips
plastic (resilient tiles or sheets) cost: moderately high	great variety of colors, patterns, textures	where durable, resilient walls are wanted, such as in play space or above kitchen counters	some need waxing; many now do not	very durable and resistant to cuts and stains; easy maintenance; can extend into counter tops	none of consequence

Table 8.1
Wall Materials (continued)

Material	Character	Use	Finishes	Advantages	Disadvantages
plastic (rigid panels, glazing; often reinforced with glass fibers) cost: moderate	opaque or translucent, often textured and colorful; thin and flat or corrugated; thicker with cores of varied materials	interior walls where durability, upkeep are important; partitions; interior-exterior walls	factory finished	similar to patterned glass except breaks less easily, lighter in weight; can be sawed and nailed	not thoroughly tested for longevity
stone cost: high	substantial, solid, impressive; natural colors and textures	around fireplaces; walls	none unless waterproofing is necessary	beauty and individuality; durability, ease of maintenance; fireproof; ages gracefully	poor insulator; reflects sound; not amenable to change
tile (clay) cost: moderately high	repeated regularity sets up pattern; great variety in size, shape, ornamentation	kitchens, bathrooms, and around fireplaces	no finish needed	can have great beauty and individuality; very durable, easily maintained; resistant to water, stains, fire	hard and cold to touch; reflects noise; can crack or break
wallboard (gypsum, sheetrock) cost: moderately low	noncommittal; joints show unless very well taped and painted	any room	paint, wallpaper, or fabric	not easily cracked; fire-resistant; can be finished in many ways	visually uninteresting in itself; needs protective surface
wallboard (plastic laminates) cost: high	shiny, mat, or textured surface; varied colors and patterns	kitchens, bathrooms, or any hard-use wall	none needed	very durable, unusually resistant to moisture, stains, dirt; cleaned with damp cloth	although wear-resistant, can be scratched or chipped; reflects noise
wallboard (pressed wood) cost: moderate	smooth, mat surface with slight visual texture; also great variety of patterns	hard-wear rooms	needs no finish but can be stained, waxed, painted	tough surface is hard to damage	none of importance
wall covering (plastic) cost: moderately high	many patterns; pleasing textures; mat or glossy surfaces	good for hard-use walls	none needed	very durable; resists moisture, dirt, stains; cleans with damp cloth	none of importance
wallpaper and fabrics cost: low to high	tremendous variety of color and pattern	any wall	usually none but can be protected with lacquer	inexpensive to costly; can give decided character; some kinds very durable and easy to keep	must be chosen and used carefully
wood (boards, plywood, shingles) cost: moderate	natural beauty and individuality of grain and color	interior-exterior walls	needs protective finish to seal it against water, stains, dirt	fairly durable, easily maintained; good insulator; adaptable; ages well inside	few kinds are weather-resistant unless treated; burns; attacked by termites

194. Wood is available in numerous colors and grains. Shown here are different woods for interior use. (*Photographs courtesy American Plywood Association; Bangkok Industries; Expanko Cork Co., Inc.; Potlatch Corp.; and U.S. Plywood*)

sheets of plywood is the most used today. It is fairly easy to apply, covers large areas, and can range from smooth to rough-sawn, with a noticeable or quiet grain. Some plywood is grooved to resemble boards with beveled joints.

Solid boards can be applied with either flush, tongue-and-groove, or beveled joints, laid vertically, horizontally, or diagonally. These variations set up quiet or decided rhythms.

Some other possibilities include shingles or cork, which bring special textural and insulation qualities.

Wood with a clear protective finish is extremely durable, slow to soil, and capable of being refinished. Unfinished wood acts as a base for other wall materials—paint or wallpaper being the most common.

Wood does have a few disadvantages. When anything is hung on a plain wood wall, that section will eventually change color due to fading and dirt. The wood can be refinished, but this is costly.

Wood is a flammable material, but it can and should be treated to be fire-resistant.

195. Ceramic wall tiles are durable and easily cleaned. At top is tiling that might be suitable for a bathroom; the tiles above would be appropriate in a kitchen. (*Photographs courtesy American Olean; and Country Floors, Inc.*)

Masonry   Except for stone or brick fireplaces, and an occasional fireplace wall, masonry is seen mostly on bathroom or kitchen walls. Here, as tile, ranging from small inch-square mosaic tile to larger sizes, masonry can be a colorful, plain or patterned, and very durable wall surfacing.

Tile is rather noisy and can crack or chip, but its easy maintenance, imperviousness to water, and lately, do-it-yourself possibilities recommend it to many people. Although tiles still can be handset, they now come in mesh-backed sheets that are set in place with adhesive instead of grout. The larger tiles are available with peel-and-stick backing for easy application.

In warmer climates, concrete blocks are used as structural walls. On the interior they are finished as wallboard is, with paint, wallpaper, or a surface layer of plaster masking the obvious joints. The main objection to them, other than their rather institutional look when painted, is that their hard dense surface makes it difficult to add enrichment in the form of paintings or wall hangings.

Plastics   *Rigid plastics* are being used for walls with increasing frequency, as in the laminated plastic panels mentioned under wallboards, and even as formed plastic shower or bath enclosures. Colorful and durable, they are an asset wherever hard use and easy maintenance are factors. Repairing or refinishing, should this become necessary, would be very difficult, although buffing will take care of minor scratches.

Resilient tiles and *sheets*, affixed to base wall surfaces, add sound- and temperature-insulating qualities to the other advantages of plastics, as well as a softer look. They are a great do-it-yourself, peel-and-stick material, often useful in remodeling.

Glass   The place of glass as a wall surfacing divides into three categories: it can be the wall itself in what is popularly known as a window wall; it can be part of the wall design as windows and doors; or it can be a wall-surfacing material as mirrors. For the first two, glass can be colorless and transparent, tinted to reduce glare and heat, or patterned for privacy.

Window walls are the result of a long evolution of ever larger and larger windows. Some forego the function of movable window entirely and concentrate on opening up the home visually to its surroundings.

This approach brings dividends. A room with one wall of glass seemingly enlarges to take in at least a portion of the outdoor scene. The effect of unbroken space may be so complete that it becomes necessary to call attention to the glass in some way, so that people will not walk into it by mistake.

Window walls are a decisive factor in the overall interior design scheme. They flood rooms with light—or glare, heat, and cold. Thus, they influence color schemes, bring curtaining and insulation problems, and determine possible furniture arrangement. Table 8.2 lists some of the special factors associated with window walls and what the designer can do about them.

Mirrors used as wall surfacing offer unique characteristics. They enlarge a room visually by reproducing the interior, and they create brilliant patterns of reflected light.

These qualities make mirroring very useful as a design device, especially if a room is small and dark and the mirror used is the usual variety with a silvery, unobtrusive backing. The wall itself disappears as space seemingly flows through it, and light can be brought deep into the room to bounce back from what is actually a solid surface. These ambiguities keep us guessing. We do not see glass as a material, only the effects produced.

Mirrors are fairly easy to install—the large ones with clips, smaller mirror tiles with double-face tape.

Wall Finishes

The wall surfacings discussed so far are hard surfacings. They are or could be complete in themselves. We now turn to wall *finishes,* surfacings that are applied to the basic wall material to make it more durable and more attractive.

Plaster One of the most popular wall finishes for many centuries, plaster is generally applied on a lath (a lattice of thin strips of wood or metal grilles) or on special types of wallboard or even concrete blocks. Its great advantage is that it can smoothly cover simple or complex surfaces with no visible joints. Plaster will accept texturing, coloring, or painting; it can be covered with wallpaper or wall fabrics, and is moderate in cost.

Plaster's potential for enrichment, not often used these days, can be seen in the intricate moldings of some older houses. Many of these are being preserved or restored, but the artisans who can do new and contemporary versions of this type of ornament are rare.

Like any material, plaster has some disadvantages. Cracks and chips are common unless precautions are taken, and cracks will be conspicuous on almost any colored walls. Plaster soils easily, but light soil responds to cleaning, and repainting is simple. Although not expensive,

196. Large glass walls look out onto a deck, visually enlarging the space in this home. The clerestory windows at right add even more to the open feeling. Moore, Grover, Harper, architects. (*Photograph: Norman McGrath*)

197. The side wheel steamer *China* was restored by Fred Zelinsky for use as a waterfront cottage. Ornate moldings and decorations of wood and plaster adorn the walls and ceiling. (*Photograph: Philip L. Molten*)

the original cost of plaster is higher than for many of the hardboards, which provide better insulation against heat, cold, and noise.

Paint By far the most common wall finish is, of course, paint, which goes on over all the surfacings mentioned. It is also the most flexible and versatile—a surface coating that can have tremendous impact or recede into the background. (See Plate 31, p. 170.)

Paints are made from natural and synthetic substances selected for special properties—whether for application to wood, masonry, plaster, metal, or wallboard. They are available in mat (flat), eggshell, semigloss, and gloss finishes, and some are even textured. In general, the glossier they are (enamels), the harder and more durable, but this is not the only criterion. Enamels may seem too glossy in many situations, but they are a good choice for hard-wear areas, such as doors and door frames.

Painting a room seems so easy, but getting the correct paint, and the right color, can be frustrating and difficult. Color, as discussed in Chapter 6, is not stable. It varies with light and with surrounding hues. A small spot of color looks quite different from a large wall of the same color. Too many people have chosen a soft green from a color chip, only to have it become a sickly green on the wall. A few simple tests will help to avoid costly mistakes.

- Paint as large a sample as feasible, then place it against the different walls of a room, if possible in a corner or against a molding to cover the effect of the present wall color.
- Observe the sample at different times of day and night to see what daylight and electric light coming from different directions do to the color.
- Place the sample against other colors of paint, fabric, and wood that will be used in the room.
- Form a frame with your fingers or a piece of cardboard, and squint at the color. This will give some idea of the color when spread over a greater surface and seen alone.

Some color effects should be kept in mind:

- Color intensifies in large areas, and especially so when it is bounced back from other walls of the same hue.
- Colors are changed by reflections from nearby walls.
- Glossy paints make color seem more intense; flat paint colors are more subdued.

Paint has other attributes besides color that make it important. It gives a uniform surface to whatever it covers. Sometimes smooth paint will not cover all blemishes, and occasionally smoothness is not wanted. Paint can then be:

- stippled with a stiff brush to obliterate brush marks and to provide a soft mat finish.
- textured by applying with special rollers or by going over wet paint with a sponge or whiskbroom. Special textured paints go on with a roughened or sandy surface.

These finishes are useful as easy and inexpensive ways to cover plaster cracks or gypsum board joints, and they create unique surfaces.

Paint makes an excellent, unobtrusive background for furnishings, art, and people, but a distinctive color or combination of colors can be dynamic design in its own right.

Wallpaper   Wallpaper is akin to paint in that it must be applied over another surface, but it opens up other possibilities in design. Papers vary from the plain colored variety (which is simply another means of applying color) to elaborate mural scenes that seem to open up a room to other vistas. Among the more useful characteristics of wallpaper are that it can:

- minimize architectural awkwardnesses by illusion or camouflage
- hide disfigured walls
- distract attention from miscellaneous or commonplace furniture
- make rooms with little furniture seem furnished

198. A series of colorful postcards creates an effective border frieze in this child's room. The wallpaper is a delicate diamond pattern, and other subtle patterns appear elsewhere in the room. Mary Emmerling, owner-designer. (*Photograph: Robert Perron*)

Added to these is the fact that it is available in colors, patterns, and textures that can be tested for their effects in advance by borrowing large samples.

Wallpaper provides a quick, easy, and often inexpensive way to establish the character of a room. It is also fairly easy to change that character with prepasted or self-adhesive (peel-and-stick) types.

Because wallpaper is such a positive factor, it must be chosen with care. It can make a room seem to shrink or swell, gain height or intimacy, become more active or subdued, more or less formal. Where paint is generally a background, almost ignored, wallpaper often advances and becomes a design statement impossible to overlook. If the pattern is bold, it does not take kindly to other enrichment, such as paintings. Furnishings in the room must be keyed to such paper, or the effect is chaotic.

Wallpaper is available in a wide price range and an equally wide range of textures, both actual and simulated. Most have a dull mat finish that may or may not be washable, but some are glossy, flocked, or marbleized. Metallic papers bring luster. It is also possible to get wallpaper and fabric patterns that are identical or blended—an easy way to achieve harmony.

Many of the comments about paint apply equally to wallpaper. If at all possible, obtain a large sample that can be tested in all kinds of light and with other furnishings. Small pieces simply do not have the same effect as a wall-size swatch.

The line between wallpaper and plastic wall coverings is very thin these days, because wallpaper may have a vinyl coating to make it washable, more durable, and soil resistant.

Vinyl Wall Coverings   In general, vinyl wall coverings are tougher than wallpaper, because they are made of a fairly heavyweight vinyl film and often backed by a fabric. They tend to be more expensive than most wallpapers, but they have more endurance. Originally appearing as simulated leather, they are now available with patterns similar to wallpaper or with heavily textured effects that add another dimension to flat surfaces.

The heavy weight and toughness of vinyls enable them to hide serious wall defects, even to holding cracked plaster in place. Some

199. This angular room with a strong light source has reflective Mylar wallpaper. The sleek lines of built-in furniture blend with the lustrous wallcovering for a modern look. Baskets and accessories provide variety. Charles Moore and Dimitri Vedensky, designers. (*Photograph* © *Morley Baer*)

left: 200. The vinyl wallcovering *Zizahne* has a reverse-pattern matching fabric that can be used for drapes. (*Photograph courtesy Woodson Wallpapers*)

below: 201. Linen is an excellent fabric for wallcoverings because of its dimensional stability, solidarity of color, and acoustical properties. These wall linens are paperbacked for extra stability. Top two examples by Gilford Inc.; bottom by S.M. Hexter. (*Photographs courtesy Belgian Linen Association*)

vinyls have special sound insulation backings, and many can also be used as upholstery—a harmonizing effect that must be used with care.

Wall Fabrics   The use of fabrics on walls goes back a long way, to the time when fabrics *were* the walls of nomadic tents or were hung on stone walls to counteract their coldness. Wallpaper, in fact, evolved as an inexpensive substitute for the tapestries of the wealthy. Today, wall fabrics fall into two main categories: fabrics that actually surface a wall in the manner of wallpaper; and those that are draped loosely on a wall.

Almost any fabric can be made into a wall finish by tacking it to the wall, but this approach is often frowned upon because it mars the original surface. A better approach is to stretch the fabric on a wood frame, which can then be attached to the wall in just a few places. The use of double-face tape or a vinyl adhesive allows the fabric to be stripped from the wall without defacing it.

Fabric can also be hung in soft folds, perhaps as a continuation of window drapery, or for its own sake as a supple alternative to patterned wallpaper. This approach can be useful as a way of hiding an unwanted window or door without actually blocking it out.

Two more alternatives are possible:

- Grasscloth, loosely woven grasses and reeds affixed to a paper backing, can be handled like wallpaper. Textures range from smooth to bold; a number of colors are available, but natural or muted tones seem most appropriate.
- Carpeting is also applied to walls. As mentioned, it provides both sound and cold insulation, a soft sensuous texture, and continuity.

A textile can also *become* a wall, when it is used as a room divider, separating areas visually, either hanging from the ceiling or stretched on a frame that can be placed as a screen.

The problem of cleaning wall fabrics should be thought out in advance. Texture will play a role—the rougher the texture, the more dust will cling to it, but the less dirt will show. A fabric actually applied to a wall may be impossible to clean without dismantling. A draped fabric can be taken down and washed or dry cleaned. The list of fabrics in Chapter 10 will give some indication of how quickly a textile will soil.

The present availability of sheets in colors and patterns has sparked a renewal of interest in fabrics as wall material. Sheets are undoubtedly the quickest way to change color and mood in a room, as well as being relatively inexpensive.

Any textile used as a wall covering will bring in softness and act as a moderator between people and architecture.

Table 8.2
Special Considerations for Window Walls

Problem	Solution
loss of privacy	Choose window wall facing toward private part of property or above sight lines. Build fences or plant hedges. Use curtains and draperies, and potted plants indoors and out.
glare of light	Light should be balanced with windows in other walls or with skylights. Overhanging roof or trellis will help. Plant suitable shade trees nearby. Use glass curtains and hanging plants.
excessive heat or cold	Look for orientation toward south or southeast, insulating glass, overhead protection or trees. Use insulating draperies that can be drawn when necessary.
more glass to clean	No easy solution; use professional window-washer's techniques.
greater quantity of curtaining	Look for window wall placed so that curtains are not essential.
furniture arrangement	Plan room so that major furniture group is related both to window wall and another dominant unit, such as a fireplace.
color schemes	Take account of relationship between colors inside and those seen through the glass.
danger of being mistaken for an open door	Use proper design—a raised sill, obvious supports, or colorful stick-on designs—to indicate physical presence of a window wall. Arrange furniture and/or floor materials indoors and out to steer traffic to a door, not a window.
fading of colors	Choose colors that do not fade or that fade pleasantly. Exclude sun with projecting roof, planting, or curtains.
black and cold at night	Illumine window with lighting trough above it. Light terrace, balcony, or garden outside. Use draperies or reflective glass.
design and maintenance of landscape	Plan at least the immediate landscape architecturally to harmonize with interior; use paving, fixed outdoor furniture, sculpture, and plants that will remain attractive all year with little care.

Windows

Walls create spaces. Windows and doors relate these spaces to one another, both visually and physically. As elements of wall design, they are often the most noticeable part, creating lines and forms that decisively affect the character of a room. Evenly spaced tall windows set up a definite formal rhythm; broad fixed windows may almost disappear in a less formal joining of indoors to the outdoor scene.

Windows and doors have four practical functions—they admit air, light, vision, and people, to varying degrees. How well they perform these functions is a result of their design, placement, and treatment. We can evaluate their effectiveness in these functions, and we can also hide, improve, or accentuate their design by the control devices used—curtains, draperies, shades, and so forth.

202. Windows create lines and forms that affect a room's character. A diamond-shape window in a room designed by Hank Bruce has special striped curtains that roll up and down from the center. The round window just visible at left adds another interesting shape. (*Photograph: Philip L. Molten*)

The roles of windows and doors are currently being reevaluated. With the coming of the energy shortage, air-conditioning is no longer looked upon as a viable and preferred alternative to movable windows functionally designed in relation to site orientation, sun and rain, heat and cold.

Windows can be classified in two general categories.

- **Fixed windows** are meant essentially for light and views.
- **Movable windows** combine the first two functions with ventilation.

Today we often find a combination of the two types in one unit.

Each type of window (Table 8.3) has certain advantages and disadvantages which influence not only the treatment but also the furniture arrangement nearby.

Beyond the design of the individual window units, their placement in the architectural shell is a factor of great importance for function and design. They can establish an incipient rhythm and balance both space and light. Their scale and proportions indicate character. Often a variety of window sizes and types must be blended to create a unified design statement.

Design of Windows

Any assessment of windows should take in the following considerations.

Views and Privacy   Is there a view, and if so should it be an important factor in the interior design scheme? Can it be enjoyed without loss of privacy, in the daytime, and at night? What are the possibilities for ensuring privacy? Table 8.2 gave some answers under the discussion of window walls. But we must also consider what should be done with viewless windows.

- If a view is attractive, concentrate attention on it by leaving the window(s) bare and uncurtained as much as possible. Orient furnishings toward the window.

Table 8.3
Types of Windows

	Advantages	Disadvantages
double hung single hung vertical slide	sashes slide up and down so they can be opened top and/or bottom for ventilation; weatherproofing is effective; do not get in way of people or curtains; usually taller than wide	only half can be opened at one time; little protection from rain; difficult to clean from inside, unless sash can be removed or pivoted; inconvenient to operate with furniture under them
horizontal sliding	advantages and disadvantages similar to above, except for horizontal slide often combined with fixed glass to give broader horizontal proportions; furniture can be placed under fixed portion	
casement	panels hinged at one side, swing in or out; whole area can be opened; panels direct breezes, reduce drafts; crank-operated hardware easy to use over furniture	usually fairly small panels, larger may warp; in-swinging interfere with furniture; out-swinging hazardous if at ground level; little protection from rain
awning or projected	similar to casement but hinged at top and occasionally at bottom; give precise, draft-free ventilation, block rain or snow	similar to casement, but collect dust when open; look institutional
jalousie	similar to awning type but with narrow, un-framed strips of glass, plastic, even wood; take little space, and can be made to fit odd shapes; excellent, precise control of ventilation	many small panes difficult to clean and weatherproof; may interfere somewhat with view
fixed glass	free design from constraints of standardized shapes and sizes; need no screens or hardware; easy to wash if accessible; furniture usually stands away from wall, lessening usable space, increasing visual space	hard to control light and heat, and to clean inaccessible areas; attention must be called to glass in some way to prevent collisions
skylights and clerestories	bring light and air into center of house; balance light and remove air efficiently; introduce light from unexpected source to give new dimensions to form and space	difficult to control light and heat; difficult to clean; special hardware needed if operable

- A need for some screening suggests thin translucent curtains or a heavier curtain of plants to veil the inward view.
- When the outward view is a nearby blank wall or an unappealing scene, consider creating the view with a greenhouse window, or decisively patterned but translucent fabric, grille, or shutter treatment. Orient furnishings away from the window.
- Complete privacy can be assured by opaque materials.

Light Natural light is both cheerful and saving of energy that is more costly than the free sun. Window treatment provides the ultimate but flexible control of light by means of draperies, shades, and so forth. These treatments are considered later in the chapter.

Ventilation In choosing a home, cross ventilation throughout the house or apartment can be the decisive factor in future comfort. It is an old but more than ever useful substitute for air-conditioning. Next to cross ventilation, the most efficient ventilation system lets stale air out near the ceiling, where it rises naturally, and fresh air in at floor level.

An exhaust fan placed at the top of a window will vent stale air and draw fresh air into a room through other openings, but care should be taken to make this flow of air as draft-free as possible. Larger exhaust fans high up in the home (perhaps in an attic) do an even better job, ridding the home of the hot blanket of air that gathers under the roof and radiates its heat downward.

Openings with movable opaque louvers or panels are a useful alternative to windows.

Heat and Cold Most colorless transparent materials are poor insulators. Special types of glass are available that modify this tendency, and also modify the temperatures transmitted through windows. Double

203. Louvered doors are a practical alternative to windows in a tropical climate. They can be opened in good weather to allow for cross-ventilation, thereby decreasing the need for air conditioning. Oda McCarty, architect. (*Photograph: Julius Shulman*)

204. Double-glazed windows warrant their expense in cold climates. Moisture condensation on the window at right comes from warm air hitting cold glass. Twin panes on the left keep cold out, warmth in, and the window free from condensed moisture. (*Photograph courtesy Pittsburgh Plate Glass Company*)

insulating glass (Thermopane) keeps cold air out, warmed household air in. Glass that reflects solar heat is useful for summer cooling.

Orientation of windows, however, is the best solution to problems of heat and cold. Again, curtains and draperies can be of great help by their flexibility—modifying heat and insulating against cold as needed.

Maintenance   Windows need cleaning. How often depends on the cleanliness of the atmosphere and whether or not the windows can be reached by small children and dogs, both indoors and out.

205. The unique angled window in this home has a large fixed pane of glass at the center. Casement windows on either side of the center open to make cleaning easier. The outside glass of the small skylight at right would be more difficult to clean. Alfredo De Vido, architect. (*Photograph: Steve Rosenthal*)

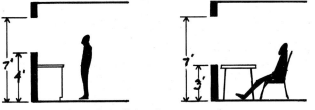

206. Practical windowsill heights vary with room use and furniture arrangement. These three heights meet most needs.

Large panes of glass are the easiest to clean if access is available. Clerestories and skylights bring special cleaning problems, lessened somewhat if they are translucent rather than transparent.

Indoor access to windows is often a matter of furniture placement.

Furniture Arrangement   The more openings in the walls and the larger the openings are, the harder it is to place furniture. Points to keep in mind are these:

- Windows above the usual table height of 27 to 30 inches allow furniture to be placed beneath them (Fig. 206). But the furniture may limit access for opening, closing, and window cleaning.
- Windows that extend to the floor make indoor and outdoor space seem continuous, but they lose most of their value if heavy furniture is placed in front of them—which also makes cleaning difficult.
- Many small windows at regularly spaced intervals lessen usable wall space and make it more difficult to arrange furniture.
- Skylights and clerestories present few problems in furniture arrangement except to avoid sky glare that might be uncomfortable at certain times of the day.

Two opposing schools of furniture arrangement are often seen today, influenced at least in part by the type and placement of windows in a room. One idea places most furniture around the perimeter of the room, under windowsill height, making the most of usable space. This may require some nimbleness for cleaning and adjustment of windows and draperies. The other idea groups furniture away from walls and windows (which may be wall-wide), reducing the area of interaction, but often increasing the visual sense of space, as well as providing ready access to the windows.

These two very different types of arrangements require quite different window treatments.

Window Treatment

Some windows may need no "treatment," but they are few. We cannot ignore the changes in outdoor light and temperature, and the needs of people indoors for privacy, control of light and sun, heat and cold.

The architectural design of windows can be changed by remodeling or by the insertion of a new and more pleasing window unit. Mostly, however, we use what is there and make changes by way of window treatment. Window treatments, in essence, are controls on windows. They have great design potential as sources of beauty and character.

207. There are many window treatments that do not utilize curtains. These are called hard window treatments. Fabric roman shades (**a**) come in a variety of patterns and can be made to match other fabrics in the room. Bamboo roll-up shades (**b**) let in light, air, and a view. Venetian blinds (**c**) can be either horizontal or vertical. Both styles offer maximum light control compared to other hard treatments. Shutters (**d**) act as a layer of indoor insulation and provide varying degrees of privacy and light. Japanese shoji panels (**e**) are made of translucent paper over a wood frame. They allow diffused light to enter the room and slide to open completely.

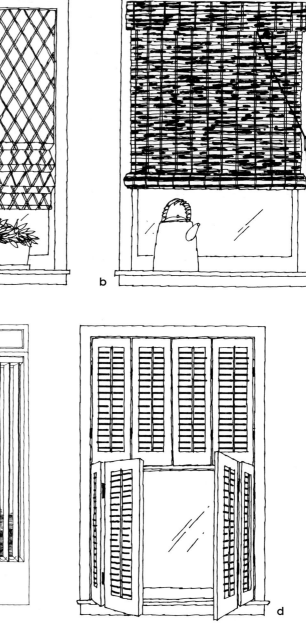

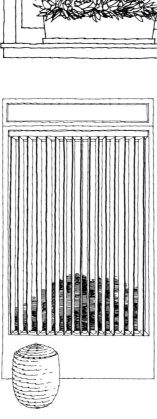

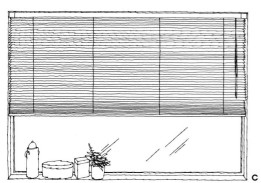

The first solutions that come to mind when we are considering window treatments usually are curtains and draperies. Other kinds of controls are possible, however, and often better for certain situations.

Hard Window Treatments

Shades   Shades come in two basic categories.

Fabric roller shades are inexpensive and can be flexibly adjusted to cover as much of the window as wanted at a particular time. They can be translucent, letting in some light; or completely opaque.

Shades are available in many colors, textures, and patterns, although neutral white or off-white, fairly smooth fabrics are standard. They can be personalized by laminating a fabric to a ready-made shade.

Bamboo and woven-wood shades, once considered rustic and informal, are increasingly available in a variety of materials and weaves. Slat shades have several advantages. They let through some light and air and allow a view outward, but not inward, according to the tightness of the weave or size of the slats or sticks. This one-way vision will be reversed at night, however, when indoor lights are on.

Slat shades can be very plain or enlivened by the form and size of the materials and by interwoven colored yarns and tapes. Some are made of washable plastic, handy for bathroom use.

Most importantly, they have a greater architectural character than fabric shades or draperies.

Venetian Blinds   Venetian blinds are made of wood, metal, or plastic slats in horizontal or vertical configurations. They are popular for their almost complete control of air, light, and views. While usually low in price and innocuous in color, some custom-designed blinds come in decisive colors and patterns. The new very thin slat versions can even be of different colors on the two sides. (See Plate 32, p. 170.)

208. Woven wood shades cut glare and allow light to enter. No window treatment is needed for the large clerestory window, however. It is high enough so that privacy is not a problem, and it admits maximum light. Fisher-Friedman Associates, architects. (*Photograph: Joshua Friewald*)

209. Venetian blinds allow easy control of light and view. The vertical kind have a special fluidity and give a fresh look to a room. They are easier to clean than horizontal blinds. Joan Lane, designer. (*Photograph: Robert Perron*)

Their major disadvantage is their affinity for dust and the difficulty of really cleaning them. The thin-slat and vertical versions do better in this respect.

Shutters Shutters consist of movable wood slats on a framework. In sections, they can provide varying degrees of privacy and light control and can be completely open or closed. They also act as a possible layer of indoor insulation over windows.

Although their initial cost is high, shutters last almost indefinitely, and for many people they have pleasant associations with the past. They are tiresome to dust, but their wood is generally sealed against soil.

Shoji Panels Grilles or screens of wood with a translucent backing, called *shoji* by the Japanese, deserve consideration when the windows are not well designed and there is no view. They will mask the windows but allow diffused light to enter, giving some privacy during the day but not at night.

The treatments considered above are "hard" treatments, although they vary in their degree of rigidity. Two other possibilities, one hard, one soft, should be mentioned before we take up the traditional "soft" window treatments.

Bare Windows Architecturally exciting window design, complete privacy, and no need for sun or temperature control may eliminate the need for any further window treatment. These situations are rare, but treasured, and even they will benefit by outdoor lighting to counteract the blackness of windows at night.

Plants Some people turn windows into actual greenhouses, complete with temperature and humidity controls for good plant growth. Others simply place plants in windows to catch the sun and more or less incidentally give some privacy without shutting out light. A dedicated gardener is needed to keep the plants happy—and the gardener will probably be kept happy by the constant need to water, prune, repot, shift, and generally keep busy in order to have the window treatment looking its best at all times.

Soft Window Treatments

Curtains and draperies are the designer's and homemaker's delight. Imagination can take flight with colors, textures, patterns, styles, at prices ranging from the down-to-earth to the stratosphere.

Not only are the design possibilities exciting, but curtains and draperies fulfill very important functions.

- They give flexible control of privacy, light, and heat.
- They soak up noise in proportion to the area they cover, the thickness of the fabric, and the depth of the folds.
- They can add color and pattern.
- They cover bareness and furnish without furniture.
- They can change the apparent size and shape of a room, or conceal architectural mistakes.

Curtains and draperies can suit moods—bright curtains to provide cheer or a gentle unobtrusive pattern for tranquility.

With all these faculties, they are perhaps the most easily manipulated elements to set and underline the character and style of a room. They can "make" a room, literally and figuratively.

A few definitions will help to clarify the terminology of "soft" window treatments.

- **Glass curtains** are of thin materials and hang next to the glass.
- **Sash curtains** are a type of glass curtain hung on the window sash. They can be stretched taut between rods on the top and bottom of window sashes or hung in loose folds.
- **Draw curtains,** usually of translucent or opaque fabrics, are mounted on traverse rods. In the past, they came between glass curtains and draperies; nowadays they are more often used alone.

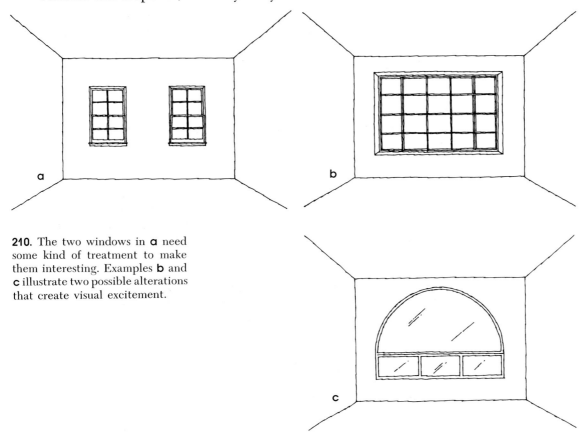

210. The two windows in **a** need some kind of treatment to make them interesting. Examples **b** and **c** illustrate two possible alterations that create visual excitement.

211. There are many types of soft window treatments. Glass curtains (**a**) are often made of filmy, transparent material. They hang next to the glass and are not meant to be opened. Sash curtains (**b**) hang on the sash of the window and are an abbreviated form of glass curtains. Draw curtains (**c**) are mounted on traverse rods and are of heavier material than glass curtains. The term *draperies* (**d**) usually refers to heavy curtains that hang loosely at a window. Cornices (**e**) are rigid bands used to conceal the tops of curtains and the rods from which they hang. Valances (**f**) perform the same function as cornices but can be made of fabric.

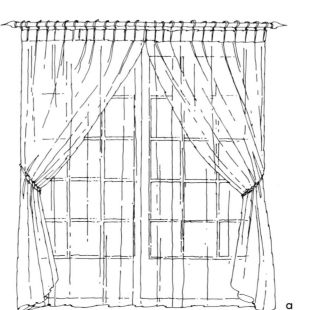

a

b

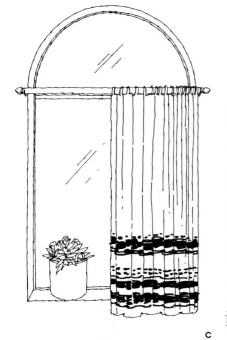

c

d

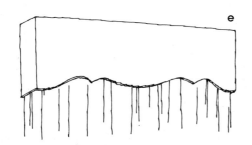

e

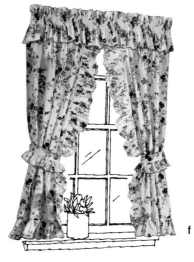

f

200   *The Shell: Walls, Windows, and Doors*

- **Draperies** are any loosely hung (not stretched) fabric. Thus, the term really includes all curtains. Generally, though, draperies are thought of as heavy fabrics that can be drawn or that stand idly at the sides of windows purely for decoration.
- **Cornices** are rigid horizontal bands several inches wide placed at the window top (or the ceiling) to conceal curtain tops and the rods from which they hang. They are somewhat architectural in feeling and relate window treatment to walls and ceiling.
- **Valances** are of fabric draped across, or covering, a shaped form at the top of a window. They perform the same function as cornices but are allied more closely with the drapery than with the wall. The two terms sometimes are used interchangeably.

Glass Curtains   When it is desirable or necessary to diffuse light, provide some privacy, and soften the hard glitter of glass, glass curtains are a good solution. They blend the windows into the rest of the room, especially if they are color-cued to the walls.

Glass curtains make one almost unique visual contribution: they bring light into the room *through* color and pattern. Color is especially important, because the light filtering through will take on this tint and pass it on to the room's aura. In appropriate situations glass curtains could be pink or yellow to warm a room, pale green or blue to cool a hot one.

Customarily, however, they are a neutral, light color, and identical or similar in all rooms because they are conspicuous from the outside.

Draperies and Draw Curtains   *Flexible* control of light, temperature, and privacy are the primary functions of draw curtains and draperies. The distinction between them is not too important, but draw curtains, as the name implies, are designed to be drawn back and forth across the windows as needed. Draperies, on the other hand, can be pulled across the window but at times they simply are draped on either side (and perhaps across the top) of a window, without the draw feature. Both types differ from glass curtains in that they do not veil the view.

212. Heavy dark draperies, when open, emphasize the corners of this dining room. On cold evenings they can be pulled shut to give extra insulation and warmth. Designer and photographer: Philip L. Molten.

213. Draperies can be an integral part of a design. The fabric of these echoes the pattern of the sofa upholstery. The fabric and wallpaper are harmonious, although the darker fabric is more emphatic than the lighter wallpaper. (*Photograph courtesy Schumacher*)

In practice, draw curtains and draperies tend to be heavier than glass curtains to withstand the constant pulling back and forth or to hang gracefully and create a soft but distinct frame for the window.

The choice of material is wide, ranging from bedding through dress and upholstery fabrics to bamboo and woven wood. Equally wide-ranging are the design effects possible with the different materials. In color and pattern, they:

- are least noticeable when related to the walls
- become more conspicuous if they repeat or echo the color and character of upholstery or carpeting
- make emphatic statements when they are in strong contrast to any of the other elements in the room.

It is a matter of deciding what degree of dominance and subordination, harmony or contrast, will be most appropriate.

Design of Window Treatments

Curtains and draperies of all kinds have aesthetic functions that are important in both interior room design and exterior harmony.

What shows on the exterior is often the last consideration that comes to mind, but it is first in the sequence of approaching and entering the home. To avoid a checkerboard effect, thought should be given to having the colors that show at various windows either identical or similar. In fact, many apartment houses and condominiums now write such requirements into their contracts, white or off-white usually being specified.

This may sound confining, but it should be remembered that glass curtains customarily are neutral in color anyway. Draw curtains and draperies often are lined to give them more body and to shut out more light, heat or cold, and color. These linings tailor the reverse side so that hems and hardware do not show, and again are usually neutral in color so that they do not fight with the face fabric.

If no restrictions exist, then the choice is wider, but consideration should still be given to the total effect on the exterior.

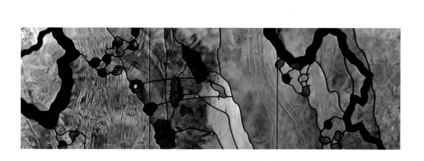

Plate 33. This set of stained glass windows and the hand-carved door add a rustic touch to a home in Virginia. Handcrafted items make a personal statement about the home's owners. The door was carved from laminated teak plank, with a shallow relief to make the design. Windows by Joan Machiz and Michael Lien, door by Tony Marcus. M. Dean Jones, architect.

left: Plate 34. An exposed brick wall, along with unpainted window frames and floor, contributes to the warmth and character of this New York City living room. Hugh Hardy, designer. (*Photograph: Norman McGrath*)

below: Plate 35. Several possibilities of form in ceramics are shown in this dining area. Decorative painted glazed tiles frame an arched storage area where handmade ceramic dinnerware is displayed. Glazed tiles top the counter in the kitchen area, and large, unglazed tiles are used for flooring. (*Photograph: Robert Perron*)

214. Folding doors serve primarily for decoration in this
playroom. They frame the doorway but can also be closed
to control noise. Venetian blinds are used on the glass
doors leading outside. Charles Moore and Dimitri Vedensky, designers. (*Photograph © Morley Baer*)

It is in interior design that window treatment can be most effective.
It can accentuate architectural qualities or disguise them. It may be
helpful to consider three questions first:

- Should the windows be emphasized or deemphasized?
- Should each window be treated separately or should groups of
  windows be combined into units?
- Should the windows be given a horizontal or vertical treatment?

After these basic considerations have been decided, then the designer's imagination can take over.

Doors

Light, sounds, smells, breezes, warmth, and cold—and we ourselves—go
into and out of the house, and from room to room through doorways.
Doors control this movement. They can be heavy, opaque, swinging
barriers of wood or sliding transparent ones of glass that are part of the
architectural shell. Folding doors of wood, bamboo, or fabrics can be in
place or added later as needed.

In rented apartments or in a home already built, you can do less
about the doors than about windows, but you can:

- remove unneeded doors to create greater openness
- seal up or cover with a wall hanging doors that are unnecessary for
  circulation and may be unattractive.

215. The decision to leave an old door where it was in a renovated home creates a whimsical effect. The door is unnecessary and leads nowhere, but it now acts as a divider wall. Carl Pucci and Ben Benedict, Bumpzoid, architects. (*Photograph: Robert Perron*)

- refinish doors and their frames so that they blend with walls, or so that they stand out in shape, texture, and/or color
- use decorative devices (such as a stained glass panel) so that the doors become dominant features

Design of Doors

The doors most often seen today are visually simple. They may be utterly plain doors of plywood sheathing a light but strong core, or of glass framed unobtrusively with metal, plastic, or wood. Many units are little more than sheets of glass that function as both window and door, calling attention not to themselves but to what they reveal.

Glass doors can be a danger, however, unless care is taken to alert people to the glass barrier. This can be done by decals on the glass and by furniture and plant arrangement.

216. Boards are angled to provide accents and contrast at various points in this home—a staircase and a door, for example. The door also has a tall, thin shape that catches the eye. M. Dean Jones, architect. (*Photograph: Philip L. Molten*)

Occasionally, doors may be accented by panels outlined by moldings. Folding doors by their nature—the repeated vertical lines—or by their material—wood with a pronounced grain, or a fabric—can provide some visual interest with their textures and patterns.

A door also can be a more emphatic design statement. This is seen in the occasional entrance door of heavily carved wood, in interior doors framed by heavy moldings, or in recycled or newly designed leaded or stained glass doors that are used for dramatic effect.

Further treatment of doors is seldom seen, except when sliding glass doors are part of a window wall and then are included in the total curtaining design.

There are other possibilities:

- A fabric can be hung to replace a door.
- Fabric can be laminated to one or both sides of a door. If fabric is used on both sides, it should harmonize with both rooms.
- Mirrors in panels or tiles can be attached on one or both sides.

These are some of the aesthetic potentials. But mostly we think of doors quite prosaically and concentrate on their functional aspects.

Functional Aspects of Doors

Circulation   Doors govern traffic paths. As with highways, traffic paths are best when short and direct, and when they disturb areas for work or relaxation as little as possible. The fewer doors in a room, and the closer together they are, the less the room will be crisscrossed by people and animals traveling from one part of the home to another. This can have a decided effect on the arrangement of furniture.

Furniture Arrangement   Because space free of furniture—a path—should be left between each pair of doors and for the arc of a swinging door, the space allotted to furniture is somewhat circumscribed. Major furniture groupings should be away from main entrances and exits, not only for direct circulation but also to leave free space for the milling around that often accompanies coming into and going out of a room. At the same time, a traffic path, preferably two or three paths for easy circulation, should lead fairly directly to an important furniture group from any doors.

Views and Privacy   Opaque doors are needed where privacy is a factor, such as at the entrance. Here we want to see out, but we may not want people to see in. A peephole is the standard answer to this problem. A well-placed door into a bedroom will shield the bed or dressing area from full view when open; into the kitchen the door should hide major work areas.

Glass doors, particularly when combined with windows, give two-way vision between indoors and the private garden or balcony.

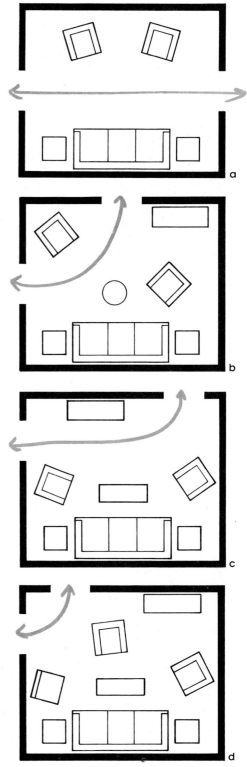

217. The location of doors affects furniture placement and circulation paths. Doors opposite one another (**a**) result in a poor furniture arrangement, since traffic through the middle of the room is heavy. Another poor solution would be having doors in the centers of two adjacent walls (**b**). Especially in a small room, circulation paths would be disruptive. Doors in the corners of adjacent walls (**c**) provide a path for traffic away from conversation groups. Two very close doors (**d**) allow for a maximum amount of furniture and minimal disruptive traffic. This is a particularly good arrangement for bedrooms, workrooms, or places where quiet is desired.

218–219. The two angled partitions contain large paintings that slide out to divide a large space into separate living areas. Osborn/ Woods, architect. (*Photograph: Joshua Friewald*)

218. When retracted, the paintings barely jut out from the partitions.

Climate Control   Heat-cold transmission is similar to that for windows and walls—and the same comments apply. Of particular importance, however, is the weatherstripping around outside doors, an inexpensive but very effective way to conserve heat. In extremely cold climates, storm doors more than repay their cost.

At the other extreme, in very sunny, hot climates, we might take example from Mediterranean countries and hang a heavy fabric outside the doorway as a sun screen, with the door itself left open for air.

The design of doors and windows themselves has been downplayed in this century, with only the softer treatments assuming much importance. In many historic homes these elements gave architects and craftsmen a unique opportunity to use their inventiveness in enriching walls through the design of their openings. In recent years, some of these potentials are once again being explored.

219. In the opposite view, one painting has been extended to create a private place.

Hard
Materials

9

The first concern of an interior designer is to satisfy the basic needs of the people for whom he or she is designing. Each material has its own range of characteristics, possibilities, potentialities, and limitations. What material will best meet the demands of the user for the particular object being designed? The one chosen will to a great extent determine the object's form, as well as its practicality and useful life, its beauty, and eventually its disposition.

- A chair should be comfortable to sit on.
- A plate should hold food and be washable, but not break easily.
- A goblet should fit the hand, be easy to wash, and perhaps add sparkle to the dining table.

From this short listing, it becomes obvious that a designer must know something about materials in order to decide which is best for any given purpose.

To evaluate the objects we choose for a home, it will help us to learn some of their characteristics. We can then seek out those furnishings that most closely meet our particular needs and desires.

Wood

Wood and masonry have served us since human beings first sought shelter, but only wood continues its central role as a material suitable for everything from the house shell to its furnishings.

As a material, wood has many useful qualities. It has great tensile strength, making it suitable for spanning gaps, and considerable strength in compression so that it can support fairly heavy loads. But, more importantly, it has great potential for beauty of form, texture, and ornament. It is therefore our most valued material for furniture.

Wood is relatively easy to shape and light in weight, warm and responsive. It is comparatively inexpensive in original cost, can be maintained economically, and requires relatively little care. Also it can be refinished, almost indefinitely. We seem to have a natural affinity for wood, a material that was once living and always bears the marks of nature's infinite variety. No two pieces of wood are ever exactly alike.

Wood has some major limitations in that it can burn; it is subject to rot, decay, and invasion by insects; and it may swell, shrink, or warp with changes in humidity. But these factors can be minimized by judicious choice of wood (Table 9.1) and proper preservatives and finishes (Table 9.2).

220. Wood is used in this sofa in a very straightforward way. The frame, inspired by a shipping crate, is solid wood with no ornamentation other than the natural grain and the structure. (*Photograph courtesy This End Up Furniture Company*)

Table 9.1
Qualities of Selected Woods

Name	Source	Color and Grain	Character	Uses
alder (red)	one of few native hardwoods in Pacific Northwest	pleasant light colors from white to pale pinks, browns; close, uniform grain	lightweight, not very strong; resists denting, abrasion; shrinks little; stains well	chairs, other furniture
ash (white)	central and eastern United States; Europe	creamy white to light brown; prominent grain resembling oak; emphatic elliptical figures in plain-sawed or rotary cut	hard, strong; wears well; intermediate to difficult to work; intermediate in warping	furniture frames requiring strength; exposed parts of moderate-priced furniture; cheaper than most durable hardwoods
beech	central and eastern North America; Europe	white or slightly reddish; inconspicuous figure and uniform texture, similar to maple	strong, dense, hard; bends well; warps, shrinks, subject to dry rot; relatively hard to work, but good for turning; polishes well	middle-quality, country-style furniture; good for curved parts, rocker runners, interior parts requiring strength; also floors, utensil handles, woodenware food containers
birch	temperate zones; many species; yellow birch most important	sapwood, white; heartwood, light to dark reddish brown; irregular grain, not obtrusive; uniform surface texture; undulating grain	usually hard, heavy, strong; little shrinking, warping; moderately easy to work; beautiful natural finish; stains, enamels well	plywoods; structural, exposed parts of furniture, usually naturally finished (esp. Scandinavian); can be stained to imitate mahogany, walnut
cedar	north Pacific coast and mountains of North America	reddish brown to white; close-grained	rather soft, weak, lightweight; easily worked; little shrinkage; resists decay; holds paint; red cedar repels moths	shingles, siding, porch and trellis columns, vertical grain plywood, cabinetwork, interior paneling
cherry	United States, Europe, Asia	light to dark reddish brown; close-grained	strong, durable, moderately hard; carves and polishes well	associated with Early American and Colonial furniture; now often used as a veneer
cypress (southern)	southeastern coast of United States; southern Mississippi Valley	slightly reddish, yellowish brown, or almost black; weathers silvery gray if exposed	moderately strong, light; resists decay; holds paint well	doors, sash, siding, shingles, porch materials; occasionally outdoor furniture
elm	Europe and United States	light grayish brown tinged with red to dark chocolate brown; white sapwood; porous, open, oaklike grain; delicate wavy figure	hard, heavy; difficult to work; shrinks; swells; bends well	somewhat sparingly in furniture; curved parts of provincial types; extensively used now for decorative veneers
fir (Douglas)	Pacific coast of United States	yellow to red to brownish; coarse-grained, irregular wavy patterns, especially in rotary-cut plywood; "busy"	rather soft, quite strong, heavy; tends to check, split; does not sand or paint well	plywood for exterior, interior walls, doors; cabinetwork; interior, exterior trim, large timbers, flooring; low-cost furniture, especially interior parts
gum (red or sweet)	eastern United States to Guatemala	reddish brown; often irregular pigment streaks make striking matched patterns; figure much like Circassian walnut	moderately hard, heavy, strong; tends to shrink, swell, warp; susceptible to decay; easy to work; finishes well	most-used wood for structural parts, with or imitating mahogany, walnut; also exposed as gumwood

Table 9.1
Qualities of Selected Woods (continued)

Name	Source	Color and Grain	Character	Uses
mahogany	Central and South America, Africa	heartwood pale to deep reddish brown; darkens with exposure to light; adjacent parts of surface reflect light differently, giving many effects; smallscale, interlocked, or woven grain; distinctive figures	medium hard, strong; easy to work, carve; shrinks little; beautiful texture; takes high polish; always expensive	most favored wood for fine furniture in 18th century; much used in 19th century; used today in expensive furniture finished naturally, bleached, or stained dark
maple (sugar, and black, both called hard)	central and eastern United States	almost white to light brown; small, fine, dense pores; straight-grained or figures (bird's-eye, curly, wavy)	hard, heavy, strong; little shrinking, swelling if well seasoned; hard to work; has luster; takes good polish	Early American furniture; now used as solid wood for sturdy, durable, unpretentious, moderate-priced furniture; good for hardwood floors
oak (many varieties; two groups: white and red)	all temperate zones	white oaks: pale grayish brown, sometimes tinged red; red oaks: more reddish; both have quite large conspicuous open grains; fancy figures rare	hard, strong; workable, carves well; adaptable to many kinds of finishes	standard wood in Gothic period, Early Renaissance in northern Europe, continuously used in United States; suitable for floors, wall panels, plywood; furniture, solid and veneer
Philippine mahogany (actually red, white Lauan, and Tanguile)	Philippines	straw to deep reddish brown according to species; pales when exposed to light; pronounced interlocking grain gives conspicuous ribbon figure	about as strong as mahogany, less easy to work; greater shrinking, swelling, warping; less durable, harder to polish	extensively used for furniture in past few decades; also plywood wall panels, which should be fireproofed
pine (many varieties similar in character)	all temperate zones	almost white to yellow, red, brown; close-grained	usually soft, light, relatively weak; easy to work; shrinks, swells, warps little; decays in contact with earth; takes oil finish especially well, also paint; knotty pine originally covered with paint	used throughout world for provincial, rustic furniture; in Early Georgian furniture for ease of carving, also paneled walls; often is painted or has decorative patterns; now used for inexpensive cabinet-work, doors, window-sash frames, structural members, furniture
poplar	eastern United States	white to yellowish brown; close-grained, relatively uniform texture	moderately soft, weak, lightweight; easy to work; finishes smoothly; stains and paints well	siding; interior, exterior trim; inexpensive furniture, cabinetwork, especially when painted or enameled
redwood	Pacific coast of United States	reddish brown; lightens in strong sun; becomes gray or blackish if allowed to weather; parallel grain in better cuts, contorted in others; decorative burls	moderately strong in large timbers, but soft and splinters easily; resists rot and decay	exterior siding, garden walls, outdoor furniture; some use for interior walls, cabinetwork

Table 9.1
Qualities of Selected Woods (continued)

Name	Source	Color and Grain	Character	Uses
rosewood (several species, grouped because of fragrance)	India, Brazil	great variation from light to deep reddish brown; irregular black, brown streaks in fanciful curves	hard, durable; takes high polish	extensively used in fine 18th-century furniture, chiefly veneers, inlays; 19th-century solid wood; increasing use in furniture today
teak	Asia (India, Burma, Thailand, and so on)	straw yellow to tobacco brown; striped or mottled in pattern	heavy, durable, oily; works and carves well; takes oil finish beautifully	widely used in Far East, both plain and for ornately carved furniture; now often used by Scandinavians for sculptural qualities
Tupelo gum	southeastern United States	pale brownish-gray heartwood merges gradually with white sapwood; lack of luster makes interlocking grain inconspicuous	hard, heavy, strong; good stability; moderately easy to work; tendency to warp	same purposes as red gum, although it is somewhat weaker, softer
walnut (American or black)	central and eastern United States	light to dark chocolate brown, sometimes dark irregular streaks; distinctive, unobtrusive figures of stripes, irregular curves; or also intricate, beautiful figures	hard, heavy, strong; warps little; moderately easy to work, carve; natural luster; takes good finish	in America from earliest times for good furniture, but especially in 19th century; now in high-grade furniture, paneling
walnut (Circassian) (also called English, Italian, European, Russian, and so on)	Balkans to Asia Minor, Burma, China, Japan; planted in Europe for wood and nuts	fawn-colored; many conspicuous irregular dark streaks give elaborate figures; butts, burls, crotches add to variety	strong, hard, durable; works, carves well; shrinks, warps little; takes fine polish	a leading furniture wood since ancient times; used in Italian, French, Spanish Renaissance; in England, during Queen Anne period, 1660–1720, called age of walnut; imported for American furniture

Varieties of Wood

Wood derives from plants ranging in size from pencil-thin bamboos to tall Australian eucalyptuses and giant California redwoods. Table 9.1, however, lists those most often used domestically, as building materials, or for furniture—the more familiar mahoganies, pines, oaks, and walnuts. Differences in strength, hardness, durability, and beauty indicate possible uses.

In selecting wood, it is important to keep in mind that its potential use should be a guide. Every piece does not have to be top quality in all respects. Wood must be strong enough to do its job, but for some purposes, such as the interior framework of cabinets, relatively soft wood will do. Hardness is an advantage when wood is subject to wear, when a high finish or beautiful grain and figure is desired. This is especially true of furniture wood.

Table 9.2
Wood Finishes

Name	Composition	Application	Result	Use
bleach	various acids, chlorine compounds	brushed on (if bleaching agent is strong enough to affect wood, it will also affect skin)	lightens wood, neutralizes color, usually makes grain less conspicuous; not dependably permanent; wood loses some luster	to make furniture and inferior wood paneling pale, blond; also used on outdoor furniture and siding to give a weathered look
enamel	varnish mixed with pigments to give color, opaqueness	brushed or sprayed over undercoat since it has less body and covering power than most paints	generally hard, durable coat, like varnish; usually glossy, may be dull; wide range of colors	chiefly on furniture, cabinets, walls getting hard use and washing; also on floors
lacquer	cellulose derivatives, consisting of resins, one or more gums, volatile solvents, a softener, and a pigment (if colored)	regular lacquer best applied with spray since it dries rapidly (15 min.); brushing lacquers dry slowly, make brush application feasible	hard, tough, durable; resistant to heat, acids; not suitable for outdoor wood because of expansion, contraction; glossy, satiny, or dull	transparent lacquers much used on furniture, walls; opaque on furniture
oil	boiled linseed oil or various other oils; usually thinned with turpentine	brushed or wiped on, excess wiped off, allowed to dry, sanded or rubbed; between five and thirty coats—more the better; hot oil sinks into wood, brings out grain	penetrating, very durable finish with soft luster; darkens and yellows wood somewhat at first, considerably in time; protective, not conspicuous; must be renewed	oil, often mixed with beeswax, used in Europe from early times to 17th century; now used on indoor and outdoor furniture and on siding
paint	pigments suspended in linseed oil or, more commonly now, in various synthetics and water; usually contain a drier to hasten hardening	brushed, rolled, or sprayed on	opaque coating, varies from hard, durable gloss to softer dull finishes; hides character of wood; new types dry quickly with little odor, are easy to apply and have good covering power	protects and embellishes; painted furniture popular in ancient Egypt, the Orient, Europe since Middle Ages; much Colonial furniture was painted; widely used now on exterior and interior walls and furniture
shellac	resinous secretion of an insect of southern Asia, dissolved in alcohol	brushed, rubbed, or sprayed on; dries rapidly; many thin coats, each rubbed, gives best finish	changes character and color of wood very little; soft satiny to high gloss finish; fragile; wears poorly; affected by heat, moisture; water spots	primarily as an easily applied, quick-drying undercoat
stain	dye or pigment dissolved or suspended in oil or water	brushed, sprayed, or rubbed on	changes color of wood without covering grain (often emphasizes grain or changes surface noticeably); usually darkens wood to make look richer	frequently used to alter color of furniture woods thought unattractive, or in imitation of expensive woods; outdoors compensates for weathering
synthetics	wide range of polyester, polyurethane, polyamide, vinyl; liquid or film; newest type finish; continuing new developments	usually factory-applied; *liquid* impregnates wood; *sprays* form a coating; *film*, typically colored, is bonded to wood with laminating adhesive	durable, long-lasting finish; resistant to abrasion, mars, chemicals, water, or burns; clear or colored, mat to glossy surface; film type difficult to repair	exterior siding; interior walls, floors, furniture; very good wherever abrasion, moisture, or weathering is a problem

Table 9.2
Wood Finishes (continued)

Name	Composition	Application	Result	Use
varnish	various gums, resins dissolved in drying oils (linseed, tung, or synthetic), usually combined with other driers; dye or pigment makes varnish-stain	brushed or sprayed on; many thin coats best; dries slowly or quickly, depending on kind, amount of thinner used	thin, durable, brownish skin coating, little penetration; darkens wood, emphasizes grain; dull mat to high gloss; best when not thick, gummy	known by ancients; not used again until mid-18th century; widely used today on furniture, floors, walls, chiefly interior
wax	fatty acids from animal, vegetable, mineral sources combined with alcohols; usually paste or liquid; varies greatly in hardness, durability	brushed, sprayed, or rubbed on, usually several coats; often used over oil, shellac, varnish, but may be used alone	penetrates raw wood; darkens, enriches, emphasizes grain; soft to high luster; must be renewed often; may show water spots and make floor slippery; other finishes cannot be used	very old way of finishing wood; generally used today as easily renewed surface over more durable undercoats; some liquid waxes used alone on walls, floors, furniture

Form in Wood

Since wood is so responsive, so easily shaped, its potential forms are almost infinite.

Solid Wood   Solid wood—wood all the way through—can be turned on a lathe or carved, or refinished in case of damage. It is still one of the basic materials for the skeleton and outdoor siding of homes, the unseen but necessary structural framework of cabinets and cupboards. For furniture, solid wood is probably the most desired, offering great possibilities of shape and ornament, luster and long life.

Layered Wood   Veneers, plywood, and laminated wood are layered constructions with unique design possibilities. They are based on the fact that wood can be sliced, sawn, or rotary cut into very thin sheets, then glued as a surface on less expensive materials. Layered woods have added greatly to the repertoire of wood forms.

The popular idea that veneers and plywoods are cheap substitutes for solid wood is a misconception. They are usually less expensive, because the more costly wood goes much further as sheet than solid form. However, they also have distinctive advantages.

221. A stacking chair of molded plywood is an example of wood's versatility. The wood can be finished or varnished to suit any interior. The base of chromium-plated steel lightly supports the seat and back, which are shaped for comfort. Poul Pedersen, designer. (*Photograph courtesy Cado/Royal System, Inc.*)

215

222. A simple hallway is transformed by the use of wood. Highly polished plank flooring has a warm glow, and the unique carved bannister adds a strong focal point. Tom Murphy, designer. (*Photograph: Joshua Freiwald*)

Layered woods:
- are available in much larger pieces than solid wood
- are usually stronger than solid wood of the same thickness
- are less likely than solid wood to shrink, check, or warp excessively
- are less susceptible to splitting by nails or marring by sharp objects
- give almost identical grain on several pieces, which can then be matched to produce symmetrical figures
- permit the use of fragile, highly figured woods that, if solid, might split apart or shrink irregularly
- lend themselves readily to curved and irregular forms

Veneers and plywood are widely used today because of their superior and in some cases unique performance, both as structural materials and for their ornamental possibilities.

Ornament in Wood

Wood possesses a unique kind of inherent, structural ornament in its grain, figure, texture, and color. It is not something introduced; it just has to be revealed. Each species of wood has its own general pattern of grain, some of them amazingly intricate figures that are loved by designers. Different aspects of these patterns can be brought to light by careful cutting.

Texture The surface texture produced by the way in which wood is cut offers a kind of ornament in itself, and determines the effectiveness of grain. Roughly sawn wood has an uneven, light-diffusing texture that minimizes grain. It is usually reserved for exterior application or to produce a rustic character. Resawn wood is considerably smoother, with a soft texture somewhat like a short-pile fabric; it reveals but does not emphasize grain. Smoothly finished wood reflects light, emphasizes figure, is pleasant to touch, and is standard for furniture.

Color   Each wood has its own distinctive color, from white birch to dark ebony, and often a variety of colors within one piece. Designers sometimes contrast the different wood colors in such techniques as inlay and parquetry. And, of course, wood takes color in paint both for beauty and as a preservative.

Joints   The way in which pieces of wood are joined creates structural patterns of possible interest. Wood joints can be emphasized in furniture for the sheer beauty of shape against shape, pattern against pattern. (Most important, however, is the structural stability of a joint, taken up in Chapter 11.)

Carving and Turning   Since the earliest humans started to whittle wood, *carving* has been a favored form of wood ornamentation. The great periods of design are known as much for their carving as for their more basic qualities. *Turning*, an early form of machine carving, means that a piece of wood is shaped into distinctive profiles while being turned on a rapidly rotating lathe.

A diminished art today, carving is still capable of arousing the interest of the handcrafter and appears on much furniture, both good and bad. Carving as architectural ornament is, however, almost totally absent, with a few exceptions (Plate 33, p. 203).

Pieced Design in Wood   There are several techniques that combine different woods—and sometimes metals, ivory, or shell—in such a way that contrasting colors and textures make patterns on a flat surface. These are fascinating forms of ornament, although not too often used in woodworking today.

- **Inlay** is a term that covers the general methods.
- **Intarsia** consists of pieces inlaid in solid wood.
- **Marquetry** applies to designs inlaid in veneers and then glued to a solid backing.
- **Parquetry** indicates geometric patterns, often in floors and tables.

223. Salvaged wood, from heavy beams to small strips pieced together, creates a warm, rustic interior. The parquet table and concrete aggregate floor contribute to the natural theme. Alex Riley, designer. (*Photograph: Philip L. Molten*)

Wood Finishes   Most woods need a protective finish to preserve the wood itself and to give it an easy-to-clean surface. Appropriate finishes may be a kind of ornament, enhancing the grain, changing the color, or hiding unattractive color and grain. Table 9.2 lists the typical wood finishes, their characteristics and uses. In general, however:

- **Opaque** finishes hide the wood character, give a smooth uniformity, and offer great possibilities for color.
- **Transparent** finishes reveal the character of the wood and absorb minor damage that comes with use.
- **Penetrating** finishes, such as linseed oil, produce a soft surface that may absorb stains but will not chip or crack.
- **Plastic-impregnated** finishes harden wood, give it greater density and strength, and can make it almost impervious to damage.
- **Glossy** finishes reflect more light than dull ones, are more durable because of their hard, dense surface, and facilitate cleaning, but they also show blemishes more readily.
- **Many coats** of any finish, sanded or rubbed between coats, give a more durable, attractive result than one or two thick coats.

Despite great advances in plastics, glass, and metal, wood remains one of our most useful, beautiful resources. A house built of wood seems most natural to us, and furniture of wood is still the standard.

Masonry

Stone or brick laid up by a mason—masonry—seems of the earth, timeless, enduring, protective. It takes many shapes, from the strict rectangularity of brick to the irregular shapes of natural rock. Masonry has many natural textures and colors, can be laid in many patterns.

Except for fireplaces and an occasional wall or a patio floor, most masonry today is seen but not noticed, or unseen and strictly utilitarian. This is because the term masonry also covers concrete, stucco, and plaster—materials that in themselves are formless, colorless, and often hidden in the structure of a building.

The materials of masonry come from inorganic mineral compounds of crystalline structure, and typically are hard, dense, and heavy. They are extremely resistant to fire, rot, and decay, and they require little maintenance. They retain their shape under pressure, but are not very strong in tension. They will chip and crack and can be difficult to repair. Also, most masonry offers poor insulation against cold and dampness and reflects rather than absorbs noise.

Form in Masonry

Masonry can be divided into two major categories—*block* and *moldable* materials. These categories largely determine the finished forms.

Block Materials   *Stone, bricks,* and *concrete blocks* can be assembled in forms ranging from the rugged informality of rocks piled up almost at random to the pattern of rectangular forms laid up in precise shapes.

Block materials can also be used in other ways. *Travertine,* a form of limestone, is a favorite for tabletops, as is the heavier and often more variegated *marble. Slate,* a rock that splits easily into thin sheets with smooth surfaces, is an attractive flooring material.

Moldable Materials   Concrete, plaster, and stucco share common qualities. They are shaped at the building site from a semiliquid state, cover large areas without joints, and can take almost any form.

Concrete was introduced as long ago as the Roman Empire, but its use as a home building material is definitely of this century. Its great virtues are its plasticity when wet and durability after hardening—qualities no other material combines to the same degree.

Concrete appears mostly in foundations and in slab floors that are then covered with a surface flooring material, often wall-to-wall carpeting. In apartment buildings, it may be the unseen structure, walls, and floors. However, its great plasticity suggests that almost any form is possible, a quality that some architects are beginning to investigate.

Plaster and stucco are mostly finishing materials, rather than structural ones. Plaster is a thick, pasty mixture of treated gypsum and water, sand and lime. Stucco is a weather-resistant variation most often used on exteriors. Both are applied on a lath or on any masonry surface that is rough enough to hold them.

Plaster will hold any shape given it before it hardens. Today it is used mostly as a smooth, seamless cover for walls and ceilings. It ensures an undemanding background for paintings, wall hangings, or sculpture.

left: 224. A working farmhouse on Long Island, by architect Alfredo De Vido, makes use of stones found on the building site. The chimney shown, as well as walls elsewhere in the house, are constructed of stone. Other walls are oak strip flooring. (*Photograph: Ernest Silva*)

right: 225. Painted stucco encloses a brick-lined fireplace and contains a convective heating system that transfers heat to other places. The hearth is sandcast concrete. The Oriental mode of the fireplace harmonizes with the Japanese-inspired design of the rest of the home. M. Dean Jones, architect.

226. Ceramic surfaces can add warmth and character to an interior. Highly glazed floor tiles and a collection of old bean pots enhance the clean design of a home by Hayes, Howell & Associates. (*Photograph: Gordon H. Schenck, Jr.*)

Ornament in Masonry

The distinction between block and moldable forms in masonry holds for ornament as well. The block forms in general provide their own ornament. The very colors and shapes of rocks, plus the way they can be built up into a wall or fireplace, provide structural ornament. They can also be shaped for patterned placement. (See Plate 34, p. 204.)

Bricks have a little less inherent character, but they come in a range of colors and shapes that can then be laid in a variety of patterns.

Concrete blocks have a character that is generally more unpleasant than pleasing, so they are usually covered with paint, plaster, or some kind of wall covering. But they can be made in more interesting colors and shapes than the familiar chilling gray cube.

Ornament in concrete and plaster can be introduced by embedded materials—pebbles, chips, rocks. Surface interest can be created by the texture of the form into which concrete is poured, or by the way plaster is finished—smooth, rough, swirled, stippled. Both take paint well.

Still other possibilities exist. Concrete can be hardened in molds that create sculptural forms either on the surface or as integral shape. Plaster is a natural for the most intricate of molded ornament.

More than any other material, masonry lends itself to recycling. Since earliest times stones and bricks from old walls have provided raw material for new structures. This link with the past has timeless charm.

Ceramics

Objects made of clay hardened by heat have a long history. They have, in fact, carried much of our history down to us, often in fragments, but evocative in the insights they give of early civilizations. Ceramics are at the same time usually quite fragile but almost imperishable. The object itself may be easily broken, but the pieces remain.

Ceramics have retained a central position in our daily life. They are still the most common material of dinnerware, and appear in many other forms—vases, cooking vessels, flooring, counter and wall tiles, handcrafted pots, and sculpture.

The processes in making ceramic objects have changed very little over the years, although machines have long since speeded actual work in many cases. Essentially, the technique consists of choosing the proper clay, shaping it, then firing and glazing it to make it hard and waterproof. The process may also involve painting or carving to enrich the basic shape.

Clay Bodies

Clays differ in many properties—in colors, textures, the temperatures they will withstand at the firing stage. Ceramic items, therefore, have characteristics dependent on the clay used in their construction, and the interior designer should be aware of differences. For convenience, ceramic bodies can be grouped into four major types.

Earthenware   Coarse clays fired at comparatively low temperatures typically have produced a thick, porous, fragile, and opaque ware, often red or brown, suitable for bricks, flowerpots, and some ovenware. Much folk pottery is earthenware. Glazing, however, can make it nonporous, colorful, and appropriate for dinnerware. In the 18th century, Josiah Wedgwood produced a cream-colored earthenware called Queensware that raised this humble product into the realm of fine ceramics and was the predecessor of much of today's tableware.

Stoneware   In general, finer clays, fired at medium temperatures result in stoneware. This ware, like a similar material called *ironstone*, is strong, waterproof, and durable. Stoneware is the material of most medium-price dinnerware.

Porcelain   A white ware fired at extremely high temperatures, porcelain is completely vitrified (the clay particles are fused together into a glassy substance) and often translucent. It is thin but strong, takes a hard, impervious glaze, and is expensive.

227. Earthenware casseroles by Römertopf, excellent for preserving nutrients, are decorated with traditional designs. (*Photograph courtesy Bloomingdales*)

above: **228.** Stoneware from the *BLT* collection designed by Niels Refsgaard is decorated in "iron earth" glazes with brown speckles. (*Photograph courtesy Dansk International Designs*)

right: **229.** The limits of any material are dictated by the imagination of the designer. This porcelain mirror frame was handmade from thrown elements by Pat Probst Gilman. (*Photograph: Elizabeth Galt*)

China The word "china" is often used as a synonym for ceramic dinnerware in general, although originally it meant European ceramics that imitated Chinese porcelains. As a particular type, however, the term "china" covers a range of dinnerware that is fired at only a slightly lower temperature than porcelain. Some manufacturers produce a ware called *fine china, English china,* or *bone china* that is indistinguishable from porcelain. *American vitreous china* is unusually break-, chip-, and scratch-resistant.

Glazes

Glazes are glassy coatings joined at high temperatures to clay objects. They are important because they give ceramics a hard, durable, easily cleaned, and usually waterproof surface. Beyond this, the textures and colors of glazes are primary sources of beauty. In addition they play a role in protecting colored designs applied to a clay body:

left: 230. Bone china comes in numerous patterns. Shown here is *Grasmere* by Minton. (*Photograph courtesy Royal Doulton*)

below: 231. Glazed ceramic tiles form an easy-to-clean, impervious top on a breakfast table and match the unglazed floor tiles. Rough-cut cedar boards on the walls add another natural touch. Alfredo De Vido, architect. (*Photograph: Maris-Semel*)

- Underglaze designs are applied before a final transparent glaze that protects them from scratches and wear.
- Overglaze patterns, as the name suggests, are applied on a finished surface, although they may be fused with the surface in a second firing at a low temperature.

In dinnerware, overglaze decoration may be a disadvantage. Often found on inexpensive ware, overglazes are not so durable as underglaze patterns. But for decorative pieces, this objection may be overshadowed by the possibility of greater color range and intensity.

Form in Ceramics

Ceramics are a prime example of the influence of material on form. The physical properties of clay determine the methods by which it can be formed and the shapes it will take. Clay originates as a formless mass or powderlike or granular particles. Water makes it malleable, more water a liquid capable of being poured into a mold. Firing sets the form. After firing, clay is hard and brittle, with little tensile strength.

Ceramics are now made by hand and by machine, and the differences in these techniques also influence form. Almost any shape is possible in clay, but most household ceramics are round and compact, as they come naturally from the potter's wheel and industrial equivalents. These shapes have a minimum of edges to chip, they are easy to hold, and they provide a counterpoint to the basic rectangularity of most homes. Utility may demand spouts and handles, but these are the first to chip and break.

Angular shapes do appear in bricks and tiles, where only their flat surfaces are subject to much wear, and these can be protected by the application of hard glazes.

As mentioned earlier, this age-old material still plays a very useful role in homes today. Tile counters, wall surfaces, floors, even tile roofs are satisfactory in use and also, because they are traditional materials with a long history, they add elements of continuity and nostalgia to their own inherent beauty.

Ceramic dinnerware still seems the most satisfactory to most of us. Centuries of use let us know what to expect; centuries of design have given us traditional patterns of great beauty and proven quality. Modern techniques and artistry have added to the repertoire. The craft revival brings a living art into our homes in a very useful form.

Ceramic accessories continue to enrich our homes, from lamp bases to major pieces of sculpture. (See Plate 35, p. 204.)

Glass

Almost as old as ceramics, glass has had its role as a material expanded from that of a semiprecious substance to a more commonplace, relatively inexpensive material. The invention of the blowpipe led to hollow receptacles, vases, and goblets that eventually descended into the glass tableware we use today.

Further research into glassmaking formulas and techniques resulted in other forms and possibilities. Ways were found to draw glass into flat sheets that became, first, small windows, and then the window walls so common today. Technology has expanded the range to most unglasslike applications, such as the spun fibers in fiberglass and heat-resistant types of glass suitable for ovenware.

The versatility of glass as the result of the various formulas and methods of manufacture is almost unimaginable. Glass can:

- be shatterproof
- be given sound, heat, cold, and glare control
- have reflective qualities, as in mirrors
- be lighter than cork or almost as heavy as iron
- be made into fabrics or fabricated house panels
- transmit heat or electricity, or block it
- survive extremes in temperatures and even sudden temperature changes
- be clear or colored, transparent, opaque, or anything in between
- automatically darken and lighten according to light exposure

Composition

The basic ingredient in glass is sand (silica) plus soda and lime, and various other substances that give special qualities. Crystal, the finest glass, contains lead. Color comes with the addition of appropriate minerals. Such special forms as glass fibers and insulation are the result of other chemicals or of the way in which glass is treated.

Form in Glass

When the combined ingredients are melted at very high temperatures, they fuse into a molten mass that can then be shaped, while still hot, by one of these methods:

- pressing, casting, or molding into almost any shape
- blowing into a bubble by hand or machine for glassware
- drawing and sometimes rolling to produce the most gossamer of glass fibers or ordinary window glass

232. A dining room wall made of industrial glass building blocks gives the space an open feeling. Light enters the room, but privacy is maintained. Carl Pucci and Ben Benedict, Bumpzoid, architects. (*Photograph: Robert Perron*)

233. A fresh approach to the design of etched glass resulted in these graceful goblets. The pattern is confined to the lower part of the cup. Björn Wiinblad, designer. (*Photograph courtesy Rosenthal Studio-Haus*)

Given this variety of production possibilities and the nature of the material, it is evident that form in glass can cover a wide range. The forming techniques themselves suggest appropriate shapes. The bubble seems very right in a goblet, the flat sheet in window glass.

The possible transparency of glass, an almost but not quite unique quality (some plastics now achieve this), reminds us that an exciting union of form and space can be achieved with glass. This quality is often exploited in handcrafted objects, and architects have used it to devise a totally new style of architecture—the glass-walled building.

Of all the materials, glass is the one most responsive to light. Light seems to come alive, both within the form itself and on the surface. It is this attribute that designers often use in enriching basic shapes.

Ornament in Glass

Glass has another rare quality: it allows us to see ornament within it, as well as on the surface. Especially in transparent glass, form, texture, and ornament are closely intertwined.

The glass form itself can be so complex that it serves as its own ornament. Globs of molten glass can be "laid" or "dropped on" in the practical shapes of handles or purely as fluid decoration. Molded or pressed glass takes its texture and ornament, as well as its form, from the mold in which it is processed. This industrial process offers a quick and easy way to achieve enrichment.

In addition to these structural types of ornament, there are various ways of embellishing glass that take advantage of its transparency and response to light.

- **Cutting** gives many surfaces to catch and break up light, a technique much admired by the Victorians but still popular today for crystal goblets and other tableware.
- **Engraving** produces a shallow intaglio that often seems to be in relief, an effect due to optical illusion.
- **Etching** is done with acid or sandblasting and results usually in less firm and less subtly modeled designs than does engraving.
- **Enameling** and **gilding** are achieved by burning colored enamels or gold or silver onto the surface. They are rarely seen today.

These techniques only begin to explain the decorative possibilities of glass. Its versatility, its marvelous ability to transmit and break up light, its affinity with color, have led designers in many directions.

The stained glass revival, for example, has brought a renewed appreciation of colored glass as an art medium. Stained glass needs light to be effective, hence its use as windows or panels, or as lamp shades or decorative objects containing a light source.

It is almost impossible to imagine a home today without glass. Glass is still the standard material for tumblers and goblets.

Architectural glass, covered in more detail in Chapter 8 on windows, is still the primary transparent material that allows us to see the outdoors while enjoying the protection of our homes.

Glass mirrors are a source of visual pleasure as well as a device for expanding the size of a small room. They spread light throughout a room and bring sparkle to dark corners.

Glass table tops have the dual advantage of hardness and transparency. They look light and airy, but give a solid surface that will withstand the action of most liquids.

Fiberglass, the latest invention, is now seen almost everywhere. From insulation to rigid panels, cast in molds for integral tub, shower, and wall installation, or made into molded furniture, fiberglass is fast becoming a common material for home use.

Metals

It is hard to imagine a world without metals. Steel construction has given architecture a new character. Other metals have made possible

234. Open glass shelves store and display crystal stemware while adding a decorative touch to the home. Jonathon Bulkley, designer. (*Photograph: Joshua Freiwald*)

235. Pierced Mexican tin makes a delicate shade for a hanging fixture in this country kitchen. Peter Rocchia, designer. (*Photograph © Morley Baer*)

household appliances and systems of plumbing, heating, and lighting that greatly add to our comfort and health. Metal utensils are by far the most durable.

The metals most often seen in the home, their qualities, and their applications are given in Table 9.3. Many other metals could be listed—brass, bronze, tin, gold—but their uses are more limited. They can, however, add unusual touches, such as brass fittings in a fireplace or stamped Mexican tinware.

Table 9.3
Metals

Metal	Color and Finish	Special Characteristics	Uses
aluminum	whitish, oxidizes to a soft gray; highly polished or brushed to silvery gray; anodizing gives satiny surface in bright metallic hues	light weight; easily worked; does not deteriorate; impervious to water	cooking utensils, pitchers, and trays; screens, sliding doors; maintenance-free indoor-outdoor furniture
chromium	blue-white; takes and keeps high polish; can be given brushed finish	hard; resists corrosion; cold, glittery unless brushed; often used as thin plating	faucets; toasters and other small appliances; lighting fixtures; maintenance-free furniture
copper	orange color quickly oxidizes to dull greenish brown or lively blue-green; must be kept polished to retain orange hue	soft, easily shaped, but durable; good conductor of heat, electricity; impervious to water	water pipes; electrical wiring; eave troughs and roofs (expensive); cooking utensils, often displayed for beauty of finish
iron	grayish; galvanized with zinc coating, painted to resist rust	strong; worked easily by hand or machine	cookware, railings, decorative hardware
steel	iron alloyed with carbon, also needs painting except for special types	harder than iron but still easily formed by machine	cookware, window and door frames, painted or enameled furniture
stainless steel	addition of chromium makes pleasant blue-gray color	resistant to rust and staining	cooking utensils, flatware, counter tops
silver	whitest of metals; takes beautiful polish; reflects light; can be plated over alloy base	soft until hardened with copper (sterling silver); ductile, malleable; tarnishes, but easily cleaned and polished	flat and hollow tableware, decorative accessories

236. The properties of metal allow it to be formed in many ways. A hanging sculpture in the home of Charles F. Pensinger moves and casts shadows that are hard to differentiate from the curved elements themselves. Sculpture by Robert Seeburger. (*Photograph: Robert Seeburger*)

Form in Metal

Metals will take almost any imaginable form, with a minimal chance of breakage. One quality has distinguished the forms that have, in general, become associated with metal—that of tensile strength.

The ability to withstand stress is metal's most distinctive quality, the one that permits quite slender shapes and thin-walled forms. When used expressively, metal contributes a precise thinness that is much more durable than would be possible in any other material. Although metals can be dented or bent out of shape, they can also be returned to their original form.

Ornament in Metal

The surface treatment of metal acts as basic ornament, giving reflections or distortions, varied dark and light patterns, or three-dimensional

237. Stainless steel is often used for flatware. These serving pieces, from a pattern called *Variation V*, have a particularly clean, fresh design. (*Photograph courtesy Dansk International Designs*)

right: **238.** Metal can be a source of beauty as well as strength. A gracefully arching lamp offsets the many rectangular elements in this living room. It acts as a connecting line between the floor and high ceiling. Tom Murphy, designer. (*Photograph: Joshua Freiwald*)

below right: **239.** Plastic reinforced with fiberglass can be formed into light, multipurpose stacking chairs. (*Photograph courtesy Stendig*)

textures. But ornament in metal can go far beyond this, due again to the nature of the material.

Except in the kitchen, most metal in the home is hidden. When we think of metal as a household material, we usually envision silverware, surely one of the most useful of the many forms that metals take. Although other metals appear in eating utensils, such as stainless steel, "silverware" has become almost a generic term.

Useful as silverware is, however, it accounts for only a very small part of the total tonnage of metal in the average home. From all manner of kitchen utensils and household appliances, through the umbilical cords that convey energy throughout the house, to structural members and frames, even at times to siding and roofing, metals are an integral part of the home. Think of the thousands of nails, screws, bolts and brads, and other connective devices that hold it all together.

For all their serviceability, metals are also an important source of beauty. We love copper for its lustrous, gleaming reddish-orange tone; silver for the deep polish and wide range of ornamentation; wrought iron for the intricacy of design that is possible; steel for the restrained but appealing contours it can assume.

Plastics

The newest of materials, plastics are also the most varied, because they are created by chemists to meet specific needs and end-uses. Plastic resins, principally carbon compounds in long molecular chains, come to forming machines as powders, granules, compressed tablets, or liquids, which under heat and/or pressure can be shaped as designers wish. Many techniques exist. Plastics can be compressed in molds, extruded through dies, injected into cavities, sprayed over forms of any desired shape, blown full of gas or air, rolled to desired thicknesses, or laminated to other materials and pressed into a single sheet or panel.

Although innumerable plastics exist, most of those used in the home fall into the categories outlined in Table 9.4. Each family of plastics shares certain characteristics, but specific types may have considerable diversity of form and application. More and more resins are being cross-bred to produce plastics with unique traits. Four terms associated with plastics explain some of their distinctions:

- The terms **plastic** and **synthetic** can be applied to the same basic material: molded nylon is called a plastic; nylon thread a synthetic.
- **Thermoplastic** substances can be softened and resoftened by heat and pressure, short of the point of decomposition.
- **Thermosetting** plastics cannot be modified after the initial (chemical) change during the curing process.

Form in Plastics

What does a designer do with such a range of amorphous materials, without historical precedent to start the process of creative design? The designer goes back to basics: that the purpose of design is to satisfy needs. Thus, need is the starting point. A material then can be formulated that will meet a potential use, real or imagined.

For example, the search for a floor covering that looks clean and shiny and is easy to keep that way, that is slightly resilient and therefore comfortable to stand on for lengthy periods, that is colorful and adaptable to almost any home and style, long wearing, durable, not very expensive—the list goes on. Resilient vinyl flooring is the result.

This broad potential calls for unusually close, steady cooperation among chemist, manufacturer, and designer. But the designer is freed from stereotypes of past forms, from preconceived notions of what is proper for any particular material.

This does not mean that shapes *must* be invented anew simply because the potential exists. The contours of plastic dishes and tumblers resemble those of clay or glass, because these shapes have been found well-suited to their end-use and pleasing in form. The great diversity of plastics has, however, allowed breakthroughs—whole new vocabularies of form and function, such as the chairs in Figure 239. Also, some of the simplest forms assume a new quality when translated into plastic.

240. Lucite is particularly adaptable for household objects because of its clarity and light weight combined with strength and durability. (*Photograph courtesy Georg Jensen, Inc.*)

Table 9.4
Families of Plastics

Name	Characteristics	Uses
ABS (Acrylonitrile, butadiene, styrene)	tough, hard, great tensile strength; resistant to scratching, chemicals, weather; moldable; lightweight	"fitting" ability leads to everything from plumbing systems to modular furniture that can be assembled in various configurations
ASA (Acrylonitrile, styrene, acrylic)	good integral color; cross-bred for specific applications and for plating, alloying	
acrylics Plexiglas Lucite Perspex (also acrylic yarns)	strong, rigid, light in weigh, excellent color; exceptional clarity, ability to pipe light; resistant to weathering, temperature changes and extremes; may scratch but can be buffed; molded into rigid shapes, then carved	domes and skylights, furniture, tableware, sculpture, paint (much used by artists)
FRP (fiberglass-reinforced plastics, often polyester)	stiff to flexible, hard to soft; good color range; resistant to chemicals, weather	patio covers, luminous ceilings, light-transmitting panels, walls, skylights, furniture, sculpture
melamines Formica Micarta Melmac	hard, durable, transparent to opaque; resistant to scratching, chipping, water, food stains, heat, fading; thin layer used in laminates shows material underneath; thicker molded, opaque; extensive color range	high-pressure laminates for countertops, tabletops, and as wood substitute for case goods; dinnerware
nylon generic term for group of plastics; also trade name and nylon yarn	thin layer transparent, thicker opaque; relatively rigid, high tensile strength; resistant to many chemicals, but not to food stains, coffee, tea; to abrasion but not to scratches or weathering; good color range; can be frozen, boiled	tumblers, dinnerware, kitchenware; especially useful for long-wearing gears, bearings, rollers; furniture
polyethylenes	flexible to semirigid, often waxy surface; semitransparent to opaque, lightweight; resistant to breakage, chemicals, freezing, boiling water, but cannot be boiled; good color range	kitchen bowls, dishpans, squeeze bottles; more rigid form used for molded, nonupholstered chair shells
polystyrenes	hard, rigid, but will break under bending, impact; resistant to household chemicals, foods (except citrus fruits, cleaning fluids), but not to abrasion; transparent types pipe light; range of translucent, opaque colors	kitchenware to modular furniture
urethanes cellular plastics so called because of structure, ability to foam (also as nonwoven fabric)	can be given any density, degree of hardness, from resilient to rigid; hard can be worked, finished, repaired like wood; can be foamed in place, bonded to any surface; good insulating properties, light weight	cushioning material, covering fabric, to furniture itself; insulation
vinyls (also as nonwoven fabric)	rigid, nonrigid, foam or cellular types; transparent, translucent, opaque; tough, strong, lightweight; resistant to foods, chemicals, normal use; cuts readily, may stiffen in cold; cellular form a wood substitute; can be embossed, printed in wide range of colors and textures	upholstery, wall coverings, lamp shades, luminous ceilings, counter surface; vinyl floor coverings combine most wanted characteristics in single material

Ornament in Plastics

Structural ornament seems to be in the nature of the materials and the processes used to form them. The inherent possibilities for varied colors, different degrees of transparency, translucency, opacity, embedded materials, molded forms and surface texture, open up many avenues for exploration and design.

The traditional materials also have these possibilities, but a plastic can combine some of these characteristics in a different way or may add

241. Different types of plastics have been developed to meet specific needs. This sink counter has been molded of a solid plastic called Corian. It has no dirt-catching crevices, and the surface is easily cleaned and repaired. (*Photograph courtesy E.I. duPont de Nemours & Co.*)

other qualities that are desirable, usually that of durability and/or ease of maintenance.

Applied ornament has not been as successful, although much molded ornament that resembles carved wood has come on the market. Perhaps because we *know* it is a plastic, it seems weak and imitative.

As yet, little applied ornament has been developed for plastics that intensifies a unique quality, as cutting heightens the sparkle of glass or intricate ornament throws into relief the luster of silver. We are seeing increasingly effective design in plastics, as their nature becomes more fully understood.

The introduction of plastics has had enormous impact on today's homes. Plastic surfaces on furniture, counters, walls, and floors lighten housekeeping and reduce noise. Plastic furniture is light in weight, easy to move around the house and from house to house. Plastic houses of the future may change many concepts of home planning and furnishing. The structure and most of the furnishings may be simply sprayed in place. Even now, many of the familiar components in the traditional house may be of plastic, from the piping, to insulation, to wall panels. Artists have accepted it as an exciting new medium, and many are busy exploring its potentialities. We cannot deny we are in the age of plastics, a 20th-century material that meets many of our 20th-century needs.

Fabrics

O f all materials, fabrics are the most pliantly responsive to our needs. They have one property shared by no other material: they can be adjusted or readjusted easily to an endless variety of forms. Moreover, we can do this adjusting ourselves, without calling upon experts. A snip of the scissors will shorten and shape fabrics; needle and thread will lengthen and shape fabrics.

Fabrics relate and accentuate forms within the home—floors to furniture, walls to windows, room to room. The same textile can be used as a bedcovering, a wall covering, upholstery on a chair, or drapery. Different fabrics establish a bond through their tactile softness—for example, a rug to sofa upholstery. Window drapery can call attention to the window form and moderate it at the same time. Or, conversely, it can hide a window altogether, if this is necessary to the overall design of a room.

Since earliest times fabrics have acted as an inexpensive means of energy conservation. A layer of heavy, well-padded carpeting warms a concrete floor; draperies come with thermal linings to cut the inflow of cold in the winter through large windows; fabric shades can stop the penetration of hot summer sun.

Fabrics answer our need for adornment. We choose household fabrics for color, pattern, and tactile interest as well as for comfort.

It is relatively easy and inexpensive to replace the fabrics in a room or an entire home. Thus, they answer our desire for change in the same surroundings with a minimum of cost and fuss.

As in the previous chapter on hard materials, we shall focus here on fabrics as material: the fibers and compounds that are the basic substances; the processes by which they are transformed into fabrics; and fabric design. Other chapters consider the potential integration of fabrics with walls, windows, floors, and furniture in more detail. We never can isolate them totally from other components of the home.

Some explanation of terms might be appropriate here:

- **Fabric** is a general term referring to anything manufactured by hand or machine, but it has come to be applied especially to fabricated material that is pliable and supple.
- **Textile** originally referred only to woven fabrics, and some purists still retain this distinction. A broader definition covers any *fabric made from fibers*, whether assembled by weaving or by any other interworking process.
- **Film** is produced originally in sheet form, rather than as fibers.

The Basic Substances

Fabrics can be categorized in two different ways: by the *substances* from which they are made, either natural or manufactured; and by the *processes* by which they are formed.

- **Natural** substances are fibers from sources such as reeds and grasses, flax (for linen), the wool and hair of animals, the seed coverings of plants (cotton), or the cocoons spun by silkworms.
- **Manufactured** substances are produced by machine from chemical compounds that can be formed into filaments or directly into films.

Fibers are made into yarns that are then interlinked by weaving, knitting, felting, knotting, lacing, tufting, or any other interworking process. Sheet forms—films—come from machines as a finished product.

242. Two 19th-century quilts hang in the living room of a renovated barn on Long Island, warming it physically and visually. Owners Anne and George Crawford wanted to preserve the character of the barn, so the natural materials of brick and stone remain exposed. (*Photograph: New York Times/ Hausner*)

Fibers

The term fiber covers any threadlike filament. Natural and manufactured fibers differ in the processes necessary to make them ready to be spun into yarns. Cotton, linen, silk, and wool fibers must be cleaned and drawn out (spun) so they are more or less even. Manufactured fibers, such as nylon, originate as clean, continuous, parallel filaments.

Both types of fibers must then be twisted together to make yarns—strands long enough and sufficiently strong for weaving or other fabric construction processes.

243. Fabric has been used here in unique ways. Stretched over beams it gives scale to the height of the ceiling. Moore, Grover, Harper, designers. (*Photograph: Norman McGrath*)

244. The yarns of a fabric determine many of its characteristics. Notice the differences in texture of these fabrics: screenprinted linen (**a**), knitted cotton in a drapery weight (**b**), a Jacquard wool weave (**c**), hand-printed silk (**d**), Jacquard fabric made primarily of rayon (**e**), nylon fabric woven of textured yarns (**f**), textured yarns of viscose and nylon (**g**), and a fiberglass fabric (**h**). (*Photographs courtesy Schumacher; Jack Lenor Larson, Inc.; Cohama Decorative Fabrics; and E.I. duPont de Nemours & Co.*)

Each fiber has its strong and weak points, and fibers differ from one another in many ways: strength and elasticity; resistance to abrasion, stains, sun, moisture, insects, and fire; and tactile and visual qualities. New developments create new fibers, familiar ones are modified, and processing and finishing techniques are constantly improved.

Yarns

Yarns vary in the kinds of fibers used either alone or in combination, in the type or tightness of twist, in the number of strands in the yarn (the ply), and in the size of the finished yarn, from spider-web thin to heavy cords. For example,

- **Long fibers** (called *filament fibers*) laid parallel to one another and tightly twisted produce smooth, strong yarns.
- **Short fibers** (*staple fibers*), somewhat randomly arranged and loosely twisted, result in softer yarns, such as *spun* silk or nylon.

right: Plate 36. This group of Jacquard fabrics is made of nylon. Because of their construction, Jacquards are often heavy fabrics suitable for upholstery material. (*Photograph courtesy Schumacher*)

below: Plate 37. Polyester/cotton blend Marimekko screenprinted fabrics provide the main color interest among the otherwise neutral-colored furnishings in a bedroom. Reprinted from *Bride's*. Copyright © 1978 by The Conde Nast Publications Inc. (*Photograph: Norman McGrath*)

Plate 38. A loft apartment can be a cold place, with large open spaces and bare brick walls. This one is made warmer with wall-to-wall carpeting, velvet textured upholstery on modular sofas, floor pillows covered with quilted fabrics, handmade pillows, and a wall tapestry in the background. Lolita Shalleck, owner/designer. (*Photograph: Anita Baskin*)

Many other variations are possible, such as *bouclé*, which has tight loops projecting from the yarn at intervals; or *slub*, in which sections of yarn are twisted loosely to produce an occasional soft, fluffy effect. *Bulk* or *textured* yarns come from inherently bulky fibers or have been treated in such a way that they have greater apparent volume than conventional yarn. *Stretch* yarns have stretch capability either from the type of fibers, such as Spandex, or from special manufacturing techniques introduced in the spinning process.

Of great importance now is the mixing of fibers to produce a fabric superior in some respect to a single-fiber fabric. For instance, cotton is mated with polyester to give us no-iron sheets. This can be done either in the yarn stage or later, in weaving.

The world of fabrics is constantly changing, but fortunately, Federal regulations for labeling fabric content and care give us some help in selection. Careful reading of this information and collating it with the general qualities of specific substances should prove useful in assessing fabrics. Such knowledge is an aid, but the feel or "hand" and appearance of a fabric, and a close look at the actual structure, will help determine its satisfaction in use.

Table 10.1 gives some of the basic facts about the qualities of the more important fabric families. Some are more versatile than others, but none is ideally suited to every purpose.

Form in Fabrics

There are five basic methods of fabric formation, divided according to the ways the fibers are worked together or the films handled. Each has special advantages and end results.

Felts

Felting is the matting together of fibers to form a web. It is a very old process but has recently been updated. Traditional felts of wool, hair, or fur fibers are matted by moisture, pressure, and heat that induces shrinkage and increases density. This results in a continuous dense cloth that is firm, slightly fuzzy, and of comparatively low tensile strength. Felt has no *grain*, or direction, so it can be cut, sewn, or draped in any way. Its edges usually need no hemming.

Films

As mentioned before, films are produced originally in sheet form—by extrusion through a wide die, casting or forming in molds, or calendering (rolling between rollers). The forming may stop there. The sheet is the finished product, but even this can be highly varied. Thin and transparent, thick and opaque, smooth as leather, suedelike in softness, deeply molded for three-dimensional patterns—it seems only imagination limits the effects.

The newest techniques in fabric construction eliminate the cut-and-sew and even the sheet stage and go right to the finished product—a film on the form.

- **Vacuum-formed** fabrics can be shaped into a single molded piece of upholstery.
- **Liquid vinyl** flows onto polyurethane foam and becomes bonded to it in a no-seams, fitted, durable surface.

Table 10.1
Fabric Families

Substance	Appearance	Uses	Maintenance	Resistances	Special Characteristics
acetates (cellulose diacetate) *Acele Avisco Celaperm Chromspun*	drapes well; good color range	bedspreads, curtains, draperies, rugs, upholstery	fair soil resistance; dry-clean or wash; dries quickly; iron with *cool* iron	*poor* to abrasion, aging, heat, sunlight, wrinkling *good* to felting, insects, pilling, shrinking, static electricity, stretching, and to fire if treated	integral color in fiber in newer processes, increasing resistances to sunlight, cleaning
(cellulose triacetate) *Arnel*	pleasant luster; drapes well; excellent color range	draperies, upholstery	slow to soil; dry-clean or wash; dries quickly; little ironing at medium temperature	*good* to abrasion, insects, pilling, static electricity, stretching *excellent* to aging, felting, fire, mildew, shrinking, wrinkling, sunlight	excellent retention of heat-set pleats and creases; good for high humidity areas
acrylics (acrylonitrile and other monomers) *Acrilan Creslan Orlon Zefran*	warm, bulky, woollike touch; good color range in some types	blankets, curtains, rugs, upholstery	slow to soil; easy to spot-clean, dry-clean, or wash; dries quickly; little ironing, under 325°	*poor* to fire, pilling, static electricity unless treated *good* to abrasion, felting, shrinking, stretching, sunlight, wrinkling	warmth without weight; retains heat-set pleats and creases; tightly woven will melt rather than flame; loosely woven, napped need fireproofing
modacrylics (modified acrylics) *Acrilan Dynel Verel*	warm, bulky, heavy, dense	blankets, draperies, rugs, upholstery	similar to acrylics, but iron at low setting if at all	*poor* to heat, shrinking unless stabilized by heat-setting, sunlight (*Dynel*) *good* to abrasion, pilling, static electricity, wrinkling *excellent* to aging, felting, fire, insects, mildew, sunlight (*Verel*)	special processes result in dense, furlike pile, textured, three-dimensional effects; will burn in direct flame, but self-extinguishing, without drip; added to other fibers for this quality
cotton (cellulose)	pleasant, soft, dull surface; fair drape; excellent color	bed and table linen, bedspreads, draperies, rugs, towels, upholstery	soils, stains, wrinkles unless treated; dry-clean or wash; irons easily	*poor* to felting, fire, mildew, shrinking, wrinkling *good* to abrasion, aging, fading, insects, stretching, sun *excellent* to pilling, static electricity	mercerizing increases luster, softness, strength, dry absorption; special treatments, blends for washwear, spot, wrinkle resistance
glass (silica sand, limestone, aluminum, and borax) *Beta Fiberglas Uniglass Pittsburgh PPG*	lustrous, silky; good drape; fair color range in dyes, printed many hues	bedspreads, curtains, draperies, wallpaper	slow to soil; easy spot removal; handwash, hang with no ironing; dries quickly	*poor* to abrasion, flexing (nonelastic) but new processes increase flexibility *excellent* to aging, chemicals, felting, fire, insects, mildew, shrinking, stretching, sunlight	*Beta* yarn one-half size of any other fiber; can be woven into very sheer fabric; fireproof, impervious to moisture and salt air; shed fibers can cause skin rash
linen (cellulose, from flax)	clean, fresh, lintless; fair drape; good color range	curtains, draperies, household linens, rugs, upholstery	soils and wrinkles easily; washes and irons well	*poor* to fire, shrinking, wrinkling unless treated *good* to abrasion, mildew, pilling, stretching, sunlight *excellent* to aging, insects, static electricity	stronger when wet; *sanforized* to reduce shrinking; can be made wrinkle-resistant

Fiber	Appearance/hand	Uses	Care	Resistance	Characteristics
nylon (polyamide) 6; 6,6; 501 *Antron Caprolan Cumuloft*	natural luster; good drape; good color range	bedspreads, rugs, upholstery	slow to soil; easy spot removal; dry-clean or wash, dries quickly; little ironing at low heat	*poor* to pilling, static electricity unless treated, sunlight *good* to fire *excellent* to abrasion, aging, felting, insects, mildew, shrinking, stretching, wrinkling	outstanding elasticity strength, and lightness; can be heat-set to keep permanent shape; sometimes damaged by acids; may pick up color and soil during washing
olefins (ethylene, propylene, or other olefin units) *Herculon Vectra*	woollike hand; fair color range	blankets, rugs, upholstery, webbing	slow to soil; spot-clean or wash; little ironing, at *very* low heat	*poor* to heat, shrinking, static electricity *good* to abrasion, felting, fire, stretching, sunlight, wrinkling *excellent* to insects, mildew, pilling, aging	lightest fiber made; excellent heat insulator; transmits humidity well; is very cohesive (can be made into nonwoven carpets); low cost
polyesters (dihydric alcohol and terephthalic acid) *Dacron Fortrel Kodel*	crisp or soft, pleasant touch; good drape; fair color range	bedding, curtains, draperies, rugs, upholstery	soils easily; dry-clean or wash; dries quickly; very little ironing, moderate heat	*poor* to dust, soil, pilling; very electrostatic *good* to abrasion, fire, sunlight *excellent* to felting, insects, mildew, shrinking, stretching, wrinkling	lightweight; ranges from sheer, silklike to bulky, woollike; as strong wet as dry; retains heat-set pleats and creases; picks up colors in washing
rayon (regenerated cellulose) *Avril Cupioni Enka Fortisan*	bright or dull luster; drapes well; excellent color range	blankets, curtains, draperies, rugs, table "linens," upholstery	fair soil resistance; dry-clean or wash; iron like cotton or silk, depending on type, finish	*poor* to felting, fire, mildew, shrinking, wrinkling *good* to abrasion, insects, stretching (poor when wet) *excellent* to pilling, static electricity; all resistances greatly improved by blending, finishes	most versatile fiber—can resemble cotton, silk, wool; absorbs moisture and swells when wet unless specially processed; reduces static electricity in blends; low cost; wash-and-wear and spot- and wrinkle-resistant finishes
silk (protein from silkworm cocoon)	lustrous, smooth, unique crunchy softness; drapes well; excellent color range	draperies, rugs, upholstery	good soil resistance; dry-clean or hand-wash; irons easily, moderate heat	*poor* to fire (but self-extinguishing), static electricity, sunlight *good* to abrasion, aging, felting, insects, mildew, shrinking, stretching, wrinkling	most desirable combination of properties of any fiber; smoothness, luster, resiliency, toughness, adaptability to temperature changes
wool (protein from sheep or goat and camel families)	soft or hard finish; dry, warm touch; drapes well; good color range	blankets, draperies, rugs, upholstery	good soil resistance; spot-clean, dry-clean, or wash in cold water; press over damp cloth at low heat	*poor* to insects, felting, shrinking unless treated *good* to abrasion, aging, fire, mildew, pilling, stretching, static electricity, sunlight *excellent* to wrinkling; new processes improve resistance to soil, stains, water, wrinkling	notable for warmth, absorbency (without feeling wet), resiliency, durability; wool-synthetic blends reduce shrinkage but have tendency to pill

Knitting

An old hand process now updated by machine technology, knitting is a process by which blunt rods or needles are used to form a single continuous yarn into a series of interlocking loops. Patterns result from plain, rib, and purl stitches, plus many variations.

Machine knitting can be much faster than weaving and produces dimensionally stable knit fabrics. New fibers and techniques offer good stretch recovery, wrinkle resistance, and form-fitting characteristics.

Twisting

The process by which nets, macramé, and laces are made, twisting is the intertwining and sometimes knotting of yarns that run in two or more directions. Fresh and imaginative designs in lace are appearing.

Weaving

Weaving is the interlacing of warp (lengthwise) and filling (crosswise) yarns, usually at right angles. It can range widely from the simple to the intricate. Weaves can, however, be considered under three general headings—plain, twill, and satin—according to the way the yarns are interwoven.

246. Net curtains veil but do not obscure a view. The texture of the curtains complements a room in which many textures interact. Robert Lyles, architect. (*Photograph: Gordon H. Schenck, Jr.*)

247. Shown in diagram form are the basic weaves. The dark boxes represent warp yarns, the white filling yarns. The patterns are plain weave (**a**); basket weave (**b**); twill weave (**c**); herringbone, a variation of twill (**d**); and satin weave (**e**).

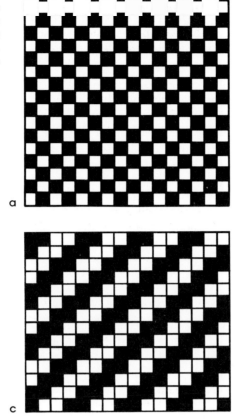

- **Plain weave** is simply one filling yarn carried over one warp yarn in a regular pattern. When woven from a mixture of heavy and thin yarns, the result is a definite ribbed texture (*rep*) or an undefined surface texture. If the weave is extended so that two or more filling yarns cross two or more warp yarns, there is a noticeable pattern (*basket weave*). Plain-weave textiles tend to be firm and sturdy.
- **Twill** weaves have a definite diagonal line or wale on the surface. The filling yarns "float" across a number of warp yarns in a regular pattern. Twills resist soil, wrinkle less, and are more flexible and drapable than plain weaves of similar quality.
- **Satin** weaves have yarns that make longer, less regular floats on the surface of the fabric. This minimizes the over-and-under texture and may result in a smooth, light-reflecting surface.

248. Plain-weave textiles, such as these wools, are sturdy enough for use as upholstery. (*Photograph courtesy Schumacher*)

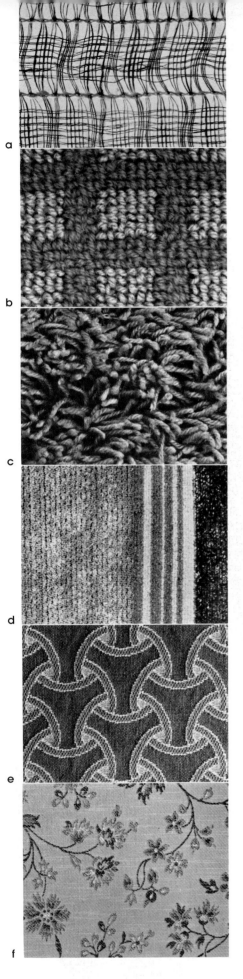

There are special variations of these weaves particularly useful in the home. *Lace weaves* (as distinct from laces produced by twisting alone) result when the warp (or the filling) yarns are crossed or twisted at certain points to create an open effect (*leno*).

Pile weaves add a third set of yarns to the basic warp and filler. The pile yarns protrude from the background to make a three-dimensional fabric. Sometimes the pile is a single continuous yarn that leaves loops on one side of the fabric; the loops may be left uncut (terry cloth), or cut for velvet, plush, and the like. A variation, *tufting*, has loops of pile yarns inserted through an already constructed backing. The handcraft version is called *hooking*. Certain fine carpets (rya and Oriental rugs) have yarns hand-tied onto the warp between rows of filler. Patterns are made by cutting some loops and not others, by mixing high and low pile, or by different colored yarns.

Jacquard weaves are usually complex pattern weaves produced on the Jacquard loom, which operates something like a computer. *Damasks* and *tapestries* are made this way. (See Plate 36, p. 237.)

Finishing the Fabric

After they have been formed, most fabrics need further processing to give them a pleasing appearance and add useful qualities. *Shrinking*, for example, lessens the tendency of most fibers to contract when exposed to moisture. Thus, it pays to know whether a fabric has been preshrunk before making it into curtains that are to be washed. *Mercerization*, a chemical finish applied to cellulosic fibers such as cotton, strengthens the fabric, adds luster, and improves dye receptivity. Many other processes help to turn lifeless textiles into attractive ones.

Some of the newer special treatments, however, notably change the behavior of fibers and fabrics. They are important when choosing fabrics for home use.

Textiles can be made:

- **Antistatic** to prevent the buildup of static charges and reduce soiling.
- **Bacteria-, mildew-,** and **moth-resistant** in varying degrees of effectiveness and permanence.
- **Crease-resistant** ("wash-and-wear," "no-iron," "permanent press") by impregnating fibers with resins or with agents that either cross-link cellulose molecules or build a "memory" into the fiber, causing it to return to its original shape. Crease-resistance gives textiles more firmness and sometimes better draping qualities. But it may also weaken fibers, reduce abrasion resistance, and wash out. Dyes become more permanent, and shrinkage of spun rayons, light cottons and linens, velvets diminishes. Bonding to a foam or tricot backing also enhances wrinkle resistance.

249. Variations of basic textile weaves can serve many purposes in the home. Shown here are: leno (**a**); low pile (**b**); high pile (**c**); tufted fabric (**d**); Jacquard (**e**); and damask (**f**). (*Photographs courtesy E.I. duPont de Nemours & Co.; Schumacher; and Greef Fabrics, Inc.*)

250. An Oriental rug adds pattern and texture to a room. The macramé hanging planter in the foreground is another type of fabric construction. Kipp Stewart, designer. (*Photograph © Morley Baer*)

- **Fire-** and **flame-resistant** through chemical treatments. A worthwhile safety precaution, these processes can be durable but sometimes need to be renewed. They may make textiles heavier and stiffer but may also increase resistance to weathering and sometimes to insects and mildew.
- **Elastic** by including Spandex fiber in the blend or by inserting stretch properties through special construction techniques, such as the twisting or crimping of yarns, slack mercerization of fabrics, or heat setting.
- **Glossy** with resins that provide a more or less permanent smooth, lustrous surface. Glazed fabrics resist soil and have improved draping qualities. Glazing is usually limited to textiles meant for curtains, draperies, and slipcovers.
- **Insulating** through the application of a thin (milium) or foamed coating on the back, which keeps out the heat rays of the sun and keeps in winter warmth.
- **Soil-resistant** or **soil-releasing** by coating or impregnating fibers or fabrics with chemicals to make them less absorbent.
- **Stable,** chiefly through careful control of shrinking tendencies. In some processes, chemicals supplement moisture, heat, pressure, and tension.
- **Water-repellent** by coating or impregnating the fibers with wax, metals, or resins. Such treatment makes fabrics hold their shape better, as well as helping to keep dirt on the surface.

Ornament in Fabrics

Structural ornament is inherent in the very nature of fabrics—the over-and-under pattern of weaves, the twisted lines of laces, the textures of pile, and, of course, the colors.

Coloring the Fabric

Dyes can be introduced at several stages: in fibers, yarns, or the fabric itself. In some manufactured fibers and films, the dye is mixed with the liquid from which they are formed, resulting in a colorfast product.

The kind of dye and its hue affect colorfastness, but almost all colors will fade somewhat on exposure to sun or polluted air, washing, or dry-cleaning. It makes sense to get the most nearly fade-proof textiles available. Some mellow more gracefully than others.

- The colors most common in nature—grays, greens, browns, soft yellows, and oranges—age better than colors of higher intensity. Dark colors may lose richness and depth.
- Mixtures, as in tweeds, do not become as listless as faded solid colors.
- Textures compensate for loss of color.
- Patterns that are intricate or diffused lose less of their character than those of brilliant contrasts or precision.

Fabrics that have mellowed, however, give many of us a comfortable feeling of continuity and warmth. When we compare an antique Oriental rug with a modern version, we realize that the softening of colors, textures, and patterns can result in harmonious richness.

Applied Ornament

Beyond the colors and designs in the fabric itself are the many types of applied enrichment that add pattern and intricacy.

Printing   Pigments the consistency of thick paste can be applied to a finished fabric by one of the following methods:

- **Roller printing,** a machine process, applies pigments directly from copper rollers engraved with a design, one for each color.
- **Block printing** is most often done by hand, although semimechanized methods now exist. Wood blocks, often surfaced with metal or linoleum, transfer the design to the fabric.
- **Screenprinting,** often called **silk screen,** is a type of stencil printing. A thick dye is forced through a mesh treated in some portions to resist penetration. (See Plate 37, p. 237).
- **Batik** is a *resist* printing method. A wax or paste applied to sections of the cloth prevents dye from being absorbed in those areas. After each dye bath, the wax is removed; the process can be repeated to form a design of more than one color.

above: 251. A continuous design with a fairly small-scale repeat is well adapted to roller printing (*top*). Screenprinting (*center*) generally emphasizes large patterns with broad color areas. Tie-dyeing (*bottom*), a resist technique, typically creates symmetrical forms with irregular edges. (*Photographs courtesy Boussac of France, Inc.; Schumacher*)

right: 252. Crewel embroidery is usually casual and colorful—a bright note in an informal room.

left: 253. Fabrics can set the mood in a home. In another view of the house shown in Figure 243, a strongly patterned drapery pulls around to hide the bed area. The bedspread is an India print, and the area rug is Oriental. Moore, Grover, Harper, designers.(*Photograph: Norman McGrath*)

below: 254. When choosing fabrics, you should take into consideration how a pattern will look when it is draped. The stylized flower pattern *Allegro*, by Gloria Vanderbilt, is shown hung in folds and stretched flat. (*Photograph courtesy James Seeman Studios, Inc.*)

- **Tie-dyeing,** also a resist method, uses an arrangement of pleats and knots to prevent absorption of dye in certain areas, thus creating a pattern.
- **Discharge printing** has parts of a dyed fabric treated with a chemical to remove color in certain areas.

Stitchery   Stitchery is a general term covering such enrichment as embroidery, appliqué, quilting, needlepoint, and other types of needlework. It adds small-scale, intricate design that seems, and often is, more personalized than any of the other types of applied ornament.

Fabrics in the Home

Undoubtedly, fabrics are used more in the home today than ever before. With the availability and acceptance of carpeting as wall-to-wall floor covering (sometimes moving up the wall), the wide windows that need curtaining for privacy and warmth, the cushioned furniture that must be covered with fabric, we live surrounded, almost cocooned by fabrics. The elements of softness and warmth that fabrics bring to the home are probably their major attraction. (See Plate 38, p. 238.)

Not only is there great choice in fabrics, but we can instantly change a room by changing fabrics. A bedroom can be visually cooled in summer by blue and white bedcoverings and curtains, and warmed in winter by a switch to a persimmon color scheme. Nothing in the home offers the freedom of design that comes naturally in fabrics.

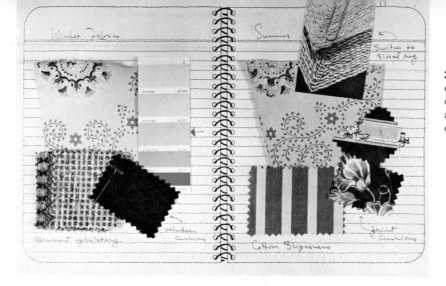

255. Fabric selection is easier when all the elements of a room are seen together. Collages of upholstery and carpet materials, and perhaps a wallpaper or paint sample, can be tested with different drapery fabrics.

List of Fabrics

The following pages list some of the fabrics most frequently used in the home. They have been divided into five categories, based primarily on thickness, which is an important factor in determining their applications. However, there is quite a range within each category and some overlapping between categories.

Most of the fabrics can be woven from a number of different fibers, but a few are made from only one. Some are *blends* of different fibers, in combinations too numerous to mention. The cotton-polyester blend is the most common.

Fabric names constitute a strange miscellany, being based on the fiber, such as *linen,* which has come to mean a special kind of linen textile; the weave, such as *satin;* the early use, such as *monk's cloth;* or a trade name, such as *Indian Head.*

Very Thin   Almost transparent fabrics are suitable for glass curtains and sometimes for summer bedspreads, table skirts, and table coverings. Most can be made from cotton, silk, synthetics, or even wool.

Bobbinet   A fine and sheer to coarse open plain lace with hexagonal meshes. Soft yet with character; most effective when very full; coarser types best for straight folds; sheer types well suited to tiebacks and ruffles. White, cream, ecru, pale colors.
Cheesecloth   Cotton in loose, plain weaves, very low thread count. Very inexpensive; short-lived; informal. Usually off-white.
Dimity   Fine, tightly twisted, usually combed cotton; plain weave with thin cord making vertical stripe or plaid. Often mercerized. Fine, sheer, crisp. White, tints, or printed patterns.
Filet   Square-mesh lace knotted at intersecting corners. Fine to coarse but usually giving a bold effect. White, cream, ecru, and plain colors.
Marquisette   Leno weave in many fibers. Sheer and open; soft or crisp; fine to coarse. Serviceable; launders well. White, cream, or pale colors; sometimes printed or woven patterns.
Net   Any lace with a uniform mesh, such as bobbinet or filet; fine to coarse, sheer to open; made of almost any fiber.
Ninon   Plain voilelike or novelty weaves. Very thin; smooth, silky, pleasant sheen. Best in straight folds. Plain colors; self-colored stripes or shadowy figures; sometimes embroidered.
Organdy   Cotton in plain weave; like sheer, crisp muslin, but crispness washes out unless specially treated. Folds keep their place. Often used

without draperies; frequently tied back. Many plain colors; also printed or embroidered designs.

Point d'esprit   Variation of bobbinet with dots that give it more body. White, cream, and pale colors.

Swiss muslin (dotted swiss)   Cotton in plain weaves; usually embroidered or patterned in dots or figures. Fine, sheer, slightly crisp. Can be used alone, usually draped; effect generally informal. White and plain colors, usually light; figures may be colored.

Theatrical gauze   Linen or cotton in a loose, open, crisp weave with a shimmering texture. Often used without draperies for colorful, informal effect. Wide range of plain colors, often two-toned.

Voile   Open, plain weave, sheer and smooth. Drapes softly; gives more privacy than marquisette. Various textures; many colors, usually pale; sometimes woven patterns.

Thin   Translucent fabrics are suitable for glass curtains or for draperies. They have sufficient body to be used alone and give a measure of privacy, although not at night. Thin fabrics can also be used for table skirts, table coverings, and summer bedspreads.

Batiste   Delicate and fine, plain weave, usually cotton or Dacron, often with printed or embroidered designs. Needs fullness to be effective; when embroidered, has considerable body. Light and dainty. White or pastel colors.

Casement cloth   Almost every known fiber in plain or figured weaves. Flat and lustrous. Often ecru, but can be other colors. Frequently used alone as draw curtains.

Fiberglass   Glass fibers in varied weaves and weights, from sheer marquisette to heavy drapery fabrics. Translucent to opaque; can be washed and hung immediately without shrinking or stretching. Good range of colors; plain or printed.

Films (plastic)   Smooth or textured, plain or printed, thin or thick. Used for shower curtains, table coverings, upholstery, or wall coverings. Waterproof; wipes clean.

Muslin   Cotton in a soft, plain weave; light to heavy qualities. Bleached or unbleached; also dyed and printed. Inexpensive, durable, informal; often used alone at windows.

Osnaburg   Cotton yarns, coarse and uneven, in an open, plain weave; similar to crash. Usually medium weight, natural color, but can be light or heavy weight, any color, printed patterns. Strong and long-lasting; rough-textured; informal.

Pongee   Wild silk in plain weave with broken crossbar texture caused by irregular yarns; also imitated in cotton and synthetics. Fairly heavy; often used without draperies. Shrinks unless treated. Usually pale or dark ecru, but can be dyed. Also called tussah, antique taffeta, and doupioné (duppioni).

Sheeting (cotton or blend)   Smooth, plain weave, lightweight. Inexpensive and informal. White, colors, or printed.

Silk gauze   Plain weave with a slight irregularity in threads, making an interesting texture. Hangs well; is never slick. Wide range of colors.

Lightweight   Light fabrics are suitable for draperies, bedspreads, table skirts, pillows, screens, wall coverings, table coverings, and slipcovers. They sometimes serve for upholstery in the heavier grades. Many can be made of cotton, silk, wool, synthetics, or a cotton-polyester blend. They come in a wide color range and can be washed.

Antique satin   Variation of smooth satin, with a dull, uneven texture. Variety of weights but usually heavier than satin. Widely used for upholstery and drapery materials.

Broadcloth   Cotton, a blend, or silk in plain or twill weaves; spun rayon or wool in twill weaves. Varies greatly in terms of fiber and weave. Cotton and synthetic types used for draperies, bedspreads, tablecloths.

Calico   Cotton or a blend in a plain weave, printed with small figures. Inexpensive and informal.

Challis   Wool, synthetic, or cotton in a soft, plain, firm weave. Usually printed with small floral designs but sometimes a plain color.

Chambray   Cotton or a blend in a smooth, close, plain weave. White-frosted appearance on wide range of colors.

Chintz   Cotton in a close, plain weave, usually with a printed design and often glazed. Washing removes glaze in many types.

Drill   Blend in diagonal twill weave. Firm, heavy, very durable textile. Typical color is gray, but other colors available.

Faille   Plain weave with decided flat, crosswise ribs. Difficult to launder, but wears well if handled carefully. Varies from soft yet firm to quite stiff.

Gingham   Cotton or a blend in light to medium weight, plain weave; woven from colored yarns. Strong; launders well. Checked, striped, and plaid patterns.

Homespun   Irregular yarns woven in loose, plain weave. Texture somewhat rough and irregular; informal character. Plain colors, dyed, or woven of mixed yarns.

India print   Printed cotton cloth from India or Persia with characteristic intricate design in clear or dull colors. Inexpensive and durable. Fades, but pleasantly.

Indian Head   Plain weave, firm and smooth. Trade name for a permanent-finish cotton, vat-dyed, colorfast, shrink-resistant. Inexpensive and durable.

Insulating   Fabrics coated on one side with metallic flakes to reflect heat or with foam plastic to trap heat.

Jaspé cloth   Plain weave; varied yarns give unobtrusive, irregular, blended stripes. Generally firm, hard, and durable. Can be in any color, but usually fairly neutral, medium dark, and monochromatic.

Linen   Flax in a plain, firm weave. Cool to the touch, good body, launders well; wrinkles easily unless specially treated. Often has hand-blocked designs.

Moiré   Ribbed, plain weave with a watermarked appearance. Most moiré finishes can be steamed or washed out—more permanent on synthetic fibers.

Oxford cloth   Plain basket or twill weave, light to rather heavy weights. Durable and launders well.

Piqué   Plain weave with narrow raised cords running in one direction or at right angles to each other (waffle piqué). Durable; interesting texture.

Poplin   Plain weave with fine crosswise ribs. Firm and durable.

Rep   Plain weave with prominent rounded ribs running crosswise or lengthwise.

Sateen   Cotton or a blend, usually mercerized, in a satin weave; flat and glossy, with a dull back. Durable, substantial, but with a tendency to roughen. Often used for lining curtains.

Satin   Satin weave, smooth, delicate fabric with very high sheen. Durable; somewhat slippery.

Seersucker Plain weave with woven, crinkly stripes. Durable, needs no ironing.

Shantung Plain weave with elongated irregularities. A heavy grade of pongee, but with wider color range.

Stretch Knit or woven of cotton, rayon, or other synthetic with special stretch properties, or of Spandex. Smooth to rough textures. Valuable for slipcovers and contoured shapes.

Taffeta Close, plain weave, slightly crossribbed. Crisp; sometimes weighted with chemical salts; cracks in strong sunlight. Antique taffeta has unevenly spun threads.

Medium Weight Fabrics of medium weight are suitable for heavy draperies and upholstery, as well as for wall coverings and pillows. Some also adapt to slipcovers, bedspreads, screens, and table coverings. Made of heavier fibers of cotton, flax, hemp, jute, linen, silk, synthetics, or wool, they are available in a wide color range; some are washable.

Bark cloth Blend in a firm, plain weave with irregular texture due to uneven yarns. Plain or printed. Durable.

Brocade Woven on a Jacquard loom; raised designs are produced by floating some of the filling yarns. Usually has a multicolored floral or conventional pattern.

Brocatelle A Jacquard weave similar to brocade but with a heavier design. Used mostly as upholstery on large sofas and chairs.

Burlap Loose basket weave. Heavy and coarse; interesting texture. Often fades quickly.

Canvas Cotton or blend in a plain, diagonal weave. Heavy, firm, and durable. Strong solid colors, as well as stripes or printed designs. Often used for awnings, outdoor curtains, and upholstery.

Crash Plain weave with a rough texture caused by uneven yarns. Often hand-blocked or printed.

Cretonne Cotton or blend in a firm plain, rep, or twill weave. Fairly heavy texture and bold design. Similar to chintz but heavier, never glazed. Patterns are usually more vigorous.

Damask Any combination of two of the three basic weaves; flat Jacquard patterns. Firm, lustrous, reversible. Similar to brocade but design is not in relief. May be referred to as figured satin. One or two colors used.

Denim Cotton or blend in a close twill weave. Warp and filler often in contrasting colors; can have a small woven pattern. Inexpensive; washable; Sanforizing prevents shrinking; reasonably sunfast.

Duck Cotton or blend in a close plain or ribbed weave. Often given protective finishes against fire, water, mildew. Similar to canvas.

Hopsacking Loose, plain weave. Coarse, inexpensive, and durable.

Laminated Any fabric bonded to a lightweight foam backing, or two fabrics bonded together. Wrinkle-resistant; good for upholstery, slipcovers, insulating draperies.

Mohair Hair of Angora goats (now often mixture of synthetic and wool) in a plain, twill, or pile weave or with a woven or printed design. Resilient and durable. Novelty weaves, sheer to very heavy.

Monk's cloth Jute, hemp, flax, usually mixed with cotton or a blend in a loose plain or basket weave. Coarse and heavy; friar's cloth and druid's cloth similar but coarser. Not easy to sew, tendency to sag. Usually comes in natural color.

Sailcloth Plain weave. Heavy and strong. Similar to canvas or duck. Often used on summer furniture.

Serge   Twill weave with a pronounced diagonal rib on both face and back. Has a clear, hard finish.

Terrycloth   Cotton or blend in a loose uncut-pile weave; loops on one or both sides. Very absorbent; not always colorfast; may sag. Not suitable for upholstery, but useful for draperies and bedspreads.

Ticking   Cotton or blend in a satin or twill weave. Strong, closely woven, durable. Best known in white with colored stripes, but may have simple designs. Not always colorfast but washable.

Heavy   Heavy fabrics are perfect for upholstery because of their weight and durability; in lighter grades they make draperies, pillows, bedspreads, slipcovers, wall coverings, even table coverings. Most are available in a variety of fibers and a wide color range. Few are washable.

Bouclé   Plain or twill weave. Flat, irregular surface, woven or knitted from specially twisted bouclé yarns; small spaced loops on surface.

Corduroy   Cotton or a synthetic in a pile weave, raised in cords of various sizes giving pronounced lines. Durable, washable, inexpensive.

Expanded vinyl   Plastic upholstery fabric with an elastic knit fabric back. Stretches for contour fit.

Felt   Nonwoven fabric of wool, rayon and wool, or synthetics. Nonraveling edges need no hemming. Available in intense colors; used for table coverings, pillows, even for draperies.

Frieze   Also called *frizé;* heavy-pile weave. Loops uncut or cut to form a pattern; sometimes yarns of different colors or with irregularities used. Usually has a heavy rib. Extremely durable.

Matelassé   Double-woven fabric with quilted or puckered surface effect, caused by interweaving to form the pattern. Needs care in cleaning, but otherwise durable.

Needlepoint   Originally handmade in variety of patterns, colors, and degrees of fineness. Now imitated on Jacquard loom. At best, has pronounced character, from delicate (*petit point*) to robust (*gros point*); at worst, looks like weak imitation.

Plastic   Wide variety of textures from smooth to embossed; used for upholstering and wall-covering. Resists soil, wipes clean. Not for use over deep springs unless fabric-backed, which is more pliable, easier to fit, less likely to split.

Plush   Cut-pile weave. Similar to velvet but with a longer pile. Sometimes pressed and then brushed to give surface variations; sculptured by having design clipped or burned out of pile, leaving motif in relief. Also made to imitate animal fur.

Tapestry   Weaves with two sets of warps and weft; woven on a Jacquard loom. Heavier and rougher than damask or brocade. Patterns usually pictorial and large.

Tweed   Soft, irregularly textured, plain weave. Yarns dyed before weaving; often several or many colors combined.

Velour   Short, heavy, stiff cut-pile weave. Slight luster and indistinct horizontal lines. Durable.

Velvet   Pile weave with loops cut or uncut. Luxurious but often shows wear quickly. Lustrous or dull; light to heavy grades; plain, striped, or patterned.

Velveteen   Cotton or a synthetic woven with a short, close, sheared pile. Strong, durable, launders well.

Webbing   Cotton, jute, or plastic in narrow strips (1 to 4 inches) of very firm, plain weave. Plain, striped, or plaid design. Jute used to support springs; cotton or plastic interlaced for webbed seats and backs.

Furniture

11

Furniture acts as a mediator between architecture and people. A room is empty space until furniture gives it meaning, a role, whereupon the space becomes a bedroom or a dining room.

The function of furniture is mainly supportive—of our bodies, our actions, and our way of life. But furniture is also somewhat dictatorial. It exists to make living comfortable, easy, and pleasurable, but it often ends up influencing our actions.

Chairs and beds ease the pull of gravitational forces by supporting our bodies at many points rather than at just our feet. Tables bring food up to a convenient level for eating, or a typewriter to a height for easy typing. Shelves, cupboards, and drawers store things not in immediate use, keeping them clean and out of the way but accessible.

We are in almost constant touch with furniture—sitting, sleeping, working. Therefore, a major factor in its selection is use. Does it fulfill its function in an easy, comfortable manner? How does it feel?

Since furniture is in such constant use, an important consideration is the amount of work necessary to keep it in condition. How much maintenance does it require, in terms of time, effort, and cost?

Furniture has great potential for enhancing the beauty and individuality of our spaces. It enables us to express our personal tastes and to make a home our own, even when the space may be architecturally the same as that next door. One of its special qualities is that it can be rearranged easily, without additional cost. Many people work out some of their frustrations by moving furniture about. We may not be able to change our lives, but we can change the physical aspect of our homes. This symbolic act acknowledges that furnishings influence our lives.

256. Furnishings reflect the life style of a home's owners. A large piece of furniture, such as this rolltop desk, can be the keynote for an entire room. Smaller pieces, however, must complement the larger. The chairs are too formal for the massive desk, making it seem out of place; the other accessories are delicate.

257. The desk of Figure 256 works better with more rustic furnishings, giving the room a single theme.

This last point is important. Does the furniture chosen for a particular home fit in with and reinforce the life style of the people who will live there? Too often people furnish in a traditional style because it is familiar and established. It has been sanctioned by years of use and needs little imagination to put it all together. Others let themselves be talked into the latest style simply because it is "in." This may result in a dead level of fashion unrelieved by personal touches. The interior designer must beware of imposing his or her own taste on clients who may not be able to live with it.

Whether a given piece of furniture has beauty and character is a subjective appraisal. Everyone differs in tastes. Here, once again, you need to know yourself or your client. The profile in Chapter 1 will have started you off on this quest. Your reactions to many of the furnishings illustrated in this book or others, in magazines and stores, will add to your self-knowledge. A conscious effort to see and evaluate differences will help establish your scale of values—a personal aesthetic.

The profile questionnaire in the first part of the book will, we hope, have given information on the types and sizes of furniture that might be needed, how the furniture might be arranged, the space available, and the makeup of the household: adults, young, older, or handicapped; children; even animals. All these will influence furniture choices. And, of course, the life style of the household members will affect, and be affected by, the furnishings chosen.

There are four basic criteria for choosing furniture:

- **Use**—Does it give comfortable support for its particular function?
- **Economy**—Is it worth the original cost, plus the time, energy, and money necessary for its maintenance?
- **Beauty**—Does it give pleasure to the eye and the touch?
- **Individuality**—Does it suit the household in question so well that it belongs in the home, but at the same time have special qualities of character and spirit?

Types of Furniture

The home-furnishings industry often divides furniture into soft goods and case goods—in other words, into pieces relatively soft to the touch, such as upholstered chairs and sofas; and hard pieces, tables and chests of drawers made of rigid materials.

Although the word "case" originally referred to receptacles, in the trade it has been broadened to include tables, desks, chests of drawers, even wood chairs. There is a lot of crossover between the two types. We will consider furniture in terms of tasks: sofas, chairs, and beds for supporting bodies; tables and desks at which to eat, work, or play; and storage units for keeping things.

Seating: Sofas and Chairs

Reducing physical strain to a minimum is the major purpose of sofas and chairs, to varying degrees. For many of us today, the greater part of our waking hours are spent sitting down: working, studying, relaxing, talking, eating, and traveling. Leading such sedentary lives, we should by now have produced the perfect seating unit. Unfortunately, this is not the case, perhaps because we ourselves come in so many sizes and shapes, padded or not, aware of comfort or stoic.

A number of studies indicate that maximum comfort results when weight and pressure are distributed to ease tension. Figure 258 illustrates some of the salient points, adapted to the average person. How-

258. New studies have caused some designers to reevaluate the ideal proportions for comfort in various furniture pieces. In these diagrams, the first number is the one currently recommended. The number in parentheses is the dimension considered standard up to now. (*Adapted from* Nomadic Furniture 1)

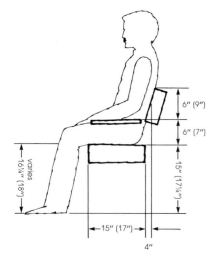
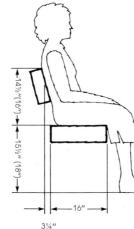
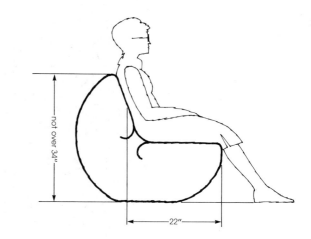

259. Soft, cushioned seating is comfortable for children as well as adults. It invites relaxation. Dan Solomon, designer. (*Photograph: Joshua Freiwald*)

ever, very few of us fit a norm. We have to pick out seating units that come nearest to the general sizes in a particular household, and then adjust them as much as possible with cushions. We need a diversity of sizes and types for different people and situations.

Some seating, of course, is adjustable, notably sofas on which we do the adjusting, squirming around and perhaps swinging our legs up. Reclining chairs allow a person to take a nap, then snap back upright to talk to friends or watch television. Typists' chairs, although seldom beautiful, can also be adjusted for different people, to ease the strain of long desk work.

Rocking chairs provide a different kind of adjustment, by constantly shifting the sitter's weight onto different pressure points in a predictable rhythm. Many people find them enormously soothing and physically relaxing. Another kind of adjustment is found in swivel chairs.

No doubt the most adjustable of all seating units are to be found in some cars, with electrically powered bucket seats and backs that slide around, up and down, at different angles, and sometimes even with different contours and degrees of resiliency in the back support, all at the touch of a button or two. Perhaps it is just as well we are not quite so mechanized at home, but the idea does suggest possibilities.

You should begin the task of choosing seating units by deciding what *kind* they must be. For that you need to know what you want them to do. What are they going to be used for? Activities can be classed in two groups: those meant to be physically relaxing and those that require more mental alertness.

Relaxed Activities   If possible, it is best that each person who regularly uses a room have comfortable seating in which to relax, read, talk, watch television, or simply be quiet. Most well-cushioned lounge or arm chairs, as well as recliners and sofas, adapt to a certain extent—if the potential user is kept in mind. A small person in an oversize chair may feel the need to curl up; the very tall person may spill out of a small piece.

260. Sofas can be found to meet practically every design need.

chesterfield

studio couch

divan

For guests, these lounge chairs will suffice if there are enough of them. Otherwise, you can add a few easy chairs, sometimes called side chairs, that are smaller yet comfortable. Mobility is a plus here. Chairs, perhaps on wheels or light enough to be moved, can join different furniture groupings, as the need arises.

Alert Activities   Dining, working, and games require easily moved chairs, sturdy enough to withstand constant shifting, with relatively upright backs for support. Seats and backs that are shaped or lightly padded lessen pressure; abrasion- and dirt-resistant upholstery lessens maintenance.

Group dining spaces need enough chairs or built-in seating to accommodate the entire household; some other pull-up type chairs, not necessarily identical, should be available for larger gatherings.

Many dining room "sets" come with chairs that have a definitely dining room look. More useful are those that are right for dining but equally attractive if used in other areas for extra seating.

Having decided on the type of seating desired, you can proceed to examine the various choices in more detail.

Sofas

We will use the term *sofa* to refer to a seat for two or more people, but it goes by many other names, conveying shades of meaning.

- **Chesterfield**—A large overstuffed, upholstered sofa.
- **couch**—Originally a long upholstered piece, with one raised end, for reclining; now most often used in the term *studio couch*, a combined sitting-sleeping unit.

traditional lounge

traditional love seat

settee

modern lounge

modern love seat

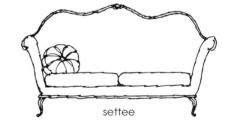
early American settee

traditional sofa

Lawson

modern sofa

traditional convertible sofa

tuxedo

■ **Davenport**—A term used in the United States to describe an upholstered sofa often convertible into a bed.

■ **divan**—A Turkish term for large, low couches without arms or backs that developed from piles of rugs for reclining.

■ **lounge**—From the verb meaning to relax indolently, today the term indicates either a flat padded surface on which to stretch out, or any supercomfortable seating unit.

■ **loveseat**—A small sofa or double chair for two people.

■ **settee**—A double seat with a back and sometimes arms, often lightly upholstered.

■ **settle**—An all-wood settee, with a high back and arms, used in Colonial days before a fire to trap heat.

■ **sofa**—Originally from the Arabic, sofa has become the favored term to describe any long upholstered seat for more than one person. A Tuxedo sofa has arms and back the same height; a Lawson has arms lower than the back.

■ **convertible sofa, sofa-bed, sleeper, studio couch**—Dual purpose units used for both sitting and sleeping.

■ **sectional unit,** or **modular sofa**—Pieces easily assembled into various and changeable sizes and shapes, or separated into individual chair units.

■ **seating platforms**—These often look built-in, are of almost any dimensions, and merge with the floor and wall.

■ **floor pad**—A mattress placed directly on the floor, often heaped with cushions, for relaxed lounging.

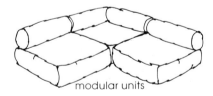

modular units

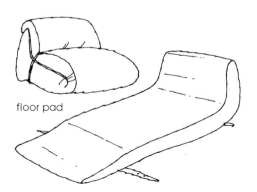

floor pad

Selecting Sofas   The first question to ask is whether you really need a sofa. Most of us think we do, because we are used to the idea. Sofas have many good points: we can sit on them or stretch out on them; they provide a variable number of people with a place to sit, in varying degrees of comfort. They are a good solid center of interest, stabilizing a main furniture group in the sea of space.

The main disadvantages of sofas are that they tend to be large and cumbersome, heavy and difficult to move, unadaptable to changing circumstances. This is undoubtedly the reason why sectional furniture has become so popular. The sofa dissolves into a series of chairs, or two or more smaller sofas. If furniture will be moved often—around the room or to another home—sectional pieces are a good choice.

When shopping for a sofa, keep the following in mind. For different situations, people will need a sofa:

- long enough to stretch out on—6 feet or longer for most people
- low and deep enough for relaxation but high and firm enough so most people feel well supported and can get up under their own power
- fitted with arms for comfort
- convertible into a bed if extra sleeping space is required
- upholstered for comfort in a material that combines beauty and durability

It is helpful also to imagine the sofa in use: people talking to people, the textural comforts of different kinds of upholstery. These matters will be taken up in detail later, but they are major considerations in the choice of sofas.

It is imperative that you try out a variety of sofas, not just by sitting primly upright, but also by lounging. Both are important, because a sofa is used by different people, for different occasions, subject to different whims and moods.

Last but by no means least is the size of the sofa in relation to the space it will occupy and its passage into and eventually out of the room. The size of doorways, the angles of halls and stairs, even the dimensions of the freight elevator in a highrise building may limit the size of the unit. No doubt these considerations have added to the popularity of

261. Multi-use furniture adapts to today's needs. Pushed together these two pieces become an informal lounging area. The sofa section converts to a double-size bed, and the matching chaise can be used as a twin bed. (*Photograph courtesy Simmons Company*)

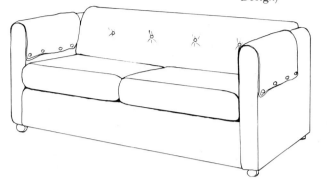

262. A sofa designed with detachable flaps that snap over the arms eases maintenance. (*Photograph courtesy Sausalito Design*)

modular sofas. The sections are lighter and more manageable for those who move themselves.

Careful measurements of possible placements in the room are important. If a sofa is to go parallel to a wall section, is the wall section long enough to allow convenient side tables and to avoid a squeezed-in look? If it will project into the room, will it block traffic lanes? Alternative routes to seating positions allow people to move about at will.

The sofa, or sofas, usually set the scale for the rest of the room furnishings. Size alone is not the determinant, but the general treatment will be influential. The checklist for sofas will serve as a handy guide in actual selection.

Checklist for Sofas

1. How deep is it from front to back? _____
   Some sofas are so deep the short-legged cannot bend their knees if they sit back. Others are so shallow the long-legged have no support under the front part of the upper leg.
2. How low or high is the seat? _____
   Can you get up without support, or is it so high that you feel perched on it?
3. How soft or hard is it? _____
   Do you wallow in it, feel supported, or slide around on it?
4. How high are the arms? _____
   Some arms are at a convenient height for resting human arms while allowing access to a side table, but some are at shoulder height, protective but hemming the sitter in.
5. How high is the back? _____
   Does it give support to the shoulders or even the head?
6. How many people will it hold comfortably? _____
   A loveseat is adequate for two, who can then turn slightly toward each other and talk easily. A three-seat sofa will hold three people, but the middle person is apt to be left out of conversation. This is the most popular size, however, because it is long enough to stretch out on. A four or more seater compounds the problem of conversation for those in the middle and may give sitters the appearance of sparrows perched on a wire. Fronting such a long sofa with a long coffee table adds to the problem, effectively fencing the middle people into their isolation. Smaller coffee tables and facing seats will help.
7. How sturdy is the upholstery? _____
   A sofa gets a lot of use. The less wear and soil it shows, the longer it will remain attractive.
8. Are the arms upholstered, or of wood or other rigid material? _____
   Padded arms are, of course, comfortable, but people will put their hands on them, sitting and rising, and soil soon builds up. Wooden arms will be much easier to clean. Upholstered arms can be covered with small slipcovers, *if* the shape will allow it.

263. Chairs, even more than sofas, should be chosen for specific uses.

lounge chair/recliner

lounge chair/swivel

traditional easy chair

modern easy chair

wing chair

traditional pull-up chair

Chairs

Much that has been said about sofas applies to chairs as well, with this difference: Chairs are not so all-purpose, but they are more mobile. Their types include the following:

- **Lounge chairs** may be multiadjustable to recline, rock, swivel, even jiggle, with or without head and foot rests. Others are simply deeply upholstered, fairly large in size, and sometimes have a matching ottoman. Lounge chairs require a set placement in a room to allow for the stretched-out position of person or chair.
- **Easy chairs** are similar to lounge chairs but somewhat less cumbersome and without the mechanized functions. They are useful as comfortable but not competitive adjuncts to a sofa grouping.
- **Wing chairs** are a specialized type of easy chair that has been continuously popular in various versions since their introduction in the late 17th century. They support and protect the head and shoulders by a high back and adjacent wings.
- **Pull-up chairs,** as the name implies, are moved to where they are needed. They are often made of wood, metal, or plastic, with simple padding, shaped or slightly resilient seats. Pull-up chairs should be easy to grasp, light to lift, and strong enough to withstand carrying around.
- **Dining chairs** have for many years been sold in sets to match dining tables and often look out of place when moved to provide seating elsewhere. Whether the chairs match in style is less important than how the seat height relates to the table height to allow comfortable space for legs in between, and how much support they give for the fairly upright posture most of us like for eating.
- **Ottomans** are low upholstered seats without back or arms. They often double as leg rests, really a more comfortable use.
- **Floor cushions,** if they may be listed under chairs, work as padded seats on the floor for overflow crowds, or as pillows for floor lounging.

Choosing Chairs   Even more than sofas, chairs should be sat upon when buying them. The proportions shown in Figure 258 are general guidelines, but the actual design of the chair is all-important. How many times has a chair back poked into your backbone, provided support at the wrong places, or none at all? Many large chairs have casters for ease in moving them. Even more important, for the elderly or the handicapped person, might be casters on dining chairs to facilitate the double motion of sitting down and sliding the chair in—and its reverse.

Other than these guidelines, the generalizations about sofas apply.

modern pull-up chair

traditional dining chair

modern dining chair

chair with ottoman

Chairs for specific functions or of specialized type should be chosen with that in mind. A chair used for playing games at a card table will generally be more comfortable with a lower seat than a dining chair, because card tables are lower than dining tables. A desk chair should fit into the kneehole of a desk. A chair for use at a 36-inch-high kitchen counter will need to be higher than usual. A child's dining chair is best scrubbable and tip-proof. A delicate but valued antique should be placed where it can be seen but not too often abused by a heavyweight.

Beds

The bed is the most personal of all furniture. Individuals differ in their ideas about sleeping comfort, so the only way to find out whether a bed is right for you is to try it. You may find it hard to relax in the middle of a showroom floor, but it will be worth any slight embarrassment.

We have been conditioned to believe that a bed should have a springy foundation and a resilient mattress. The typical combination consists of a bulky box spring foundation topped by an innerspring or foam mattress. This is not the only possibility. Lightweight flat springs are less bulky, and often used in sofa-beds and bunk beds. A flat plywood foundation can also be comfortable if the mattress is thick enough, particularly for those who enjoy a very firm surface. Indeed, this is often a necessity for anyone with back trouble.

Innerspring Mattresses   Innerspring mattresses are still the most popular, probably because we are familiar with them. They vary in the number of coils, their design, whether or not the coils are individually pocketed, and their padding. All this affects their conformity—the way in which they respond to distributed body weight, which is an individual

265. A platform bed gives the user firm back support and becomes an integral part of the room's design. The emphasis here is on straight lines and uninterrupted areas of color, with variety provided by plants and the patterned bedspread. Chimacoff/Peterson, designers. (*Photograph: Norman McGrath*)

matter to be determined by trial. They are fairly heavy in weight and need to be turned to equalize wear.

The mattresses vary in firmness, with names (such as soft or orthopedic) supposedly giving guidance. There is no industry-wide agreement about what these terms mean.

Foam Mattresses   Lightweight in proportion to their size, and therefore more easily moved, foam mattresses harbor no insects or allergy producers. They, too, come in various degrees of resilience and actual inner design. They can also be made to order—cut to size in thickness and density desired, or even built up of layers of foam in different densities for greater comfort. The latter are particularly useful for custom installations, such as sleeping platforms.

The least expensive mattresses are thin pads of polyurethane foam that can be rolled up and stored when not in use.

Box Springs   With either innerspring or foam mattresses, if box springs are used, the industry strongly suggests getting coordinated sets, on the supposition that they are matched in firmness and probable length of service. The springs usually are supported on simple wood legs or on the more convenient metal frames on casters that permit easy moving.

Waterbeds   Once thought to be a fad, waterbeds remain a popular choice. They consist of a heavy-duty plastic water bag, a solid frame that supports the bag, a watertight liner between bed and frame to guard against floods, and a special heating pad to warm the water to a comfortable temperature. (The heating pad should bear the Underwriters' Laboratories label of safety testing.)

Waterbeds are firm and strongly supportive. They shape themselves to bodily contours, but quickly react to changes in position, which some people find disconcerting. They weigh a lot (1600 pounds for a standard-size model). This weight, however, is distributed evenly over the covered section of floor, rather than at spaced pressure points. Still, you may find it difficult to persuade a landlord of their safety. They present some problems in filling and emptying and need special sheets and bedcoverings.

Newer models have a smaller water bag encased in foam rubber, lightening the weight and easing bedmaking.

Buying Beds   These are some of the possibilities for the bodies of the beds. The actual beds chosen bring up many more decisions, most of them related to size.

From the smallest studio bed to the largest king size set, the space available is the main criterion. Figure 266 shows the most common sizes. But there are some other points to remember.

- People feel most comfortable in a bed at least 6 inches longer than they are tall.
- In double beds of any dimension, some people like more elbow room than others.
- Head and footboards add to floor space needed.
- Space for bedmaking is a factor, especially if the bed or one section at a time must swing out.

long king 76" x 84"

cot 30" x 75" | single 36" x 75" | twin 39" x 75" | ¾ size 48" x 75" | full 54" x 75" | queen 60" x 80" | king 76" x 80"

above: 266. Standard mattress sizes. (*Adapted from* Nomadic Furniture 1)

below: 267. Bunk beds are especially popular in children's rooms. These not only save space but take advantage of the placement of windows in the room. The fabrics on the beds add texture and liveliness. Kipp Stewart, designer. (*Photograph* © *Morley Baer*)

- Bunk beds make use of vertical space but require agility to make up the top bed.
- For safety's sake, a mattress should carry a label stating that it conforms to the flammability standard established by the Consumer Product Safety Commission *and* any state laws that apply. But the fire hazard is an extremely complicated problem, and it should be remembered that *cigarettes and any open flame* are potentially dangerous.

Checklist for Beds

1. Is the bed comfortable? _____
   This should be tested at the store by the person who will be using it, if at all possible.
2. Does the mattress have handles for ease in moving and turning? _____
3. Does the mattress have air vents to prevent mildew and odors? _____
4. Is the box spring finished on the underside with a layer of cloth to keep out dust? _____
5. Is there a written warranty, and for how long? _____
   Most are for ten or fifteen years.
6. Do the mattress and box spring meet flammability standards? _____

Tables and Desks

A flat surface supported above the floor at a convenient level is the essence of table design. Because we sit so much of the time, tables are inevitable. We need our food, eating implements, and working utensils up where we can reach them easily. This has resulted in a variety of tables that differ in specific function and therefore in size, shape, height, and materials. But some criteria remain constant. A table should have:

268. The table in this seaside home has a base taken from a barber stool. The table top can be raised or lowered as the occasion requires. Louis Mackall, architect. (*Photograph: Robert Perron*)

- the necessary strength, stability, durability for its task
- supports out of the way of legs and feet
- adaptability to its use or uses

Dining Tables   Figures 269 and 270 show standard sizes of rectangular and round dining tables, indicating the number of people they can seat. Beyond these specifications are some points on tables themselves:

- They should be sturdy and stable, not easily jarred.
- Supports should be spaced so that they do not interfere with the diners' legs; and the table height should allow leg room between the chair and the underside of the table.

The surface of a dining table is important. Much of the time it stands uncovered, a large noticeable expanse, so it should be pleasing and easy to keep looking its best. These days, many tables are set for dining with place mats, or even without, so appearance is always a factor. Ease of maintenance must also be considered, and this largely depends on the material. Wood and plastic surfacings of many kinds are the most common choices. Wood is expensive but beautiful; it needs polishing but can be refinished. Plastic is more durable, easy to wipe clean, less expensive, and often very attractive; but it is probably nonrepairable. The choice depends on circumstances.

Most dining tables are rectangular, from a basic square to elongated extension tables. They harmonize with the usual shape of the space and can be pushed snugly against a wall or into a corner. A round or oval table may seem more friendly and brings a welcome circular element. Round tables often can be extended to ovals by inserting leaves.

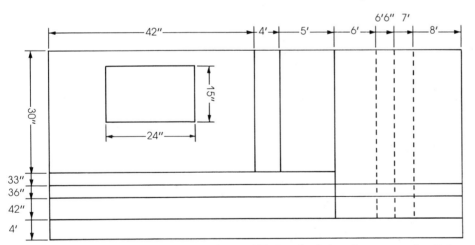

above: **269.** Standard sizes for rectangular dining tables. (*Adapted from* Nomadic Furniture 1)

below: **270.** Standard sizes for round dining tables. The figure in the center of each shows the number of people that can be seated comfortably. (*Adapted from* Nomadic Furniture 1)

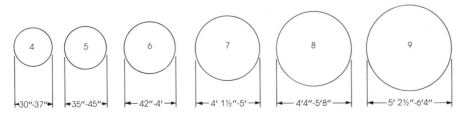

271. This square dining table could seat eight people comfortably. The director's chairs slide under the table even though they have arms. The hammock in the foreground emphasizes the casual feeling of the home. John Saladino, designer. (*Photograph: Norman McGrath*)

Any table that can be extended, either by inserting or raising leaves, should be tested for ease in manipulation and stability when extended. Also, check to see that the leaves match the table surface.

Coffee Tables Perhaps coffee tables should be called *sofa* tables, because no sofa seems complete without one these days, and they are only occasionally used for coffee. They are extremely useful, however, as a temporary resting place for snacks and any kind of drink. They also hold ashtrays, books, magazines, and accessories, as well as plants and sometimes flowers. Obviously, such tables need durable tops.

Height depends on the sofa, allowing for a comfortable reach with some footroom underneath. Length is another matter. If in scale with the sofa, a long table will block traffic, especially for the middle seating position(s). This problem can be overcome by substituting a number of smaller modular units that can be placed together or separated along the length of the sofa, as desired.

Some storage space—a shelf or drawers—will add to usefulness.

Occasional Tables We seem to need a surface, however small, within easy reach of each seat in a room. Occasional tables come in many sizes, shapes, and forms:

- **End** or **lamp tables** for use at the sides of sofas and chairs. These look better if they are about the same height as the arms of the unit they serve. But a somewhat lower or higher level may make them easier to reach and prevent spillage of liquids.
- **Console** or **sofa tables** are higher, longer, and designed to fit snugly against a wall or in back of a sofa.

- **Nesting, stacking,** and **television tables** that can be collapsed simplify entertainment, as do clusters of cubes or any other shapes that will fit together.
- **Cushions** in some modular furniture systems provide table space within the grouping.

Card and Game Tables Most people find it more comfortable to play cards or games at tables several inches lower than the standard dining table. Space permitting, a permanent card table, with at least two chairs handy, could be a fixture when games or casual eating are frequent. The old collapsible card table is ideal for occasional games, bridge luncheons, buffet suppers, and supplementary serving at dinner. Newer models have been updated in looks and sturdiness.

Kitchen Tables Once almost banished, kitchen tables have staged a comeback both as work tables (often butcher block) for meal preparation, and for eating in a family kitchen. They are, or should be, more durable and even more stable than dining tables, and they may have some storage built in. Kitchen tables should be accommodated to the height of the principal cook.

Desks Falling somewhere between a table and a storage unit, a desk serves as both. It can be a writing surface with only one or two drawers, a compartment in a modular storage unit, or a piece of furniture designed for writing, record keeping, and storage of papers and supplies.

The surface should be steady and well supported, particularly if it folds or slides out of the way, and at a convenient height for the person who uses it most frequently. These points should be well checked! (Most office desks are 29 inches high, a typewriter desk or pull-out shelf $26\frac{1}{2}''$. This may or may not be appropriate.)

A vertical file will store compactly all the pieces of paper related to household operations. It can be part of a desk; or a two-drawer file unit is a well-known means to an instant desk, with a piece of plywood for the top and a support of some kind at the other end.

The size and deployment of desks depends on the household. Some people find a small kitchen desk counter sufficient for their needs; those who do a lot of writing and record keeping may want more privacy, in their own room or a study. This is especially true for the older student. Young children may do better working around a kitchen or dining table, in the old-fashioned way.

A discussion of desks leads naturally into storage.

272. Simplicity of design places emphasis on the beauty of the wood and the way it has been joined. This is particularly noticeable in the round coffee table. (*Photograph courtesy John Adden Furniture*)

Storage Units

We store things by standing them on floors or shelves; by hanging them on clothes hangers, spaced on closet poles, or on hooks attached to walls; or by putting them in drawers or chests. Which of these solutions is best depends on the use, size, shape, fragility, and value of the objects. The profile in Chapter 1 should have established storage needs.

Efficient storage should be a part of architectural design. Most homes provide kitchen cupboards that range from barely adequate to superabundant and meticulously planned. Bathrooms usually have some storage provided, even if only a medicine chest.

Beyond these, we look for as many closets as we can find. With the disappearance of attics and basements, generous closet space is a neces-

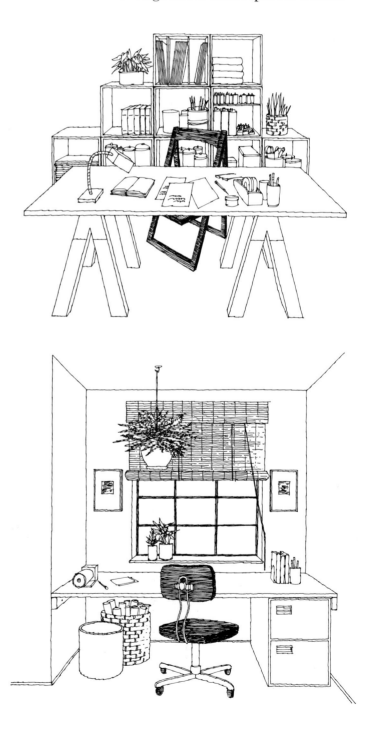

273. Desks can be made fairly easily. The desk above is nothing more than a piece of plywood resting on a file cabinet and a shelf unit. The trestle table (*above right*) is constructed from sawhorses and a board. An alcove provides a good setting for a work area (*right*). The desk is built in. Supports are hammered into the wall and a large board placed on top.

left: 274. A desk is often useful in the kitchen. This one takes up a minimum of space and might seem confining were it not for the opening onto the living room. Phyllis Martin-Vegue, designer. (*Photograph: Philip L. Molten*)

right: 275. Wire shelving creates a contemporary environment within an otherwise fairly traditional living room. Hugh Hardy, designer. (*Photograph: Norman McGrath*)

sity. Lacking enough closets, storage space can sometimes be devised by installing a wall of sliding doors across one end of a room, or more simply, by draping a curtain across the space.

But we also need more specific types of storage.

Shelves   Nearly every room can profit from some shelves—the simplest kind of storage unit. Books, art objects, collections, and stereo units go on open shelving that may be attached to the wall, part of a modular system, or a substantial bookcase unit. The important points to check are the stability of the shelves and the entire unit, coupled with flexibility. Shelves need to be adjustable to accommodate the various sizes that books come in and the often changing needs of an evolving music system. Sometimes a piece of sculpture will need an oversize space.

Although bookcases and stereo-television shelf stands (often called entertainment centers) come readymade, many people prefer to assemble them themselves from the variety of brackets, spacers, and shelves available at hardware and furniture stores. Modular systems consisting of shelves and matching cupboards and drawers are an excellent way of providing for mixed storage needs. (See Plate 39, p. 287.) Shelving can be an architectural asset, too:

- Low bookcases can double as tables and partial walls.
- If sufficiently long and well planned, a bookcase will unify a wall.
- A ceiling-height bookcase becomes a forceful wall element.
- Shelves can frame and relate doors and windows, or serve as freestanding partial or complete dividers.

Shelves are very revealing in more ways than one. Books and magazines, records and tapes, the extent of a music system, art objects or plants, perhaps the size of a television set, the neatness or disarray, say a lot about the household members to the discerning person. Sometimes, it is better to hide some of this behind closed doors—in cabinets.

276. This glass-front teak cabinet, by Scan, consists of modular units. The top keeps china free from dust. Separated, the bottom piece becomes a buffet. (*Photograph: Bengt Carlen*)

Cabinets   Shelves enclosed by doors, which may be either opaque or transparent, have the added advantage of keeping objects relatively free of dust, thus lessening maintenance. They have the same requirements of adjustability and stability that other shelving does.

- Swinging doors work easily and accept narrow storage racks on their inner surfaces, but they get in the way when open.
- Sliding doors open only part of the cabinet at a time and cannot be shelved, but they are a good solution when space is limited.

Kitchen and bathroom cabinets are now commonplace and almost always built in. Television and music system cabinets have had a short but erratic history. Because, unlike chairs and beds, they originally had no historical precedent, they have often been awkward in size and shape and are constantly being updated. We are coming more and more to take them for what they are—functional, highly engineered pieces of technology that can be attractive on their own terms. We accept the blank screen of the television set just as we do the unlit fireplace.

Chests and Drawers   The chest was the original piece of storage furniture, useful at home and easily carried along when traveling—no packing of bags required. Nowadays it is seen as a toy chest in a child's room and occasionally as a blanket chest in the bedroom. But a chest or trunk easily can double as a table in the social spaces.

Perhaps people became tired of delving into the depths for an elusive article and came up with the idea of dividing one large chest into a series of smaller ones, which could slide out and expose their contents. Chests of drawers now are available in a variety of stacked configurations and should be checked for these points:

- The drawers should be strongly joined and dustproof.
- They should slide easily and have handles that can be grasped without difficulty.
- Some shallow drawers are a convenience, as are flexible dividers.
- Modular units that can fit together in different combinations are space saving and simplify placement in changing situations.

These are the principal types of storage, supplemented, of course by closets, which are enclosed recesses in the shell of the house. Closets, however, can be fitted with any of the storage types mentioned, so that they become built-in furniture.

Built-In and Modular Furniture   The kitchen pioneered in the concept of built-in furniture. We now take for granted that specially designed drawers, cabinets, and closets with integrated kitchen appliances will line the cooking area. This system makes use of as much wall space as possible, while minimizing dirt-catching crevices. The idea moved on to other kinds of spaces as its usefulness became apparent, and may now include tables and seating or even sleeping units. Built-in furniture reduces the visual clutter of isolated pieces, stays in place, and becomes an integral part of the architecture. (See Plate 40, p. 287.)

The concept of built-in furniture—that everything fit exactly together—is the basis of modular furniture. Modular furniture, however, offers the added advantage of mobility and flexibility. Because the component pieces can be assembled into larger units, as desired, without any waste spaces between, they leave more free floor space.

1. Does the material look and feel smooth and clean? _____
2. Is the finish evenly applied, without a gummy buildup in crevices? _____
3. Is the grain uniform? _____
    Does it seem to flow over the surface? _____
4. Is the wood or other material all of the same color (unless designed to be otherwise)? _____
5. Are wood joints strong and reinforced by glue? _____
    Larger joints should be reinforced by triangular blocks screwed and glued in place to provide stability.
6. Are metal joints smooth and strong looking, or solidly riveted? _____
7. Are plastics smoothly molded in one continuous piece? _____
8. Do drawers move smoothly? _____
    Side and bottom guides help in this.
9. Are drawer pulls easy to grasp and firmly attached? _____
    Larger drawers should have two pulls so that the unit glides out without binding. If the pulls are indentations, they should be checked for ease of inserting fingers and applying pulling pressure.
10. Are drawers smoothly finished inside? _____
    This will prevent any snagging of contents.
11. Does the unit stand firmly on the floor and resist effort to make it wobble? _____
12. Are shelves adjustable and stable when repositioned? _____

Materials and Construction

Consumer groups long have advocated that manufacturers provide specifications with their products, so that we can have more information on what we are buying. Lacking these guidelines, you should look at every piece of furniture literally from every angle, applying what you already know about materials and construction. Then gather all possible information from salesclerks, and try to purchase from reputable stores that will stand behind their merchandise. Furniture can be no better than the materials, the joinings, and the finishes that go into its construction. Each material has its own qualities.

Wood

The standard furniture material is still wood. We keep coming back to wood, for nothing else seems quite to take its place. The different kinds of wood, their qualities and aptitudes have been covered in some detail in Chapter 9.

Here we will first focus briefly on furniture construction in wood—the ways wood can be joined. Whether done by hand or machine, this critically affects the durability and appearance of furniture (Fig. 278). This is particularly true of wood furniture, because wood has a tendency to expand, contract, and even change shape with temperature and age.

Until a few decades ago wood joints were a good sign of the level of craftsmanship. After a period in which joinings declined in both interest

277. Wood probably is used more than any other material for furniture. This chair, designed by Poul Cadovius, is made of varnished oak on beech laminate with wool upholstery. It exploits the ability of laminated wood to be bent and boldly exposes the lamination as a form of structural beauty. (*Photograph courtesy Cado/Royal System*)

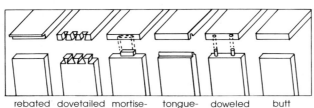

rebated dovetailed mortise- tongue- doweled butt
                     and-tenon and-groove

left: 278. The ways wood is joined critically affect the durability and appearance of furniture. The most typical joints are shown here, from the relatively weak butt joint to the strong dovetail.

and quality, we are now beginning to see again an emphasis on joints as part of structural design and beauty.

In the end, it is the exposed surface that is important. Fine hand-carving is beautiful but costly; machine carving has a uniformity that eventually is tedious. Much good-quality furniture relies chiefly on the finish of its handsomely grained, plain surfaces for its appeal.

A fine surface involves successive rounds of sanding, staining, glazing, oiling or waxing, and rubbing, rubbing, rubbing, as anyone who has refinished a piece of furniture well knows. This treatment results in a variety of finishes, according to the ingredients used, from the soft satiny sheen of an oil finish, through the glowing patina of wax, to the high gloss of so-called French polish. Each finish has its own beauty, its own degree of upkeep and durability (Table 9.2).

Metal

Metal seems to lend itself to mass-produced furniture; its construction is more suitable to machining than to handcrafting. As discussed in Chapter 9, it is relatively inexpensive, strong and durable, but not bulky.

Metal can be joined by welding, riveting, bolting; or it can simply be shaped. Most metal furniture is so much stronger than normal household use demands that its construction generally presents little of a problem to the consumer. However, repairs are much more difficult.

Steel with a baked-enamel finish is familiar in kitchen and bathroom cabinets, and is also popular for indoor-outdoor furniture because of its resistance to moisture. It is often mated with plastic either as melamine tops or vinyl upholstery, for hard-use areas such as family rooms. Steel comes in many colors, is easy to wash, and maintains its good appearance if not kicked or banged.

Chromium-plating gives steel lasting protection and surfaces that range from glittering hardness to pewterlike mellowness. Aluminum is rainproof, sunproof, and cool to the touch, lightweight, and available in color—ideal for terrace furniture.

Occasionally, metal is used for more formal furniture. It has been fashioned into original designs based on the sculptural potentialities of the material. More often, the rigidity of metal even when thin has prompted its use as lamp bases, the frames of glass tables, and the supports of some modular storage systems.

279. The Miës van der Rohe lounge chair, designed in the 1920s, is constructed with a polished stainless steel frame and saddle leather straps supporting leather-covered foam upholstery. It is a perfect example of metal's tensile strength and sculptural potential. (*Photograph courtesy Knoll International*)

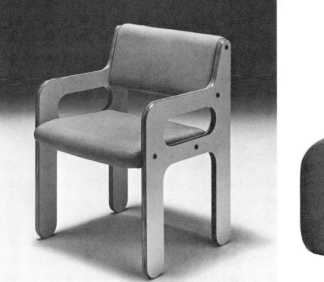

Plastics

Synthetic materials have markedly affected furniture design and maintenance. As suggested in Chapter 9, plastics can be invented to meet almost any kind of need. Vinyl upholstery and laminated melamine table tops are durable and wipe clean. Plastic chairs and tables can be lightweight, strong yet slightly resilient, and molded in one piece, thus eliminating the need for joining. Transparent or translucent plastics, such as Plexiglas and Lucite, offer designers opportunity for a totally new vocabulary in furniture design.

Foamed plastics have revived the bulky look in furniture, but it is bulk without weight. These cellular plastics are very versatile. Density can be controlled to produce either rigid structural parts or soft cushioning. Or shaped slabs of foams in different densities can be assembled and glued together. Integral-skin foams eliminate separate upholstery.

All these offer exciting possibilities for new design and above all for low-maintenance furniture. But we do not have all the answers yet. To date, repair or refinishing runs from difficult to impossible. Problems resulting from flammability—from actual flames or toxic gasses—and ultimate waste disposal have still to be worked out.

To be sure, these are common problems with wood and metal also, but the natural materials have been around longer, so their dangers, their environmental insult probabilities, and recycling possibilities, are fairly well known. With plastics we must learn as we go, always insisting on more thorough testing and disclosure.

Upholstered Furniture

The term "upholstery" comes from the same root as "uphold," and that is just what it does. It may be a simple piece of fabric stretched across a frame to hold us up in a seated position, or an extremely complicated assemblage of springs, padding, and fabrics that insulates our bodies from a hard chair. Different upholstery results in varying comfort.

Fabrics Stretched on a Frame   One of the earliest types of chairs—furniture with backs and seats of leather or fabric—is still useful today. Such a piece provides lightweight, inexpensive resilience, can often be folded up for moving or storage, and is extremely easy to reupholster.

Woven cane, rush, wicker, or rattan for furniture seats and backs, often teamed with the same materials made into the framework, are also popular. These materials provide the natural look and a slight resilience,

left: 280. The Karin armchair, designed by Gunter Eberle, is made of plywood laminated with melamine for easy maintenance. (*Photograph courtesy Vecta Contract*)

right: 281. Modular furniture has gained in popularity, largely because of the ease with which it can be moved around. This chair, from the Tappo Seating System designed by John Mascheroni, is upholstered in wool. Additional units can be put together to form a sofa. (*Photograph courtesy Vecta Contract*)

282. The back and seat of this chair are canvas, stretched on a frame of beech. This type of furniture is useful because of the way it can be taken apart for storage or moving. It remains practical after centuries of existence. (*Photograph courtesy Cado/Royal System*)

283. Stuffing-and-spring upholstery has several components, shown here in a cross-section drawing.

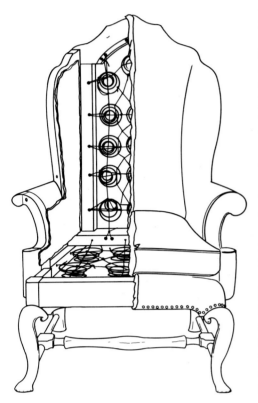

in a range of prices from very low to quite expensive. Intricate caning, for example, is costly and becomes very formal in some applications.

Separate cushions, if desired, will add to comfort. In any event, the frame on which the fabric or caning is stretched should be strong as well as attractive (since it is so visible), the upholstery durable and securely fastened to the frame but easily removable if that is the design.

Simple Padding   The next step in comfortable seating would be padding of thin layers of resilient materials, covered with fabric and secured to a frame. Until recently, long curled hair was the best padding, with kapok, moss, and cotton used for less expensive pieces. Today, various types of foam padding are more common, placed on a plywood base, on webbing, or on a sling of fabric.

The great versatility of foam has resulted also in much thicker pads, which have taken the place of springs and stuffing for many sofas and chairs. The pads are supported simply by plywood or webbing. Sometimes foam pads become a piece of furniture in themselves, of one piece, or perhaps held together by buckles or straps.

For either of these types, removable covers (either zippered or the newly popular shirred—gathered and tied) make cleaning and replacement easy.

Stuffing and Springs   Furniture designers began to place springs under stuffing during the 18th century. But it was not until about 1914 that massively overstuffed pieces came into fashion. The materials and steps of this complicated process are shown in Figure 283. The exact number of steps will vary with the manufacturer and the cost. Except for the covering upholstery, it is all hidden from view anyway, but it does have a bearing on comfort and durability.

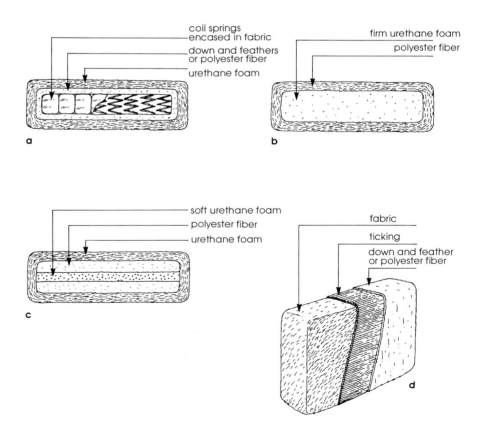

284. Seat and back furniture pillows can be made of coil springs encased in fabric, covered with foam, down, and other stuffing (**a**). Less expensive pillows are made of firm foam between two layers of soft foam (**b**) or dense foam with polyester fiberfill (**c**). Back pillows (**d**) may be down- and feather-filled or filled with polyester fiber or bits of foam.

Cushions and Pillows   Where once most upholstery was firmly fastened to the frame, now separate cushions may be used for the seat and back, even arms, to make the piece of furniture even more comfortable and adjustable to the human body. Down (and feathers) remain the most luxurious stuffings, but they retain their squashed look long after the sitter has departed.

Newer types of cushions may have a core of coil springs or firm urethane foam covered by softer layers of foam and perhaps a wrap of polyester or even a layer of down encased in ticking (Fig. 284). Different versions and densities may be used for sitting and support cushions. Back and arm cushions are often softer and perhaps filled with ground-up foam or polyester fill. One of the main benefits of their design is that they spring back to their original contours.

Loose pillows, often added as enrichment, serve a useful purpose in filling in hollows and giving support for individual positions. They tend nowadays to be of some sort of fiberfill or of foam.

Upholstery Fabrics   Fabrics become almost an integral part, and the most conspicuous part, of the furniture to which they are fastened. They are what we touch. Some furniture today is completely upholstered, covering even the legs.

The least we should expect is that upholstery look comfortable to sit on, feel good to hands and arms, and resist abrasion and soil. Visual relationship to the shape it covers and the setting in which it is placed

285. The same piece of furniture can take on very different characteristics depending on the upholstery fabric used. Velvet (*left*) seems more plush, appropriate, perhaps, for a bedroom or parlor. Leather (*right*) gives a rugged look to the same chair, which now fits in with the furnishings of a den.

lifts it above mere usefulness. Beyond this are fabrics with their own distinctive character, used creatively.

To assess the role of upholstery in the overall look of a piece of furniture, we have only to look at a chair covered with different fabrics (Fig. 285). In choosing upholstery, remember the effects of color hue and value, of emphasis and scale in design, both for individual pieces and as part of an ensemble. The total identity of a room can be altered with different covers. This transformation is sometimes used to advantage when furniture is slipcovered for a cool summer look or for a change.

Most important is deciding on the fabric itself. Chapter 10 discusses many of the fibers and weaves available. Then it is a matter of searching for a textile that is pleasing to you or your client, within the range of acceptable fibers and weaves. Finally, you must assess a fabric for its intended use.

Recently, the International Fabricare Institute announced a voluntary code to be adopted by manufacturers to guide consumers in cleaning and caring for upholstered pieces. It was suggested that a tag be attached to each piece, labeling the fabric as follows:

- **W**—Clean with the foam only of an upholstery shampooer or other water-base cleaner specifically designed for upholstery. Do not use laundry products, household cleaners, or solvents.
- **S**—Clean with a water-free solvent dry-cleaning product. Do not use detergent or water-base solvent cleaners, which may cause excessive shrinking or permanent stains. (Petroleum-distillate-base products should be used in a well-ventilated room. Avoid products containing carbon tetrachloride, which is highly toxic.)
- **S-W**—Clean with only the foam of an upholstery shampoo or use a water-free solvent dry-cleaning product.
- **X**—Clean by frequent vacuuming or brushing only. Do not use water-solvent or detergent-base cleaners of any kind, for they can cause shrinking or fading.

All upholstered pieces should carry this information: manufacturer, fiber content, composition of fiber fill and cushioning, care instructions, colorfastness, shrinkage and spot-stain resistance.

Cost will be a deciding factor in choice of upholstery. The price range is wide, but cost should be pro-rated, within the bounds of the budget, over its probable life. The life of upholstery, however, is not limited to its physical condition. Perhaps a change of taste or circumstance will suggest a change of upholstery before the original is worn.

Checklist for Upholstery

1. Does the upholstery fit properly along the edges of the piece and at corners? _____
2. Do cushions align properly with the edges? _____
3. If there is a skirt, does it fall cleanly? _____
4. Does the fabric fit smoothly over the surface (unless intentionally gathered)? _____
5. Are cleaning instructions provided? _____
6. Has the fabric been treated for soil resistance? _____

This chapter has dealt with furniture in a general way. We turn now to a consideration of the specific furnishing needs for different types of rooms or spaces, and the ways in which furniture can be arranged.

Social
Spaces

12

The social spaces in any home are the gathering places where people come together to talk, to eat, to play games, to entertain and be entertained. Most homes, throughout history and around the world, have centered on such spaces where the family assembles and friends are welcomed.

Our needs for companionship and recreation take many forms—parties, reading, making or listening to music, watching television, various home crafts and hobbies, children's play. Each activity makes different demands on space and the arrangement of furniture in that space. After deciding which activities apply to the household in question, the designer should think through the requirements and possible consequences of them. The profile in Chapter 1 should have answered many questions about the uses of this space.

The emphasis given to each group pursuit varies from individual to individual and from household to household. Furthermore, priorities inevitably change as the years pass. The social space that makes ample provision for small children's play should assume a different character when those children are grown.

286. Social spaces should be designed so that the entire family, as well as guests, will be comfortable. A large room can be divided into areas for different activities.

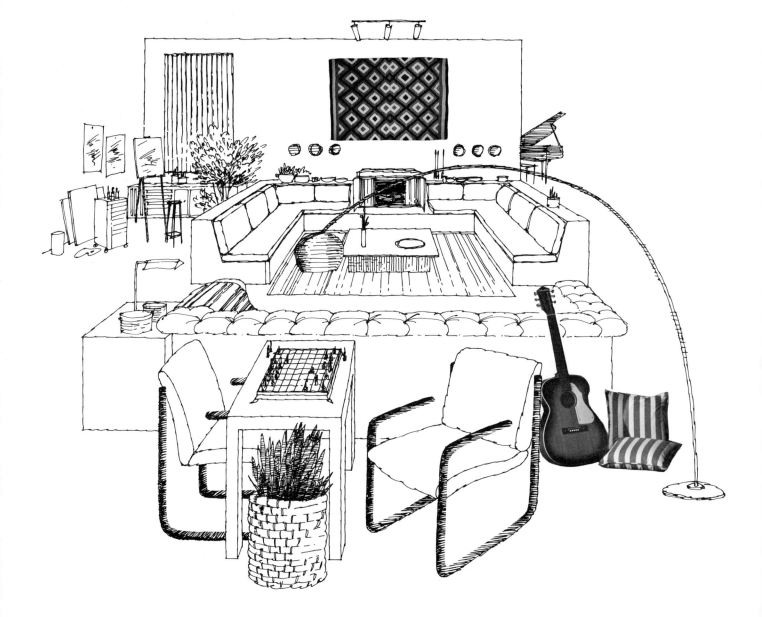

Because none but the very wealthy can provide for all kinds of activities equally well, most people must decide which should be given priority, then plan accordingly. The placement of the furnishings can then be designed so that the space will function well both for daily living and for special occasions.

Arranging Furniture

A working knowledge of the sizes and shapes of specific pieces of furniture helps in evaluating and planning a room, as does familiarity with recommended clearances between pieces, between furniture and walls, and so on.

Figure 287 shows a selection of typical furniture pieces drawn to a scale of $\frac{1}{4}$ inch equals 1 foot. Table 12.1 lists a range of furniture sizes

Table 12.1
Furniture Sizes and Clearance Spaces

Living Room	Small			Large	
	depth	width		depth	width
sofa	2'6″	× 6'	to	3'	× 9'
love seat	2'6″	× 4'	to	3'	× 5'
easy chair	2'6″	× 2'4″	to	3'4″	× 3'3″
pull-up chair	1'6″	× 1'6″	to	2'	× 2'
coffee table, oblong	1'6″	× 3'	to	3'	× 5'
coffee table, round	2' diam.		to	4' diam.	
coffee table, square	2'	× 2'	to	4'	× 4'
occasional table	1'6″	× 10″	to	3'	× 1'8″
card table	2'6″	× 2'6″	to	3'	× 3'
flattop desk	1'6″	× 2'8″	to	3'	× 6'
secretary	1'6″	× 2'8″	to	2'	× 3'6″
upright piano	2'	× 4'9″	to	2'2″	× 5'10″
grand piano	5'10″	× 4'10″	to	9'	× 5'2″
bookcase	9″	× 2'6″	to	1'	× —
clearances					
traffic path, major	4'	to 6'			
traffic path, minor	1'4″	to 4'			
foot room between seating units and edge of top of coffee table	1'				
floor space in front of chair or sofa for feet and legs	1'6″	to 2'6″			
chair or bench space in front of desk or piano	3'				

Dining Area	Small			Large	
	depth	width		depth	width
table, square, 4–8 people	2'6″	× 2'6″	to	5'	× 5'
table, rectangle, 6–12 people	3'	× 5'	to	4'	× 8'
table, round, 4–10 people	2'7″ diam.		to	6'4″ diam.	
straight chairs	1'4″	× 1'4″	to	1'8″	× 1'8″
arm chairs	1'10″	× 1'10″	to	2'	× 2'
buffet	1'8″	× 4'	to	2'	× 6'
serving table	1'6″	× 3'	to	2'	× 4'
china cabinet	1'6″	× 3'	to	1'8″	× 4'
clearances					
space for occupied chairs	1'6″ to 1'10″				
space to get into chairs	1'10″ to 3'				
traffic path around table and occupied chairs for serving	1'6″ to 2'				

287. Becoming familiar with furniture sizes and shapes is an important early step in planning arrangements. Here, each square represents 1 foot. (*Adapted from a drawing by Victor Thompson*)

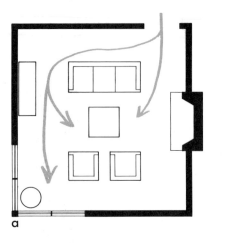
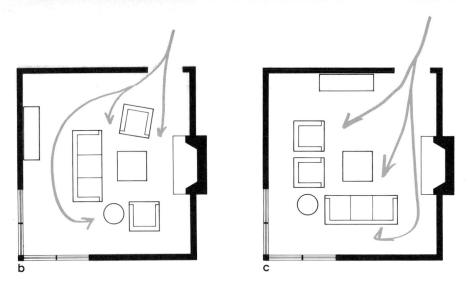

288. Furniture placement creates traffic patterns within a room. The arrangement in **a** is cumbersome. The sofa blocks the main view into the room. Although privacy is afforded for conversation, moving around would be difficult. In **b** the sofa is better placed, since there is room for circulation. A living room should welcome people into the conversation area; the best arrangement is shown in **c**.

and shapes. It must be remembered that these are usual sizes, commonly available in stores. Custom, built-in, and free-form pieces vary widely.

The first step in planning furniture arrangements is to list all the activities that need to be provided for, the furnishings and equipment each requires. Then, using the knowledge gained in Chapter 2 about drawing to scale, you can begin to plan specific room arrangements.

Finally, there should be an evaluation of the results in terms of both practicality and aesthetics. The individual arrangements should meet the requirements, should work as a whole, with good traffic patterns. A pleasing design should be evident.

Successful interior design requires more than simply the practical application of knowledge. Imagination and perhaps some role-playing enable us to test the results of different placements and find which work best. Put people into a seating arrangement. Are those in certain positions hemmed in? How easy would it be to pass snacks? Could small chairs be pulled up to enlarge the major group if desired? This brings us back again to the role of activities.

Leisure and Entertainment

What will people be doing in the social spaces of the home? Here they spend a good part of their leisure time. What activities will they engage in? How should one arrange furniture to support these activities?

Conversation

The most pervasive social activity is conversation. When people get together, they talk—anyplace in the home, but especially in the social spaces. This is so natural an activity that we take it for granted and do not always consider the specific situations that make for pleasant and easy dialogue among family and friends.

Studies of small-group interaction have shown that people like to sit opposite each other when talking, at some slight angle, unless there is too much space between. Then they choose to sit side by side.[*] The elements encouraging conversation are:

- **Arrangement of seats and tables** in a generally circular or elliptical pattern so that each person can look at others easily and talk

---

[*] Robert Sommer, *Personal Space: The Behavioral Basis of Design*, p. 66.

289–290. These two living rooms are in the same housing complex but have been arranged and personalized differently. Fisher-Friedman Associates, architects. (*Photographs: Joshua Freiwald*)

right: 289. A sofa facing the fireplace gives the effect of intimacy by closing off space.

without strain. A diameter of 8 to 10 feet across the seating area has proved the most desirable.

- **Comfortable seats** for each person—a minimum of one good seat for each household member and additional ones for guests.
- **Surfaces**—tables, shelves, and so on—on which to rest things.
- **Light** of moderate intensity with highlights at strategic points.
- **Space** sufficient for the usual number of people who are present. This is fairly easy to arrange in the average home in what we might call the primary seating group.

Primary Seating Group The major conversation center is typically the primary and dominant seating group in the home. The furniture is usually, although not always, stabilized in some way around a sofa. It could be in a corner, around a window wall or fireplace, or built up into a substantial arrangement.

290. This arrangement is more open than the one in Figure 289, encouraging people to walk in and sit down, as well as stimulating conversation.

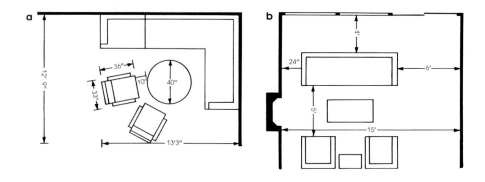

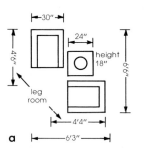

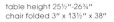

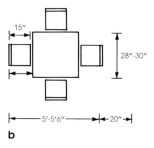

above: 291. Furniture in the major group space can be arranged in different ways depending on the desired effect. The grouping in **a** shows a large corner sofa with coffee table and occasional chairs. In a room with a fireplace (**b**) the sofa and easy chairs face each other and are at right angles to the fireplace.

below: 292. Special needs can be met in a room large enough to have a secondary seating group. Two easy chairs flank a table with a reading lamp (**a**); in **b** a game table with four chairs is set up.

When a home has only one such relaxation area, this grouping must also serve for music, television, reading, buffet suppers, even games.

Secondary Seating Group   In large rooms, the dominant seating arrangement is often supplemented by a secondary conversation or reading group. Centering on a recliner or two, or a few comfortable but smaller chairs, such a grouping occupies a subdominant position.

Such arrangements also are useful in encouraging the ebb and flow of a successful party, offering as they do alternative seating possibilities.

Reading

Some people can read anywhere, under any circumstances. But most of us prefer tranquility when we read. Quiet and comfort seem essential:

- **Seating** that is resilient but not sleep-inducing. It should give adequate support to the back and, for maximum comfort, to the neck and arms as well.
- **Light** coming over one shoulder, either moderately strong daylight or artificial light that illuminates the room and concentrates fairly intense but diffused light on the reading material.
- **Security** from distracting sights, sounds, and household traffic.

Tables or other surfaces nearby, accessible shelves to hold books and magazines, and enough space to stretch the eyes occasionally add to reading comfort. Such conditions, which are adequate for more or less casual reading, can be provided in most living rooms. More demanding reading or study may suggest retreat to a den or bedroom.

Music

For many today, music is a major part of life. It may come from a small radio or cassette player, but increasingly, music in the home has become centered on a complex arrangement of stereo components that require considerable space. Further, the space must be flexible, because the number and shape of the parts change as new designs become available and as the listeners' sophistication increases.

Many people enjoy playing instruments—making their own music. Small instruments, such as guitars, pose few problems. The placement of a piano, however, is a major design consideration. Should it be in the living room, a family room, studio, or den? How should it be placed? The curved side should always face the listeners. When the top is raised, this will project sound toward them.

Serious musicians may want a separate music center—in a corner, an alcove, or even a whole room—where everything can be kept together and out of the way of other activities.

People who have great concern for the quality of sound may wish further refinements. The arrangement, composition, and shape of a room are important acoustically. Recommended are:

- **Seating** so arranged that listeners hear a *balanced* projection from instruments or multiple speakers.
- **Space** shaped to enhance sound. Sound engineers have long known that musical sounds have a finer quality in rooms whose opposite walls are not parallel to each other, or in which the space is broken up in some way.
- **Materials** chosen and placed for their acoustical qualities. Materials are sound-reflecting or "live" if they bounce sound, as does plaster or glass; and sound-absorbing or "dead" if they soak up sound— heavy draperies, rugs, books, cork, or other so-called acoustical materials. Too many live materials give strident amplification and reverberation. Too many dead surfaces rob music of its brilliance. For best results, live surfaces should face dead surfaces.

293. A living room can also be a place to enjoy live music. Ideally, a piano should be placed as far away as possible from windows and radiators. The piano in this living room is well-placed either for casual listening or for an arrangement in which chairs can be pulled up for a more formal concert. The bare floor and lowered ceiling directly above the piano are acoustically good. (*Photograph: Ezra Stoller © ESTO*)

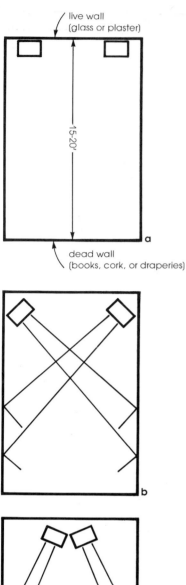

294. Stereo speakers should be mounted on a live wall, such as plaster, that reflects sound (**a**). Speakers also should face a dead wall—one with books, cork, or draperies. A length of 15 to 20 feet between walls is preferred. In a small room, speakers work best on the shorter wall. Movable speakers (**b**) permit various positionings. Common box loudspeakers should be placed in corners facing into the room. They could also be placed to reflect off side walls or toward the ceiling at a 45-degree angle (**c**).

Placement of Stereo Components   For the dedicated stereo buff, the placement of the various components can become a science beyond the scope of this book. In general, however:

- The tuner and record player and/or tape deck should be separated from the speakers, so that the operator can balance the sound—next to impossible when they are close by. This also lessens annoying vibrations.
- The speakers should be mounted in or placed against a live wall facing a dead one. Their exact placement depends on the size of the room and the positions of the listeners, among other factors.
- Storage space for a growing library of records and tapes will help keep them in good condition.

Television, Movies, and Slides

The theater, movie house, concert hall, sports field, and even the classroom have come into our homes and altered our living patterns. Television primarily, but also movies and slides, have become important sources of home entertainment. This is a problem we have not always come to terms with. Television viewing is often treated as an afterthought, even though it may be a major home activity. As a result, the set is not well integrated into the total room design, from the standpoint of style, placement, or viewing.

Placement demands are fairly simple but may well shift the main focus of the room:

- **Seating** requirements are much like those for conversation and reading, except that the seating should be placed within a 60-degree angle of the screen to avoid distortion. Easily moved or swivel chairs offer flexibility; backrests or cushions on the floor increase a room's seating capacity.
- **Height of screen** should be as near eye level as possible.
- **Lighting** of low intensity is desirable, especially for watching television, but the light should shine neither on the screen nor in the viewers' eyes.
- **Acoustical** control primarily relates to those who do not care to listen. This can mean placing the television set in the family room, leaving the living room free of its pervasive presence, or having smaller sets in bedrooms or kitchen.

The design of television cabinets is only beginning to catch up with design of the inner components. Small sets are accepted as functional, modern pieces of equipment, but many of the larger console sets are still cumbersome boxes whose styling rarely fits well into any home. This limits their placement. According to size and design, the following are possibilities:

- **Mounted in walls,** a set can be treated as part of the wall design or hidden behind doors. Provision must be made, however, for venting, to allow heat generated during operation to escape.
- **Mounted on a portable stand,** a set can be pushed from place to place as needed. This precludes a permanent hookup to an outside antenna and may expose the unpleasant back of the set to view.
- **Mounted on a swivel base,** a set can be turned to face in several directions according to viewers' needs.

right: Plate 39. Built-in shelves serve not only for storage but also for displaying paintings, ceramics, and other objects. Moore/Turnbull, architects. (*Photograph: © Morley Baer*)

below: Plate 40. Sofas were built into the wall to frame the fireplace. Ceramic tile was used for the sofa supports, as well as on the floor. Charles Moore and Dimitri Vedensky, architects. (*Photograph: © Morley Baer*)

Plates 41–43. These three apartments are in a single condominium structure. Although they have the same basic layout, they show the differences in design that come from personalizing social spaces. Wong and Brocchini, architects. (*Photographs: Joshua Freiwald*)

left: Plate 41. This apartment is smaller than the other two, but the furniture was scaled down to make it appear larger. Instead of sofas, two dark brown love seats were placed on either side of the fireplace. The drop-leaf table can be expanded when necessary.

Plate 42. In contrast to Plates 41 and 43, the arrangement of the large sofas and two large lounge chairs takes advantage of the entire open space of the living area. Shallow dark bookcases surround the fireplace. They are sparsely filled, however, giving a more open effect, with shelves for the display of objects and paintings. The tile-patterned carpet adds to the casual flavor.

Plate 43. The slanted ceiling of a top-floor apartment gives it extra height. White love seats face each other over a large rectangular coffee table, while two big floor cushions provide extra seating. Tall bookshelves frame the fireplace. An ethnic flavor is provided by the rugs, cushions, and blankets.

left: **Plate 44.** A beautiful antique four-poster bed is the focal point in this bedroom. The other old-fashioned furniture contrasts with the contemporary style of the walls and the staircase outside. James Terril, architect. (*Photograph: Ezra Stoller © ESTO*)

below: **Plate 45.** A simple, old-fashioned bathroom was transformed by the introduction of bold primary colors. Robert A. M. Stern, architect. (*Photograph: John T. Hill*)

- **Relating a television set to a fireplace** usually gives an unobstructed view from the major seating group.
- **Large console sets** must go where space and a hookup are available.

Screens for movies or slides fold easily for storage. However, a permanently mounted screen that rolls up behind a cornice or other fixture near the ceiling is useful when home projection is frequent.

Home Entertainment Area   Increasingly, as home entertainment has come to involve more and more elements, a special area has evolved in which the various components can be placed and the necessary storage of equipment provided. Starting as a bookcase in which to keep reading material, this unit has grown into a storage wall housing a whole audio-visual center. It may also serve for a wide range of storage needs for games and dining, and even as display space.

Besides serving these very practical needs, an entertainment center can function as focus, perhaps balancing the fireplace wall or the dominant furniture grouping. Or it may be integrated with either of these, building up into a forceful statement.

295–296. A seating cave by owner/architect Wendell H. Lovett contains multiuse space for reading and home entertainment.

right: 295. One wall has a built-in television set; the other has stereo equipment.

below right: 296. The cave also can be used as a mini-theatre. The window shade pulls down to serve as a screen for viewing slides.

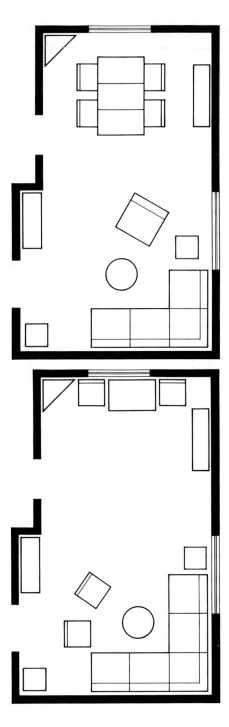

Quiet Indoor Games

Bridge, backgammon, and chess require concentration. Many other games benefit from quiet surroundings and the right furniture, such as:

- a well-illuminated table, about $2\frac{1}{4}$ feet high
- upright chairs, arranged in a spot free from distractions
- a folding card table and chairs, or the dining table and chairs

Some people never play cards, so the question of where to place such a set-up does not arise. But those for whom bridge or some other game is almost a way of life will want as permanent an arrangement as possible, perhaps in one corner of the living or family room.

Active Indoor Entertainment

Many households survive quite well without any provision for vigorous entertainment, such as dancing, ping-pong, or pool. But for those who do like such lively pursuits, the main requirements are plenty of space, a durable floor, and furniture that can be pushed out of the way.

The family room, and increasingly community social spaces, are the preferred locations.

Outdoor Entertainment

Many city balconies are used mainly for the safekeeping of bicycles and wheeled toys, but a couple of chairs, a table, and a few plants can expand limited outdoor space, both physically and visually.

A larger deck, patio, terrace, or porch, however, can function as another room, lessening the burden on the indoor space or simply as an alternative social area. Its furnishings are usually lightweight, durable, and easily cleaned, to cope with sun, rain, dust, and informality.

above: 297. If furniture is to be moved around frequently to make space for dancing or other activities, a flexible furniture arrangement is desirable. Modular furniture on casters and a drop-leaf table are particularly adaptable.

right: 298. A terrace can function as an extra room. The easy-care furniture could also be used indoors in cold weather, perhaps in a tiled garden/sitting room. (*Photograph courtesy Meadowcraft*)

Children

The ways of children change quickly from active play to quiet. They need space to interact with other children, and places in which to be alone. They may want to be with the family or secede from it. Basic needs of a child's play area are space; access to the bathroom, the outdoors, and adult supervision; light, warmth, and fresh air. Walls, floors, and furniture should take hard use gracefully.

A family room, by any name, is one obvious solution. It is generally furnished with durability and versatility in mind and may well be near the kitchen or children's bedrooms. Its aspect can change as children grow, perhaps into a retreat for teenagers, and finally into an alternative adult social space.

Furniture arrangements follow no set patterns except as they apply to activities considered earlier—with adaptability paramount.

Another solution is to make children's own rooms multipurpose. By judicious planning—bunk beds or creation of a sleeping loft, plus plenty of built-in storage—a sizable area can often be left open for active play.

Dining

Meals are often the only daily events that bring an entire household together. Entertaining friends almost always involves food, ranging from a simple snack to a multicourse dinner.

Just how open or closed the dining area should be depends on the space available and the life style of the household. In many homes, instead of one totally separate dining room, two or more dining spaces merge with other areas, to be used as circumstances indicate. A living-dining room, plus eating space in the kitchen, is a common solution.

The household that entertains frequently with rather formal dinners may want a completely separate dining space where the table can be screened from view during setting and clearing.

299. A multipurpose bedroom/playroom for children includes bunk beds (at left). A ladder at the back of the room leads to a platform in front of the window. There is plenty of storage space, including bars suspended from the ceiling to hold large toys. Charles Moore and Dimitri Vedensky, architects. (*Photograph © Morley Baer*)

300. A three-bedroom townhouse in Amherst Fields condominiums has a family kitchen on the first floor, open yet screened by high counters from the dining area. The accessories all contribute to the rustic feeling created by exposed beams and the built-in furniture. Callister, Payne & Bischoff, architects. Virginia Anawalt/Marianne Myers, interior designers. *(Photograph: Ezra Stoller © ESTO)*

A certain flexibility in dining areas is helpful today, considering the ways in which we eat. Although we still think of the family sit-down meal as the norm—or wish it could be—the National Restaurant Association predicts that, within the next eight years, the eating-out market is likely to take 50 cents of every food dollar. Even in the home, "fast food" is increasingly used, with corresponding changes in where the food is prepared and eaten.

left: 301. The transparency of glass is exploited in this dining/conservatory area. Sunlight, filtered through the plants, reflects off the glass table. Warren Platner, designer. *(Photograph: Ezra Stoller © ESTO)*

below: 302. In a dining area adjoining an open kitchen the furniture arrangement makes the space seem more flexible. The ends of the table fold down, and the table can be pushed against the wall for maximum open space. Exposed beams, hanging lights, and open shelves also contribute to the casual atmosphere. Moore, Grover, Harper, designers. *(Photograph: Norman McGrath)*

Sit-Down Meals

Ideally, there should be one adequately large, relatively permanent area planned so that the table can be set, the meal served and eaten, and the table cleared with a minimum of interference to and from other activities. This gathers the household in a way no other single activity does.

A dining area large enough to permit extension of the table, perhaps with one side opening into another portion of space, allows for celebrations and parties. The essentials are:

- **A surface or surfaces** on which to put food and utensils, usually 27 to 30 inches high but lower when indicated. The ages and physical conditions of various group members are important. Limber young people can be happy at low tables that would be uncomfortable for many older people. Small children are safer at child-size tables.
- **Seats** giving comfortable, usually upright support, such as chairs, stools, built-in or movable benches, or sitting platforms, all *scaled to the height of the table.* Chairs on casters are helpful to the elderly.
- **Light,** natural and artificial, that illuminates without glare.
- **Ventilation,** free of drafts, helps keep the space fresh.

To these essentials we quickly add that:

- Convenience to kitchen and dish storage saves steps.
- Freedom from noise gives a peaceful atmosphere.
- Pleasant surroundings and table settings add another dimension to these daily rituals.

Buffet Meals

Buffets simplify the labor of serving food and make it possible to use the entire social space for eating. All of this leads to a lively informality.

If such meals are to be handled often and successfully, cafeteria procedures give guidance:

- service counters near the kitchen
- good carrying trays
- durable dishes and glassware
- traffic paths that avoid collisions between tray-laden people
- convenient places to sit and surfaces on which to rest food

Snacks and "Fast Foods"

Some households rarely eat "meals" at all. Their life styles may call for a series of snacks, cold or heated fast-foods, for one or more people, at frequent intervals throughout the day. When members function on different time schedules, this system may be inevitable.

The primary goals in planning space for eating, then, will be speed and economy of effort. A minimum of interference with other activities is also important.

- **A counter and stools** adjacent to the cooking area of the kitchen often work well.
- **A small dining table** and chairs, near a supplementary fast-food preparation unit, either at one end of the kitchen or in a family room, will reduce congestion in the kitchen proper.

right: **303.** This kitchen area has room for two dining arrangements. A counter and stools serve for casual meals or snacks. A wonderful old plank table is used for more formal meals. Tod Williams, architect. (*Photograph: Norman McGrath*)

below: **304.** Shown are four of the many possible arrangements of dining furniture. A rectangular table (**a**) or a round table (**b**) can be placed in the center of the room. The short side of a rectangular table can be placed against a wall (**c**). In **d**, seating is built in along two sides of a table.

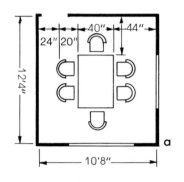

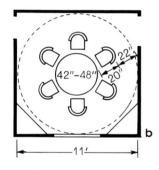

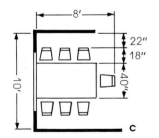

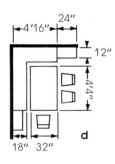

Dining Arrangements

Dining tables and seats, no matter where they are placed, can be arranged only in so many ways. Figure 304 gives furniture sizes, space needed to allow elbow room and easy access, and possible placements. Some of the latter are more workable than others, but all are somewhat dictated by the space available.

- **A rectangular or round table** in the center of a space allows easy access and simplifies serving.
- **A table with one end against the wall** takes less floor space and fits into the room architecturally.
- **A table and seating in a corner,** especially if built-in, requires minimum space but access is more complicated.
- **A series of small tables,** folding or not, allows flexibility in choosing where to eat.

In addition to tables and chairs, a serving counter or table is a useful adjunct. The counter can be allied with storage space for the many items used at the table, from covers and mats, through silverware and table accessories. If space permits, an old sideboard (which goes far beyond the implications of the name) usually gives an amplitude of storage space. Smaller modular units may fit the space better.

Besides their storage and serving usefulness, such units provide a subdominant focus in a room, balancing the major dining group.

Planning for Social Activities

The foregoing discussions, and the profile in Chapter 1, have gone into some detail about the needs and possibilities for the various social activities. From these we can formulate a generalization useful in planning the social spaces:

Social activities take place in many areas of the home. We can eat together in the living room or family room, the dining room or kitchen, or out-of-doors. We talk wherever we gather, and music often fills the farthest reaches of the home. It seems obvious that planning for these activities is more a matter of organizing space for function than of arranging "rooms."

Planning for social activities requires that the needs of everyone in the household be considered, if the plan is to be successful. When the needs of children are overlooked, for example, the quiet adult spaces of the home may be overrun.

Types of Social Spaces

Basically, two types of social spaces in the home are available:

There can be *one large open area*, suitable for a variety of purposes and used intensively, as in a one-room apartment. Here group and private living necessarily share the same space. By visually separating areas and perhaps varying levels, even this limited space can be designed to accommodate different activities with subtle distinctions.

305. When planning for social activities, storage needs must be taken into consideration. Built-in shelving provides a maximum of space and works as part of the design. It is conveniently located next to the work area by the window. (*Photographs courtesy U.S. Plywood-Champion Papers, Inc.*)

right: 306. Space in a home designed by owner/architect Jefferson Riley of Moore, Grover, Harper is open and multifunctional. Overall, the home is symmetrical, but it has many asymmetrical parts, giving it a contemporary look. Cozy spaces combine with soaring ceilings, and shadows play on the walls. (*Photograph: Norman McGrath*)

below: 307. This room doubles as a bedroom and den. When the owners' son is away at college the family gains new space, which he can easily reclaim upon his return. A diagonal platform holds a mattress, stereo components, records, and storage areas. Built-in shelves and writing surfaces, as well as the contemporary furnishings, give a denlike feeling while still performing functions needed in a bedroom. Barbara Ross and Barbara Schwartz, Dexter Design, Inc., designers. (*Photograph: Norman McGrath*)

These same devices can be used in larger homes in which group space is essentially open and multifunctional, flowing easily from sitting and entertainment areas to dining and even cooking domains.

For many homes a *second discrete social space*, however, is the only way to meet the needs of differing age and activity groups and maintain sanity. Family rooms, playrooms, multipurpose or recreation rooms, whatever name they go by, such spaces can be invaluable as alternative places in which to play or work.

As a rule, secondary spaces are informal, durable, and easily maintained. Their furnishings are functional and planned for specific activities, from card games to pool, perhaps dancing, sewing, weaving, or woodwork. These activities often will dictate, or at least suggest, the arrangement and character of the room.

Perhaps most important, by a kind of general consent, we do not expect them to be consistently neat and ordered. They can be truly relaxation spaces.

Personalizing Social Spaces

Most of this chapter has dwelt on mundane matters—the planning of social spaces for different activities, the arrangement of furniture, provisions based on the profile questionnaire. This will have gone a long way toward personalization, because a specific life style should have become evident.

But the social spaces of the home are the most highly used by the inhabitants. Moreover, they introduce guests to the life that the home

308–310. A condominium complex in California illustrates how social spaces can be personalized according to the desires of the occupants. All three rooms are used largely for conversation and entertaining. Wong and Brocchini, architects. (*Photographs: Joshua Freiwald*)

308. This apartment is slightly smaller than the other two, and the furnishings have been scaled down so they do not overwhelm. The ceiling and walls are white; carpeting and draperies are off-white, setting off the dark furniture. See also Plate 41, p. 288.

above: 309. The arrangement of furnishings in this apartment makes the most of the space. Neutral walls, draperies, and ceiling also help to open up the space. A Moroccan rug in a brown-and-white pattern picks up the shape and color of the floor tiles but adds interest. Dark bookcases framing the fireplace make this area a focal point. The bookcases are not completely filled, adding even more to the open feeling. See also Plate 42, p. 288.

right: 310. An apartment on the top floor of the complex has a slanted ceiling that makes it appear more spacious. Neutral walls and carpeting are offset by patterned area rugs and many and varied accessories. White love seats face each other over a rectangular coffee table; large floor cushions provide extra seating. Variety is the keynote here, yet all furnishings are harmonious. See also Plate 43, p. 289.

encourages. The owners will want the home to look like *their* home. Beyond the practical matters of where certain pieces of furniture will fit, and how the group areas relate to each other and the interior as a whole, there are many original design possibilities that will fulfill this desire.

Personalization involves the design elements and principles, the effects of light and color, the selection of materials and furnishings that the owners will like and that give character and individuality to the home. The personalization of social spaces is too large a topic to cover in one chapter. We have touched on it all through the book and will return again in the chapter on accessories.

For now we will just remind you that the design of social spaces should be workable but at the same time embody a kind of enrichment that makes a home unique.

Private Places

13

W e consider as private places those areas of the home designed primarily for one or two persons. Here people retreat for rest and renewal, and sometimes for concentrated work or study. These spaces may be called bedrooms, bathrooms, studios, or studies—names that indicate their primary functions. What they have in common is the privacy they provide.

Privacy is a luxury in an increasingly overcrowded world, but people have evolved many ways of achieving it. Even on a busy street or subway we maintain a feeling of detachment by avoiding other people's eyes. Many people can wrap themselves in a cocoon of sound, shutting out the rest of the world. Still others find solitude in reading, even in the midst of family life. Most of us, however, appreciate the possibility of physical seclusion for some of life's needs and rituals—for relaxation, sleep, and grooming, even for work.

Rest and Renewal

The separate sleeping room evolved quite late in human history and is even today not a world-wide concept. The bathroom is a still more recent phenomenon, but we have come to think of both as necessities. The typical advertisement for a house or apartment starts out with the number of bedrooms and baths it contains, so fundamental do we consider these spaces.

We feel we need a quiet place to sleep, if sleep is to be restful. We like privacy for the rituals of getting ready to face the day and then unwinding at night. We usually work best in an isolated spot—work that may range from simple letter writing and keeping the budget to more complicated tasks and hobbies. These physical needs often are best met in private places that may be the sole domain of one or two people. We also want a secluded place in which to be by ourselves, to collect our thoughts, explore our emotions, enjoy our dreams. These are psychic needs for which such areas are well suited.

Bedrooms

Since we spend about one third of our lives in bed, the bedroom should be planned with that in mind. Almost equally important is the bedroom's role as a place for dressing and undressing. These functions have requirements beyond the actual square footage that will permit the variety of movements involved.

Besides sleeping and dressing, a bedroom may serve other needs. It may double as a study or workroom, play area, or supplementary sitting room. Guest bedrooms in particular will usually play another role when not in use by a visitor.

The profile questionnaire in Chapter 1 has given some indication of the needs for the household. Above all comes the provision for rest.

Sleep

The major element in any bedroom is the facility for sleeping. This might include:

- **A bed or beds,** consisting of spring and mattress, with or without head and footboards, and long and wide enough for one or two persons. Since such beds are large and inflexible, convenience

311–312. This modern version of the Murphy bed presents an unusual solution to the problem of multiuse space. Joan Regenbogen, designer. (*Photographs: Norman McGrath*)

311. The bedroom has plenty of built-in storage, but the bed takes up a good part of the room.

usually dictates certain types of placement. Alternatives would range from a sleeping bag or sleeping pallet on the floor to a mattress, with or without a box spring, on a platform or loft.

- **Bedside tables,** night stands, or small chests of drawers to hold whatever might be needed at night: clock, radio, tissues, flashlight, cough drops, or television set. Sometimes such facilities are part of an extended headboard or a built-in unit.
- **A light** over the bed or on the bedside table, for reading in bed, getting up at night, or emergencies.

But a good night's sleep is dependent on more than these.

Draperies, shades, shutters, or blinds control natural light and give the privacy and darkness most of us like for sleeping.

Ventilation, efficient but draft-free, creates a comfortable climate. Windows or other ventilating devices on opposite walls encourage a through breeze in summer, which if possible, should skirt the sleeping area. A high window also draws out summer heat.

Quiet, like dark, is a normal requisite for sleep and is best achieved by isolating the bedrooms from noisier parts of the house and by using sound-absorbing materials.

312. When the bed is folded (at right), the same room is transformed into a spacious work area for an artist.

Dressing and Undressing

Dressing and undressing require both open and closed space:

- **open, uncluttered space** in which to stand, stretch, turn around, bend over
- **closed closets and drawers** in which to store clothes

In addition,

- **Lighting,** both natural and artificial, is needed for general illumination and for such specific tasks as applying makeup.
- **A full-length mirror** reveals the total effect.
- **A seat** for dealing with hosiery and shoes spares the edge of the mattress, which will eventually sag if used constantly as a seat.

Well-planned and sufficient storage space keeps clothes in good order, clean, and accessible. Some of the possibilities are shown in Figures 314 and 315, but there are no perfect solutions. The designer should make a realistic appraisal of the clothes and equipment owned, the amount of space they will occupy, and the space available.

As space and finances permit, the dressing center may grow into a separate dressing area placed between the sleeping room and the bath. Especially helpful for the two-person room, such an arrangement allows different levels of activity to take place at the same time.

313. Antique furniture, handmade quilts, and simple accessories create a cozy, personal retreat. Mary Emmerling, designer. (*Photograph: Robert Perron*)

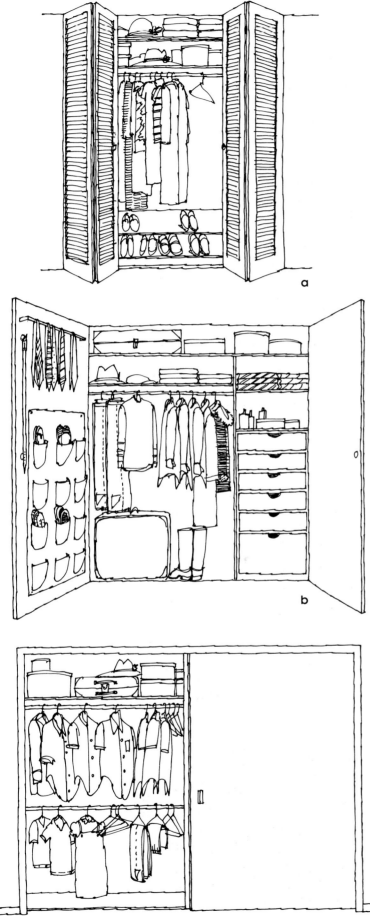

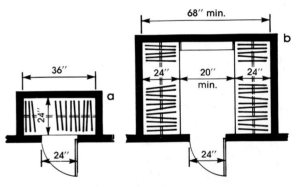

above: 314. Clothes closets should be designed to meet the needs of the person who will use them. They should provide easy accessibility and visibility. Shown are the two most common types of closets. A reach-in closet (**a**) has a rod all the way across from which clothes hang. There usually is a shelf over the rod for extra storage. It must be at least 24″ deep, but an extra 4″ of depth will make storage of bulky objects, such as coats, easier. If the rod length is more than 6″ wider on each side than the closet's opening, it will be hard to reach corners of the closet. A walk-in closet (**b**) is ideal for the person with many clothes. If it is spacious enough it can also be used for a dressing area.

left: 315. Folding doors (**a**) are often used for closets because they provide easy access to a large space. A comparable space closed off with sliding doors would not be as accessible, because half of the closet would always be hidden. However, clearance space must be left in front of folding doors. A maximum use of space (**b**) is created when drawers and shelves are built in and storage is provided for specific items. Although sliding doors (**c**) cover half of the closet at all times, they do not require clearance space in front.

left: 316. A desk is handy in a bedroom that must double as office space. The desk here is built in and also has shelves for storage and display. It is in a corner, partially closed off from the rest of the room. Lighting is concealed under a shelf. Don Loomis, architect. (*Photograph: Philip L. Molten*)

below: 317. The work space in this bedroom can be used only for light tasks without seeming cluttered. Many small pieces of furniture break up the room visually.

Private Work and Leisure

The bedroom is often the only place in the home suitable for serious work—from the homework of a student to the writing of a professional author. In between are the myriad tasks that either generate a certain amount of confusion, such as dressmaking, and/or require concentration, such as filling out an income tax return.

A desk, perhaps supplemented with file drawers and bookcases, will fit into many bedrooms if carefully planned. A simple desk is almost an imperative for a school-age child. Sewing or craft equipment is more complicated but can be absorbed. It may be more easily accommodated, however, in a family room or den.

We take for granted the fact that children's rooms will double as playrooms but sometimes forget that they should be designed accordingly. Sturdy furnishings, easily cleaned surfaces, accessible and generous storage allow for both the exuberance of high spirits and a quick return to order.

The adult bedroom as a place for relaxation and companionship supplements the more open social spaces. If there is room for a table and a chair or two, there is the possibility of a simple meal, a quiet game of cards or chess, and reading of a book or magazine.

When more space is available, the bedroom may take on some of the attributes of a private spa, merging with the bathroom and providing facilities for exercise and relaxation. For most of us, this is a dream, but bathroom suppliers are beginning to produce equipment that can be introduced into a moderate-size sleep-dressing-bathroom space.

318. Built-in or modular furniture makes the space of Figure 317 seem less cluttered. Even though the room is used for sewing, the increased amount of storage space keeps some work materials out of sight.

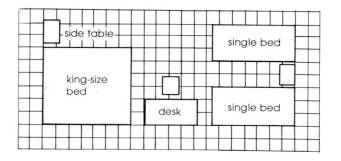

Planning Bedrooms

The number of bedrooms in a home is determined by the number of permanent household members in relation to the financial resources available. This number will also be affected by the life style and stage of family life. To some extent these factors will dictate how the bedrooms are designed.

The actual scale plan of a bedroom often controls the way it can be furnished and its comfort. Because bedroom furniture is usually large and cumbersome, wall space is at a premium. The placement of bulky beds and accompanying night stands is the first decision.

Placement of chests of drawers comes next because of their size. For convenience, they are best located near the closet(s) to create a dressing area. At times they are incorporated into the closet design where they are more inconspicuous, if not hidden entirely. Or they may be part of a modular arrangement that can include a desk and bookshelves—a space-saving solution.

Putting a chest near the entrance door allows ready access, and a small chair nearby will prove useful as a seat when dressing and as a handy drop for articles in transit.

Ideally a desk is set near a window, for natural light and perhaps a pleasant view. It usually takes whatever wall space is available, although it can be against the wall or at an angle to it, allowing a little more freedom of placement.

Last, but still important, would be a table-chair arrangement or a chaise that provides for relaxation short of sleeping. Again, the window area suggests the most pleasant spot, but any location somewhat segregated from the general traffic pattern would do. Not all bedrooms have this much space, but even one small comfortable chair will be welcome. In addition, provision for circulation and privacy should be checked, such as:

- Easy circulation between the door, closet, chest of drawers, and possibly a private bath. This is an often-used path and should be as short and direct as possible.
- Shielding the bed and dressing area against direct view from the door allows some privacy without always shutting the door.

Personalizing Bedrooms

The opportunity to make a bedroom truly the private place of its occupant opens great possibilities. Color preferences could well come first; this gives a chance to indulge in vivid colors or subdued monochromes to suit a personality. The choice of a furniture style also can be individual. Although the architectural design of the room will have some

above right: 319. The scale of bedroom furnishings must be taken into consideration. Each square represents one foot.

below: 320. Bedrooms can be arranged many ways, depending on the size of the room and its furnishings. A large bed (**a**) could be placed at a right angle to the wall. A single bed (**b**) could be set parallel to the wall, in a studio couch-like arrangement. Two single beds (**c**) placed against adjacent walls and at right angles to each other leave much open space in the room.

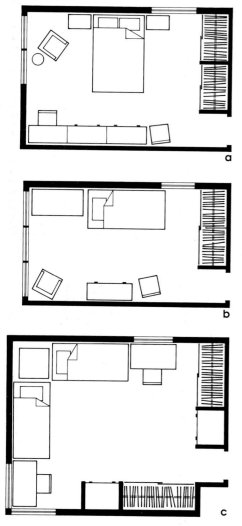

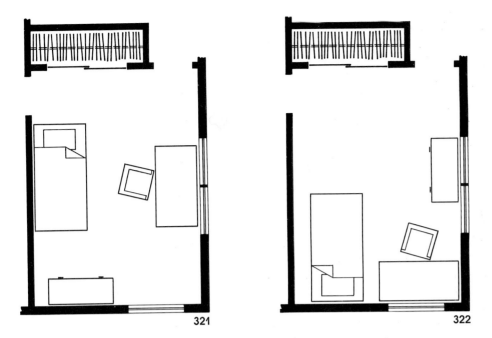

321 322 323

321–327. These floor plans show several solutions to what might seem an almost impossible problem: how to arrange furniture in a badly planned room. The first four are, for various reasons, undesirable. The last three represent somewhat better solutions.

321. This arrangement leaves no room for a bedside table. The dresser is far away from the closet, and there is wasted space in the corner.

322. The high bureau blocks one window. There is no room for a bookcase except perhaps over the left side of the desk.

323. Bookshelves could go over the desk, but there would be a draft from the windows directly onto the bed. The desk would be better placed under a window.

324. The desk is well-located, but the bureau blocks the other window, besides being at the opposite end of the room from the closet.

325. This plan represents a better solution, although not an ideal one. The head of the bed is away from the window, the dresser is near the closet, and the desk is in a good position by the window.

326. A small room looks better when it is less cluttered with miscellaneous furnishings. Built-in or modular furniture (dresser/desk/storage) is probably the best solution.

327. A built-in platform bed has drawers beneath for storage. The bed has a full-length mattress plus a smaller one at one end for lounging. Shelves above the smaller mattress could hold books or a television set.

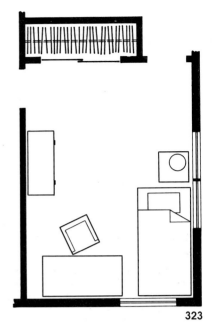

324

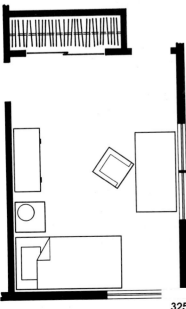

325

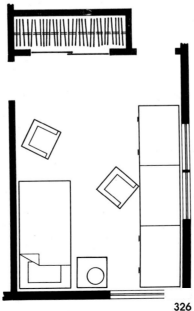

326

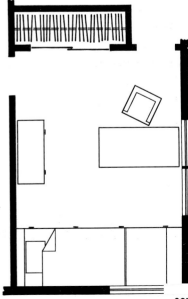

327

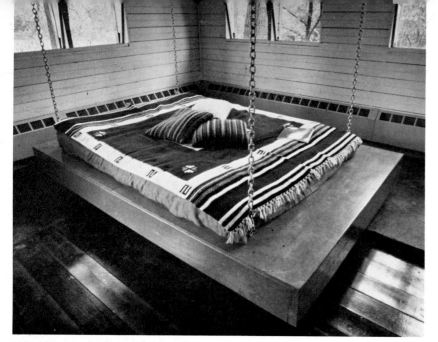

328. A hanging bed in a converted barn provides a dramatic focal point. Byron Bell, designer. (*Photograph: Robert Perron*)

influence, modern or traditional furniture can be treated in ways that fit in with the setting or use it as a foil. (See Plate 44, p. 290.)

Equally important in creating the mood and character of a room is the way in which the walls, windows, and floors are handled. Fluffy or restrained, natural or formal, these elements, their finishes and treatments should be the choice of the occupant. In addition, almost everyone has at least one collection of objects that are cherished and particularly meaningful to the owner. Counters, shelves, or open cupboards for their display, separate or integrated with other units, become a focal point of interest and an expression of personality. In children's rooms, especially, sturdy walls or bulletin boards provide for changing exhibits.

The design of a bedroom for a couple is more challenging and should start with communication between the two involved. Only in this way will the inevitable differences in expectations be brought out into the open and compromises worked out. With a little give and take it should be possible to choose a color scheme that is pleasing to both and to decide on the kind of furniture and treatments with which both will be comfortable.

329. A child's bedroom can be personalized with a bed on a high platform accessible by stairs. A shelf nearby holds books, while a built-in closet has plenty of space for toys. The compact design leaves an open area for play. Turner Brooks, architect. (*Photograph: Robert Perron*)

Bathrooms

Almost since the beginning of the bathroom as a separated space, it has been thought of in strictly utilitarian terms. The smallest room in the house, finished with laboratory-like efficiency and often chilling materials, the bathroom was not a place to linger.

Now, however, renewed interest in bathing rituals as a therapeutic pastime, although perhaps not quite as social as the Roman baths or the Victorian spa, is changing the look of bathrooms. For most people this means more colorful, somewhat larger bathrooms, perhaps merging into a dressing area, and sometimes including such relaxing devices as the sauna, the hot tub, or the whirlpool bath.

Planning Bathrooms

Bathroom fixtures, because they must be hooked up to plumbing lines already in place in the structure, are not easy to move around. This is a limiting factor in interior design. Unlike most furnishings, fixtures usually are built in. They come in a range of set sizes and with optimum clearances that are also design determinants. Table 13.1 lists standard

Table 13.1
Standard Bathroom Fixture Sizes and Clearances*

Fixture	Small Depth	Width	Large Depth	Width
bathtub	30″	× 48″	42″	× 66″
soaking tub	40″	× 40″	60″	× 60″
washbasin	15″	× 18″	24″	× 30″
toilet	24″	× 22″	30″	× 24″
bidet	25″	× 14″	28″	× 16″
shower	30″	× 30″	42″	× 60″
bathinette	21″	× 35″	24″	× 36″
vanity cabinet	30″	× 24″	32″	× 26″
Clearances				
space between front of tub and opposite wall	30″	—	42″	
space in front of toilet	18″	—	24″	
space at sides of toilet	12″	—	18″	
space between fronts of fixtures	24″	—	36″	

* Luxury fixtures are available in larger sizes.

above: 330. A skylight brings natural light into a bathroom but maintains privacy. Twin wash bowls and lots of storage, separated from the bath area, make a dressing room. James Caldwell, architect. (*Photograph: Philip L. Molten*)

below: 331. Hot tubs are gaining in popularity, especially in warm climates where they can be installed outdoors. (*Photograph: Matthew Kelleher, courtesy Spring Mountain Hot Tubs*)

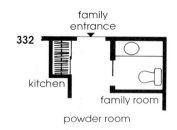

332

family
entrance

kitchen

family room

powder room

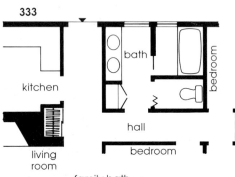

333

kitchen

bath

bedroom

hall

living
room

bedroom

family bath

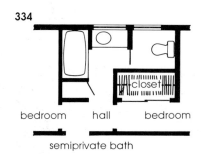

334

bedroom   hall   bedroom

closet

semiprivate bath

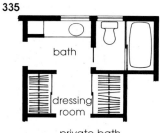

335

bath

dressing
room

private bath

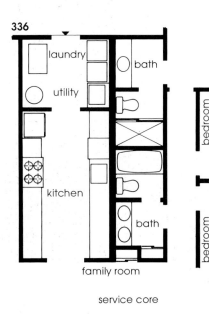

336

laundry   bath

utility

bedroom

kitchen

bedroom

bath

family room

service core

top to bottom: 332–336.   Various types of bathrooms can fulfill different functions.

332.   A powder room near the main entrance to a house is often useful for quick cleanups, especially in a two-story home.

333.   A family bathroom should be large and centrally located, but out of sight of the social spaces.   Since all family members use this room, dividing the space to increase simultaneous use is often a good idea.

334.   A semiprivate bathroom, planned for two or three members of the family, should be near bedrooms but entered from the hall.

335.   A private bathroom for one or two persons is entered from a bedroom. A second entrance is useful if guests use the room as well.   Dividing a private bathroom gives even more privacy.

336.   A service core concentrates all plumbing—bathrooms, kitchen, and laundry—and centralizes the inevitable noise. Construction costs are also lowered.

sizes and clearances. Figures 332 to 336 show a few possible layouts in response to typical house plans.

Few of us can design the total bathroom, but we all are forced to evaluate a bathroom in use. Sometimes we can remodel a bathroom, and a few observations may help.

Size   A minimum $5\frac{1}{2}$-by-6-foot bathroom allows use by only one person at a time and leaves little space for storage. A few more square feet are usually well worth their cost, as is a divided room with perhaps a wash basin in the dressing area.

Windows and Doors   Window design is not so important as it used to be but often is much more interesting. Since the introduction of vented fans, an operable window is no longer necessary. Good artificial illumination has almost cancelled our need for daylight and made possible complete privacy.

However, a skylight, a bathroom window—or even a window wall with a sliding door opening onto a protected balcony or garden area—will visually and perhaps even physically enlarge this smallest of rooms.

The angle at which the door opens is important. Since the door usually is left partway open for ventilation when the bathroom is not in use, it should shield from view as many of the fixtures as possible.

below: 337. A small bathroom is visually enlarged by a window wall. A mirror behind the shelves reflects the outdoors. Emily Keady, designer. (*Photograph © Morley Baer*)

Finishes   Almost anything can be made waterproof these days, greatly expanding the range of materials suitable for use on floors and walls. Wood, paint, and plaster, soft plastic wall coverings and hard laminated plastics, as well as the favorite tile—all are or can be made practically impervious to dampness. The varieties of patterns and colors are almost overwhelming and give great latitude in designing.

Vinyl flooring provides interest underfoot, waterproof wood adds a nostalgic note, nylon or other synthetic carpetings are soft and warm, and surprisingly practical.

Fixtures   Although the design of fixtures is fairly standard, they now are available in a wide range of colors. However, fixtures will set the color schemes possible for a number of years, so care must be taken in deciding whether to use white or some other hue.

left: **338.** Unglazed ceramic tiles cover the floor and shower stall in a remodeled house. The tub enclosure and walls are various types of wood, varnished or painted to be moisture-resistant. Ben Thompson, owner-architect. (*Photograph: Ezra Stoller © ESTO*)

below: **339.** A custom-made bathroom with a sunken tub has a tile shower, walls, and floor. Peter Hamilton, designer. (*Photograph: Robert Perron*)

Fixtures constantly are being refined and reshaped for ease and safety, within the narrow standard bounds. Among the things to look for, according to particular needs are:

- **Tubs** may be deeper and larger than usual for leisurely soaking. Non-skid bottoms and grab rails foster safety. Wide ledges are useful for sitting upon when bathing a child, a dog, or one's own feet.
- **Showers** with two separate shower heads or a flexible shower spray will accommodate people of different heights. Integral seats in shower stalls are especially appreciated by the ill or elderly, allowing them to walk in and sit down rather than climb into a tub.
- **Wash basins** often are built into a counter with storage space over, under, and sometimes beside them. Newer still are modern versions of the old-fashioned pedestal sink, but with ample rims. Counter space is built in elsewhere, usually in the dressing area. The truly efficient basin is one placed at a comfortable height for the user.
- **Faucets** offer a ripe area for design. Many new faucets seem to have little regard for ease of operation. Mentally, try to turn off a round, slightly grooved ball with a wet soapy hand. These are among the easiest parts of the bathroom to replace, so a little first-hand experimentation pays off.
- **Mirrors** should be well lighted, especially when used for shaving and makeup. Side light illumines the face without shadows, but the source should be shielded or outside the field of vision. Top lighting casts shadows, particularly under the chin. A flexible shaving mirror will help in this case.

left: 340. An inventive bathroom was created from an old tub, sunk into the floor, a simple shower fixture, built-in shelves and vertical wallboards painted a bright yellow, and an old sink. Ben Thompson, architect. (*Photograph: Ezra Stoller © ESTO*)

right: 341. The warm feeling wood gives is apparent in this bathroom. The fixtures are dark, and a patterned rug adds to the warmth. Even the toilet seat is wood. Sherman Riley, architect. (*Photograph: Philip L. Molten*)

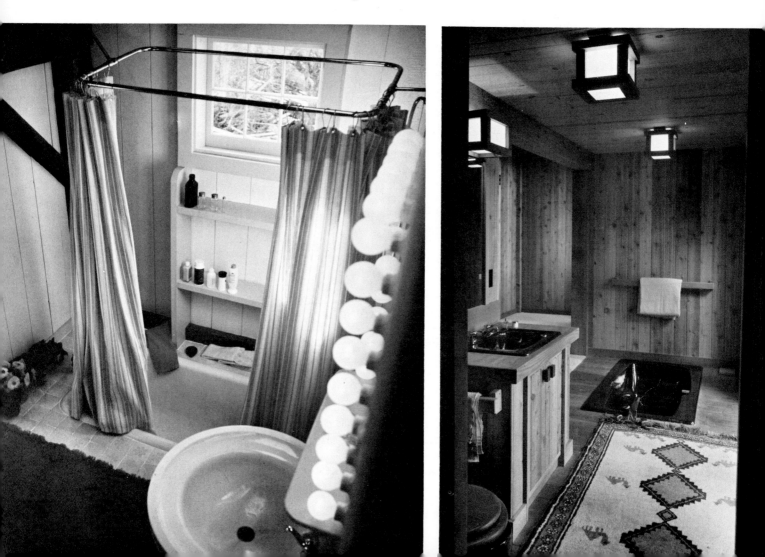

Storage   Provision for storage has become increasingly important as more and more grooming rituals take place in the bath-dressing area, and as the number of gadgets used in these rituals multiplies. This indicates that the traditional medicine cabinets should be supplemented by spacious cupboards and drawers. Storage areas for medicine or cleaning supplies need locks for safety if children are in the household.

Color   As mentioned, the color of the fixtures is basic in setting the total scheme. It should also be considered for both its visual impact and its reflectance values. There is no doubt that color in the bathroom is cheering, *but* oranges and pinks reflect a healthy tinge; blues, yellows, and greens can make people look sallow.

Personalizing Bathrooms

We have talked about bathrooms mostly from a mundane, efficiency viewpoint, even when mentioning color. But bathrooms usually are rather small, often windowless, and are used for relatively short periods of time. They cry out for color and excitement that can be much more intense than other portions of the home. (See Plate 45, p. 290.)

Colored fixtures limit the possibilities in choosing color schemes; white fixtures give more leeway. Finishes, such as waterproof wall coverings and paints, are more easily changed and come in a fabulous range of textures and effects that can truly enliven the space. Bathroom carpeting gives a feeling of luxury at little cost and warms up the room both physically and visually.

Accessories, of course, are even more adaptable. Towels and mats can vary weekly. Paintings, graphics, and sculpture, if properly steam-proofed, can be on changing display. Plants, many of them loving the warm, humid atmosphere, will thrive if well-chosen.

The height of luxury would undoubtedly be an elaborate dressing room-spa-bathroom, but even a small, quite ordinary room can take on new life, at small expense, from the addition of dramatic color.

Personal Pursuits

Crafts and hobbies are becoming increasingly important to many people, either as escape or enrichment, and sometimes as a vocation. Intermittent or small-scale activities can be absorbed in the social spaces or in bedrooms. Such pursuits as painting or woodworking, weaving or pottery, either require more concentration or result in greater physical confusion. An isolated space is almost a must. Providing a separate room allows the hobbyist or artist to leave work in an unfinished state reasonably secure in the knowledge that it will remain untouched—and untroubling to the rest of the household.

Equally, persons who must do part or all of their work at home greatly benefit from having a secluded space in which to do it.

Den or study, studio or hobby shop, perhaps even a meditation room—these are private places that may be sacred to one person alone. The furnishings are usually functional, and the equipment may provide the interest: desk and books in a study, loom and wool in a weaving studio, tools of the trade of any hobby, craft, or vocation.

In a studio, white walls and uncurtained windows make the most of natural light; in a den, darker colors may seem soothing, and draperies will provide privacy. Accessories often are limited to articles brought in as inspiration. Thus, these are truly personal places.

342. An awkwardly shaped attic room has been converted to a hobby/sitting room. This arrangement makes use of all the available space, but could be better planned.

343. The arrangement below is better, because the work area is changed to the window position, affording access to built-in storage under the eaves (to right). All the tall elements are now in the tall part of the room, while the low couch is under the low section.

Work
Spaces

I n housekeeping activities, three trends are apparent: one related to cooking, another to cleaning, the third to conservation.

The kitchen is in a state of evolution that in many ways seems a reversion to its past status—as the main gathering place in the household. The separate laundry or utility room, on the other hand, is often broken up and scattered, no longer a distinct place.

Our growing awareness of the need to conserve energy pervades all parts of our lives. It follows that we not only have to consider how to "keep" the house and furnishings, we must also be aware of energy consumption in doing so.

Cooking

Once again the kitchen, instead of being a completely shut-off room devoted almost entirely to cooking and cleanup, is broadening into a family kitchen—another social space. It often has a dining setup and perhaps a sitting area complete with fireplace, barbecue facilities, probably a television set, and even a greenhouse. The cooking center itself is expanded to take care of simultaneous cooking-cleanup activities by two or more people.

In another direction, but with the same motivation, the cooking center is simply a strip along one end of a much larger social space. It might be part of the living-dining area or the family room, opening out over a counter to the social activities, or completely exposed.

The reasons seem obvious. Many cooks have rebelled against the role of unpaid servant. Quite rightly, they want to be part of the social group while they are plying what may be to them a hobby and delight, or, if a chore, one that can be lightened by the companionship of other people. In some households cooking is a shared activity, which means that the kitchen must be planned with that in mind, if the cooks are not to spoil the broth by getting in each other's way.

At the same time, kitchen equipment is being viewed with a different eye. Manufacturers are offering new colors, materials, and designs that allow appliances, cupboards, counters, and floor coverings to blend with other parts of the home. The white sterile look is gone, although the starkness of white may be used as a color comment. From

left: 344. A kitchen can be an integral part of the larger social space. Shelves here are open to display dishes, connecting the kitchen visually to the dining area. Herb Kosovitz, architect. (*Photograph © Morley Baer*)

right: 345. An open kitchen plan does not separate the cook from the conversation area. This townhouse, belonging to Ivan Chermayeff, is spacious and airy because interior walls are low and windows are uncovered. Skidmore Owings & Merrill, designers. (*Photograph: Norman McGrath*)

346. In another view of the home shown in Figure 188, an old gas stove is the focal point of the kitchen. Like most of the home's furnishings the stove has been recycled. Designer and photographer: Philip L. Molten.

mellow wood cabinets to brightly colored appliances, kitchen equipment is emerging from the laboratory to take its place in the overall design scheme of the home.

Another trend is the appreciation of culinary objects as interesting in themselves. Pots and utensils hang on the walls or overhead, dinnerware is ranged on open shelves, food ingredients exposed in see-through containers or fruit left out in the open to ripen. Instead of hiding these objects as much as possible, people display them for visual appeal. Old equipment may be recycled: an ancient gas range repaired and made useful again; an old cabinet refinished; antique gadgets hung for their intriguing shapes and associations. (See Plate 46, p. 323.)

All of this has positive design implications. In most households, however, the cooking area often is the most work-intensive of any space in the house. In terms of use, safety, and comfort, physical aspects assume primary importance.

Physical Factors

The profile questionnaire in Chapter 1 has provided you with an array of statistics about the people in the household, the spaces they have to work in, the tools they work with. The emphasis here is on *work*—physical exertion. People will work in the kitchen; the kitchen must work for *them*.

In other parts of the house, furniture sizes, clearances between pieces, traffic paths and their widths all are pertinent. In the kitchen they assume a dominant role. Unless the people who do the cooking and cleanup are physically comfortable, the work will be tiring. A 36-inch counter height may be just right for a tall person rolling out pie dough; it could be awkward for a short person. There must be sufficient space to open the oven door without bumping into anyone else standing in the room, for safety's sake.

A set of dinnerware for twelve takes more cupboard space than one for eight, and two sets will strain the capacity of a standard kitchen unless special provision is made. Again, these physical facts must be taken into consideration.

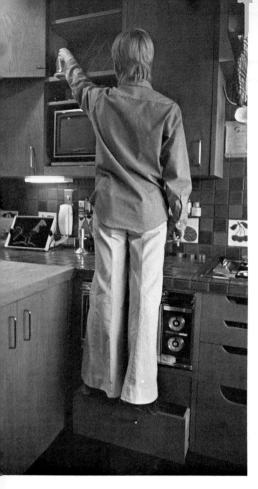

left: 347. When planning a kitchen it should be remembered that storage areas are often difficult to reach. Designer Mandy Haas solved the problem with a specially made drawer strong enough to stand on. (*Photograph: Philip L. Molten*)

right: 348. A convenient work counter is created by a pull-out leaf in the center of a kitchen. The leaf is positioned at a good height for sit-down work. (*Photograph courtesy Poggenpohl*)

These situations are individual for every household, but kitchens usually are designed for the "norm." It will be up to you, the designer, to evaluate how a given kitchen will work or how it can be remodeled or easily refitted to suit the users.

Considerable research has been done on functional kitchen planning at Cornell University, the University of Illinois, the U.S. Department of Agriculture, and other centers. Some of the formulas that have emerged from these studies are shown in Figure 349.

It should be remembered that they are based on averages: average needs, average people, the average amounts of space available to average people. But from these studies there also emerged three concepts that can be used to adapt the averages to specific situations:

- The **physical limitations** of the person or persons most involved is a primary determinant.
- The principle of **first use**—storing items where they will be needed rather than by category—fosters efficiency.
- **Work centers** provide the basis for organizing the kitchen.

Physical Limitations   In general, physical limitations vary with a person's height. It follows that normal work curves—the space within easy reach of the hands—will also vary accordingly (Fig. 349a). This probably is most important in establishing the height of the work counter and the upper shelves in cupboards for storage of often-used items (Fig. 349b). But it relates also to, for example, the placement of the dishwasher within the normal work curve of the person cleaning up at the sink (Fig. 349c). To take it a step further, the cupboard for storing the cleaned dishes within an easy work curve would also be energy-efficient.

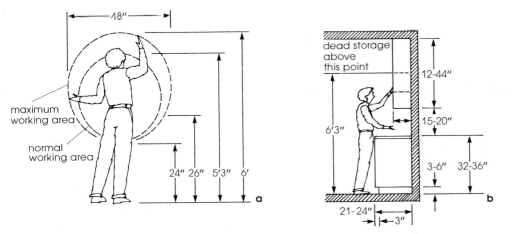

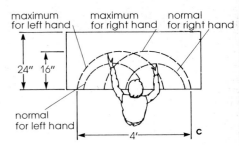

349. Kitchen dimensions should be based on the height and reach of the person who will use the room most. The dimensions given in these drawings are for the average individual.

First Use The idea of storing items where they will be at hand for the first step in their use seems quite obvious. But we are addicted to categorizing things. This will often lead to coffee mugs being stored with the rest of the dishware rather than near the coffee maker, where they will be filled. Or we may line up all knives neatly in a knife rack by the range, when the paring knife is used primarily at the sink.

Like all principles, the principle of first use must be applied intelligently. It makes sense to store skillets by the range, flour and flour sifter in the mix center near the electric mixer. The storage of dinnerware raises another question, however—a question necessarily influenced by the life style of the household. Should the dish cupboard and flatware drawer be near the sink and/or dishwasher where the items can be easily transferred after they are dry? Or should they be placed near the dining table where they will be used? In either case, some transporting will be required, unless this problem has been solved by judicious planning. A pass-through cupboard between sink center and dining area might be the answer.

Nevertheless, the principle of first use is the base around which work centers are organized. The result is the conservation of energy.

Table 14.1
Standard Kitchen Appliance and Cabinet Sizes*

		Small				Large		
	Height	Depth		Width		Height	Depth	Width
cooktop (built-in)		21″	×	26″	to		21″ ×	36″
range (cooktop at 36″)	43″	× 24″	×	20″	to	66″	× 25″ ×	40″
oven (built-in)°°	27″	× 21″	×	22½″	to	42″	× 21″ ×	24″
microwave oven	13⅜″	× 15¼″	×	21¼″	to	16½″	× 18¾″ ×	24″
refrigerator	52″	× 24″	×	20″	to	66″	× 29″ ×	30″
refrigerator-freezer	65″	× 29″	×	31″	to	66″	× 29″ ×	60″
freezer	33″	× 25″	×	42″	to	66″	× 29″ ×	33″
dishwasher (built-in)						35″	× 24″ ×	24″
dishwasher (portable)						38″	× 28″ ×	24″
clothes washer	42″	× 25″	×	25″	to	45″	× 28″ ×	29″
clothes dryer	42″	× 25″	×	27″	to	45″	× 28″ ×	31″
ironing board	30″	× 44″	×	11″	to	36″	× 54″ ×	14″
trash compactor						36″	× 24″ ×	15″
sink	(single)	20″	×	24″	to	(double)	22″ ×	33″
cabinets, base	30″	× 25″	×	15″	to	36″	× 25″ ×	30″
cabinets, wall	12″	× 6″	×	15″	to	30″	× 13″ ×	30″

° Larger sizes are available for special installations. Dimensions do not include an allowance of 3 to 5 inches clearance behind large motored appliances and ranges.
°° Cut-out space needed for single and double units.

Work Centers

Kitchen activities divide naturally into a few categories having to do with food preparation and subsequent cleanup. Some foods have to be washed, pared, and supplied with water at a sink. Others are cooked on a range (or a cooktop or in a separate wall oven). Many foods must be stored in a refrigerator to prevent spoilage. Still others must be mixed with other ingredients before they are usable. Eventually, all the pots, pans, dishes, and utensils that come in contact with food must be washed, which brings us back to the sink.

Each of these categories suggests a special center focusing on the tasks to be performed and the equipment needed to do them as quickly, efficiently, and comfortably as possible.

The work centers evolve naturally around the three largest pieces of equipment found in most kitchens—sink, range, refrigerator—and the tasks they generate, plus one center in which the cook is the large appliance—the mix center. Cupboards and the appropriate amount of work surface, plus supplementary appliances and tools, complete the work centers.

Additional minor centers may round out the storage and work needs either within or outside the kitchen proper.

The design of work centers and their placement determines to a large extent how easily kitchen work flows and how much energy must be expended in these everyday tasks.

The Sink Center The *sink center* is usually the first one established, since it is the most used. Therefore, it suggests a central placement both pleasant for the user and convenient to the other centers.

This center serves for washing vegetables and hands, provides water for cooking, and finally takes care of cleanup. Several types of sinks available are shown in Figure 350 and some of their merits evaluated.

below: 350. There are different types of sinks to serve various purposes. A single sink (**a**) is probably the most common type. It should be large enough for washing roasting pans. A double sink (**b**) is useful for washing and rinsing dishes or when more than one person uses the kitchen. Drains and boards are available to fit over a sink not in use. The smaller sink with high faucet (**c**) is used primarily for a second sink or a bar area. It often supplies only cold water.

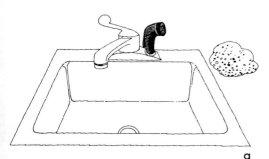

a

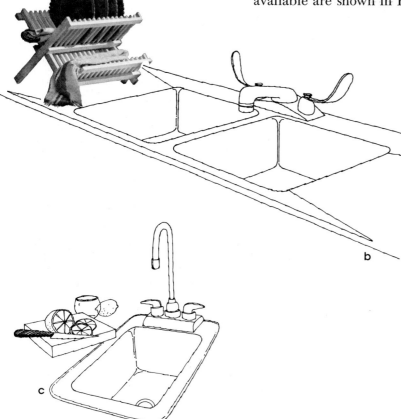

b

c

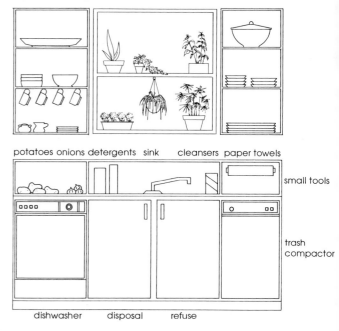

351. A sink center often is located between the cooking and mixing centers and under a window.

potatoes onions detergents sink   cleansers paper towels

small tools

trash compactor

dishwasher   disposal   refuse

Plate 46. Instead of being tucked away in cupboards and drawers, these kitchen utensils and other objects form an integral part of the design of a spacious kitchen. Alfredo De Vido, architect. (*Photograph: Ezra Stoller © ESTO*)

Plate 47. This collection of small landscape paintings is grouped over an antique cabinet. Mary Emmerling, designer. (*Photograph: Robert Perron*)

A dishwasher, disposal, and perhaps a trash compactor may supplement the sink, but more essential is adequate counter space for piling soiled dishes on one side and for draining them on the other (Fig. 351). Storage for cleaning supplies, dish towels, and sometimes for such vegetables as potatoes and onions, complete the center.

The Range Center   The *range center* is built around a gas or electric stove complete with one or two ovens and perhaps a microwave oven; or a cooktop set into a heat-resistant counter, with an oven or ovens built in elsewhere in the room. Adjacent storage for pots and pans, for small implements used in cooking, and for frequently used seasonings is useful nearby (Fig. 352). Very necessary is adequate heat-resistant counter space on which hot pans can be set. This is sometimes provided on the range itself, or a movable heat-resistant pad may protect a counter top, if such a convenience has not been built in.

An exhaust fan, either integral with the range or in an overhead hood vented to the outdoors, provides for much-needed ventilation and disposal of odors.

Built-in wall ovens or countertop microwave ovens need thoughtful placement and heat-resistant surroundings. If possible, these ovens should not interrupt the flow of counter space but should have a heat-resistant surface adjacent on which to place a large hot casserole. The oven that will have the most use should be placed so that the principal cook will be able to reach into it without stooping or stretching.

The range center has many ties to the other centers, but a good relationship to the eating space is very helpful. At the same time, placement out of the path of traffic is a safety precaution, as well as eliminating a source of annoyance.

below: 352. A range center brings together all items needed for cooking.

right: 353. These wall ovens are at a convenient height. Next to them is a heat-resistant counter on which to place baking pans or casseroles. Architect and photographer: Philip L. Molten.

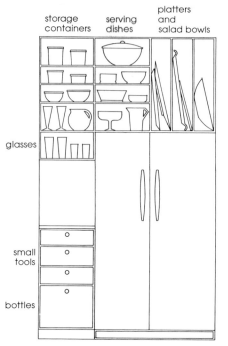

354. A refrigerator center should store not only food but glasses and other dishes as well as storage containers.

355. Specially designed storage spaces for flour, sugar, and bread—as well as for small appliances such as mixers and blenders—will often be included in the wall or base cabinets of a mix center.

The Refrigerator Center   The *refrigerator center* (Fig. 354) should be flanked by counter space on the latch side of the door and some storage space for refrigerator-freezer containers and supplies. Cabinets for glassware are most useful here. The newer refrigerators with vertical doors opening down the center pose a problem. A counter opposite is then best for the temporary resting place of food going into or out of this appliance.

Many types of refrigerator-freezers are available, with advantages and disadvantages in the placement of the different compartments. The choice is a personal one.

Most refrigerators need only a connection to a properly grounded three-pronged electrical wall outlet. The newer ones with automatic icemakers and water dispensers, however, will need a plumbing connection to supply the water.

Placement of the refrigerator is usually either first or last in the work sequence. Near the outside entrance it is handy for the first storage of food, near the dining area for the serving of refrigerated food.

The Mix Center   The *mix center* (Fig. 355), as suggested earlier in this discussion, should have as its focus the person or persons who will mix or otherwise prepare breads and pastries, casseroles and salads. It should have plenty of electrical outlets (perhaps a strip outlet) for the many small appliances that may be used here—mixer, blender, food processor—but there will still be a fair amount of physical energy expended.

Not all counters in the kitchen need be at the same level. Dropping the mix center counter a few inches below the common level will allow the user more easily to exert force on those tasks requiring it.

The height of the counter relative to the user and the placement of storage within the normal work curve contribute to the ease with which tasks can be accomplished—reaching in all directions, stirring, beating, chopping, kneading, and rolling out. A general rule is to place the most frequently used items within the work curve, with heavier objects below, lighter ones above.

Specially designed storage is helpful here, of a kind that often can be added to a standard kitchen. Small shelves for flavorings can be fitted under wall cabinets or on the inside of doors. Stepped-back-and-up shelving also can be inserted in wall cabinets; and file dividers, plastic pull-out drawers, or turntables in base cabinets.

A countertop of wood, marble, or laminated plastic is helpful for kneading and rolling out dough. It can be built either into the counter or on a special pull-out board at a lower height. If neither of these is provided, a separate pastry board can be purchased.

Convenient storage for electrical appliances such as blenders is essential in the mix center, or else lack of use will destroy their benefit. A special base cupboard with a pull-up shelf takes care of the mixer or food processor. Otherwise, all the small appliances may stand on the counter either in plain view or in specially built compartments.

The mix center often is combined with other centers and placed between either the refrigerator and range, or the range and sink, since it has close ties with all of these.

Other Centers   A *serve center* stores those items that go directly from storage to table—dishes, glassware, flatware, linens and accessories, condiments, and small electrical appliances that are used at the table, such as toasters. If this center is located between the kitchen and dining area, then cabinet space might well be accessible from either side.

A *pantry* or *storage wall* provides space for canned goods and bottles and often for large pieces of equipment that are too cumbersome for storage elsewhere. If at all possible, like items should be stored together, as many as possible in plain view and within easy reach. This suggests shelves tailored to their expected uses, but here again, with a little ingenuity, much can be done to improve existing shelving.

A *secondary cooking center* fits in with many a household's life style. Useful for quick snacks or simultaneous cooking, this center may be as simple as a portable barbecue or as elaborate as a fully equipped wall kitchen. A barbecue could be built up with counter space and storage for fuel and utensils.

A microwave oven, electric broiler, or electric skillet often serves as the focus of a secondary center, either in the kitchen itself or in some other room. It may be supplemented by a whole array or other equipment, from a sink to a small refrigerator and cupboards for storage of cooking utensils.

A *cleaning closet* is needed to take care of a vacuum cleaner and brooms, cleaning supplies and a variety of brushes, mops, and dusting equipment. Sometimes a built-in or portable ironing board can be accommodated here. More frequently nowadays such a board migrates with the washer and dryer to wherever they are located.

A *kitchen office* may consist of no more than a telephone, a shelf for cookbooks, and the surface of the refrigerator on which notes can be attached with magnets. More useful is counter space at desk height, supplemented by a drawer or two, some pigeonholes, cookbook shelves, a tack board for temporary reminders, and perhaps a typewriter as well as the telephone. Here meals can be planned and bills paid, social and appointment calendars coordinated. If space and location permit, of course, the center may be enlarged by other drawers and files into a full-scale home office for correspondence and financial affairs.

left: 356. The mix center of this custom kitchen has special bins for dry ingredients, a marble top for rolling pastry, and a built-in two-unit cooktop. Donald Mallow, architect. (*Photograph: Norman McGrath*)

right: 357. A built-in pantry with foldout doors and revolving shelves shows an efficient use of space. (*Photograph courtesy Mutschler*)

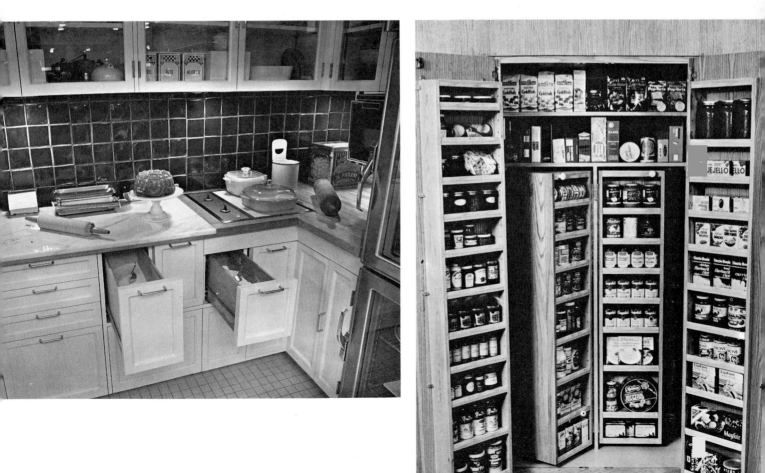

right: 358. A kitchen work island doubles as an office area with desk space, book-shelves, and storage space. Steve Davis, architect. (*Photograph: Robert Perron*)

below: 359. The most convenient storage is easily accessible and visible. Hooks on a wall store baking utensils and pots while keeping them within easy reach. A leaf added to the counter can be folded down when not needed. Small shallow shelves are handy for spices, and cook-books have their own niche—an efficient use of space. Pull-out shelves make base cabinets more accessible; some of the most convenient swing out to reveal contents at a glance. For pots and pans, pull-out shelves are particularly useful. A vertical drawer holds tall bottles.

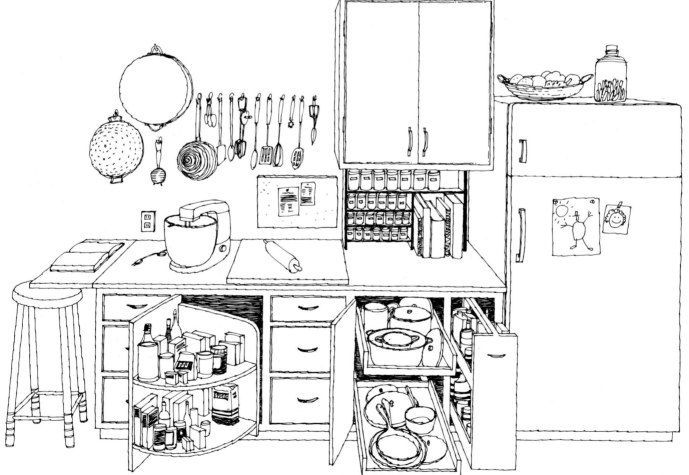

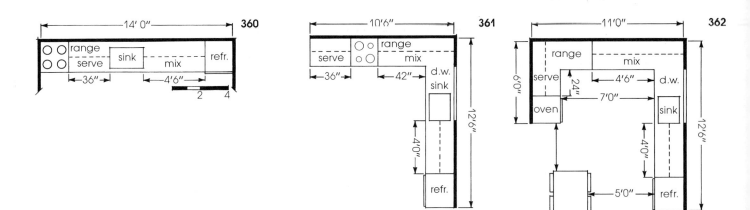

Counter and Storage Space in the Centers

Each center has its recommended amount of *counter space*. In practice, these spaces often are combined. If this is done, it is usually suggested that the widest counter of the two centers, *plus 1 foot*, will give adequate work surface for the combined tasks that will be performed there.

Storage space is another question. If the formulas for the work centers are followed, the counter space provided totals at least 10 lineal feet. Assuming that wall and base cabinets are placed above and below these counters, the resulting storage space will be adequate for most kitchen supplies but will leave space for only enough dinnerware to serve four persons. Each set of dinnerware for twelve needs an extra 5 feet of shelf space, either in the kitchen proper or elsewhere.

The quality of the storage space deserves careful consideration.

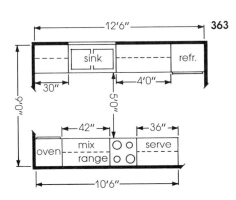

- **Visibility** suggests storing items, especially small ones such as spices, only one row deep, except for identical articles.
- **Accessibility** indicates putting frequently used items at a convenient height. The principle of first use applies here. Drawers or pull-out shelves are more convenient than fixed shelves in base cabinets. Open shelving allows easy access, as do wall or overhead hook racks for pots, pans, and utensils.
- **Flexibility** is enhanced by adjustable shelves and drawers with movable dividers.
- **Maintenance** is less with enclosed storage, but items that are used daily may well be exposed for convenience, especially in relatively clean environments.

Planning Kitchens

The *location* of the work centers within the space allotted to cooking and cleanup determines the basic working layout of the kitchen. Standard arrangements of these centers fall within four categories: strip, L-shape, U-shape, and corridor. At times these define the shape of the kitchen itself; at others they are within the context of a larger space. Occasionally, individual needs will demand a unique space.

If there is room for it, an island is often a useful adjunct, primarily for counter and storage space or sometimes as a base for range or sink.

The *placement* of sink, range, and refrigerator centers determines the so-called work triangle—the busy paths between them. Distances should be as short and direct as possible while still allowing for the counters and storage. The maximum is considered to be 23 feet.

above: 360–363. Work centers in a kitchen are usually a strip against one wall, L-shape, U-shape, or a corridor arrangement.

360. One-wall kitchens can be fitted into alcoves and concealed with folding doors when not in use. They are available in complete prefabricated units, and concentrate plumbing and wiring economically. However, if they contain standard-size appliances—rather than scaled-down "kitchenette" units—they require a great deal of walking.

361. L-shape plans have somewhat less distance between centers than one-wall kitchens. They leave room for eating and laundry and divert miscellaneous traffic to some extent.

362. U-shape kitchens generally are the most compact and efficient. They have the further grace of almost eliminating bothersome intrusion.

363. Corridor arrangements also decrease distances between work centers, but they invite unwelcome traffic when often-used doors are located at both ends.

364. An island is particularly useful in a kitchen. This one has storage space, a large sink, and extra counter space. The double wall ovens are flanked on either side by counters. There is another sink just visible at right. A pass-through window leading to the dining area is another timesaver. Campbell & Wong, architects. (*Photograph* © *Morley Baer*)

Traffic to and around the work centers is best limited to that connected with kitchen work. Miscellaneous traffic should be diverted.

Personalizing Kitchens

Once function has been dealt with, the possibilities for kitchen design are wide open. This is so even though the designs of the large kitchen appliances themselves are basically standardized. Not many people would be able to differentiate between various manufacturers' models. There is much more leeway in choosing a particular style of kitchen cabinetry, from the smoothest of clean-lined, colorful steel to the mellow look of antique wood cupboards. Beyond this, the countertop and wall materials—smooth plastic laminate or colorful patterned tile, paint, or wallcovering—greatly influence the result.

Kitchen utensils are becoming more colorful and appealing, providing their own design inspiration. More and more, the kitchen is being planned for pleasure as well as work, with well-chosen accessories.

Cleaning and Conservation

Cleaning really is a form of conservation. We keep carpets clean to make them last longer as well as look better, because embedded dirt causes fibers to break off. We polish furniture to keep it attractive but also to keep it from drying out and cracking. We wash clothes to keep them fresh looking *and* hygienic, thus conserving ourselves.

Laundry

The major cleaning devices in most homes today are the washer and dryer. In a way, they have been wandering all over the house ever since fairly compact machines were invented, looking for a permanent home. No longer relegated to the dismal basement, they appear in the kitchen, a separate utility room, in a bathroom, or in a closet in the bedroom wing of the home. Each placement has its advantages.

above: 365. Plants arrayed in this kitchen thrive on the humidity and the sun from the skylight. Herbs and spices stored by the range are conveniently placed and visible. Ceramic tiles provide easily cleaned, colorful surfaces. Paul Bradley, designer. (*Photograph: Philip L. Molten*)

above: 366. A streamlined, open kitchen has very visible storage space. Shelves are open, and the upper cabinets have glass doors. Everything is easily accessible, facilitating work and cleanup. Most of the equipment is from restaurants—the steel and glass cabinets are the type used in short order coffee shops. Peter de Bretteville, designer. (*Photograph: Norman McGrath*)

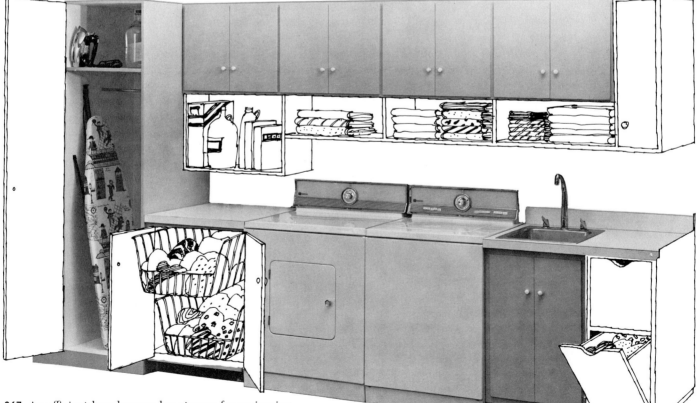

367. An efficient laundry area has storage for an ironing board and other items such as detergent. A sink is often useful here, as is a work surface for sorting and folding. (*Photograph courtesy Maytag Company*)

- In a fairly large kitchen, appliances can be situated out of the way, perhaps in a closet, within easy control of anyone working there. Some storage and an ironing board, perhaps a sink, and a work surface for sorting and folding complete a *laundry center.*
- In a bathroom, again often within a closet, appliances are near the source of most of the soiled laundry—beds, baths, and people—and easily returned when cleaned. This placement is feasible because not many people do their laundry at night when others are trying to sleep. During the day, doors and distance diminish the sound.
- In a bedroom hall closet laundry fixtures are a little more accessible and can be integrated with linen storage facilities.
- A separate laundry is, in many cases, the ideal situation. Washer and dryer can be supplemented by a tub for presoaking laundry, cleaning up adults and children after work or play, and watering plants. Space for drip-drying is readily available and often counter space for arranging flowers or repotting plants. An ironing board can be left in place, and storage space for out-of-season or seldom-used items may be built in.

None of these features may be necessary in apartment houses with laundry facilities on each floor or a large common laundry room. Such communal laundry spaces also appear in condominium housing.

Cleaning and Maintenance

An important consideration for interior designers, whether planning for themselves or for clients, is *how much time and energy* household members are willing to spend on maintenance. Many people still enjoy the homely tasks of polishing furniture and silver, dusting bric-a-brac, or keeping brass surfaces gleaming. For them, the designer can exercise free rein in working with hard-to-clean materials.

At the other extreme, houses and apartments actually have been designed with sloping floors, central drains, and waterproof furnishings, so that the whole interior space could be hosed down periodically.

Most households will fall somewhere in the middle. The preference usually leans, however, toward minimum care. Designing for those who do not mind cleaning is easy. Planning an interior for a relatively maintenance-free life style takes a bit more forethought:

- a maximum of fixed objects that stay where they belong
- ample storage to keep seldom-used articles out of the way
- broad, simple forms, with a minimum of moldings and crevices
- furnishings that come down to the floor
- smooth, impenetrable surfaces
- fibers that naturally do not absorb dirt or that have been treated to resist soil and stains
- colors, textures, and patterns that do not show dirt or scratches

Many decisions will be guided by the answers to the profile questionnaire. For example, a household actively pursuing outdoor sports such as skiing may need a special place to remove clothing and boots so that mud is not tracked through the house. A beach house presents unique problems in controlling sand. And the family with large, shaggy dogs or long-haired cats can offer a real design challenge in terms of maintenance. As in every other area, the particular needs of the people involved must be considered.

The Personal Home: Accessories

15

Accessories is a term that includes most of the additional furnishings needed to make a home livable in all senses. Many people think of an "accessory" as something subordinate. Subordinate calls to mind a collection of small, dispensable objects used for their decorative appeal—if any. We prefer to think of accessories as supplementary, "something that completes."

A home could not function without the many smaller furnishings, such as tableware and lamps, that are needed to make dining, reading (or even seeing) possible. Nor would it function well as a personal retreat without the plants, pottery, graphics, or paintings that are extensions of our personalities. These objects are supplementary to architecture and furniture. They complete both, and they express the identity of the home and its occupants.

We have only to recall a motel room, with perhaps one undersized, undistinguished print and one overscaled lamp, to realize the part that accessories play in expressing individuality.

Accessories also can be thought of in terms of concentrated enrichment. We use smaller furnishings as likely subjects for this kind of enrichment, from the actual form of a beautifully shaped vase, which is a concentration of line, to a painting—forms and colors brought together, focused, and isolated.

Functional Accessories

The objects to be considered in this section serve very specific utilitarian purposes—for eating, drinking, seeing—but all come in a diversity of designs that can be concentrated forms of enrichment.

Tableware

Very few households today follow the routine of three set meals a day at which the whole family is expected to gather. Our time schedules are too diverse. However, experiments, and our personal experiences, have shown how the environment in which we eat can affect our health and happiness. Dining with companions, either family or friends, enhances the pleasure of eating for most of us, and many elements enter in: people, the actual food served, the general setting, and the implements used. These should fuse together, complement each other.

Meals are significant in any kind of group living, possibly being the only time the household congregates. The giving of food is a tradition in almost all cultures, a gesture of friendship. For these reasons, the atmosphere and the various implements for dining deserve more than casual treatment.

The household's preferences in kind of food and method of serving—their life style as indicated in the profile questionnaire—have a direct bearing on the selection of tableware. Will there be dinner parties, buffet meals, or many casual snacks? While the same tableware could work for each, selection based on use would be more successful.

Because tableware is seen only a few hours a day and often in different contexts, it seems a natural outlet for great freedom in choosing patterns and colors that might seem too demanding if always on view. The designers of tableware present us with a wide range of choices.

China Plates, cups and saucers, bowls, and serving dishes of all kinds have come to be grouped under the generic term "china," even though

368. Accessories complement the fairly simple, austere architecture of this home. The table setting, flowers and plants, and a neon sculpture soften and brighten the spaces. Moore, Grover, Harper, architects. (*Photograph: Norman McGrath*)

they may be made of porcelain or earthenware, even glass or plastic. They usually come in sets and because they are the most conspicuous part of table equipment, often establish the character of the entire table setting.

In selecting china you should keep in mind that only rarely does a piece stand alone. Relationships to other table appointments, furniture, and life style, even to food itself are at least as important as the beauty of the pattern seen alone.

In general, originality and personalization will derive from the way in which china is combined and arranged. In this respect, flexibility is a great asset, enabling the same china to be used in different ways, in changed surroundings and moods.

below left: 369. Fine china would seem out of place on a checkered tablecloth. Fabrics should be selected with this in mind. The choice of centerpieces, flowers, and so on, should also be coordinated with the overall design. (*Photograph courtesy Royal Doulton*)

below: 370. Sturdy stoneware, on the other hand, looks wonderful on a country-type cloth. Here stainless steel flatware with wooden handles complements the effect. (*Photograph courtesy Dansk International*)

below left: 371. Selecting glassware can be a problem if the other table accessories are wood. Here heavy colored goblets blend with the other textures. Wooden dishes and utensils are placed directly on a large planked table. Linen table mats and napkins are used for each setting.

below: 372. Plastic is the most difficult material to match with other table accessories. It works best with drinking and eating utensils of a similar plastic material arranged on fairly smooth surfaces—patterned vinyl, for example. (*Photograph courtesy Dansk International*)

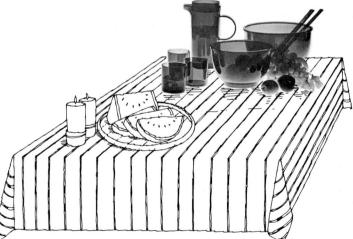

Silverware   As with china, "silverware" tends to be used almost as a generic word, covering not only knives, forks, and spoons made of silver but also those of stainless steel or pewter. Wood, bone, and plastic occasionally appear. Sometimes the term *flatware* is used, but this leaves out the items that are not flat, such as teapots, which may then be called *holloware*. By whatever name, silverware is probably the most enduring of all furnishings. With proper care, it lasts for generations, often growing more beautiful with use. Because of its high original cost and its potential longevity, it should be chosen with care. The patterns available range from the most simple shapes to highly embossed designs—something to suit every taste and situation.

The nature of the material, metal, brings a different beauty to the home. It adds elongated forms and soft sparkle, highly concentrated surface enrichment or beauty of outline and shape. Silverware is interchangeable. Not all the flatware in a place or table setting need be of the same pattern. Variety will add interest.

Glassware   Almost everything said about china and silver applies to glassware, with only a few very important exceptions. Drinking vessels of all kinds can be made of unbreakable aluminum, stainless steel, transparent or opaque plastic, silver, or pottery. However, the nature of glass seems to have a special affinity for liquids.

Glassware can be opaque, as in the metal or plastic varieties, but the special beauty of glassware is its transparency. It can be utterly plain, a pure curving of line, or deeply cut, delicately etched, or of deep rich color. Stemware has a buoyant quality. Goblets are a pleasure to hold and give airiness to a table setting. The patterns available attain individuality by the way they are allied with other table equipment.

Table Coverings   Comparatively inexpensive table coverings offer a greater chance for variety and individuality, in contrast to the other tableware. Table mats and tablecovers can be bought readymade—or are fairly easy to make or have made from an immense spectrum of colors and patterns in dress or household fabrics. They often can be found at craft studios.

Aside from their usefulness as protection for the surface of the table, table coverings give a fresh look to the same old china, change its character, key a table setting to a room's scheme, or assert a theme of celebration.

Table Settings   When all these small pieces of equipment are brought together in a table setting, they supplement each other and become a whole. This arrangement, in turn, takes its place in the interior space and complements it. An unused dining table can be left bare, but we often feel that it looks barren and incomplete. So we finish it with a piece of sculpture, a flower arrangement or plant.

Table settings can be a creative experience, one that we encounter every day or only once in a while. With a limited array of dishes, glassware, silverware, more varied table coverings and incidental pieces, we create a temporary design that will give those who gather a pleasant experience.

The incidental enrichment causes the smaller pieces of equipment to coalesce into a design. The table covering is the decisive unifying factor. Mats will circumscribe each place setting, their repetion set up a rhythm. A large table cover acts as an area rug does, framing the total composition. Some transitional pieces are often needed: serving dishes,

salt and pepper shakers, perhaps candles. These can bring in variety, contrasts of material, color, and texture.

The dominant enrichment factor in any table setting, however, is apt to be what is commonly called the "centerpiece," although it may not be in the center. It is usually, but not always, purely decorative, and it is the most personalized part of the setting.

The diversity of objects that can be used is endless—flowers or leaves, live plants or dried weeds, fruits and vegetables. Rocks and shells, a piece or two of sculpture, or a cluster of candles can be renewed by the addition of transient items, such as a flower or two.

The design and scale of the centerpiece in relation to the rest of the setting, as well as to the size of the table and the room, are all important. Any arrangement should be low enough to permit those at the table to hold cross-conversation without interference. It should be attractive from all sides if people sit around the table, or walk around it at a buffet.

Bed and Bath Accessories

The time has long since passed when we could speak of bed and bath *linens*, most of which were white. These accessories are now often the most colorful accents in the home and come in many different fibers.

Sheets and pillowcases, in their array of colors and patterns, allow us to change from one day to the next as the mood takes us. They offer an easy way to bring in color and pattern, not only to the bed but throughout the room.

Bed coverings strongly affect the bedroom's total design. They dominate the large pieces of furniture that are nearly always the focus of the room, because of their size and placement. Bedspreads and quilts

above left: 373. A sparkling formal table setting that promises gourmet dining is consistent in its use of delicate, curvilinear forms played against the rectangular framework of the table and the diamond-shape motif of the supports that show through the glass tabletop. (*Photograph courtesy Tiffany & Co.*)

above: 374. An attractive handmade quilt is the perfect accessory for this rustic bed, also made by hand. Louis Mackall, designer. (*Photograph: Robert Perron*)

above: **375.** The shape and placement of a lampshade should have a pleasing proportion in relation to the base. The shade should not be too high (*left*), or the fixture will be visible.

above: **376.** A cylindrical base of basketry is better complemented by a shade of similar shape and rough texture (*right*) than by a squat, very flared shade with a silky texture.

above: **377.** An Oriental vase is cheapened by a rough, woven lampshade (*left*), but is enhanced by the simplicity of a flared, pleated shade.

above: **378.** A frilly shade (*left*) is inappropriate for a stoneware base, but a randomly textured shade results in a very straightforward combination.

suggest a personal expression. Stores carry a fair choice, but spreads are quite easy to make or have made, or they can be sought out at craft and hobby shows, country fairs, and import outlets.

Bath accessories—towels and shower curtains, often matched to bath mats—are also a good way to introduce color and design, subdued or flamboyant. Here, too, the effect is temporary and easily changed. Because they are exposed to so much water and steam, the colorfastness of bathroom fabrics is a point to consider. Fading will mar the effect of decisive colors and patterns.

Other bath accessories—hampers, and such—are usually keyed, not matched, to the dominant color in the room.

Lamps

Chapter 5 dealt with lighting in general and with permanent lighting fixtures, chiefly in terms of their overall effects. These are usually part of the architectural shell. While the designer can occasionally choose a permanent fixture, or replace one, there is much more leeway in selecting movable lamps.

Lamps are absolutely indispensable accessories in most social and private spaces today, because in many instances built-in fixtures are simply not provided. Only in kitchens, bathrooms, and hallways can we be sure of general lighting.

Portable lamps, then, must provide for some ambient lighting in a room, and for direct lighting for specific tasks, such as reading, writing, or sewing. They may be floor, wall, or table lamps, or movable ceiling fixtures, and there are many variations of a base, bulb, and shade.

Base and shade, although different in function and usually in material, are parts of one visual unit. This suggests a fundamental agreement between the two, some qualities in common without exact repetition. The bulb or bulbs are usually hidden, being too bright for our eyes, unless they are of the new variety that are meant to be exposed as a source of scintillating light.

Scale relationships will be very important, first between base and shade. You do not want the shade to overpower the base, nor look like a too-small hat. Equally important will be the relation between a lamp and perhaps the table on which it sits, or the floor area and surrounding furniture if it is a floor lamp. A wall lamp will have to be considered as part of the total wall design, as well as relating to the furniture.

Many functional requirements enter into the choice of a lamp: how stable it is, whether it spreads its light over the required area and is capable of delivering the amount of light necessary. Since almost every room needs ambient lighting, some lamps should be chosen that spread light up as well as down. The more lamps a room has, the smaller each can be, but too many will create clutter.

Lamp cords can be a nuisance, unattractive and hazardous. If light is needed in the center of a room, a ceiling installation may be the answer. Possibilities include a pin-up hanging fixture that can be placed where needed, or one of the plug-in track systems, with a variety of fixtures that can direct light in various places.

In choosing lamps as accessories, the designer must regard them as decorative also. The light in a lamp usually illuminates first the base, bringing out the beauty of wood, metal, or ceramic form and color. The shades themselves can be decorative, although this is an area that can easily be overdone. Some of the most successful shades are those that rely on the effect of light coming through the material.

379. Track lighting provides a variety of fixtures to direct light on different places. The table and work surfaces are lit by green-shaded lamps hung from ceiling tracks. In addition, bare globe bulbs provide general lighting. Tom O'Toole, designer. (*Photograph: Robert Perron*)

Color is a factor here. The color of a translucent shade will change when lit from within and will spread its hue around; the color of an opaque shade will seem darker when the lamp is lighted.

Screens

Unlike lamps, screens are not necessary, but they can be very useful adjuncts, as well as decorative ones. They have had a long history as ornamental space dividers and are especially welcome today in open-plan homes or simply as supplementary walls in any room.

By definition a covered frame, a screen is usually movable and often foldable, easily changed and adjusted. It creates a wall without completely shutting out what is behind. Almost like a traveling architectural unit, it changes the shape of a room. There are no limits to the possible materials—paper, fabrics, glass, plastics; clear, translucent, or opaque.

380. Screens can be anything from elegant to simple to extremely useful. The type of screen shown in **a** is very expensive, but less costly ones of rattan and bamboo are also available. Screens can be homemade very easily with a simple frame with fabric stretched or tacked on. Another type of homemade screen can be made by hinging together tall shutters (**b**). A screen made of stronger materials can hold decorative items as well (**c**).

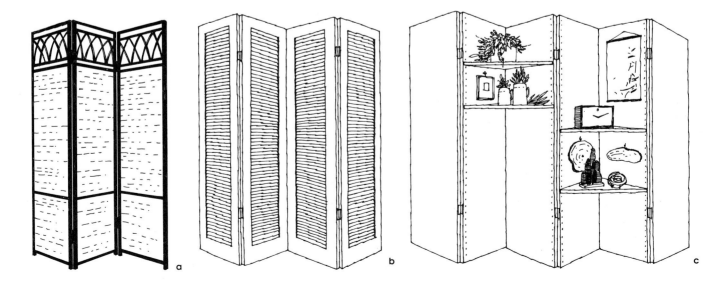

Nonfunctional Accessories

Some accessories bridge the gap between the primarily functional and the purely decorative. Books might be one example. Only occasionally is a book cover handsome in itself, but books in quantity, filling a bookcase or a whole wall, make a strong statement. A grouping of candles or a line of small animal figures, a toss of pillows or an assemblage of antique artifacts, if well displayed, add up to more than the sum of their parts.

Crafts

Many craft objects are available today—handcrafted by a neighborhood potter or weaver or handblown at a glassblowing factory; knitted or stitched by yourself, a friend, or an ancestor. Not only local crafts but those made by peoples all over the world are tremendously popular now. They add freshness and vigor to otherwise bland interiors.

A quilted bedcover can be beautiful in itself, a ceramic vase may be virtually a piece of sculpture, a handhooked rug no less important than an oil painting—the line is thin between craft objects and art objects.

However, crafts are, in general, less expensive and more accessible than good paintings and sculpture. In many homes they have begun to replace pictures on the wall. (See Plate 48, opposite.)

Plants and Flowers

Plants   The use of plants as decorative objects is widespread. We seem to feel the need to bring something natural and alive into the most urban of environments. There have been fashions in plants as in all other aspects of interior design. Grandmother's Boston fern was supplanted by the aspidistra of the twenties and the split-leaf philodendron of the forties. Now we search for plants that will survive in our particular indoor environment, while completing and complementing the design of a room. In fact, in many cases, plants will take the place of nonexistent furniture, physically and visually filling the space.

There is good reason for this. Plants contribute colors, textures, and casual forms that contrast pleasantly with over-controlled parts of the interior. They also give the emotional satisfaction of watching something

right: Plate 48. The brightly painted stairs in this renovated barn form a natural display for a collection of ceramic jugs. Byron Bell, designer. (*Photograph: Robert Perron*)

below: Plate 49. Modern graphics, together with rejuvenated furniture, helped give a new look to an antebellum house in Savannah, Georgia. The strongest image is centered over a main focal point—the fireplace. (*Photograph: Elliott Erwitt, Magnum Photos*)

341

Plate 50. Old office furniture was painted and given a new life in this New York apartment, in one of many possibilities for recycling. Malcolm Holzman, designer. (*Photograph: Norman McGrath*)

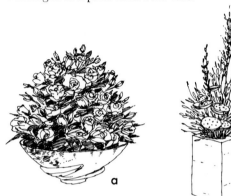

left: 383. Architect Mark Mills designed a composition in texture in the entry of this California house. (*Photograph © Morley Baer*)

below: 384. When arranging flowers you must consider colors, proportions, textures, and the suitability of the vase to the flowers. An **a,** roses—the most elegant of flowers—have been set off by the simple elegance of the glass form. Plain white porcelain shows off delicately colored flowers to good advantage. Some flowers—chrysanthemums, zinnias, marigolds—are well suited to rougher textures and more decided colors, such as stoneware. In **b,** a group of dried plants collected in the fall are arranged in a plain stoneware vase.

grow and change and develop. This brings up two points: First, does someone in the household have a green thumb? Second, plants grow larger, change shape, and may bloom, a distinct change in physical appearance that is unique in home design.

As visual design, a plant can be a dramatic outline against a wall or a soft mass filling a bay window. It can be a small tree occupying otherwise empty space or a cascade of vines from hanging baskets.

Each plant has its own requirements of light, heat, soil, water, and humidity for best growth. Almost none like dark, hot, poorly ventilated rooms any more than people do, but a few will survive almost any conditions. All will need water at some time, which brings up the question of containers.

Plant containers contribute to ornamental value and the physical health of the plants. They range from the classic unglazed pottery, through highly glazed, decorative ceramic, to glass and plastics. Usually, the container is subordinate to the plant, but this is not necessarily so. A rush basket containing a potted fern will make a balanced statement; a fanciful Italian urn may be just the thing for a citrus tree.

Fresh Flowers   Flower arrangement can be everything from stuffing a few blossoms into any vase, to a fascinating art in which a container is meticulously selected to show off to advantage a few perfect blossoms. The flowers, branches, and leaves at hand suggest possible arrangements. Each plant has its own character and habit of growth. Flowers will cooperate up to a point, but arrangements that emphasize the personalities of the materials used are most likely to be successful.

The relation of flower to container is important. Very often, a bowl or a vase, simple glass, ceramic, or metal, is chosen to show off a mass of colorful blossoms. But to a dedicated flower arranger, total composition is the goal—container and contained are part of a unified whole. This is flower arrangement brought to the level of an art.

Dry Arrangements   Beautiful as fresh flowers can be, their limited life is a disadvantage. Dry arrangements usually are composed of everlasting dried flowers, weeds and seedpods, leaves and bare branches, supplemented by driftwood, shells, and rocks.

They often cost little or nothing and require little or no care, other than the tedious and sometimes impossible job of dusting. They serve well for those who are not good with plants or flowers.

Dried flowers and weeds or branches often are subservient to their containers, and even to their place in the design picture. They enhance or supplement, rather than taking precedence. Spindly branches will complement a large round pot; feathery weeds will contrast with the solidity of walls or the rectangularity of windows.

Art

Paintings, drawings, prints, photographs, and sculpture differ from the other categories of decorative accessories in that they carry a heavier emotional charge. They usually carry a heavier price tag, too. In terms of home design, three factors must be considered: choosing works that evoke a special response; framing them appropriately if this is necessary; and deciding where and how to display them to best advantage.

Paintings

Original works done in oil, tempera, watercolor, acrylics, or other pigment bases on canvas or similar backing—these may be the most

385. A child's drawings, simply framed for display, would be a cheerful decoration in any part of the house. Charles Moore and Dimitri Vedensky, architects. (*Photograph © Morley Baer*)

expensive works of art one can buy. Few of us are in a position to purchase paintings of museum caliber, but it must be remembered that the vast majority of paintings initially were sold to discerning collectors for a tiny fraction of their current value. (See Plate 47, p. 324.)

We can find paintings that please us and evoke personal responses if we seek them out—at local art shows and galleries, art schools, even auctions. But we need to educate ourselves first, if we are to choose works that will continue to please and perhaps have some intrinsic value. If you are designing for yourself, the choices will be a bit easier. Working with clients means selecting paintings that create an aesthetic experience for *them*.

Perhaps the greatest mistake people make in choosing paintings is in buying a picture because it "goes with" the other furnishings in a room, either in color or in style. It may speak with the furniture, but if it does not speak to the viewer, it soon becomes boring. But a painting *can* be used in reverse. It may suggest a color scheme or a general theme because its statement is so intense.

Drawings

Works done in pencil, crayon, charcoal, or ink on paper are generally less expensive than paintings, even when done by recognized artists. Often preliminary sketches for larger works, they may be more relaxed, a direct revelation of the artist's concept. Or they can be full-bodied statements, as developed as a painting.

Since they are smaller, usually, both in size and cost than paintings, they are a good introduction to buying original works of art.

Prints

Prints are impressions on paper resulting from such processes as woodcut, etching, drypoint, lithography, and silkscreen. They are often called *multiples*, because a number of copies are struck in sequence. When they come directly from plates or screens made or supervised by the artist, they are considered original works. They are numbered according to their place in the sequence of prints made, and signed or authorized by the artist.

Prints by established artists are within the range of many collectors and could represent a sound investment. Also, being relatively inexpensive, works by developing artists are a fertile field for exploration.

Photographs

A medium of expression uniquely of the 19th and 20th centuries, photographs range from those conceived as artistic statements to those personal snapshots of significance only to family and friends. Either is valid as a means of home enrichment; it depends on what is sought.

Sculpture

Sculpture brings the intensity of the artist into three-dimensional expression. It can add a wealth of irregular, unexpected forms to our basically rectangular, predictable environments. We want to touch it, grasp and feel its shape, trace its outline with our hands, and experience its texture. The process of acquiring sculpture is the same as that for buying any works of art.

Stained Glass

Stained glass as an art medium is unique in the way it brings together color and light. Although the glass itself is colored, it comes alive only when the work is displayed so that light penetrates it.

Rescued pieces from old houses become windows or suspended panels in new houses. Modern stained glass appears in lamp shades, screens, or freely hanging works that can be considered craft objects or even fine art.

Art Fabrics

The resurgence of interest in fiber as an art medium has brought a whole new dimension to art in the home. Fiber art includes the silkscreen-printed fabric stretched taut on a frame, as well as the one-of-a-kind hand-fabricated piece that may well be as forceful an aesthetic statement as an oil painting.

Weaving is the traditional technique, as in the tapestries of the Middle Ages, but the form has exploded in all directions. We still find handsome woven tapestries that lie flat against the wall, but there are also woven three-dimensional creations that project to become space sculptures or even whole environments.

Knitting, crocheting, hooking, knotting, tying—any technique possible with fibers can be used, alone or in combination, to create an art fabric that will enrich an interior design in its own particularly warm and human fashion.

Art fabrics can be attached to the wall or hung from the ceiling. Only rarely will such a piece stand alone, self supported. Such fabrics also can be used as area rugs on the floor if the piece is readily cleanable.

below: 386. A panel of recycled stained glass brings color and light together in a special way. Wong & Brocchini, architects. (*Photograph: Joshua Freiwald*)

below right: 387. A printed fabric is stretched on panels that pull across to screen off the kitchen area. Fisher-Friedman Associates, architects. (*Photograph: Joshua Freiwald*)

Reproductions

Paintings reproduced in quantity by commercial processes have no direct connection with the artist. They do not have the impact of original works, for they lack the full range and brilliance of color, the special interests of texture and materials.

But if someone has particular empathy with a certain painting or drawing, or a particular artist, and reproductions are all that one can afford, they are a valid means of bringing enrichment into the home. They also will brighten up temporary quarters. It must be remembered, however, that no reproduction made without the supervision of the artist can ever be considered "original," regardless of the cost. The only value of a reproduction is the visual pleasure it may give us. It rarely, if ever, has investment value.

Protecting Art

Most of the art media discussed need some kind of backing, support, or protection, with the exception of sculpture and stained glass which are self-supporting and relatively durable. (Casual prints or posters, of course, can be tacked up and allowed to deteriorate.) For valuable works, stretchers, frames, mats, and glass are the protective means.

Stretchers Stretchers are the framework to which a painted canvas, a piece of fabric, or a photograph is attached to keep it taut. They can be bought ready-cut and easily assembled, or they may be custom cut to size. In many cases they are the sole support, covered with a fabric, a photograph, or even a painting for a decisive statement on a wall.

388. A framed poster becomes the major focal point on a wall with a precut post and beam. Hugh Kirley, architect for Saw Mill River Post and Beam. (*Photograph: Robert Perron*)

Frames Visually enclosing pictures—paintings, drawing, prints, or whatever—frames form a boundary or transition between the art work and its architectural background. They may contribute to the importance and effectiveness of the subject. Their first duty is to enhance the work, their second to relate to the setting.

Anyone who has had a picture framed knows the difficulties. There are so many possibilities, from readymade frames through custom-designed types. The framer often will know how to choose a frame that will complement the size, scale, character, and color of what it encloses without overpowering it. The client knows where the work is going and needs to keep this in mind. A work of art in the home is not the same as one in a museum or gallery. Inevitably, it will become part of the interior design.

Heavily carved, assertive frames or those that project at the outer edges set off pictures from their backgrounds. Those of moderate width, simple design, and neutral color relate to the wall. Usually the latter will also focus attention on the work itself, not the entire composition.

Mats and Glass Watercolors, drawings, pastels, graphic prints, and photographs need more protection than paintings in oil or acrylics.

Mats enlarge small pictures and surround them with rest space as a foil. This is especially important if the picture is delicate or if the wall

389–390. Accessories should be balanced for the best possible effect. The painting shown here is by Marlene Rothkin Vine.

below: 389. The form of the mirror on the left is too much like the painting of the same size and general shape; the repetition is monotonous.

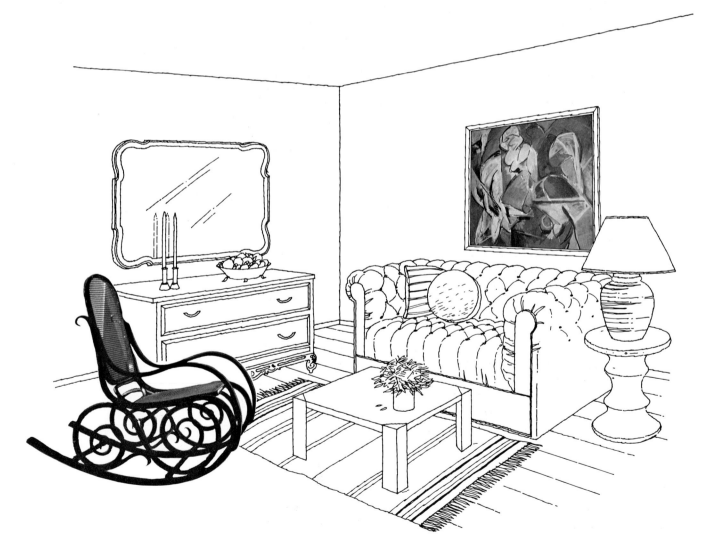

background is competitive. Mats usually are white or pale-hued, but they can be of fabric or patterned paper, cork, or metal, and have pronounced color.

In size, mats vary with the size and character of the picture, as well as with the frame and location. There is no set formula for the proportions of a mat. The illusive interaction of form, line, and space, as a total composition and with its intended placement, determine the result.

Many works also need glass as a protection from surface dirt, moisture, and abrasion. Glass seems to intensify colors, but it can also produce annoying reflections. Nonreflective glass, Lucite, or Plexiglas solves this problem, but these tend to gray and soften the art.

Many aspects of matting and framing are quite technical. A good framer needs both expertise and aesthetic sensitivity. There are also do-it-yourself framing shops where you can do the framing under guidance and with professional equipment. Before attempting such projects, however, a little research is recommended.

Displaying Art

First you decide where you wish to place works of art. Then you find out *if* and *how* you can. But the latter really comes first. You must investi-

390. The large mirror has been replaced by a grouping of smaller pictures, which complement the larger one and provide more variety of shape.

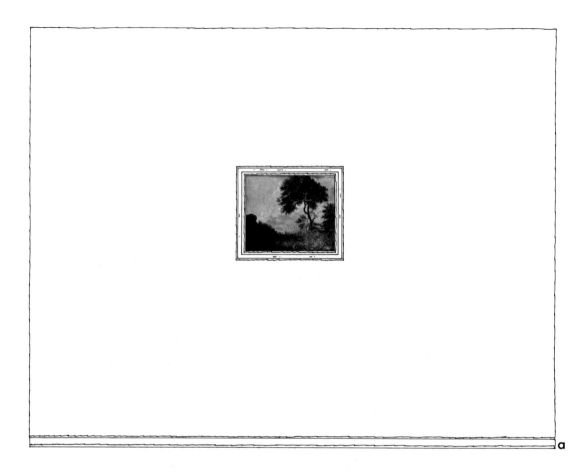

391. A rather small framed picture would show to better advantage if there were furniture underneath to anchor it in space (**a**). In a very tall room, pictures can be positioned higher than normal, to bring the ceiling height down (**b**). In a low-ceilinged room, a picture can be positioned lower than usual (**c**), to emphasize the horizontal space.

gate the kind of walls and ceilings you have, to determine what kind of supports are possible.

- Nails and hooks can be driven or screwed into some types of walls. In frame houses with interior walls of plaster or wallboard, the wooden studs (upright structural posts) must be located in order to anchor the nail into something solid. Studs are most often 16 inches apart, which may place them just where you do *not* want to hang a picture. The traditional method of finding studs is to pound on the wall with your knuckles. The wall will sound hollow everywhere *except* over the studs. If this method does not work, a "stud-finder" can be purchased in a hardware store.
- Certain types of bolts expand when they are pushed through plaster or wallboard, which prevents them from falling out. There are also plugs that can be driven into concrete, leaving a projection on the surface. Many landlords frown on these solutions, as you may yourself. However, although plugs disfigure the wall, the resulting holes can be closed up again and become invisible when the wall is next painted.
- If nails and bolts are unacceptable, there are picture hooks on superheavy tapes that will adhere to the wall, if it is not too rough, nor the picture too heavy.
- In general, pictures should be hung flat against the wall, with no wires or hooks showing, unless the hooks are decorative.

b

c

- Ceiling installations present similar problems. Plaster, a common ceiling material, covers a network of thin boards, which in turn are attached to heavier joists. These must be located, in order to hang objects successfully. Wallboard or concrete ceilings can be treated in much the same way as comparable walls.

Where to hang paintings, drawings, photographs, and prints, stained glass, and wall hangings involves aesthetic decisions. The works become part of the total room design and will relate to the nearby furnishings. They are often placed over something—a sofa, table, or fireplace—to complete the upward movement from floor, through furniture and wall, to culminate in a focus that should be in pleasing or exciting proportion to that part of the wall. (See Plate 49, p. 341.)

- Placing paintings at eye level lets them be seen comfortably, relates them to furniture, and emphasizes the room's horizontality.
- If a painting is large and dominant enough, it can be placed alone on a wall, either over a sofa or even on an otherwise blank space.
- Smaller, more modest works can be grouped for larger impact.
- An in-the-round art fabric hung from the ceiling brings art out into the room.
- Stained glass must be hung where light can come through it, which means over a window or with a source of artificial illumination within or behind it.
- Sculpture, being three-dimensional, can benefit from a placement out in a room, on a table if small. Large, freestanding pieces can be treated as articles of furniture, filling floor space and allowing viewing from all angles.
- Collections of related subjects may suggest a special display area.

These are, of course, generalizations. A specific application may be quite contrary but effective. Anyone who spends a lot of time lying down, either by choice or necessity, might appreciate a painting on the ceiling. Some of the most beautiful paintings in Venice are ceiling frescoes.

An empty space high over a doorway could be just the spot for a long horizontal painting. A tiny but intense miniature will be seen to advantage if placed on a small easel by itself on a table.

Imagination is called for in the placement of works of art, supplemented by quite a bit of preliminary trial and error. The glass on a watercolor may reflect light if the painting is placed near a window; but if it is mounted across the room, the distortions will disappear. Two drawings with the same subject matter may be quite out of scale with each other.

Sometimes it is a good idea to let works of art stand near each other for a few days before hanging them, to see how friendly they become, or how their juxtaposition adds excitement.

Most art is mobile. It can be moved around from one place to another, and this is a practicality that should be made use of. Retiring art, bringing it out, and switching it around will freshen it in your eyes and those of your guests. Moving a painting from one location to another may make it seem almost wholly new by bringing out different aspects. Friends may even say that they have never seen a certain object before, when the truth is simply that it has not caught their attention. Arranging art, an art in itself, offers infinite possibilities for change, renewal, and creativity.

Costs and Budgets

16

Costs and budgets mark neither the beginning nor the end of interior design, but are constant factors in the process and are of the utmost importance in planning a home. A discussion of costs and budgets is usually not entertaining, but it need not be depressing. Designing within a budget is a problem-solving situation and one that poses many challenges.

It is here that an interior designer can be of tremendous help. A designer should know what types of furnishings are available in all price ranges, where they can be purchased and how durable they are, and how rooms will look when the choices are assembled. The professional designer, either independent or in association with a furniture or department store, deals with clients at various income levels and different stages of the life cycle. For example, the designer may be asked to assist young clients in creating rooms in stages, to evolve with their tastes and budgets. People with a moderate-to-high budget allowance, who are about to make major purchases, may request assistance on how to select furnishings and colors, assemble and finish entire homes.

All of this can be done by individual homeowners, if they have the time and inclination. To many people, design is a fascinating hobby.

Price tags on home furnishings are determined by many factors: materials and construction, excellence and individuality of design, supply and demand, and durability. Handmade objects and those with superior workmanship are usually high in price. Durable items often are more costly than those with a shorter life span. However, price alone is not a certain factor in wearability. For instance, wool upholstery usually wears better than cotton, but an expensive silk damask would probably not withstand as much hard wear as would firm, heavy cotton.

left: 392. The banquette in the living room is actually a hand-built platform covered with fabric and oversize cushions ($135). The coffee table is simply a basket with a round piece of glass on top ($52). The banquette platform is hollow, providing space for storage.

below: 393. An old restaurant table is camouflaged by a print fabric topped by a circle of glass. The rug was the leftover end of a roll of industrial carpeting ($89). The chairs were puchased from a friend who was about to throw them out ($34). The canvas on the wall, as well as the one in the living room, was done by Mr. Manning.

392–393. This entire apartment was furnished from scratch with $1565—and some ingenuity on the part of the owner-designer, **Tony Manning.** (*Photographs: The New York Times/Gene Maggio*)

left: 394. The main living area is also used for dining and sleeping; almost every space in the house has multiple uses.

below: 395. The house was built in two sections with a spacious breezeway between them. The living area occupies one wing and a small drafting studio the other.

394–395. This house near Phoenix was built for a total cost of $13,000. It was constructed with very simple, inexpensive materials (plywood, corrugated galvanized metal sheeting); however, the owners have given it enough of a personal statement so that the materials add rather than detract from the design. William P. Bruder, architect. (*Photographs: Neil Koppes*)

left: 396. A homeowner with a special talent in carpentry or other craft areas can create especially unique effects for very little money. This handmade copper sink is a textural contrast to the wooden counter where it is installed. The entire house was built from recycled or salvaged wood. Alex Riley, architect. (*Photograph: Philip L. Molten*)

Costs and Budgets **355**

397–399. This comparison demonstrates that good design can be achieved on almost any budget.

above: 397. Expensive furnishings create an atmosphere of luxurious elegance. Multi-pillow sofa, $700; chrome and velvet armchair, $219; glass and brass-plated lamp or side table, $200; brass-finish metal table with beveled glass top, $850; floor lamp of polished chrome, $150; glass and chrome etagère, $500; large mirror, $359. Total cost: $2978.

opposite above: 398. The furnishings of this room give a similar effect but are not quite so expensive. Multi-pillow sofa in Haitian cotton, $525; chrome-plated metal frame cocktail table, $120; chrome folding lounge chair, $40; metal and wood etagère, $195; chrome-framed print, $125; glass lamp base, $68; side tables, $100. Total cost: $1173.

opposite below: 399. A third version of the room takes on a completely different look with quite inexpensive furnishings. Wicker loveseat, $110; plastic frame mirror, $30; beanpot lamp, $30; sisal and cane stool, $30; wicker telephone stand, $25; Italian folding cane seat, $25; wicker table, $95; wicker etagère with glass shelves, $150; wicker suitcases for storage, $17.50 each. Total cost: $530.

Costs of New Furnishings

Before we begin to attach prices to the wide range of furnishings available, it is important to remember not to equate only the more costly items with good design. Working with less expensive furnishings and achieving the desired effect is a successful design solution to the problem of a limited budget.

The following survey of the most common furnishings will supply some of the raw data with which to begin the task of planning for costs and budgets. In many instances, top prices could be multiplied several times over for the very high in quality or for individualized pieces. A good sale can put costs below the lower figure.

Floor Coverings

Hard Floor Coverings   Installation costs are more for tiles than for sheet flooring, but there is usually greater waste of sheet material. However, tiles can be installed by the owner without professional help. *Costs given are per square yard uninstalled.*

	Tiles, 12″ x 12″	Sheet Flooring, 12′ wide
vinyl asbestos	$ 2.00 to $10.00	
vinyl, cushioned	6.00 to 20.00	$2.00 to $20.00
ceramic	20.00 to 50.00	
wood parquet	20.00 to 50.00	

Soft Floor Coverings   Wall-to-wall carpeting, because of installation and cleaning costs, is more expensive than an almost wall-to-wall rug that

can be sent to the cleaners, turned to equalize wear, and moved to a new home. Fiber and density of fiber determine long-term durability—a major factor in total cost. Carpet tiles, self-adhesive or not, are the least expensive and can be replaced as necessary, but are usually of low quality and are a short-term solution.

	Per square yard	9' x 12' rug (approximately)
Flat Surface		
braided wool or nylon		$90.00 to $ 250.00
olefin, indoor-outdoor	$ 5.00 to $20.00	40.00 to 75.00
Chinese maize, jute, sisal	10.00 to 40.00	90.00 to 500.00
Pile Surface		
Dacron polyester	$ 9.00 to $25.00	$ 90.00 to $ 300.00
nylon	9.00 to 40.00	120.00 to 500.00
wool	15.00 to 75.00	120.00 to 1500.00
Rug Cushions or Pads		
sponge rubber	$ 2.00 to $10.00	$24.00 to $ 120.00
foam (polymeric)	3.00 to 10.00	25.00 to 130.00

Wall Surfacings

Installation costs for wall surfacings vary greatly according to the material and whether it is applied professionally or nonprofessionally. To estimate the amount of surface to be covered, measure with a steel tape the width of the wall (or the perimeter of the room if all walls are to be covered), and multiply this figure by the height of the ceiling. Deduct 15 square feet for every average-size window and door, or the actual square footage of larger openings. The remainder is the total square footage. *Costs given are for materials alone.*

Paint   Some paint labels indicate "spread rate"—the number of square feet 1 gallon will cover. A good paint dealer can give this information.

flat or semigloss	$ 9.00 to $25.00	spread rate: 400 to 500 sq. ft.
enamel	10.00 to 25.00	400 to 500 sq. ft.
textured	7.00 to 15.00	80 to 120 sq. ft.

Wallpaper or Vinyl Wall Covering   Wallpaper and vinyl wall coverings usually are sold in double or even triple rolls. They vary in width but also in length, so that each roll averages 36 square feet. In order to estimate the number of rolls needed, use the formula given under "Paint" for measuring walls, and then divide the total square footage by 30. This allows for cutting and trimming; however, large patterns will require more rolls to allow for matching repeats.

plain wallpaper	$ 2.00 to $ 30.00 per single roll
prepasted wallpaper	2.00 to 20.00
vinyl-coated paper	8.00 to 50.00
vinyl-coated, fabric-backed	10.00 to 30.00
photo murals	50.00 to 500.00
cork	30.00 to 50.00
grasscloth	20.00 to 150.00

Window Treatments

The following costs are based on a window 48 inches wide and 54 inches high, but most of the treatments will be floor length, 84 inches long. Fabrics are mostly varying blends of cotton, rayon, polyester, acetate, and silk, woven or knit.

Glass Curtains

Dacron marquisette, sheer	$ 4.00 to $ 20.00	48″ wide, 84″ long
Dacron ninon, semisheer	10.00 to 25.00	
acrylic or polyester, open weave or knit	10.00 to 50.00	

Draw Draperies

cotton and/or a blend, unlined	$13.00 to $ 50.00
open weave, knit, lined	22.00 to 80.00
cotton-blend, foam-backed	15.00 to 75.00
woven bamboo, reed, wood	20.00 to 100.00

Blinds

Venetian blinds, 1 inch slats	$50.00 to $100.00	48″ wide, 54″ long
roller shades	10.00 to 50.00	
Roman shades	22.00 to 80.00	
vinyl roll-up	8.00 to 20.00	
bamboo or wood roll-up	22.00 to 75.00	

Furniture

The cost of furnishings varies tremendously and is, of course, always subject to inflation. The following prices should be considered as guidelines only.

Sofas

sofa-bed	$250.00 to $1000.00
daybed	120.00 to 300.00
sofa, 6′	200.00 to 1500.00
modular, 6′ of units	300.00 to 1500.00

Chairs

upholstered easy chair	$100.00 to $1000.00
recliner/lounge	200.00 to 1000.00
padded pull-up	45.00 to 500.00
director's, sling seat	30.00 to 100.00
cane	25.00 to 200.00
plastic pull-up	10.00 to 150.00
dining	50.00 to 500.00

Tables

dining	$ 50.00 to $1000.00
end or coffee	20.00 to 1000.00
entertainment center	50.00 to 1000.00

Desks

$75.00 to $1000.00

Storage

bookcases, approx. 30″ wide, 72″ high	$ 75.00 to $ 500.00
cabinets, approx. 30″ wide, 72″ high	100.00 to 1000.00
room divider, 9′ wide	500.00 to 2000.00
chest of drawers	30.00 to 600.00

Beds

innerspring set	$120.00 to $ 500.00
foam rubber set	120.00 to 500.00
foam rubber pad for platform bed	40.00 to 300.00
headboard	40.00 to 300.00
head, footboard set	80.00 to 500.00
metal frame on casters	20.00 to 50.00
studio couch, 30″ wide	120.00 to 300.00
waterbed	290.00 to 1000.00

Lamps

floor	$ 50.00 to $ 200.00
table	25.00 to 200.00
pin-up wall	20.00 to 150.00
track (two-fixture)	30.00 to 200.00
swag plug-in	25.00 to 100.00
desk	20.00 to 150.00

Upholstery Fabrics

Prices for upholstery fabrics can go much higher than those given, but the fabrics may or may not be more durable. *Costs are per yard,* usually 36 inches wide for slipcover material, 54 inches wide for heavier upholstery grades, although these widths may vary.

cotton and blends for slipcovers	$ 5.00 to $50.00
upholstery grades of rayon/cotton blends, olefin, polyester, nylon, wool	10.00 to 75.00
vinyl, fabric-backed	5.00 to 50.00

Bedding

Prices given for bedding are for twin-size beds and standard 20-by-26-inch pillows.

Bedspreads

cotton	$10.00 to $150.00
polyester blend	15.00 to 100.00
quilt comforter	25.00 to 300.00

Pillows

feather, various types	$15.00 to $ 50.00
down	60.00 to 150.00
fiberfill (nonallergenic)	10.00 to 40.00

Sheets

cotton percale	$12.00 to $ 16.00
cotton and polyester percale	7.50 to 12.00

Blankets

wool	$40.00 to $100.00
Acrilan	15.00 to 60.00
electric	25.00 to 100.00

Tableware

In the upper ranges of prices and beyond, tableware costs often are attributed to ornateness of pattern, sometimes to whether pieces are handcrafted or ornamented with gold or silver. *Costs given are for five-piece place settings* for silverware and dinnerware. Service pieces may be purchased individually to complete a pattern. Complete sets (from 20 to 50 pieces) of dinnerware and silverware are available at much lower cost but tend to be of lower quality.

Dinnerware   Costs are for a five-piece place setting of dinner plate, bread-and-butter plate, soup/cereal bowl, cup, and saucer.

stoneware	$10.00 to $100.00
earthenware	5.00 to 100.00
bone china	50.00 to 200.00
porcelain	40.00 to 300.00

Silverware   Costs given are for a five-piece place setting of knife, fork, salad fork, soup spoon, teaspoon. Some settings consist of four pieces.

sterling silver	$200.00 to $400.00
silverplate	30.00 to 75.00
stainless steel	10.00 to 25.00

Glassware   Costs are per piece.

stemware	$5.00 to $25.00
tumblers	.60 to 25.00

400. Recycled materials take on a new look in this strikingly contemporary New Haven apartment designed by owners Andrus Burr and Peter Rose. The old table top rests on a new base of heavy plywood, chairs have been freshly painted, and empty wine bottles without labels serve as a decoration. The dining light is an industrial fixture. (*Photograph: John T. Hill*)

Table Coverings   Costs are for a table approximately 36 by 48 inches, seating four to six people.

mats for four place settings	$ 2.00 to $40.00
cloth, 52″ x 70″ cotton or cotton blend	9.00 to 30.00
linen and polyester	12.00 to 30.00
vinyl cloth	8.00 to 20.00

Recycled Furniture

An alternative to buying new furniture exists for people who are willing and able to spend the time "scavenging"—that is, collecting old furniture for nothing or next to nothing and restoring it to furnish their homes. Salvation Army outlets, junk shops, garage sales, even the street where trash is left for collection sometimes offer bargains for the patient and imaginative shopper. Often, all that is required is a coat of paint to transform a rejected table or chair into a functional, attractive piece of furniture. The individual who has acquired caning and slipcovering skills can achieve dramatic results, starting with a dilapidated chair or a sofa whose upholstery is in sad shape. (See Plate 50, p. 342.)

Budgeting for Furnishings

Budgeting entails wise planning to meet the expenses incurred in buying furnishings and, perhaps, the fees of professional interior designers.

As a beginning to a discussion of financial planning, the following generalizations can be made:

- No ready-made budget will fit all people.
- No suggested proportional expenditures can be applied to all situations.
- Each household has to decide, after thorough consideration of all factors, what percentage of income will be used for the many items that make up a budget.

As a rule of thumb, furnishing costs usually total about one-half of one year's income. It is wise money management to have one-fourth of the total furnishings budget in cash to furnish the first home. This allows the purchase of a few necessary pieces and cuts down on credit costs.

Furniture budgets tend to be divided as follows:

living room	30 to 40 percent
dining space	15 to 20 percent
master bedroom	15 to 20 percent
child's bedroom or guestroom	10 to 15 percent

The amount available for each room is likely to be apportioned as follows:

furniture	60 to 70 percent
floor covering	10 to 20 percent
window treatment	5 to 10 percent
accessories	2 to 7 percent

Countless factors can alter these proportions:

- The money available for each room is in part determined by the number of rooms to be furnished.
- Good hard-surfaced flooring (asphalt, wood, or vinyl tile) minimizes or eliminates the need for rugs and carpets.
- A separate dining room usually costs more to furnish than does dining space in the living room or kitchen.
- One or two rooms unusually large or small in relation to the others make a difference.
- Even a few pieces of inherited, cast-off, or bargain furniture affect the expenditures for the rooms in which they are used.

Many factors determine the percentage of income available or needed for *replacing* furnishings:

- family size
- stage of family cycle (Usually there is less money available for this purpose from the time children arrive until they become independent than there is before or after.)

401–403. Another approach to equipping a home would be to improvise furnishings at first, then gradually add more expensive items.

below: 401. An inexpensive sofa can be made from large rectangular cushions with bolsters that form a back rest against a wall. A simple hanging lamp provides light. The floor is left bare but painted a bright color.

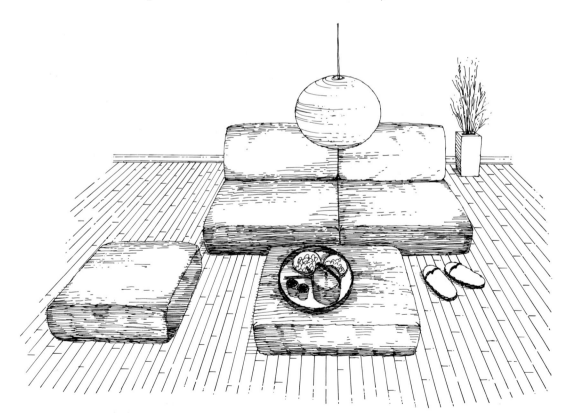

above: 402. Over the course of time, the sofa could be provided with a platform built by the owner, and perhaps a coffee table as well. A framed print, weed pots, and small cushions add enrichment.

left: 403. Some years later, an area rug and a handsome lighting fixture could be added, while retaining older things that were carefully chosen to wear well. The original sofa could be rejuvenated by new slipcovers, and art can be changed or added for more variety.

- amount and kind of entertaining
- durability of original furnishings
- kind of use and care given the furnishings
- amount of labor undertaken by family—repairing, refinishing, and remodeling furniture, making draperies or slipcovers

Planned Buying

The acquisition of furnishings over a period of time should be planned at least as wisely as color schemes and furniture arrangements. A sensible approach suggests buying the large essential pieces first, then filling in gradually with smaller and less costly items. Designing an interior in this manner—*planned buying*—forces you or your clients to compare present life styles with how you or they may be living in the future. Planned buying should be flexible enough to evolve with future tastes and incomes, and designed so that the best use is made of the furniture already chosen. Over the first two years of planning, it might work out like this:

First Year	Second Year
Living Room	
sofa or mattress on a platform	one or two chairs
one easy chair and one side chair or two of either type	occasional tables
	desk
coffee table	draperies if needed
carpet or area rug	accessories
a lamp or two	
flexible window treatment	
Dining Space	
table	two more chairs
four chairs	additional storage units if needed
carpet or rug	draperies if needed
window treatment if needed	accessories
Bedroom(s)	
springs and mattresses on legs or frames, or mattresses on platforms	bedside tables
	room-size rug, if desired
chest of drawers for each person	draperies if needed
mirror	accessories
one chair	
lamps	
area rugs	
window treatment	

Obviously, this particular plan will not work equally well for everyone. Many individuals and households are perfectly willing to spend a year or two living with foam pillow furniture and bare windows in order to afford an extraordinary Oriental rug they will have for a lifetime—to give only one possible example. It is really a matter of what people consider most important.

Planning a home is an important challenge. Successful interior design serves the needs of the people who occupy the space, allows for expression of individuality and life style, and accomplishes this within the limits of costs and budgets.

Glossary of Period Styles

French

X-Chair (1600–50) Chairs of this type, with leather backs and seats, were originally constructed to fold; later versions became fixed by the addition of a permanent back. X-chairs were universal throughout Europe during the Middle Ages and early Renaissance.

Louis XIII Armchair (1610–43) The profusion of spiral turning on the legs, arms, and stretchers of this armchair is characteristic of the Louis XIII style. About this time, upholstery of leather or cloth appeared. Dark woods were extremely popular.

Louis XIV Chair (1643–1715) The high back and ample seat of this chair are completely upholstered, providing greater comfort than before. The Louis XIV, or Baroque, style was a combination of large proportions and ornate decoration, including veneers, lacquers, inlays, gilded wood, and sculptural accents of brass and other metals. The sofa and chaise longue made their first appearance about this time. From the mid-16th to the 20th century, French fashion dominated international taste.

Louis XV Armchair (1715–75) The Louis XV, or Rococo, style was essentially a lightening of the Baroque. It emphasized delicate, stylized, curved forms with smaller units of ornament. Shapes and structural parts were made to flow smoothly into one another. The Rococo introduced asymmetry in textiles, achieving balance in subtler ways than before. Light-color woods, such as rosewood and fruit woods, partially replaced the darker ones previously in favor; light colors also prevailed in textiles.

Louis XVI Side Chair (1774–92) Strict symmetry and the clear separation of one part from another characterized Louis XVI, or Neoclassical, furniture. An emphasis on slender, straight lines developed, and chair backs took on medallion, rectangular, or shield shapes. Upholstery was simple, in light colors, often with satin stripes.

Directoire Armchair (1793–1802) Named after the group of men who governed France between the Revolution and Napoleon's assumption of power, the Directoire style reflects the austerity of those times. It was essentially an extreme simplification of the Louis XVI style, with few metallic or inlaid decorations. The arms and legs of this chair are gently curved, and the simple seat is upholstered in leather. Continuing in the Neoclassical trend, it shows the influence of the "Etruscan" mode.

Empire Armchair (1804–15) Napoleon's expedition to Egypt and his adoption of Roman motifs inspired a growing sensitivity to archaeological correctness, leading to stricter imitation of classical sources. Dark woods continued to be favored, together with strong, contrasting colors in upholstery. Chairs combined gentle curves with straight, thick lines and flat surfaces, often at the expense of comfort. Decorations and supports were often in the form of antique motifs, such as swans.

Second Empire Armchair (1848–70) During the Second Empire period, many older styles were revived, including Louis XIV and Louis XV (shown here). This chair, made about 1860, features the overstuffed upholstery popular at the time. Many different kinds of settees for two or three people were developed. Increasing mechanization, begun during the First Empire, caused a lowering of quality in furniture.

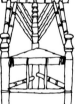

Hector Guimard Armchair (c. 1899) Guimard was the leading designer in the Art Nouveau style (1890–1905), a reaction against the increasing vulgarity of design. This armchair, part of a chaise longue, features sweeping sinuous lines interspersed with bulbous knots derived from plant forms. Motifs were abstract, but not geometric, and gentle pastel colors were favored.

English

"Thrown" (or Turned) Chair (1600–50) The arms, legs, and backs of thrown chairs were fitted together by means of sockets in the framework. About this time, chairs without arms, called back stools, were first introduced.

Jacobean Armchair (1603–49) Geometric patterns and stylized floral motifs, inlaid with holly, cherry, and stained woods, enhance the charming design of an oak armchair of the Jacobean, or Early Stuart, period. Furniture during this time became smaller and lighter with shallower carving than before. Compare the Colonial wainscot chair shown in the American period styles section.

Restoration Armchair (1660–88) Not until this period, also called Carolean or Late Stuart, did Baroque styles begin to have influence in England. Exuberant, dynamic curves and deep carving permeate the design of this armchair. Caning became popular, and walnut began to replace oak. Chests of drawers on stands, and elongated chairs, or "daybeds," were introduced.

William and Mary Armchair (1688–1702) Furniture became smaller and more comfortable during this period, while Baroque details were adapted to English tastes. Typical are the joined stretchers at the base. New types of furniture included writing and dressing tables, often embellished on their flat and curving surfaces with veneers and marquetry.

Queen Anne Arm Chair (1702–14) During the Queen Anne period furniture was ornamented by long flowing lines, rather than applied decoration. Seemingly frail cabriole legs supported sturdy, comfortable chairs. This example has an upholstered seat and is made of walnut. During this period china cabinets and small, low tables for serving came into vogue.

Chippendale Side Chair (1714–50) During the Early Georgian period, several furniture makers became renowned for their designs. Thomas Chippendale's furniture reveals a combination of strength and grace. Stout cabriole legs rest on ball-and-claw feet; the open back has slender, flaring sides and a carved "ribbon" back. Chippendale combined Baroque and Rococo curves, Gothic linearity and pointed arches, elegant Queen Anne work, and Chinese fretwork.

Hepplewhite Armchair (c. 1788) The designs of George Hepplewhite are known for their elegance and grace. Chair backs were oval-, heart-, or shield-shape, with festoons, rosettes, or flower petals. The delicacy of these designs was influenced by Robert Adam, whose interior designs seem perfect settings for Hepplewhite furniture.

Sheraton Side Chair (1791–94) Thomas Sheraton's designs were similar to Hepplewhite's with their moderate scale, slender forms, and straight legs. However, his emphasis was on rectilinear qualities, along with more complex surface detail. Sheraton's later work became much heavier and led directly into the Regency style.

Regency Armchair (1810–20) The influence of Greek, Roman, and Egyptian models, combined with a desire for archaeological correctness, helped shape the design of Regency furniture. This armchair, in the "Egyptian" mode, displays the heavy proportions, large-scale composition, and flat surfaces that characterize the style.

Arts and Crafts Movement Armchair (c. 1890–1900) A reaction against the poor quality and vulgarity of contemporary designs, the Arts and Crafts movement stressed honesty of construction and genuineness of materials. William Morris was one of its leading exponents, and his firm designed the armchair shown here. Its simplicity of design is a perfect foil for complex patterns of upholstery; Morris' floral and foliage patterns were famous.

Eastlake-Style Side Chair (c. 1880–90) Making an eloquent plea for honest crafting, Charles Eastlake advocated that materials be treated to reveal their essential character and that design grow from function. The influence of his ideas is present in this chair, the rectangular frame of which is sturdy but not too heavy; joints are stressed to indicate structure.

American

Carver Armchair (1650–1700) This chair is typical of the Early Colonial period in its similarity to those made throughout Europe at the time. The simple yet sturdy construction is somewhat relieved by a few turned ornaments on the legs and back, and by the rush seat. Although this example is made of ash, oak and hickory were also favored for their strength.

Wainscot Chair (1650–1700) Sturdy construction is combined in this Colonial chair with a profusion of shallow decorative carving. The stubby columnlike supports recall English furniture of the early Stuart period (1603–49).

Baroque Side Chair (1675–1700) As increased trade brought closer contact with European fashions, more contemporary influences began to be felt. Vigorous, complicated turnings harmonize with the swirls and S-curves in this example. The caned back and elaborate scrolls derive from English prototypes of the Restoration period (1660–88).

William and Mary Style Bannister-Back Armchair (1688–1702) This chair features more delicate construction than had previously prevailed, in response to a demand for greater comfort and beauty in furniture. The perforated back, slender arms and legs, and tasteful carving and turning exemplify furniture of this period.

Chippendale-Style Wing Chair (1750–79) This type of chair, first made in England in the late 17th century, remained fashionable through the 19th century. Stuffed upholstery nailed to the frame gives a maximum of comfort; the wings coming forward from the back protect the sitter's head from drafts. The cabriole legs and ball-and-claw feet derive from the Queen Anne style (1702–14).

Comb-Back Windsor Chair (c. 1760) The braced spindle back was the most distinctive feature of this type of chair; hoop, fan, and bow shapes were also popular. Based on the traditional everyday furniture of unpretentious homes in England, it combined lightness and strength in a lean, functional design. The seat, which is saddle-shape for comfort, supports the arms, back, and braces. The Windsor chair became the standard form of seating throughout North America.

Shaker Rocking Chair (early 19th century) Supposedly a Shaker invention, the rocking chair was a much-simplified version of 18th-century models. The spare, clean lines and sturdy but delicate proportions are characteristic of Shaker furniture, which became famous for being soundly crafted.

Duncan Phyfe (1795–1845) Lyre-Back Side Chair Beginning with free variations on Sheraton designs, Phyfe's furniture became an assimilation of Directoire, Empire, and Regency styles (1793–1820), with the proportions becoming heavier as the Victorian taste emerged. It is notable for its taut elegance and simplicity of design.

Gothic Revival Side Chair (c. 1830–40)

The Gothic revival was just one of many revivals of period styles that occurred throughout the 19th century. The Middle Ages provided few furniture models for designers to emulate; one solution to this problem was to take architectural motifs from the great cathedrals and apply them to furniture. This chair reflects the influence of Gothic pointed arches and tracery windows.

Rococo Revival Armchair (c. 1850) This example is similar to the work of John Belter, who perfected a process of laminating wood, with extra pieces added for high relief. The elaborate carving and perforated back are typical of this period, while the curved, flowing forms are reminiscent of the Rococo style (1700–50). Dark woods, such as rosewood and mahogany, were also popular.

Mission-Style Armchair (early 20th century) "Mission" furniture was an outgrowth of the Arts and Crafts movement in England and America, which emphasized simplicity of design and handwork. This style was inspired by the original Mission furniture of the Southwest, which was supposedly made from rough-hewn timbers and joined by pegs and dowels, with no nails or glue. It features a rigidly rectangular strucure with leather upholstery. Wood was stained or waxed, allowing the grain to show through; dark colors were preferred.

Modern

Thonet Side Chair (1876) The inventor of the bentwood chair, Michael Thonet, first mass-produced this version, which is still in use today. A single section of beechwood, bent through a steam process, forms the rear legs and back. Thonet successfully combined principles of honest construction and genuine materials with mass-production techniques in an elegantly functional design. Variations included an armchair and rocking chair.

Frank Lloyd Wright Side Chair (c. 1895) This early Wright design reflects the influence of the Arts and Crafts movement, which advocated handwork and light, simple styles with few historical references. The severe construction contrasts with contemporary fashions, while the natural qualities of the wood show clearly beneath a simple stain.

Rietveld "Red-Blue" Chair (1917) Gerrit Rietveld created the Red-Blue chair as a deliberate break with traditional furniture design. The back is painted red, the seat blue, and the remaining pieces black with white ends. The chair's rectilinear structure, flat panels of wood, and paint concealing the natural grain suggest a machine aesthetic rather than the individual handwork that produced the chair.

Breuer Side Chair (1928) One of the earliest cantilevered chairs, this example demonstrates the strength of steel even in very thin tubes. The simplicity of its design is consistent with the stylistic ideals of the Bauhaus, the school of design in Germany (1919–33) of which Breuer was a member and which emphasized work with the machine to combine art and technology. This chair has become a modern classic and is still in production today.

Le Corbusier Armchair (1929) Le Corbusier replaced the term "furniture" with "equipment," which for him consisted of three basic forms: chairs, tables, and open or enclosed shelves. The frame of this chair is made of chromium-plated steel tubing; the seat, armrests, and back are made of stretched canvas. The back is adjustable. It was Le Corbusier who popularized the Thonet bentwood armchair by using it in his interior designs.

Miës van der Rohe "Barcelona" Chair (1929) Named for the city in which it was first shown, the Barcelona chair is one meter in all directions. The gentle curves of its X-shape supports are a perfect expression of luxurious comfort. Miës, director of the Bauhaus (1930–33), came to America in the late 1930s and helped spread its message in what has come to be known as the International Style.

Aalto Armchair (c. 1934) Designed by Alvar Aalto, this armchair has a laminated bent frame and one-piece seat and back, which results in a strikingly modern form. The natural grain and color of Finnish birch shines through the finish. About this time, there was a renewed interest in wood, and Scandinavian furniture with its handcrafted quality came into favor.

Eames Side Chair (1946) Charles Eames' work combines the best qualities of natural and industrial materials. Metal rods provide a strong, lightweight support, while seat and back are molded to human comfort in plywood. Rubber disks joining the two elements add resilience. Eames was one of the first of the American furniture designers of the Modern period.

Saarinen Armchair (1958) A graceful continuity of line enhances the single-pedestal chair designed by Eero Saarinen, an American born in Finland. The one-piece seat, back, and arms, made of molded plastic reinforced with fiberglass, rest on a base of cast aluminum. A thin rubber pad covered with fabric softens the seat.

Glossary of Terms

Terms italicized within definitions are themselves defined in the glossary.

ABS (acrylonitrile, butadiene, styrene) A tough, lightweight, highly moldable *plastic* compound especially suited to fitted parts and interlocking components; major uses include *modular* furniture, luggage, plumbing systems.

abstract design Broadly, nonrepresentational; not recognizable as a known object.

acoustics A science dealing with sound as it is produced, transmitted, and controlled. Often refers specifically to the optimum perception of musical sounds.

acrylics Rigid, durable *plastics* that are very clear and transparent and have the unique ability to "pipe" light. Trade names include Lucite, Plexiglas, and Perspex.

analogous Referring to colors adjacent on a *color wheel.*

appliqué A fabric-decorating technique in which various *shapes,* colors, and types of material are stitched onto a background to create a design.

area The two-dimensional measure of a surface; in home design, usually the square measure of large planar elements—walls, floors, or the whole enclosure.

ASA (acrylonitrile, styrene, acrylic elastomer) A *plastic* compound with properties similar to those of *ABS.*

asymmetrical balance Distribution of weights so that visually they are equal but not identical.

awning windows Windows hinged at the top or occasionally at the bottom that swing in or out to open.

balance Distribution of weights, either physical or visual. (See *symmetrical, asymmetrical,* and *radial balance.*)

batik A form of resist dyeing for fabric in which nonprinting portions of a design are "stopped out" with wax to prevent color penetration.

bay window A window set in a frame projecting outward from a wall to create an interior recess. Usually of fixed glass, the window may have movable sections.

blend A mixture of *fibers,* often of natural and manufactured origin, to produce a fabric with the good qualities of each fiber.

block printing A printing method in which a block of wood or other workable material has been carved away leaving a raised design, which is then used to transfer ink or dye to a material.

bow window A *bay window* taking the form of an unbroken curve.

brick A clay block hardened by heat, often used as a building material.

broadloom Floor *textiles* woven on looms more than 36 inches wide.

buffet A counter on which to set out food so that people can serve themselves. Often with a cabinet underneath for storing dinnerware and table linen.

cantilever In architecture, any horizontal member—a beam, floor, or other surface—projecting beyond its support.

carpet A soft-surface floor covering available by the yard and blanketing the entire floor. Increasingly, the term is used to embrace partial floor coverings, or rugs.

casement window A window hinged at one side to swing inward or outward.

cast To mold a substance while it is in a malleable, usually liquid state, allowing it afterward to set or harden. Also, the result of such a process.

cement A finely powdered composition of alumina, silica, lime, iron oxide, and magnesia which, when combined with water, sets to a hard, durable mass; the binding agent for *concrete.*

ceramics Objects shaped from clay and heated (fired) in a kiln to make them hard and durable.

chaise longue An elongated seat for reclining with a raised backrest and sometimes with arms.

china Fine white *ceramic* ware fired at a very high temperature; the material of figurines and much expensive dinnerware.

clerestory A window or bank of windows inserted between two roof levels to bring light high into a room.

closed plan An architectural *plan* that divides the internal space of a structure into separate, discrete rooms. (Compare *open plan.*)

color wheel A circular arrangement of colors that expresses their relationships according to a particular color theory.

complementary colors Colors opposite one another on a *color wheel,* which, when mixed together in equal parts, form a neutral, or, in the case of light, form white light.

concrete A material consisting of *cement* mixed in varying proportions with sand and gravel or other aggregates. With the addition of water, the mixture become moldable, capable of assuming almost any shape. Concrete dries to a heavy, stonelike mass of great strength.

condominium A multiunit living complex—usually of the apartment-house type, but sometimes organized as a group of separate dwellings—in which residents own their individual units. Services and mainte-nance are provided by a management company, which charges a fee to residents.

cornice The topmost horizontal member of any structure. In interior design, a horizontal band at a window top or ceiling that conceals curtain or *drapery* tops and rods.

coved ceiling A ceiling that curves into the supporting walls, rather than meeting them at right angles.

crystal In common usage, *glass* of superior quality containing lead.

daybed An elongated chair or *chaise longue;* more generally, a convertible couch in which the mattresses serve as the seating surface.

dead storage Holding space either beyond unaided human reach or otherwise inconveniently situated.

dome A hemispherical roof or vault. In theory, the result of rotating an arch about its vertical axis.

dormer A window structure projecting outward from a sloped roof.

double-glazing The process of providing windows with two thin sheets of *glass* hermetically sealed together and trapping air between them; often used for window walls because of the superior cold *insulation.*

double-hung windows Windows having two vertically movable *sashes.*

draperies Loosely hung, often heavy *fabric* curtains.

drop-leaf table A table the top of which has one or more hinged "leaves" that can be folded down.

dropped ceiling That portion of a ceiling lowered below the actual functional level or below other sections of the ceiling within the same space. Often, a dropped ceiling serves to articulate specific segments of a room, such as a dining area.

drywall construction A common type of wall construction in which the interior walls are of some kind of *wallboard* panels, as opposed to *lath* and wet *plaster.*

earthenware A relatively coarse red or brown *ceramic* ware fired at a low temperature; typically brittle and fragile, porous if unglazed. Can be glazed and fired at higher temperatures for more strength.

embroidery The technique of decorating *fabric* by use of colored threads worked in a variety of stitches.

fabric Cloth; more specifically, a construction of *fibers,* not necessarily woven.

fiber A material of natural or synthetic derivation capable of forming a continuous filament such as *yarn* or thread.

fiberglass Any number of *plastic* resins, such as polyesters, polypropylene, or *nylon* reinforced with segments of *glass* fibers.

filaments Very fine, long threads or *fibers*, such as silk or manufactured fibers, that produce smooth, strong yarns.

film As applied to *textiles*, an extremely thin sheet of *plastic* produced by extrusion, *casting*, or calendering (compression between rollers or plates). Films are used as *fabrics* or as bonding *laminates*.

flatware The implements of eating and serving food—knives, forks, and spoons.

fluorescent lighting Artificial lighting that results when electrical current activates a gaseous mixture of mercury and argon within a sealed *glass* tube to create invisible radiation, which is then absorbed by the tube's interior surface coating of fluorescent material to yield visible *luminescence*.

FRP *Fiberglass*-reinforced *plastics* in thin, translucent sheets; often used for patio roofs, light-transmitting walls and ceilings, and furniture.

gabled roof A double-pitched roof; a roof that comes to a point and forms a triangle; also describes the interior ceiling.

glass A mixture of silicates, alkalies, and lime that is extremely moldable when heated to high temperatures—permitting blown, molded, pressed, and stretched forms—and cools to a rigid, nonabsorbent, transparent or translucent substance.

glass blocks Hollow, bricklike forms of *glass* available in a variety of shapes and sizes. They can be set together or joined to other materials with *mortar*.

glaze A protective and/or decorative glassy coating bonded to a *ceramic* piece by firing.

grain Disposition of the vertical *fibers* and pores in a piece of wood. More generally, *texture*, from fine to coarse, resulting from the particle composition of the material. (See *hardwood, softwood*.)

gypsum board Also known as wallboard or plasterboard, an interior wall surfacing consisting of thin panels of a *plaster*like material. The boards are not decorative, so they must be painted, wallpapered, or covered with another material.

hardwood Finely *grained* wood types from broad-leaf, deciduous trees such as maple, oak, and walnut. Hardwoods are for the most part harder than *softwoods;* they are also more expensive and accept fine finishes and intricate shapes more readily.

harmony Orderly or pleasing arrangement of parts.

high-tech Short for "high-style technology," a design trend in which *prefabricated* industrial components are used as materials, furniture, and accessories.

hue The pure state of any color; the name by which a color is called.

incandescent lighting Artificial radiant lighting created by heating a filament—usually of tungsten in common house bulbs—to a temperature at which it glows. (Compare *fluorescent lighting*.)

inlay A general term for techniques of decoration whereby pieces of wood, metal, ivory, or shell combine in patterns of contrasting color and/or *texture*, either as insertions in a background material or applications to a solid backing, to result in a continuous surface. (See *marquetry, parquetry*.)

insulation The prevention, by means of certain materials, of an excessive transfer of electricity, cold, heat, or sound between the inside and the outside of a structure or between portions of a structure; also, the materials themselves.

intensity The relative purity or grayness of a color. Colors that are not grayed are said to have "high intensity," and the converse.

Jacquard loom A complex power loom capable of producing elaborate patterned *weaves*.

jalousie windows *Louvered* window units of narrow, adjustable *glass, plastic*, or wood strips, most often arranged horizontally.

lamination The process of bonding together, generally with glue, thin sheets or small pieces of material to create a substance having properties the material would not otherwise possess, such as strength, durability, or intricate form.

lath A framework of thin wood or metal ribs integral with a building skeleton for the support of *tiles, plaster*, reinforced *concrete*, *plastic* foams, or the like.

line Technically, the extension of a point in a single dimension. More generally, the outline of a form or *shape*. In the language of design, the general disposition and dominant direction of elements.

load-bearing wall A structural wall that carries the weight of upper stories or the roof or both to the foundations.

loft An upper story of a warehouse or factory recycled for use as living space. Also an enlarged balcony used as a living area.

louvers Overlapping, sloping slats over an opening. Often they can be adjusted for the control of light, weather, and privacy.

luminescence Visible light produced by friction or by electrical or chemical action, as opposed to *incandescence* produced by heat.

macramé A *fiber*-construction technique in which form is achieved by knotting strands into varied patterns.

marquetry An elaborate *inlay* technique in which pieces of wood, shell, and ivory are set in a wood *veneer*, which is then glued to a firm backing.

masonry Architectural construction of stones, *bricks, tiles, concrete* blocks, or *glass* blocks joined together with *mortar*. In broader usage, construction, as of a wall, from *plaster* or *concrete*.

melamines High-melting, transparent-to-translucent *plastics* noted for the exceptional durability they bring to *laminated* counters and tabletops and molded dinnerware. Common trade names are Formica, Micarta, and Melmac.

mobile home Originally, a small, compact dwelling capable of being towed by an automobile or truck. Today the term applies to any *prefabricated* home equipped with axles. The basic *module* can be no more than 12 feet wide, although frequently two sections are bolted together at the site.

modular Built of *modules* or according to standardized sets of measurements.

module One of a series of units designed and scaled to integrate with each other in many different combinations to form, for example, a set of furnishings, a system of construction, or whole buildings. In current usage, the term is most often applied to *prefabricated*, mass-produced units.

molding An ornamental strip of wood or plaster that protrudes from a ceiling or wall surface.

monochromatic Having only a single *hue*, possibly with gradations of *value* or *intensity*.

mortar *Cement*, lime, or *plaster* combined with sand and water. When wet, the substance is moldable; it hardens to form the binding agent of *masonry* construction.

naturalistic design Recalling natural objects as they actually look.

nonobjective design Having no resemblance to natural forms or objects.

normal value The *value* of any color in its pure, unmixed state.

nylon The generic term (as well as trade name) for a family of *plastics* exhibiting high tensile strength in *fiber* form, sheet form, or molded form.

open plan An architectural *plan* organized with few fixed partitions to provide maximum flexibility in the use of interior space. (See *closed plan*.)

orientation In architecture, the placement of a building with regard to the sun, prevailing winds, and views.

ottoman A low upholstered seat without arms or back.

paneling Thin, flat wood boards or other similarly rectangular pieces of construction material joined side by side to form the interior and usually decorative surface for walls or ceilings.

parquetry *Inlay* of wood that takes the form of geometric patterns; used primarily for floors and sometimes for tabletops.

pile weave A *weave* characterized by protruding tufts or loops of fiber.

plain weave A basic *weave* characterized by a regular alternating sequence of one-up, one-down interlacings of *yarns.*

plan The configuration of spaces and rooms, walls and openings in an architectural structure; also, the graphic representation of such an arrangement.

plaster A paste, usually of lime, sand, and water, which hardens as it dries. Often used as a finish for the surfaces of interior walls and ceilings.

plastic Describing a maleable, ductile material. More specifically, a member of any of the several families of synthetic polymer substances.

plate glass Ground and polished *glass* sheets formed by spreading molten material upon an iron table mold with rollers.

plywood A composite sheet of *laminated veneers,* some or all made of wood, with the *grain* of adjacent strata arranged at different angles to each other for increased strength. An economical alternative to plank wood.

polyethylenes A group of lightweight, flexible *plastics* characterized by a waxy surface and resistance to chemicals and moisture but not high temperatures; popular for household containers.

polystyrenes A family of rigid, transparent-to-opaque *plastics* that are durable, capable of accepting varied finishes, and possessed of good *insulation* properties.

polyurethanes See *urethanes.*

porcelain High-grade, translucent white *ceramic* ware fired at extremely high temperatures; most familiar in fine dishes and ornaments, but with many industrial applications, such as plumbing fixtures and electrical *insulators.*

prefabricate To mass-produce standardized construction parts or *modules* for later assembly and/or combination.

primary color One of the basic colors on any *color wheel,* which cannot be mixed from other colors, but which serves as a basis for mixing all combinations on the wheel.

printing As applied to textiles, the application of dyes according to a selective pattern to create a design by such methods as woodcut, silkscreen, and tie-dye.

proportion Comparative relationships between objects or between the parts of an object. (See *scale.*)

proxemics The science of human responses to space and the people in that space.

radial balance Balance achieved by the arrangement of elements in a circular pattern around a central core.

rhythm Organized movement of recurring or developing patterns.

sash A window frame holding panes of *glass;* the movable part of the window.

scale Size relative to a standard or to a familiar size.

schematic diagram The first stage in drawing a *plan;* a free-form indication of the relationships of the various areas.

screen A covered frame, movable or fixed, that serves as a partial partition to stop sight, sun, or sound.

secondary color A color created by mixing two *primary colors* on any *color wheel.*

shade As applied to color, a variation of any *hue* that is darker than its *normal value.*

shape The measurable, identifiable contours of an object.

shed ceiling A single-slope, lean-to type ceiling.

shoji panels Sliding grilles or *screens* to open or close space, made of a frame covered with translucent material.

shutter A movable cover for a window, usually of wood, sometimes completely opaque, but often a framework with movable slats that tilt for light, heat, and privacy control.

simultaneous contrast The tendency of *complementary colors* to intensify each other when placed side by side.

skylight A window in a roof admitting natural light through reinforced *glass* or some other transparent or translucent material.

softwood Coarse-*grained,* fibrous wood primarily from trees with needle-type leaves that they do not shed, such as pine, cedar, and redwood. Although they may actually be harder than some *hardwoods,* softwoods are less expensive and cannot be given as high a finish.

spur wall A freestanding wall projecting from an adjoining wall at one end.

stainless steel Durable, blue-gray steel made rust- and stain-resistant by the inclusion of chromium.

staple fiber A short *fiber,* either natural or manufactured, that can be only loosely twisted and that results in soft yarns.

stitchery Any *fabric*-decorating technique in which the thread stitches predominate on the surface and carry the major design.

stoneware A relatively fine, durable, and waterproof *ceramic* ware made from gray or light brown clays that are fired at medium temperatures, often used for medium-price dinnerware.

structural design Design concerned with the creation of basic form in an object, as distinguished from its surface enrichment.

studio A one-room apartment; a combined living/working space.

stylized design The simplification of forms to emphasize design qualities.

symmetrical balance Equal distribution of weights that are physically and visually the same.

synthetic fiber A *fiber* made from compounds formed by chemical reaction in a laboratory, as opposed to those of natural origin.

terra cotta Fired clay, usually low-fire *earthenware;* also, the reddish brown color associated with this ware.

tetrad Any four colors equidistant from one another on a *color wheel.*

textile A *fiber* construction; technically, a woven *fabric.*

texture Tactile surface quality, perceived directly through touch or indirectly through vision.

thermoplastic Descriptive of *plastics* that can be reheated and reshaped without undergoing chemical change.

thermosetting Descriptive of *plastics* that undergo a chemical change during curing and become permanently shaped.

tile Stone, *concrete,* or *ceramic* pieces, flattened and/or curved, used for roofing and as wall and floor covering. Also, thin slabs of cork, *vinyl,* or other resilient material used primarily to protect and enhance interior wall, floors, and ceilings.

tint A variation of any color that is lighter than its *normal value.*

tone A softened color achieved by mixing a pure *hue* with gray or with its *complement.*

track lighting Long tracks that can be affixed to walls or ceilings, with numerous electrical outlets that permit flexible spacing of lighting fixtures.

triad Any group of three colors equidistant from each other on a *color wheel.*

turning The art and result of shaping decorative wooden cylindrical forms through the cutting action of a fixed tool upon a piece of wood as it rotates rapidly on a lathe.

upholstery A soft covering of *fabric* on seating units, sometimes but not necessarily over padding, stuffing, and possibly springs.

urethanes Lightweight, cellular *plastics* capable of assuming nearly any density and thus any hardness from resilient to rigid. Urethane foams can be sprayed as surface coating or preformed as cushioning and *insulation.*

valance Fabric draped across, or covering the tops of, windows. It performs the same function as a *cornice* but is more closely allied with the *drapery* than the wall.

value The lightness or darkness of a color.

veneer A thin facing of decorative or protective material attached to another material, usually of inferior quality.

venetian blinds A shade composed of overlapping horizontal or vertical slats that can be tilted to open or close them, or raised by a cord to any position.

vinyls A versatile family of strong, lightweight *plastics* available in flexible and rigid, molded and *film,* foam and cellular forms.

visual texture Surface variety that can be seen but not felt with the fingers.

wallboard See *gypsum board.*

weaving The process of interlacing two or more sets of *yarns,* usually set at right angles to each other, to make *textiles.*

wing A building portion that extends from or is subordinate to the major central area.

yarn A long strand, either of *fibers* twisted together or of extruded *synthetic* material, used in *fabric* construction.

Bibliography

In addition to the following books on specific areas related to planning a home, such magazines as *Architectural Digest, Apartment Life, Better Homes and Gardens, House & Garden, House Beautiful,* and *Residential Interiors* are valuable reference tools and sources for ideas. Also very helpful are the many SUNSET books on building, remodeling, and home design.

Basic Design

Anatomy for Interior Designers, 3rd ed. Julius Panero. New York: Whitney Library of Design, 1972.

Art in the World. Stella Pandell Russel. New York: Holt, Rinehart and Winston, 1975.

Art Today, 5th ed. Ray Faulkner and Edwin Ziegfeld. New York: Holt, Rinehart and Winston, 1969; reprint 1974.

Design and Form, 2nd ed. Johannes Itten. New York: Van Nostrand Reinhold, 1975.

Design Awareness. Robert Sommer. New York: Holt, Rinehart and Winston, 1972.

Design Basics. David A. Lauer. New York: Holt, Rinehart and Winston, 1979.

Design Collection, The. New York: Museum of Modern Art, 1970.

Design for the Real World: Human Ecology and Social Change. Victor Papanek. New York: Bantam, 1973.

Design Guide for Home Safety, A. Washington, D.C.: U.S. Government Printing Office, 1972.

Design: Sources and Resources. Louise Ballinger and T. Vroman. New York: Van Nostrand Reinhold, 1965.

Design Through Discovery, 3rd ed. Marjorie E. Bevlin. New York: Holt, Rinehart and Winston, 1977.

Dictionary of the Decorative Arts. John Fleming and Hugh Honour, eds. New York: Harper & Row, 1977.

Dictionary of Design and Decoration. Robert Harling, ed. New York: Viking, 1973.

Form, Function and Design. Paul Grillo. New York: Dover, 1975.

Forms and Patterns in Nature. Wolf Strache. New York: Pantheon, 1973.

Humanscale 1/2/3. Niels Diffrient et al. Cambridge, Mass.: M.I.T. Press, 1974.

Index of American Design, The. Erwin O. Christensen. New York: Macmillan, 1950.

Man-Made Object, The. Gyorgy Kepes, ed. New York: Braziller, 1966.

Measure of Man, The: The Human Factors in Design. Rev. ed. Henry Dreyfuss. New York: Watson-Guptill, 1967.

On Designing. Anni Albers. Middletown, Conn.: Wesleyan University Press, 1971.

Organic Design in Home Furnishings. Eliot F. Noyes. 1941. Reprint, New York: Arno, 1970.

Personal Space: The Behavioral Basis of Design. Robert Sommer. Englewood Cliffs, N.J.: Prentice-Hall, 1969.

Psychology of Color and Design, The. Deborah T. Sharpe. Chicago: Nelson-Hall, 1974.

Public Places and Private Spaces: The Psychology of Work, Play, and Living Environments. Albert Mehrabian. New York: Basic Books, 1976.

Shell, The: Five Hundred Million Years of Inspired Design. Hugh Stix et al. New York: Ballantine, 1972.

Shelter. Lloyd Kahn. New York: Random House, 1973.

Spaces for People: Human Factors in Design. Corwin Bennett. Englewood Cliffs, N.J.: Prentice-Hall, 1977.

Color

Art of Color, The. Johannes Itten. New York: Van Nostrand Reinhold, 1961; reprint 1974.

Color and Pattern in the Home. Jill Blake. New York: Quick Fox, 1978.

Color in Decoration. José Wilson and Arthur Leaman. New York: Van Nostrand Reinhold, 1971.

Color: Origin, Systems, Uses. Harald Küppers. New York: Van Nostrand Reinhold, 1973.

Color Theory (Arts and Architecture Information Guide Series, Vol. 2). Mary Buckley and David Baum, eds. Detroit, Mich.: Gale Research, 1975.

Grammar of Color, A: A Basic Treatise on the Color System of Albert H. Munsell. Faber Birren, ed. New York: Van Nostrand Reinhold, 1969.

Interaction of Color. Abr. ed. Josef Albers, 1963. New Haven: Yale University Press, 1971.

Light, Color and Environment. Faber Birren. New York: Van Nostrand Reinhold, 1969.

Munsell System of Color Notation, The. Baltimore: Munsell Color Co.

Principles of Color: A Review of Past Traditions and Modern Theories. Faber Birren. New York: Van Nostrand Reinhold, 1977.

Student Handbook of Color. Charles N. Smith. New York: Van Nostrand Reinhold, 1965.

Use of Color in Interiors, The. Albert O. Halse. New York: McGraw-Hill, 1968.

Interior Design

American Interiors: Ten Years of Innovative Interior Design in the United States. Paige Resne, ed. New York: Viking, 1978.

Architectural Record Book of Vacation Houses, The. Herbert Smith. Hightstown, N.J.: Architectural Record, 1970.

Bed and Bath Book, The. Terence Conran. New York: Crown, 1978.

Converted into Houses. Charles A. Fracchia and Jeremiah O. Bragstad. New York: Viking, 1976.

Decorating: A Realistic Guide. Mary Gilliatt. New York: Pantheon, 1978.

Decorating Ideas for Casual Living. Barbara T. Bradford. New York: Simon & Schuster, 1977.

Decorating Made Simple. Mary Jean Alexander. Garden City, N.Y.: Doubleday, 1964.

Decorating with Fabric. Judy Lindahl. Altoona, Pa.: Butterick Publishing, 1977.

Decoration Defined. José Wilson and Arthur Leaman. New York: Simon & Schuster, 1973.

Decorative Art in Modern Interiors. New York: Viking, yearly 1971–1975. New York: Van Nostrand Reinhold, 1977.

Drawing Plans for Your Own Home. June Curran. New York: McGraw-Hill.

Good Housekeeping Decorating and Do-It-Yourself. Albert Jackson and David Day. New York: Hearst Books, 1977.

Good Lives. Jeffrey Weiss and Herbert H. Wise. New York: Quick Fox, 1977.

Good Shelter: A Guide to Mobile, Modular and Prefabricated Houses, Including Domes. Bernard Rabb and Judith Rabb. New York: Quadrangle/New York Times Books, 1975.

Graphic Guide to Interior Design. Forrest Wilson. New York: Van Nostrand Reinhold, 1977.

Handmade Houses: A Guide to the Wood-butcher's Art. Art Boericke and Barry Shapiro. San Francisco: Scrimshaw, 1973.

High-Tech: The Industrial Style and Source Book for the Home. Joan Kron and Suzanne Slesin. New York: Crown, 1978.

Home: It Takes More Than Money. Rita Reif. New York: Quadrangle, 1975.

Homes Are for People. Satenig S. St. Marie. New York: Wiley, 1973.

Homes from the Heart: How to Build Feeling into Your Living Space. Curt Lamb. New York: Quick Fox, 1978.

House and Garden's Book of Remodeling: 55 Real-Life Case Histories. New York: Viking, 1978.

House and Home Kitchen Planning Guide, The. New York: McGraw-Hill, 1978.

House Book, The. Terence Conran. New York: Crown, 1976.

House in the City, A: A Guide to Buying and Renovating Old Row Houses. H. Dickson McKenna. New York: Van Nostrand Reinhold, 1971.

Houses Architects Design for Themselves. Walter F. Wagner, Jr., and Karin Schlegel, eds. New York: McGraw-Hill, 1974.

Houses Architects Live In. Barbara Plumb. New York: Viking, 1977.

Houses Around the World. Louise L. Floethe. New York: Scribner, 1973.

Houses of the West. Elisabeth Kendall Thompson. New York: McGraw-Hill, 1979.

I.E.S. Lighting Handbook, 5th ed. John E. Kaufman and Jack F. Christensen, eds. New York: Illuminating Engineering Society, 1972.

Interior Decorating with Plants. Carla Wallach. New York: Macmillan, 1976.

Interior Design: An Introduction to Architectural Interiors. Arnold Friedman et al. New York: American Elsevier, 1970.

Interior Design and Decoration. Sherrill Whiton. New York: Lippincott, 1974.

Interior Designer's Bedspread and Canopy Sketchfile. Marjorie B. Helsel. New York: Watson-Guptill, 1975.

Interior Designer's Drapery Sketchfile. Marjorie B. Helsel. New York: Watson-Guptill, 1969.

Interior Space—Interior Design: Livability and Function with Flair. Virginia Frankel. Garden City, N.Y.: Doubleday, 1973.

Interiors for Old Houses. Jacques Debaigts. New York: Van Nostrand Reinhold, 1973.

Instant Decorator, The. Frances Joslin Gold. New York: Crown, 1977.

Kitchen Book, The. Terence Conran. New York: Crown, 1977.

Lamp and Lighting Book, The. Thelma R. Newman. New York: Crown, 1976.

Lifespace: Designs for Today's Living. Spiros Zakas. New York: Macmillan, 1977.

Living for Today. Karen Fisher. New York: Viking, 1972.

Living Places. Herbert H. Wise and Jeffrey Weiss. New York: Quick Fox, 1976.

Living Spaces: 150 Design Ideas from Around the World. Franco Magnani, ed. New York: Whitney Library of Design, 1978.

Living with Books: 116 Designs for Homes and Offices. Rita Reif. New York: Quadrangle, 1973.

Looking into Houses: 60 Solutions to Design Problems. James Brett. New York: Whitney Library of Design, 1976.

Making Your Place a Home. Kevin Ruedisueli. New York: Quick Fox, 1977.

One Room Living. Sue Rowlands. London: Design Centre, 1977.

Place of Houses, The. Charles Moore et al. New York: Holt, Rinehart and Winston, 1974.

Planning Your Lighting. Derek Phillips. New York: Quick Fox, 1978.

Putting It All Together: A Consumer's Guide to Home Furnishing. Peggy Varney Collins and Shirley Wright Collins. New York: Scribner, 1977.

Record Houses of 19—. Architectural Record. New York: McGraw-Hill, yearly.

Residential Interiors Today: An Insider's View From Residential Interiors Magazine. Catherine Crane, ed. New York: Whitney Library of Design, 1977.

Rooms for Living. Penny Radford. New York: Quick Fox, 1976.

Rooms with a View. Herbert H. Wise. New York: Quick Fox, 1978.

Setting Up Home. Nicholas Hills and Barry Phillips. New York: Quick Fox, 1976.

1601 Decorating Ideas for Modern Living. Gerd Hatje and Peter Kaspar. New York: Abrams, 1974.

Spacemaker Book, The. Ellen Liman. New York: Viking, 1977.

Style for Living. Alexandra Stoddard. Garden City, N.Y.: Doubleday, 1974.

They Chose to Be Different: Unusual California Homes. Chuck Crandall. San Francisco: Chronicle, 1972.

Woodstock Handmade Houses. Robert Haney and David Ballantine. New York: Random House, 1974.

Young Designs in Color. Barbara Plumb. New York: Viking, 1972.

Young Designs in Living. Barbara Plumb. New York: Viking, 1969.

Furniture

American Furniture: A Complete Guide to 17th, 18th & Early 19th Century Styles. Helen Comstock. New York: Viking, 1962.

American Furniture of the Federal Period, 1788–1825. Charles Montgomery. New York: Viking, 1966.

American Furniture, Queen Anne and Chippendale Periods, 1725–1788. Rev. ed. Joseph Downs. New York: Viking, 1967.

American Heritage History of Antiques from the Civil War to World War I, The. Marshall B. Davidson and the eds. of *American Heritage.* New York: American Heritage, 1969.

Antique Furniture: The Guide for Collectors, Investors and Dealers. L. G. G. Ramsey and Helen Comstock, eds. New York: Hawthorn, 1969.

Art Deco International. Robert K. Brown and Iris Weinstein. New York: Quick Fox, 1978.

Cabinetmakers and Furniture Designers. Hugh Honour. New York: Putnam, 1969.

Complete Guide to Furniture Styles. Rev. ed. Louise Ade Boger. New York: Scribner, 1969.

Concise Encyclopedia of American Antiques, The. Helen Comstock, ed. New York: Hawthorn, 1965.

Dictionary of Antiques. George Savage. New York: Praeger, 1970.

Dictionary of English Antique Furniture. David Ash. Levittown, N.Y.: Transatlantic Arts, 1971.

Encyclopedia of Furniture, The, 3rd ed. Joseph Aronson. New York: Crown, 1965.

Encyclopedia of Furniture Making. Ernest Joyce. New York: Drake, 1971.

Furniture in England. S. W. Wolsey and R. W. P. Luff. New York: Praeger, 1969.

Furniture in Twenty-Four Hours. Spiros Zakas. New York: Macmillan, 1976.

Furniture of the World. Peter Philip. New York: Mayflower Books, 1978.

Furniture Past and Present. Louise Ade Boger. Garden City, N.Y.: Doubleday, 1966.

Habitat VI: Contemporary Furniture. New York: Universe, 1978.

History of Furniture. Martin Battersby et al. New York: Morrow, 1976.

Modern Chairs, 1918–1970. London: Whitechapel Art Gallery, Victoria & Albert Museum, 1970.

Modern Furniture. John F. Pile. New York: Wiley, 1978.

Modern Furniture and Decoration. Robert Harling, ed. New York: Viking, 1971.

New Furniture 10. Gerd Hatje and Elke Kaspar, eds. New York: Praeger, 1971.

Nomadic Furniture. James Hennessey and Victor Papanek. New York: Random House, 1973.

Nomadic Furniture 2. James Hennessey and Victor Papanek. New York: Random House, 1974.

Short Dictionary of Furniture, A. John Gloag. Winchester, Mass.: Allen & Unwin, 1976.

World Furniture. Helena Hayward, ed. New York: McGraw-Hill, 1965.

Materials

Beyond Craft: The Art Fabric. Mildred Constantine and Jack Lenor Larsen. New York: Van Nostrand Reinhold, 1972.

Carpets from the Orient. J. M. Con. New York: Universe, 1966.

Ceramics: A Potter's Handbook, 4th ed. Glenn C. Nelson. New York: Holt, Rinehart and Winston, 1978.

Complete Book of Woodwork. Charles Hayward. New York: Drake, 1972.

Crafts of the Modern World. Rose Slivka et al. New York: Horizon, 1968.

Fabric Almanac II, 2nd ed. Marvin Klapper. New York: Fairchild, 1971.

Fabric Decoration Book, The. Patricia Ellisor Gaines. New York: Morrow, 1975.

Glass. George Savage. New York: Putnam, 1965.

Glass: Handblown, Sculptured, Colored: Philosophy and Methods. John Burton. Philadelphia: Chilton, 1968.

In Praise of Hands: Contemporary Crafts of the World. Octavio Paz and the World Crafts Council. Greenwich, Conn.: New York Graphic, 1974.

Indian Blankets and Their Makers. George Wharton James. 1914. Reprint, New York: Dover, 1974.

Introductory Textile Science, 3rd ed. Marjory L. Joseph. New York: Holt, Rinehart and Winston, 1972.

Know Your Woods. Albert Constantine. New York: Scribner, 1972.

Metalworking. Oscar Almeida. New York: Drake, 1971.

Modern Pewter: Design and Technique. Shirley Carron. New York: Van Nostrand Reinhold, 1973.

Modern Silver Throughout the World: 1880–1967. Graham Hughes. New York: Viking, 1967.

Navajo and His Blanket, The. Uriah S. Hollister. 1903. Reprint, Glorieta, N.M.: Rio Grande, 1974.

Navajo Blanket, The. Mary Hunt Kahlenberg and Anthony Berlant. New York: Praeger, 1972.

New Design in Wood. Donald Willcox. New York: Van Nostrand Reinhold, 1970.

Oriental Rugs: A Comprehensive Study. Murray L. Eiland. Greenwich, Conn.: New York Graphic, 1973.

Oriental Rugs and Carpets. Fabio Formenton. New York: McGraw-Hill, 1972.

Plastics as Sculpture. Thelma R. Newman. Radnor, Pa.: Chilton, 1974.

Rugs and Wall Hangings. Jean Scobey. New York: Dial, 1974.

Sculpture in Plastics. Nicholas Roukes. New York: Watson-Guptill, 1978.

Steuben: Seventy Years of American Glass Blowing. Paul V. Hardner and James S. Plant. New York: Praeger, 1975.

Textile Fabrics and Their Selection, 6th ed. Isabel Wingate. Englewood Cliffs, N.J.: Prentice-Hall, 1970.

Textile Handbook, 4th ed. Washington, D.C.: American Home Economics Assoc., 1970.

200 Years of American Blown Glass. Rev. ed. George McKearin and Helen S. McKearin. New York: Crown, 1966.

Visual Art in Glass. Dominick Labino. Dubuque, Iowa: Wm. C. Brown, 1968.

Weaving: A Handbook of the Fiber Arts. 2nd ed. Shirley E. Held. New York: Holt, Rinehart and Winston, 1978.

Wood and Wood Grains: A Photographic Album for Artists and Designers. Philip Brodatz. New York: Dover, 1972.

World Ceramics. Robert J. Charleston. New York: McGraw-Hill, 1968.

Index